Brief Contents

Contents

Global Dimensions of Corporate Governance

Blackwell Global Dimensions of Business Series

Series Editors: David A Ricks, Bodo Schlegelmilch and J. Michael Geringer

This major new series will provide authoritative international business and management material for graduate students. Each book includes focused, topic-based summaries of the key global developments in the different sub-disciplines of business. They concentrate on the strategic and practical implications in each topic area, provide material and commentary on emergent and changing trends as well as reviewing established knowledge.

Titles assigned to date include:

Global Dimensions of Corporate Governance	Yadong Luo
Global Dimensions of HRM	Paula Caligiuri and Mark E. Mendenhall
Global Dimensions of Finance	Raj Aggarwal
Global Dimensions of eCommerce	Saeed Samiee
Global Dimensions of Strategy	Stephen Tallman
Global Dimensions of Management	Nick Athanassiou

Global Dimensions of Corporate Governance

Yadong Luo

Blackwell
Publishing

© 2007 by Yadong Luo

BLACKWELL PUBLISHING
350 Main Street, Malden, MA 02148-5020, USA
9600 Garsington Road, Oxford OX4 2DQ, UK
550 Swanston Street, Carlton, Victoria 3053, Australia

The right of Yadong Luo to be identified as the Author of this Work has been asserted
in accordance with the UK Copyright, Designs, and Patents Act 1988.

First published 2007 by Blackwell Publishing Ltd

1   2007

Library of Congress Cataloging-in-Publication Data

Luo, Yadong.
Global dimensions of corporate governance / Yadong Luo.
p. cm.
Includes bibliographical references.
ISBN-13: 978-1-4051-3707-2 (pbk. : alk. paper)
ISBN-10: 1-4051-3707-X (pbk. : alk. paper)   1. International business enterprises—
Management.   2. Globalization—Economic aspects.   I. Title.

HD62.4.L862 2006
658′.049—dc22
2005034696

A catalogue record for this title is available from the British Library.

Set in 10/12.5pt Photina
by Graphicraft Limited, Hong Kong
Printed and bound in Singapore
by C.O.S. Printers Pte Ltd

The publisher's policy is to use permanent paper from mills that operate a sustainable
forestry policy, and which has been manufactured from pulp processed using acid-free
and elementary chlorine-free practices. Furthermore, the publisher ensures that the
text paper and cover board used have met acceptable environmental accreditation standards.

For further information on
Blackwell Publishing, visit our website:
www.blackwellpublishing.com

Preface

This book aims to be a pioneering initiative to delineate corporate governance systems in international business and to address various governance and accountability issues facing multinational corporations (MNCs). The importance of corporate governance in MNCs active in global operations has never been more strong than today. Recent MNC debacles, corporate accounting scandals, and the drastic deflation of market values around the world have resulted in enormous attention to this issue. Current attempts at legislative and organizational reform for better self-governance seem to be a precursor to companies looking beyond the "earnings game." MNCs must now deal with more demanding global shareholder and stakeholder groups that seek greater disclosure and more transparent explanations for major decisions, thus increasing pressure to run global businesses in the best interests of these highly demanding groups. Many, including scholars, consultants, and managers, tend to treat corporate governance in MNCs as merely a larger version of corporate governance in regular companies, without considering MNCs' unique environments, activities, strategies, and structures that influence their two-tiers (parent and subsidiary levels) of corporate governance. This book tries to fill this void, for perhaps the first time, and provides researchers, practitioners, and students with analytical frameworks, a practical guide, and case examples on how to develop a global corporate governance system for MNCs.

This book first presents a conceptual foundation of corporate governance in international business. It explains what constitutes corporate governance for companies participating in international business and illustrates how such governance differs from that for domestic firms. Corporate governance specifies the distribution of rights and responsibilities among the various corporate participants including board members, executives, shareholders, and other stakeholders, and spells out the rules and procedures for making decisions on corporate affairs. In an international business setting, corporate governance contains not only parent-level corporate governance (how the parent company's rights, powers, and responsibilities are divided and monitored) but also subsidiary-level corporate governance (how foreign subsidiaries that have their own board of directors deal with their shareholders and other local stakeholders while simultaneously answering to and integrating with the parent firm). At either level, corporate governance mechanisms involve three categories: (a) market-based; (b) culture-based; and (c) discipline-based. Parent-level governance influences subsidiary-level governance through ownership holding, corporate support, and performance monitoring, while subsidiary-level governance channels back to the parent-level through advice provision, governance sharing, information reporting, and directorate expansion.

The design of both parent- and subsidiary-level corporate governance must attend to corporate governance practices and norms that often differ by countries. Chapter 2 discusses why corporate governance varies across nations and how such differences influence MNCs' international expansion and management. These differences affect corporate governance at the subunit level in specific host countries, corporate-level harmonization of managerial governance over all subunits around the world, and cost-effectiveness in governing internally differentiated yet globally coordinated business structures. The variation also implies that an MNC has to deal with many different local institutions that play very different roles in different countries in determining corporate governance. For example, in many parts of Asia, it is not the financial markets but various government ministries that monitor corporate performance and control financial allocation. Meanwhile, in many continental European countries such as Germany and Switzerland, and in some parts of Asia such as Japan, Korea, Taiwan, and Singapore, the banking sector as institutional shareholders monitor corporate performance and investment decisions.

Chapter 3 emphasizes how the global activities undertaken by MNCs determine or influence corporate governance design and actual mechanisms at both the corporate and subsidiary levels. It specifically articulates how an MNC's globalization attributes such as globalization scale, foreign adaptation, global competition, and international experience influence the design of governance mechanisms such as board size, board composition, executive compensation, market discipline, interlocking directorate, ownership concentration, duality, and inbreeding, as well as the design of accountability systems such as accounting information, auditing standards, and financial and non-financial disclosures. An MNC's corporate governance and accountability should be properly aligned with its international features for both information processing and agency cost reasons.

The two-tier (parent and subsidiary levels) governance structure contributes to greater complexity of corporate governance in MNCs than in regular firms. Chapter 4 explains the roles and functions of each tier, illustrating how the two tiers of governance are interrelated and mutually reinforce an MNC's global corporate governance; and presents a unified framework of the two-tier governance system. This framework explains both strong cross-links between parent management and subsidiary board and between parent management and subsidiary management and weak cross-links between parent board and subsidiary board and between parent board and subsidiary management. Since the specific links embedded in the two tiers of corporate governance vary according to the different roles played by individual subsidiaries, this chapter further reviews and discusses differing roles of foreign subsidiaries and how these roles actually affect the design and function of second-tier corporate governance. For instance, when a foreign subsidiary is more strategically important to the MNC's global expansion, this subsidiary's board and its management are expected to maintain a stronger tie and more frequent communication between the first and second tiers of corporate governance. If a foreign subsidiary is designed to become a dominant player penetrating and emphasized in the host country market, the subsidiary-level corporate governance mechanisms will have to be more strongly tailored to the host country environments and practices. If a foreign subsidiary is more organizationally autonomous, then the parent board and parent management need to encourage the subsidiary board to play a bigger role in monitoring subsidiary management.

Corporate accountability is an important part of corporate governance since governance cannot go far unless accountability is in place. Here corporate accountability is defined as the construct encompassing two interrelated components: financial reporting accountability and governance system transparency. Chapter 5 explains why international expansion of companies makes corporate accountability more difficult on the one hand and yet more important on the other. It articulates how an MNC's financial reporting accountability is influenced by its globalization attributes and how it can improve financial accountability in an effective way. Chapter 5 further elucidates how governance transparency should be properly aligned with an MNC's global competition and strategies and how MNCs can strengthen governance system transparency to meet the needs of global stakeholders.

Chapter 6 addresses how international corruption is interrelated to global corporate governance for MNCs. Anti-corruption is crucial to corporate governance because bribery and corruption damage the governance of corporations and impede efforts to develop corporate integrity. Corruption, or any illicit behavior, conducted by executives, managers, and employees can fundamentally deter the legitimate and long-term interests of internal and external stakeholders. In the international business context, anti-corruption becomes even more important to global corporate governance because MNCs confront significantly varying norms, laws, and standards pertaining to business practices in general and corruption practices in particular. For instance, bribery is culturally ingrained as an acceptable business practice in some countries, such as some regions of Mexico, and kickbacks are common in selling activities in many parts of China. To help executives cope with increasingly stringent anti-corruption laws and, more importantly, enhance the effectiveness and transparency of global corporate governance, this chapter explicates organizational behaviors displayed by corrupt MNCs, organizational consequences caused by international corruption, and organizational architecture resisting all illicit acts in international business.

The book ends with a chapter focusing on the relationship between corporate social responsibility (CSR) and corporate governance in international business. More then ever before, MNCs are now expected to account explicitly for all aspects of their performance – not just their financial results, but their social and environmental performance as well. In this last chapter, the book explains global CSR's principles, elements, standards, and practices for MNCs, discusses the relationship between global CSR and global corporate governance, and offers managerial guidelines for improving MNCs' global CSR. These guidelines include: (i) complying with global guidelines and mandates; (ii) redefining corporate values in global business; (iii) implementing corporate ethics programs by directors, executives, managers, and employees around the world; (iv) understanding the global stakeholders' needs; (v) fortifying organizational credibility and legitimacy in host countries; (vi) reformulating the key roles of both corporate and subsidiary boards; (vii) formulating a viable sustainability program that addresses global stakeholders' long-term concerns; and (viii) undertaking CSR auditing and assessment.

International business is a shifting and complex field wherein there is a seemingly endless learning challenge for academics and practitioners. To this end, this book is only a small piece, but I do hope that readers will share my enthusiasm for the rich subject of global dimensions of corporate governance.

Yadong Luo
Professor of Management and the Emery Findlay Distinguished Chair
University of Miami

Acknowledgments

The author and publisher gratefully acknowledge the permission granted to reproduce the copyright material in this book:

1. Will Eurotunnel inspire French proxy battles, pp. 1–5 from *International Law Review*, July, 2004. Reprinted with permission.
2. Alexander Borsch, Globalization, shareholder value, and restructuring: The transformation of Siemens, pp. 365–87 from *New Political Economy*, **9**(3), 2004. Reprinted with permission of Taylor and Francis Ltd (www.tandf.co.uk/journals) and the author.
3. Oded Shenkar and Yadong Luo, Riga Corporation: Collection or corruption, from *International Business* (Chichester: John Wiley & Sons Ltd, 2004). © Oded Shenkar and Yadong Luo. Reprinted with permission of the authors.
4. Stelios C. Zyglidopoulos, The social and environmental responsibilities of multinationals: Evidence from the Brent Spar case, pp. 141–52 from *Journal of Business Ethics*, **36**(1), 2002. Reprinted with kind permission of Springer Science and Business Media and the author.
5. Summary of Sarbanes–Oxley Act of 2002, from American Institute of Certified Public Accountants (www.aicpa.org/info/sarbanes_oxley_summary.htm). Copyright © 2002 by the American Institute of Certified Public Accountants Inc. Reprinted with permission.
6. The OECD guidelines for multinational enterprises, from The OECD Declaration and Decisions on International Investment and Multinational Enterprises: Basic Texts, Directorate for Financial, Fiscal and Enterprise Affairs, DAFFE/IME (2000)20 © OECD 2000. Reprinted with permission of the Organisation for Economic Cooperation and Development (www.oecd.org).
7. OECD convention on combating bribery of foreign public officials in international business transfers, from OECD Convention on Combating Bribery of Foreign Public Officials in International Business Transactions © OECD 1997. Reprinted with permission of the Organisation for Economic Cooperation and Development (www.oecd.org).

8. Sample company policies and procedures relating to the Foreign Corrupt Practices Act in the US, from Business Laws Inc. (inquiry@businesslaws.com). Reprinted with permission of Thomson/West Copyright Services.

Every effort has been made to trace copyright holders and to obtain their permission for the use of copyright material. The publisher apologizes for any errors or omissions in the above list and would be grateful if notified of any corrections that should be incorporated in future reprints or editions of this book.

Chapter 1

Corporate Governance in International Business: Concepts and Mechanisms

EXECUTIVE SUMMARY

This chapter serves as a conceptual foundation that defines various concepts pertaining to corporate governance in international business and discusses various types of corporate governance in multinational corporations (MNCs). Specifically, this chapter explains what constitutes corporate governance for companies participating in international business and illustrates how such governance differs from that for domestic firms. In a general setting, corporate governance is the relationship between the corporation and the stakeholders that determines and controls the strategic direction and performance of the corporation. It is the system by which corporations are directed and controlled. This structure specifies the distribution of rights and responsibilities among the various corporate participants including board members, executives, shareholders, and other stakeholders; it spells out the rules and procedures for making decisions on corporate affairs. In an international business setting, corporate governance contains not only parent-level corporate governance (how the parent company's rights, power, and responsibilities are divided and monitored) but also subsidiary-level corporate governance (how foreign subsidiaries that have their own board of directors deal with their shareholders and other local stakeholders while simultaneously answering to and integrating with the parent firm). At either level, corporate governance mechanisms involve three categories: market-based; culture-based; and discipline-based. Market-based mechanisms comprise: (i) ownership concentration; (ii) board composition; (iii) market discipline; (iv) board chairmanship; (v) board size; (vi) management remuneration; (vii) interlocking directorate; and (viii) inbreeding. Culture-based mechanisms include: (i) governance culture and (ii) corporate integrity, both set the moral tone for governance. Lastly, discipline-based mechanisms encompass: (i) executive penalty; (ii) internal auditing; (iii) a conduct code; and (iv) an ethics program.

1.1 Defining Corporate Governance in a General Context

Corporate governance has been attracting a good deal of public interest because of its importance for the economic health of corporations and the welfare of society. It represents the relationship among stakeholders that is used to determine and control the strategic direction and performance of organizations. According to the definition of the OECD (Organization for Economic Cooperation and Development, 1999), corporate governance is the system by which business corporations are directed and controlled. The corporate governance structure specifies the distribution of rights and responsibilities among different participants in the corporation, such as the board, managers, shareholders, and other stakeholders; and spells out the rules and procedures for making decisions on corporate affairs. By doing this, it also provides the structure through which the company objectives are set and the means of attaining those objectives and monitoring performance. Corporate governance requires developing internal processes and structures within a firm to minimize agency costs between shareholders, or more broadly, stakeholders, and top management. Corporate governance reflects and enforces the company's value and contributes to the firm's legitimacy and the credibility of its decisions and reporting.

Corporate governance structures serve to motivate managers to maximize firm value instead of pursuing personal objectives and to ensure that minority shareholders receive reliable information about the value of the firm and that a company's managers and large shareholders do not cheat them out of the value of their investments. A well-functioning corporate governance system can also create a competitive advantage for an individual firm. The improved alignment of top-level managers' interests with shareholders', or more broadly, stakeholders' interests, heightens a company's unity and cohesion, which not only minimizes agency costs but also streamlines a decision-making process and stabilizes internal operations and management. Effective corporate governance is also important to social welfare. Each nation wants the firms that operate within its borders to flourish and grow in such ways as to provide employment, wealth, and satisfaction, not only to improve standards of living materially but also to enhance social cohesion. These aspirations cannot be met unless those firms establish effective and accountable corporate governance as well as ethical and legitimate company standards.

A good corporate governance system, however, goes beyond company standards and efforts. It relies also on complex systems of supporting institutions that promote the governance of publicly traded companies. Institutions promoting the governance of firms include reputational intermediaries such as investment banks and audit firms, securities laws and regulators such as the Securities and Exchange Commission (SEC) in the United States, and disclosure regimes that produce credible firm-specific information about publicly traded firms.

In modern corporations, especially those in the United States and the United Kingdom, a primary objective of corporate governance is to ensure that the interests of top-level managers are aligned with the interests of the shareholders. Unsurprisingly, corporate governance became widely discussed following the publication of the seminal work by Berle and Means (1932), who wrote about the oversight challenges faced by owners who no longer personally managed their businesses but instead hired managers to carry out executive functions. The separation of ownership and control arose because, by that time, those who had invested in a company did not necessarily have the organizing expertise and talent to manage it. Meanwhile, talented managers did not always have the capital to start their own businesses. So, this was potentially a win–win situation whereby those who had the money invested and those who had the expertise managed. However, an intrinsic problem, discussed as far back as the time of Adam Smith, soon surfaced in modern corporations. This problem, later called opportunistic behavior, was that those who controlled an enterprise could act in ways that contradicted the interests of its owners. For example, managers could simply shirk their duties (and still get paid, at least for a while) or pursue objectives other than those directly related to enhancing a company's profitability (a relevant example is excessive pay packages for managers). Eloquently applied to the modern corporation in a landmark article on the agency theory by Jensen and Meckling (1976), agency theory implies that entrepreneurs, shareholders, and managers should find ways to minimize the loss of value that arises from the separation of ownership and management. These ways, ranging from hostile takeovers to legal requirements for the structure of boards of directors, are elements of corporate governance.

Agency theory is directed at the ubiquitous agency relationship, in which one party (the principal) delegates work to another (the agent), who performs that work. This theory is mainly concerned with resolving two problems that can occur in agency relationships. The first is the agency problem that arises when: (i) the desires or goals of the principal and agent conflict and (ii) it is difficult or expensive for the principal to verify that the agent has behaved appropriately. The second is the risk-sharing problem that arises when the principal and agent have different attitudes toward risk. In other words, the principal and the agent may prefer different actions because of different risk preferences. Due to these two problems, principals are often worried about managerial opportunism – top-level managers' self-interest seeking with guile. Opportunism is both an attitude and a set of behaviors. Top executives' reputations and past experience are an imperfect predictor, and opportunistic behaviors cannot be observed until they have occurred. Consequently, principals establish governance and control mechanisms to prevent agents from acting opportunistically. While board directors have long been a main representative of the principal (owner) governing top executives' decisions and behaviors, independent auditors and lawyers are also becoming important watchdogs, rather than just advisors, working for shareholders and other critical stakeholders. Still, directors mainly govern top executives' behaviors from an internal lens – evaluating the latter's behaviors and performances based on the standards, rules, goals, and charters set forth by the board. Meanwhile, independent auditors and lawyers largely emphasize an external lens – checking and ensuring the compliance of top executives and the companies they lead with various financial, accounting, taxation, and legal standards set forth by the regulators and legislators.

Corporate governance, nevertheless, requires an appropriate design and execution that optimally balance out the effectiveness of corporate governance with the quality of strategic decisions. In this sense, therefore, it is incorrect to presume a perfect linear correlation between the level of corporate governance and the level of corporate performance. A well-designed corporate governance system is necessary to the point that it effectively guides and monitors top executives' behaviors while not hindering the latter's flexibility and aspiration to make decisions that are in the best interest of a company's long-term growth. Put simply, companies should avoid a situation of "the best-governed but worst-managed". For instance, facing too many or too rigid governance rules, CEOs who are always second-guessed by their boards may soon become too risk-averse, opting to pursue strategies that are "safe" but ultimately suppressing a firm's long-term growth and expansion.

It is worthwhile here to define "stakeholders" in the corporate governance framework. As explained earlier, corporate governance is, broadly speaking, about the relationship between the corporation and the stakeholders that determines and controls the strategic direction and performance of the corporation. Stakeholders such as creditors and employees play an important role in influencing how corporate governance systems work in practice. In fact, many countries have called for information on material issues regarding employees and other stakeholders to be disclosed. Nevertheless, different stakeholders have different roles and power in the framework of corporate governance, and their roles and power further vary according to different countries (e.g., creditors and employees are more powerful in influencing corporate governance in Japan and Germany). Creditor rights are important in influencing both the access and terms of finance for companies, and typically arise from bankruptcy and other laws and the contractual relations established under them. Employee rights may derive as much from collective agreements or from international undertakings by a government as from legal provisions. Performance-enhancing mechanisms range from explicit incentives such as share distributions and forms of performance-related pay to the establishment of a corporate culture to motivate employees, employee consultation, and representation on the boards. In addition, customers and suppliers are sometimes identified as stakeholders if they make costly and specific commitments to the company and are closely involved in contributing to its success. However, their influence on corporate governance tends to be weaker than that of creditors and employees since their interests are usually handled outside the framework of corporate governance via private contractual arrangements and other market mechanisms. In most advanced market economies, relational transactions are more the norm than the exception to define customer–supplier relationships. Surely, such relationships will depend not only on trust but also on efficient methods of contract enforcement including a framework for conciliation and arbitration. The OECD *Guidelines for Multinational Enterprises* – an OECD voluntary code of conduct setting forth government-backed recommendations for MNCs – provides standards and principles for dealing with *inter alia*, the complex stakeholder issues.

1.2 Understanding Corporate Governance in MNCs

The importance of corporate governance in MNCs has never been more evident than today. Recent MNC debacles, corporate accounting scandals, and the drastic deflation of market values in the US and around the world have resulted in extra attention to this issue. Current attempts at legislative and organizational reform for better self-governance seem to be a precursor to companies looking beyond the "earnings game".

MNCs must now deal with more demanding global shareholder and stakeholder groups that seek greater disclosure and more transparent explanations for major decisions, thus escalating pressure to run global businesses in the best interests of these highly demanding groups. Although external regulations are one way to improve governance, the prime responsibility for good governance and accountability should lie within the company rather than outside it.

Recent publications tend to treat MNCs as merely large versions of regular companies, without considering their unique properties or differentiating them from large domestic firms, resulting in limited understanding of corporate governance for firms engaging in international expansion and operations. In the context of an MNC, corporate governance is the system that not only monitors the relationship between executives and stakeholders (including shareholders) but also directs its various globally dispersed businesses and pinpoints the distribution of power, rights, and responsibilities among critical participants in the corporate-level decision-making process that affects worldwide corporate affairs. Corporate governance in publicly traded MNCs generally contains two related tiers:

1. Parent-level corporate governance – how the parent company's rights, power and responsibilities are divided and monitored.
2. Subsidiary-level corporate governance – how foreign subsidiaries that have their own board of directors deal with their shareholders and other local stakeholders while simultaneously answering to and integrating with the parent firm.

Subsidiaries with their own board of directors are either independently listed and traded on foreign stock exchanges (in this case with local public shareholders) or they are not listed on exchanges but meet either a host country's legal requirements or a parent firm's strategic considerations for establishing such boards. This subsidiary-level board of directors governs the subsidiary as a legal entity although there is considerable variation in local and legal requirements as well as how parent and subsidiary choose to structure the role, responsibility, and use of such boards. Subsidiaries with their own board of directors are generally not wholly owned by the parent MNC. If an MNC participates in some ownership in a foreign enterprise but not to the extent that it actually controls the enterprise, then this foreign unit is not considered second-tier governance. Although subsidiaries that do not have their own board of directors are not strongly related to an MNC's overall corporate governance, they at least impact an MNC's corporate accountability in a fundamental way. First-tier governance influences the second-tier through ownership holding, operational coordination, corporate support, and performance monitoring. Second-tier governance in turn channels back to the first-tier through advice provision, governance sharing, information reporting, and directorate expansion. Figure 1.1 graphically shows this two-tier governance and accountability system.

Corporate governance is not synonymous with organizational governance; it is just a part of it. Organizational governance comprises both managerial governance and corporate governance. Corporate governance involves governance and control of corporate affairs while managerial governance emphasizes those internal processes

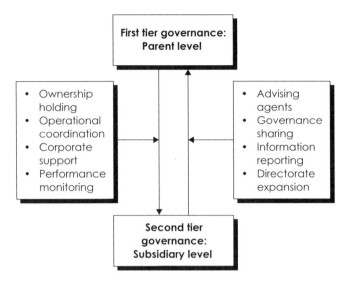

First tier governance:
Parent level

- Ownership holding
- Operational coordination
- Corporate support
- Performance monitoring

- Advising agents
- Governance sharing
- Information reporting
- Directorate expansion

Second tier governance:
Subsidiary level

Figure 1.1 Two-tier corporate governance in MNCs

and structures that regulate operational decisions and business activities undertaken by an MNC's various subunits (departments, divisions, subsidiaries, and affiliates). Managerial governance includes the systems that bring about internal adherence within the corporation to a set of strategic goals designed by top management through using corporate power or authority. Unlike corporate governance that often uses ownership concentration, board composition, board leadership, and executive compensation, managerial governance is a more direct intervention involving output monitoring, bureaucratic monitoring, and cultural monitoring (see Eisenhardt, 1985). To apply output monitoring, an MNC estimates or sets appropriate targets or outcome indicators for its foreign subunits and then monitors performance relative to these targets. Bureaucratic monitoring consists of a limited and explicit set of codified rules, regulations, or blueprints that delineate desired performance in terms of output or behavior. In this system, authority or power is exercised through control over resources.

1.3 Corporate Governance Differences between MNCs and Domestic Firms

Corporate governance in MNCs shares many common elements with corporate governance in domestic firms. Conventional mechanisms of corporate governance such as ownership concentration, board member participation, and executive compensation apply to both. However, corporate governance in MNCs differs from that in domestic firms in several ways. First, MNCs have to deal with more demanding and more diverse global shareholders and stakeholder groups that seek greater disclosure and more transparent explanations for major decisions. These highly demanding groups pressure global businesses to act in their best interests. For geographically diversified MNCs, especially those cross-listed in multiple nations, a high percentage of shareholders may be dispersed around the world with varying anticipations, preferences, and needs. This situation results in greater coordination costs and governance complexity in boardrooms and executive offices. Moreover, MNCs must respond to the needs of additional stakeholders who may influence corporate decisions. For instance, as MNCs increasingly rely on joint ventures, foreign creditors, and cross-border acquisitions, these foreign partners may shape some corporate decisions on equity ownership, capital structure, and leverage capabilities.

Second, as a growing number of MNCs become listed on multiple exchanges in multiple countries, and certain overseas units become independently listed on host country exchanges, MNC corporate governance is also becoming much more complex and subject to many more institutional constraints. For instance, MNCs that are active in Europe, North America, and Japan may have to comply with both Anglo-American (stock market capitalism) and relational-insider (welfare capitalism) governance systems simultaneously (Kim and Limpaphayom, 1998; LaPorta *et al.*, 1998). Building on agency theory, stock market capitalism favors the separation of ownership from control, financing through the stock market, and the use of an independent board of directors (Fama and Jensen, 1983; Jensen and Meckling, 1976). Building on relational rent logic or pluralistic notions of distributive justice, welfare capitalism (e.g., used in Germany, Japan, and France) favors a stakeholder-friendly policy; it uses a board that comprises representatives for large share investors who engage in collaborative decision making, or representatives for key customers, suppliers, and allied corporations on a reciprocal basis (sitting in each other's board). Even within the same system, different countries differ in their governance practices. For instance, German and French firms use two separate boards, including a supervisory board and an executive board. Typically, an outside non-executive director chairs the supervisory board, which consists of shareholders and other key constituencies (e.g., employees and bank representatives). This supervisory board is mainly responsible for overseeing management performance. The company's CEO chairs the executive board and acts as the spokesperson for management and as contact person for the supervisory board. In Japan, however, such supervisory boards do not exist and, moreover, most directors are company executives. Thus, control over management is weak in Japan and the board is often a web of interpersonal relationships that results from cross-shareholding by affiliated companies (Kim and Limpaphayom, 1998).

Third, unlike domestic firms that normally have only one board and one executive team, MNCs may have several boards or executive teams at different levels or in different countries. Many second-tier subsidiaries are legally and financially independent from their parent company and have their own boards and independent executive teams. Effective corporate governance in an independent subsidiary enhances its agent's (second-tier CEO) compliance with the principal's (subunit board and the parent company) interests by minimizing divergent and opportunistic behaviors. Often, the parent company has a representative (or representatives) in the subsidiary board to monitor second-tier executive performance. Because second-tier subsidiaries are mostly located overseas, corporate governance systems for them are likely to be heterogeneous and subject to different institutional, legal, and regulatory constraints. These multi-tier boards collectively comprise the total corporate governance structure for an MNC; yet these hierarchical tiers are sequentially interrelated. This structure leads to a large array of globally scattered principals (especially foreign shareholders), and the corporate governance framework is subject to institutional and legal constraints dispersed over many different countries. Illicit behavior by management of independently listed units at any tier will harm an MNC's image; therefore the corporate governance framework in MNCs must address the distribution of rights and responsibilities not only among the various participants (the board, executives, shareholders, and other stakeholders) at each tier but also between the two tiers within the MNC's umbrella structure.

Fourth, the corporate governance framework for MNCs includes additional governance mechanisms other than the conventional ones that domestic firms use. Domestic firms often employ ownership concentration (e.g., the percentage of institutional investors), board composition (e.g., the proportion of insider directors vs. outside directors), board leadership (e.g., CEO as chairman), board representation (e.g., the extent that other stakeholders participate in the board), and executive composition (e.g., behavior-based vs. outcome-based) in their corporate governance systems (Baliga, Moyer, and Rao, 1996; Baysinger and Butler, 1985; Chaganti, Mahajan, and Sharma, 1985; Singh and Harianto, 1989; Tosi and Gomez-Mejia, 1989). This conventional framework, tailored to the stock market capitalism and focused on the use of the shareholder governance system, is inadequate in satisfying governance needs for today's MNCs, which need additional mechanisms (Klapper and Love, 2002). As we will detail later, there should be three simultaneously operating governance systems: (i) market-based governance; (ii) culture-based governance; and (iii) discipline-based governance. Together, these three unique systems constitute an MNC's corporate governance framework for all tiers. Conventional mechanisms emphasize market-based governance and largely neglect culture-based and discipline-based approaches and instruments. While stock market-based governance does not, in large part, apply to MNCs that are not listed on exchanges (e.g., Levi Strauss), these MNCs still need to use culture-based and discipline-based schemes.

Fifth, MNC corporate governance must be designed to cope with much more complex strategies, structures, and environments than domestic corporate governance. Governance design requires not only independence, transparency, and accountability – the three core principles of governance in any country – but also a balance of effective governance and business growth. Therefore, governance design should not be isolated from an MNC's cornerstone strategies, visions, and plans; instead it should integrate them so that governance and growth mutually enhance each other. For instance, corporate governance at the second tier should be aligned with an MNC's organizational structure for managing worldwide businesses. Culture-based and discipline-based governance mechanisms must be configured properly with managerial governance systems embedded in parent–subsidiary relationships. The corporate governance framework should also be more harmonized and greatly coordinated if an MNC adopts a global strategy than if it uses a multidomestic strategy.

Finally, MNCs face heterogeneous corporate governance standards institutionalized by different countries throughout the world, whereas domestic firms in one country tend to face harmonized standards. In other words, there is no single universally accepted and implemented corporate governance standard across different countries. Although attempts have been made in formulating such "lowest common denominator" principles (OECD, 1999), there is yet little widespread compliance except by large companies who need access to capital in various markets. Where such codes of conduct or benchmark principles do exist, they are based almost entirely on the Anglo-American approach to corporate governance, which emphasizes various mechanisms to avoid potential problems inherent in a market-based governance environment, as opposed to a relationship-based environment that is present in many regions, including continental Europe and Japan. In addition, the existence of different systems of corporate governance around the world make it difficult to identify contentious issues in corporate governance specific to MNCs, which operate across borders and cultures. Just witness the case of the fundamental question about how best to achieve the effectiveness of the board of directors. There is much disagreement around the world on how the board can best fulfill its roles. In the Anglo-American sense, a well-functioning board is one that addresses tendencies of self-interested opportunism, found frequently among CEOs. For this purpose, remedies such as separation of chairman and CEO, the presence of a majority of independent members on various board committees, and transparency of pay packages of senior executives have been proposed and implemented in many corporations in the US and the UK. Although there are now many codes of conduct advocating similar principles around the world, convergence in practice does not seem to have arrived yet (Khanna, Kogan, and Palepu, 2002). In other countries, boards are viewed under a different light. Japanese corporations reflect this fact with their boards comprising company "insiders", i.e., managers and CEO, the very same people that the board is charged to oversee. Still another example is the focus on participatory mechanisms in German boards. German corporations are obliged by law to include labor representatives in the upper tier of their two-tiered boards. As these examples show, there are various ways to achieve effectiveness of the board. The implication for researchers is that work on corporate governance and MNCs needs to incorporate the heterogeneity of governance issues of host and home countries of MNCs. Figure 1.2 summarizes the main distinctions between MNCs and domestic firms with respect to corporate governance.

- MNCs must deal with more demanding and more diverse global shareholders and stakeholders.
- MNCs have more complex governance structures that are subject to more institutional and strategic constraints.
- MNCs have multi-tier or multi-level governance systems which jointly constitute their overall corporate governance framework.
- MNCs must establish and execute a larger number of governance mechanisms and instruments to cope with globalizing needs and cross-country differences in governance norms.
- MNCs must configure corporate governance with a multitude of much more complicated strategies, structures, and environments.
- MNCs face heterogeneous corporate governance standards institutionalized by different countries in which they invest and operate.

Figure 1.2 Differences in corporate governance in MNCs compared to domestic firms

1.4 Mechanisms of Corporate Governance

Conventional wisdom emphasizes that the corporate governance framework or system comprises several market-based mechanisms including ownership concentration, board member participation, and executive compensation. This is a narrow description that ignores several non-market-based mechanisms that fundamentally underpin or undercut corporate governance effectiveness. Here I categorize various corporate mechanisms into three groups: (i) market-based; (ii) culture-based; and (iii) discipline-based. These mechanisms apply to all publicly traded companies, regardless of whether they are domestic or multinational. What really sets MNCs apart from domestic firms is that the content of these mechanisms for MNCs is significantly more complex, and the execution of these mechanisms is substantially more widespread and far-reaching as MNCs' governance must be able to suppress not only corporate- or parent-level, but also regional- and subunit-level, managerial opportunism. Diversified domestic firms often use the M-form (multidivisional organizational structure) to control managerial opportunism. M-form, however, becomes much more complicated as a firm globally invests and expands. Along with internationalization, most frontline subunits are located overseas, often requiring a shift from the M-form to the matrix form. Under the traditional M-form, corporate office and board members jointly monitor managers' strategic decisions. For MNCs, internationally diversified and geographically dispersed businesses make it very difficult for corporate office and board to monitor frontline managers' strategic decisions. Instead, they have to rely on their own "agencies", namely regional headquarters executives and/or product divisional executives as well as subunit boards to oversee and control frontline managers' behavior and performance. Again, governance mechanisms themselves do not differ between domestic and multinational enterprises; but the content and context of each mechanism as well as the internal structure and external environment wherein these mechanisms are designed and executed vary significantly between domestic firms and MNCs, the issue being addressed in Chapter 4.

1.4.1 Market-based governance

In most publicly traded MNCs, market-based corporate governance mechanisms include: (i) ownership concentration; (ii) board composition; (iii) market discipline; (iv) board chairmanship; (v) board size; (vi) management remuneration; (vii) interlocking directorate; and (viii) inbreeding. These mechanisms function at both the first- and second-tier corporate governance systems. The only main difference between the two tiers is that in the second-tier ownership structure, the parent company serves as a major institutional investor or a large-block shareholder. This institutional ownership is quasi-insider in nature as the parent company legally holds the second-tier firm's investment stake and operationally coordinates the latter's activities with other corporate members in order to save common function costs, reduce financial risk, or create technological or operational synergies among them.

The first component of market-based corporate governance is *ownership concentration*, which is defined by the number of large-block shareholders (i.e., mutual funds, pension funds, and trust funds), as well as by the proportion of shares they own. These institutional owners become increasingly active in their demands that corporations adopt effective governance mechanisms to control managerial decisions. For instance, there are 10 institutional and mutual fund investors, led by Capital Research and Management Company, Barrow, Hanley Mewhinney & Strauss, Barclays Bank, and Vanguard Group, holding in total over 43 percent of Carnival's outstanding shares. Similarly, 62 percent of Nike's shares are held by institutional and mutual fund owners, led by Fidelity, Janus Capital, Wellington Management, and Barclays Bank. Ownership concentration by a small number of large-block shareholders can improve governance effectiveness because it strengthens shareholders' power when dealing with management (Mizruchi, 1983). The higher the degree of ownership concentration, the more likely managers' strategic decisions will mesh with shareholder value maximization (Tihanyi *et al.*, 2003). Institutional owners are vigilant not only of CEO behavior and performance but also of the board's effectiveness and transparency. An overly concentrated ownership structure, however, has its drawbacks. The power of small individual shareholders may be weakened when equity ownership is concentrated within a few large-block institutions. Moreover, a conflict of interest between large-block shareholders and small shareholders and between shareholders and other stakeholders may increase as executives may be more likely to maximize a few large-block shareholders' value at the expense of smaller ones or other important stakeholders.

Many pension and investment funds now scrutinize the activities of foreign firms as their holdings become more diverse geographically. In counterpoint, many firms find themselves venturing beyond national borders in the search for affordable capital. For example, about 500 non-US firms are currently listed on the New York Stock Exchange (NYSE). However, such listings often impose higher standards of scrutiny or different accounting policies. Yet the lure of capital is strong, as demonstrated by Toyota's recent decision to explore listing on the NYSE. Since the capital pools in many economies, from European to emerging economies, are limited, American funds are a prominent source of cash inflows. Continued cross-border investment means that international institutional investors become increasingly influential or powerful in shaping board and shareholder meetings.

Second, *board composition*, or the proportion of "inside" directors (executive directors) vs. "outside" directors (non-executive directors), also has strong implications on corporate governance because the board is essentially the "guardian" of the principal's interest. Inside directors participate in the decision processes and are able to access inside information. Because of their status, inside directors can be easily influenced by the CEO in the decision-making process. Having insiders on the board may cause the boardroom to be more knowledgeable, but, at the same time, having lots of insiders can make the company more vulnerable to scandals and illicit behaviors. Insiders tend to be more skewed toward the interests of the CEO rather than the interests of the shareholders. Thus, many believe that effective boards should be composed of greater proportions of outside directors (Borokhovich, Parrino and Trapani, 1996; Mizruchi, 1983; Zahra and Pearce, 1989) because outside directors can make more exhaustive and profound evaluations of strategic decisions and management behavior than inside directors (Baysinger and Butler, 1985). At Northern Trust, there is no insider sitting on the board of directors. At Lehman Brothers' 10-member board, there is only one insider (Richard S. Fuld who is chairman and CEO). In addition, outside members may include some representatives who voice opinions for other important stakeholders such as key creditors, employees, suppliers, and customers. Nonetheless, because some outside directors may lack the professional knowledge (as well as the incentives and time in some cases) necessary for understanding the firm's businesses and decisions, selecting outside directors properly becomes crucial. In general, outside directors should be competent, committed, and have character. Competence includes experience and expertise in both business and management. Commitment is the availability to fulfill important duties such as learning about the business and company, preparing for meetings, and serving on committees. Character involves possessing a good personality, vision, enthusiasm, moral integrity, and interpersonal skills. If outsider-dominated boards are not competent, especially concerning product and market knowledge, it is then necessary to have some insiders on the board. Boards with these insiders typically are better informed during board meetings about intended strategic initiatives, the reasons for the initiatives, and the outcomes expected from them. Without this type of information, outsider-dominated boards may emphasize the use of financial, as opposed to strategic, controls to gather performance information to evaluate managers' performance. In Anheuser-Busch's board, three of 15 board members are insiders. This composition seems appropriate for the company since most outside directors do not have professional experience in the industry.

As an MNC globalizes, its foreign subsidiaries will become more active in the MNC's organizing and managing worldwide activities. Accordingly, a new type of "inside" directors, namely, foreign subsidiary executives, are likely to join in the MNC's corporate board. In particular, when a foreign unit (regional headquarters, investment-holding company overseas, dominantly owned joint venture, wholly owned subsidiary) plays a strategically paramount role in the MNC's overall global expansion, or this unit's contributions to the MNC's global sales, market share, technological development, and profit have a determining impact on the MNC's overall performance, such second-tier, or subsidiary-level, executives residing in other countries may be designated as "insider" directors who lead some frontline business units that are fundamental to the MNC's global success. Companies such as Sony, Motorola, Chrysler, and Ford have already used such second-tier foreign executives sitting in the parent-level corporate boards.

Market discipline is a third component of market-based corporate governance; it is an external mechanism, namely an open market for corporate control, which becomes active when a firm's internal controls fail, its performance is poor, and/or its management is ineffective. Market discipline may involve replacing incompetent CEOs, other key executives and/or board members, or it can come in the form of a takeover (especially a hostile one) by another corporation. Under a hostile takeover, both key executives and board members may be replaced by new management and new directors. If a target firm accepts a hostile takeover, executives and directors are likely to lose their jobs; if they instead choose to fend off the takeover attempt, then they must improve the firm's performance. For example, poor market performance as well as weak corporate governance of PeopleSoft led to Oracle's $9.2 billion hostile takeover bid in 2004. More than 60 percent of PeopleSoft's shareholders voted to accept Oracle's offer of $24 a share – a healthy premium to PeopleSoft's share price at the time. But PeopleSoft's directors spurned the bid, arguing that "most" of the shareholders continued to believe that the firm was more valuable. Oracle in turn stated that PeopleSoft had abused its takeover defenses to entrench incumbent managers and directors at the expense of the firm's shareholders.

When an MNC becomes more global, especially if it is cross-listed in several stock markets in different countries, market discipline or the takeover pressure it faces becomes stronger. Other things being equal, a more globalized company is likely to be watched by more companies around the world if this company has performed poorly. Put alternatively, there will be more potential "buyers" interested in taking over this poor-performing firm. In the situation where this poor-performing company has some critical and unique assets such as brand, distribution network, and R&D force, despite its poor financial performance for years, some powerful companies from other countries may initiate a hostile takeover to acquire the company in trouble. Such takeovers could be a more cost-effective way for foreign companies to acquire some strategic assets of another company in a target host country. Such strategic assets may be too difficult, too costly, or too time-consuming to build by foreign acquirers.

Fourth, *board chairmanship* involves whether or not a firm's CEO is also the board of directors' chairperson. Because a central role of the chairperson is to monitor top management behavior, this sort of CEO "duality" is likely to seriously hinder management accountability (Baliga, Moyer, and Rao, 1996) and may inhibit the board's ability to function properly as an independent body. Agency theory advocates the separation of these two positions to protect shareholders. Duality hampers the board's ability to effectively monitor and discipline top management because board members are more likely to have emotional, attitudinal, and functional dependence on the CEO and senior executives. Feelings of loyalty or responsibility toward the CEO may restrict the directors' freedom and independence to make difficult and contrary decisions (Singh and Harianto, 1989). But still, many companies, especially those in which their CEOs personally hold a sizable percentage of the ownership, have such duality, hoping to bring real experience into the boardroom while allowing CEOs to better fulfill their strategic initiatives and plans. For instance, Richard Parson is chairman of the board and CEO of Time Warner, Robert Tillman is chairman and CEO of Lowe's Companies, and Steven Reinemund is both chairman and CEO of PepsiCo, each retaining many shares of the company. Finally, this duality may also have some industry patterns. For instance, while Richard Fuld is both chairman and CEO of Lehman Brothers, many of Lehman's competitors are in a similar position, some of which include Merrill Lynch (Stanley O'Neal is chairman, president, CEO and COO), Goldman Sachs (Henry Paulson, Jr. is chairman and CEO), and Morgan Stanley (Philip Purcell is chairman and CEO).

International expansion may have certain implications on board chairmanship. First, as an MNC globalizes, a board chairperson's international experience becomes more important. Such experience is very valuable to making some critical board decisions involving international investments, global governance, and internal control of worldwide businesses. Second, as an MNC's global operations become significantly complex, there will be a greater pressure to separate the MNC's CEO from board chairmanship. This allows the CEO and board chairperson to focus on their respective agendas, especially allowing the CEO to effectively handle complicated operations and management.

Table 1.1 Compensation summary in Goldman Sachs

| Named executive officer | Year | Annual cash compensation | | Long-term compensation awards | | |
		Salary	Bonus	Restricted stock unit awards	Securities underlying options	All other compensation
Henry M. Paulson, Jr.	2003	$600,000	$0	$20,754,337	0	$46,242
Chairman of the board and CEO	2002	$600,000	$6,253,500	$2,603,735	99,039	$54,649
	2001	$600,000	$11,550,500	$0	221,078	$53,999
Lloyd C. Blankfein	2003	$600,000	$10,244,500	$9,291,128	0	$63,997
President and COO	2002	$600,000	$8,253,500	$3,619,344	137,670	$84,686
	2001	$600,000	$9,503,000	$0	180,676	$82,985
Robert S. Kaplan	2003	$600,000	$6,494,500	$5,475,984	0	$37,275
Vice chairman of Goldman Sachs	2002	$600,000	$4,003,500	$1,461,224	55,581	$39,479
	2001	$600,000	$5,408,000	$0	99,872	$39,645
John A. Thain	2003	$600,000	$10,244,500	$9,291,128	0	$63,997
Former president and COO	2002	$600,000	$5,753,500	$2,349,853	89,382	$84,686
	2001	$600,000	$9,944,000	$0	189,378	$82,985
Robert K. Steel	2003	$600,000	$6,494,500	$5,475,984	0	$63,997
Former vice chairman of	2002	$600,000	$4,753,500	$1,842,088	70,068	$84,686
Goldman Sachs	2001	$600,000	$7,298,000	$0	137,166	$82,985

Fifth, *board size* is an important factor of market-based corporate governance since there are drawbacks when boards are either too small or too large. Too small implies a higher agency cost since the CEO is better able to influence board meetings and decisions; the board also suffers from a shortage of services and expertise. When a board is too large, despite having a bigger and more diversified pool of expertise and resources, it is also more likely to have factions that increase group conflict (O'Reilly, Caldwell, and Barnett, 1989); it may also be inefficient in taking decisive action due to frequent interruptions or coordination difficulties (Shleifer and Vishny, 1997). Thus, even though a board's expertise may increase with size, the benefits may be outweighed by resulting slower decision making and more difficult coordination (Judge and Zeithmal, 1992).

Globalization does have some impact on the size of board and/or board committees. Both information-processing demands and agency costs increase with an MNC's internationalization. As a result, a larger board, or more specialized committees within the board, may be a remedy to cope with increased needs for information-processing and agency behavior monitoring. Sanders and Carpenter (1998) argue that international firms often handle increased and more varied dependencies by adding board members who increase the overall information-processing capacity of the group either because they have valuable experience with the international constituencies or some particular expertise that applies.

Sixth, *management remuneration* as a market-based governance mechanism can be either behavior-based or outcome-based (Eisenhardt, 1989). It is a governance mechanism that seeks to align the interests of managers and owners through salaries, bonuses, and long-term incentive compensation such as stock awards and options. Tables 1.1 and 1.2 summarize compensation for top executives at Goldman Sachs and for CEOs in several financial service companies.

When managerial behaviors are well understood and evaluated, a behavior-based scheme is generally more appropriate. In such a scenario, the agent receives a fixed wage for taking well-defined actions and penalizes him or her for taking sub-optimal actions. When managerial behaviors are not well defined, outcome-based compensation plans that reward the agent's performance instead of actions are preferred. In any case, non-executive board members capable of independent judgment should set executive remuneration. Information regarding the remuneration of key executives and executive board members should be disclosed to investors so that they may properly assess the costs and benefits of such remuneration plans, incentive schemes, and stock option plans (Glenn-Hubbard and Palia, 1995). Remuneration committees composed

Table 1.2 Executive compensation summary in the financial services industry

Company	Year	Salary	Bonus/Awards	Total
Lehman Brothers (Richard Fuld)	2003	$750,000	$6,650,000	$7,400,000
Goldman Sachs (Henry Paulson)	2003	$600,000	$20,800,000	$21,400,000
Morgan Stanley (Philip Purcell)	2003	$775,000	$7,120,000	$7,895,000
Merrill Lynch (Stanley O'Neal)	2003	$500,000	$13,500,000	$14,000,000

of independent members may also be established to oversee these issues (the NYSE and NASDAQ require such independent compensation committees as part of their listing requirements). Despite differences in compensation standards across countries, it is generally agreed that: (i) executive remuneration should reflect executive responsibilities; (ii) remuneration should be reasonable and comparable with market standards; and (iii) incentive schemes should be clearly linked to performance benchmarks (Davis, Schoorman, and Donaldson, 1997; Tosi and Gomez-Mejia, 1989). Executive compensation should be organized in a formal and transparent procedure; remuneration committees, composed of independent directors, can help achieve this goal.

A seventh element in market-based corporate governance is a widely used practice whereby two or more companies exchange board members; this is known as *interlocking directorate*. Often, these companies are strategic partners such as those in long-term supply agreements, R&D consortia, joint ventures, or alliance groups. When two or more companies are cross-shareholders, interlocking directorate is even more common. Interlocking directorate can benefit member firms in several ways: information sharing among key executives or board members, collaborating and knowledge sharing among member organizations, and obtaining assistance and support from group members when a firm struggles financially or operationally (Mizruchi, 1997). However, from the agency cost perspective, interlocking directorate may obstruct decision-making independence and transparency because underperforming managers who maintain good personal ties with their interlocking partners may stay in their jobs (Zajac, 1988). It may also lead to conflicts of interests since board members may be biased due to conflicting objectives of member companies. Thus, the use of interlocking directorate should be structured in such a way that decision-making independence and transparency are not lost.

Finally, *inbreeding* is a practice whereby senior executives join the board after retiring from management. From a resource utilization perspective, this practice can enable a firm to continue to utilize and leverage the manager's expertise, experience, and personal ties; this is conducive to continuity and stability of firm evolution. However, from an agency cost or corporate governance perspective, inbreeding's negative effects may outweigh its positive effects. A board where former managers sit would probably not be proactive in detecting and correcting corporate fraud or other illicit behaviors (Lorsch, 1989). Inbreeding may also lead to emotional and attitudinal dependence on key executives, which then may impair the independent judgment of the board as whole.

1.4.2 Culture-based governance

Market-based governance mechanisms are necessary, but instilling the right culture to support corporate governance is essential. Culture-based governance, which comprises (i) governance culture and (ii) corporate integrity, sets the moral tone for governance and accountability. *Governance culture* refers to the statements, visions, slogans, values, role models, and social rituals that are unique to, and used by, an MNC's board members and key executives at both the first and second tiers to engender corporate governance, transparency, and accountability. Governance structures count for little if the culture counteracts them. For instance, board members and key executives are exemplars of best practice; they should resist opportunism and promote accountability. Once a CEO "crosses the line", employees may think it is okay to cross the line themselves. A detailed and instrumental pro-accountability and governance statement guides executives and directors in identifying, whistle-blowing, and rectifying problems associated with governance, accountability, and ethics. Vision and commitment from key executives and board members also play a significant role in improving governance and account-ability. Ethical leadership sets moral standards for the organization; leaders should be champions and role models who lead pro-governance efforts. Role models set a positive ethical climate because humans as social beings are influenced by other humans and generally strive to "fit in". An organization should also take measures to communicate its anti-corruption culture and values in an open environment that encourages par-ticipation and feedback; employees should be informed about how and to whom they should report violations.

MNCs should especially work to create a governance culture that discourages cheating. If the company culture has been compromised by cheating or if a firm is in an industry where loose practices on booking revenues and expenditures are sometimes tolerated, it is then particularly important to make a few high-profile decisions that signal change. To nourish a culture that improves corporate governance, it is also crucial to broaden and deepen disclosure on corporate websites and in annual reports. Websites should have a corporate governance section containing such information as how to get a motion to a proxy ballot and the attendance records of board meetings. Furthermore, to foster independence among non-executive directors, executive directors and key managers should develop a cultural climate in which non-executive members are encouraged to express constructive criticism or dissatisfaction with the manage-ment team. They need to collectively and frankly discuss their views about executive performance, the strategic direction of the company, and concerns about areas in which they feel inadequately briefed.

Governance and accountability also necessitate *corporate integrity* which is con-cerned with the disposition and behavior directed at realizing the wholeness of the organization. A formal structure is necessary to maintain integrity and coherently realize legitimate moral expectations. When an organization is highly globalized and decentralized, it is imperative that corporate or headquarters have an integrated struc-ture to control accountability policies and procedures. Apart from a formal structure to educate, detect, and rectify illicit behaviors, an organization may also establish com-mittees to improve governance and transparency; these committees can draft codes of conduct and educate and train employees on compliance procedures. Lastly, transparency throughout an entire organization reduces the opportunity for employees to engage in illicit behaviors that hurt governance and accountability. Thorough and extensive record keeping and reporting can document key aspects of an MNC's compliance effort and can help monitor its effectiveness. Even reporting minor incidents within an organ-ization can convey a zero tolerance policy for questionable behavior. Failure to report such occurrences may imply that such irregularities will be tolerated. Better auditing and monitoring of internal accounting also contribute to better detection of corporate malfeasance. Organizations should have clear and concise accounting policies that prohibit off-the-books accounts or inadequately or improperly conducted transactions. They should monitor accounts for deceptive book-keeping entries that may disguise illegal transactions or manipulate earnings and profit figures.

1.4.3 Discipline-based governance

Market-based and culture-based governance mechanisms are necessary but not sufficient in ensuring good corporate governance unless rules are established and executed. Discipline-based governance entails: (i) executive penalty; (ii) internal auditing; (iii) a conduct code; and (iv) an ethics program.

First, executive compensation is not enough to monitor and control agents' actions; it also requires an *executive penalty* scheme; poorly performing or ill-behaved executives should be disciplined and penalized. Financial and non-financial penalties for non-performance can be alternatives or supplements to incentive schemes. A typical executive compensation package includes a base salary, benefits in kind, an annual bonus, share options, other long-term incentive schemes, and pension rights. Penalties should be significant enough to really impact agents' incentives and influence their behavior and performance. Penalties may include base salary reduction or freeze, bonus elimination, fine payment, power downsizing (e.g., from CEO to director) and, most harshly, total dismissal. With such penalties in place, agents are less likely to "gamble" with the firm's assets. Thus, penalties can help better align the interests of shareholders and management.

Second, *independent auditing* of corporate affairs is a prerequisite for discipline-based governance: internal and external independent auditing can identify misconduct that can then be penalized. An independent auditing committee comprising only independent and non-executive directors should be established as an important arm of the board and to form a nexus for the work of the internal auditor. External auditors should be appointed not by management but by shareholders in their general meeting. Both external and internal auditing should be independent such that the auditors are not intimidated by senior management or executive directors. A governance body such as an auditing committee should regularly and frequently meet with external auditors (without management present) and discuss any contentious issues that have arisen with management during the course of the audit. The auditing committee should monitor the integrity of the financial statements, review significant financial reporting judgments, assess the internal financial control system and internal auditing function, and attempt to identify any misconduct beyond the financial statements.

Third, *conduct codes* make expectations about legal and ethical behavior clear, increase the likelihood of detection, assure the punishment of transgressions, reward desired behaviors, and discipline those who engage in illegal behavior. The codes heighten executive awareness of corporate policy and enlist their support in fighting misconduct. Codes may contain general precepts, mandate specific practices, provide clearly stated provisions to address legalities, deal with ethical concerns and detail sanctions, outline enforcement, and stipulate methods of investigation.

Lastly, *ethics programs* are organizational control systems that encourage shared ethical goals and rule compliance. Ethics and compliance training programs for board members and senior management officials should be held regularly. It is also necessary to educate overseas executives and board members about host country practices in corporate governance and accountability. It is important not to delegate too much discretionary authority to offshore executives in case they are prone to engaging in misconduct. Additional ethical practices include formalized procedures or mechanisms for evaluating ethical and legal performance and for rewarding or punishing behavior. Examples of such practices include establishing a system for auditing and reporting legal-ethical violations, having a formal ethics department for initiating, coordinating, and supervising an organization's anti-corruption guidelines, and developing a cross-functional committee for setting and assessing ethics policies and procedures. For a reporting mechanism to be effective, it should be accompanied by adequate policies on confidentiality and non-retaliation in order to foster open communication when ordinary channels fail.

CASE EXAMPLE 1.1: MICKEY MOUSE GETS TRAPPED?

The Walt Disney Company was founded in 1923 by Walt Disney, and is today one of the largest media and entertainment corporations in the world. The company's corporate headquarters are located in Burbank, California. Disney had revenues of US$22 billion in 2002.

Ownership concentration

Around early 2002, the top 10 media companies were AOL Time Warner, Disney, General Electric, News Corporation, Viacom, Vivendi, Sony, Bertelsmann, AT&T, and Liberty Media. As a media conglomerate, Disney owns many different types of media businesses through vertical integrations, and it also becomes a target for large financial institutions such as stock mutual funds and pension funds. They control large blocks of shares and impact the company's strategic decision making. By comparing the number and percentage of institutional shareholders in Disney and its main competitor, Time Warner, one may find that they both have 10 institutional shareholders who possess over 60 percent of the total shares. (Disney: 65 percent; Time Warner: 69 percent – see Table 1.3). Moreover, Disney and Time Warner share five common shareholders: Barclays Bank, FMR Corporation, State Street Corporation, Citigroup Inc., and Vanguard Group, Inc. The high percentage of institutional shareholders is a prevalent phenomenon in the broadcasting and cable TV industry, and these shareholders have large power to get together to influence and monitor company operations and performance.

Table 1.3 Ownership concentration at Disney and Time Warner

Ownership information	The Walt Disney Company	Time Warner Inc.
Shares outstanding	2.05 billion	4.57 billion
% of shares held by all insiders and 5% owners	2%	9%
% of shares held by institutional and mutual fund owners	65%	69%
% of float held by institutional and mutual fund owners	66%	76%
Number of institutions holding shares	10	10

The recent mounting shareholder activism toward the Disney board is a perfect example of this. CalPERS (California Public Employees Retirement System), a large institutional investor known for its activism, chose Disney as its 2004 "Focus List" for poor financial and corporate governance performance. Major institutional shareholders have been critical of Eisner's (Disney's CEO) autocratic management style. Disney accepted their requirement to allow pension funds to suggest nominees for the company's board in May 2004. So far, Disney has benefited from its institutional shareholders and their active disciplining efforts toward ineffective top-level managers. But it is always a question mark as to what the optimal level of such influence exercised by large institutional shareholders should be since over-influence may be counter-productive, especially in hampering top management team's decision effectiveness in a fast-paced competitive environment.

Board composition

The Certificate of Incorporation of The Walt Disney Company provides that the board of directors shall consist of no fewer than nine and no more than 21 directors, with the exact number being determined from time to time by resolution of the board. It is clearly stated that: "each director shall at all times represent the interests of the shareholders of the Company, and exhibit high standards of integrity, commitment and independence of thought and judgment. Each director shall dedicate sufficient time, energy and attention to ensure the diligent performance of his or her duties, including attending shareholder meetings and meetings of the Board and Committees of which he or she is a member, and reviewing in advance all meeting materials. The Board shall meet the standards of independence from the Company. The Board shall encompass a range of talent, skill and expertise sufficient to provide sound and prudent guidance with respect to all of the Company's operations and interests. The Board shall reflect the diversity of the Company's shareholders, employees, customers, guests and communities." The board believes that a desirable target number of directors is 12 to 15. The 11 board members in 2004 were John Bryson, John Chen, Michael Eisner (CEO, insider), Judith Estrin, Robert Iger (insider), Aylwin Lewis, Monica Lozano, Robert Matschullat, George Mitchell (chairman), Leo O'Donovan, S.J., and Gary Wilson.

Among all directors, Michael Eisner, Disney CEO, and Robert Iger, Disney president and COO, are considered inside directors because of their employment as senior executives of the company. Bryson is considered a non-independent outside director because the level of business between the company and an entity of which his wife is an executive officer exceeded the financial threshold established by the newly amended guidelines in fiscal year 2003. The rest of the directors are all outsiders. Two new members from 2003 are Aylwin Lewis, president, chief multibranding and operating officer of YUM! Brands, Inc., and John Chen, chairman, CEO and president of Sybase, Inc. Disney's largest competitor, Time Warner, has four insiders and nine outsiders in a 13-person board. Furthermore, "the board has been comprised of nominally independent folks who in fact were cronies of Eisner or know-nothing ceremonial directors," said Delaware Chancellor William Chandler, and he also gave out the strong evidence that Eisner kept bringing in his personal attorney and close friends to the board.

Although a board does not necessarily require all members to be experts in all fields, it does require care, effort, and analysis to identify and select the right team of people to help the company with its current challenges and opportunities, to take the company forward into the future and to work in partnership with senior management, providing real insight and value-adding guidance. In order to achieve this, the board should have the right mix of skills and experience and be able to work together as a team while encouraging diverse and healthy debate in the interests of the company and its shareholders. Ideally, the board as a whole should have strategic thinking, analytical skills, appropriate professional experience, effective communication skills and knowledge of the organization and industry. So, typically, a board may have a mix of directors with skills in law, finance, marketing, operations relevant to the company's activities, international experience in the key industries in which the company operates, corporate governance, human resources, risk management, etc.

Regarding board size, it is quality, not quantity that counts for a good board. A small board of directors of the highest caliber, with complementary skills and experience and a degree of independence, can make for a more effective board than just sheer numbers of individuals. Indeed, a large board can very quickly become unwieldy and limit the opportunity for individual directors to make an effective contribution. The board size should ideally reflect the needs of the organization.

Mr. Eisner used to serve the dual role of chairman and CEO of Disney, but after a surprisingly large percentage of Disney shareholders withheld their support for Michael Eisner's re-appointment to head the board, the company split the chairman and CEO roles in March 2004. Eisner retains his chief executive position while former Senator George Mitchell takes over chairman duties. The board reiterated its approval of Eisner's leadership and the company's strategy.

Although the action curbs Eisner's control over Disney and addresses the concerns of corporate governance groups who had called for the change, it will not satisfy the company's most vocal critics, ex-board members Stanley Gold and Roy E. Disney. Mitchell, another controversial choice as chairman, has also been criticized by Gold and Roy Disney as being too close to Eisner and not independent enough because his law firm had worked for Disney in the past.

Board committees

There are currently four standing committees in Disney:

- Executive Committee (George Mitchell, chair, Michael Eisner and Gary Wilson).
- Audit Committee (Robert Matschullat, chair, John Chen, Monica Lozano, and Leo O'Donovan, S.J.).
- Compensation Committee (Judith Estrin, chair, Robert Matschullat, and Leo O'Donovan, S.J.).
- Governance and Nominating Committee (Monica Lozano, chair, Judy Estrin and Aylwin Lewis).

Disney states that "Committees shall be established by the Board from time to time to facilitate and assist in the execution of the Board's responsibilities. A Committee shall be constituted to address issues that, because of their complexity, technical nature, level of detail, time requirements and/or sensitivity, cannot be adequately addressed within the normal agenda for Board meetings. Each Committee shall have full power and authority, in consultation with the Chairman of the Board, to retain the services of such advisers and experts, including counsel, as the Committee deems necessary or appropriate with respect to specific matters within its purview."

Audit Committee

The purpose of the Audit Committee is to assist the board in its oversight of:

- the integrity of the company's financial statements;
- the company's compliance with legal and regulatory requirements;
- the qualifications and independence of the company's independent auditors; and
- the performance of the company's independent auditors and of the company's internal audit function.

This committee meets at least four times a year and may call special meetings as required. Meetings may be called by the chair of the committee or the chairman of the board. The results of the meetings are reported regularly to the full board. In the area of financial reporting, the committee monitors the preparation by management of the company's quarterly and annual external financial reports. In carrying out this responsibility, the committee reviews with management the significant financial reporting issues, judgments, and estimates used in developing the financial reports, including analyses of the effects of alternative GAAP methods on the financial statements. It also reviews the accounting and reporting treatment of significant transactions outside the company's ordinary operations. It meets periodically with the company's independent auditors (in private, as appropriate) to:

1. Review their reasoning in accepting or questioning significant decisions made by management in preparing the financial reports.
2. Review any audit problems or difficulties and management's response.
3. Review any outstanding disagreements with management that would cause them to issue a non-standard report on the company's financial statements.
4. Examine the appropriateness of the company's accounting principles (including the quality, not just the acceptability, of accounting principles) and the clarity of disclosure practices used or proposed.
5. Determine if any restrictions have been placed by management on the scope of their audit.
6. Discuss any other matters the committee deems appropriate.

The committee also bears primary responsibility for overseeing the company's relationship with its independent auditors. In carrying out this responsibility, the committee is directly responsible for the appointment, compensation, retention, and oversight of the work of the company's independent auditors, in consultation with the full board. It reviews the scope and extent of audit services to be provided and the overall audit plan, including the risk factors considered in determining the audit scope, the independent auditors' annual letter pursuant to Independence Standards Board Standard No. 1, outlining all relationships that may impact their independence, and at least annually, obtain and review a report by the company's independent auditors describing the independent auditor firm's internal quality-control procedures.

The committee also has responsibility for overseeing that management has implemented an effective system of internal control that helps promote the reliability of financial and operating information and compliance with applicable laws, regulations and company policies, including those related to risk management, ethics, and conflicts of interest.

Compensation Committee

The Compensation Committee holds at least four regular meetings each year and additional meetings as may be required. Meetings may be called by the chair of the committee, the chairman of the board or any two members of the committee. The committee has direct responsibility to:

1. Review and approve corporate goals and objectives relevant to the compensation of the company's CEO, evaluate the performance of the CEO in light of those goals and objectives, and, either as a committee or together with the other independent members of the board of directors (as directed by the board), determine and approve the compensation level for the CEO based upon this evaluation.
2. Make recommendations to the board of directors with respect to non-CEO compensation, incentive-compensation plans and equity-based plans.
3. Produce a report of the committee on executive compensation as required by the Securities and Exchange Commission to be included in the company's annual proxy statement or annual report on Form 10-K filed with the Securities and Exchange Commission.

To carry out these purposes, the committee has the responsibilities set forth below:

- Overall policy: The committee shall conduct a periodic review of the company's general executive compensation policies and strategies and report and make recommendations to the board with respect thereto.
- Executive performance: The committee shall review and approve corporate goals and objectives relevant to compensation of the CEO, the COO and/or the president and any other executive officers, and periodically evaluate their respective performances in light of such goals and objectives. The committee shall have authority, either as a committee or acting together with the other independent members of the board of directors (as directed by the board) with respect to all matters relating to compensation of the CEO, to determine the compensation of the CEO, the COO and/or the president based on this evaluation.
- Section 162(m) executives: The committee shall identify, in consultation with the management of the company, persons subject to Section 162(m) of the Internal Revenue Code and/or Section 16(b) of the Exchange Act ("162(m) Executives").
- Executive salaries: Subject to the terms of any existing employment contracts, the committee shall establish the salaries of the CEO, the COO and/or the president and approve the salaries of (a) those persons who report directly to the CEO, the COO and/or the president and (b) any other executive officers.

- Bonuses: Subject to the terms of any existing employment contracts, the committee shall (a) set performance targets for eligibility for bonuses, in the case of 162(m) Executives, and (b) approve bonus awards, including any equity-based bonus awards, to 162(m) Executives and all other eligible executive officers.
- Other incentives, benefits and plans:
  - the committee shall conduct a periodic review of the company's benefit programs, individually and in the aggregate, for the CEO, the COO and/or the president and all other executive officers;
  - the committee shall review and approve all grants of equity-based compensation to executive officers;
  - the committee shall review, approve, amend, and/or make recommendations to the board relating to (i) all incentive, performance-based and equity-based plans and (ii) such other compensation, benefit, pension or welfare plans or programs as may be submitted to the committee by the CEO, the COO and/or the president (all of the foregoing being referred to collectively as "Plans").

Governance and Nominating Committee

This committee holds at least two regular meetings each year, and such special meetings as may be required. Meetings may be called by the chair of the committee or the chairman of the board. The committee's responsibilities include:

1. Monitoring the implementation and operation of the company's Corporate Governance Guidelines.
2. Reviewing from time to time the adequacy of the Corporate Governance Guidelines in light of broadly accepted practices of corporate governance, emerging governance issues and market and regulatory expectations, and to advise and make recommendations to the board with respect to appropriate modifications.
3. Identifying and reviewing measures to strengthen the operation of the Corporate Governance Guidelines, and to advise the board with respect thereto.
4. Preparing and supervising the implementation of the board's annual reviews of (i) director independence and (ii) the board's performance, as contemplated by the Corporate Governance Guidelines, and overseeing the board's processes for evaluation of the management of the corporation and making recommendations to the board with respect to such processes.
5. Identifying, reviewing and evaluating candidates for election as director who meet the standards set forth in the Corporate Governance Guidelines, including such inquiries as the committee deems appropriate into the

background and qualifications of candidates and interviews with potential candidates to determine their qualification and interest, and recommending to the board of directors nominees for any election of directors in compliance with the Corporate Governance Guidelines (including the policy that a substantial majority of directors be independent of the company and of the company's management).

6. Advising the board with respect to such other matters relating to the governance of the company as the committee may from time to time approve, including changes to the terms or scope of this charter and the committee's overall responsibilities.

Executive compensation

Disney states that "The compensation of Directors who are not employees of the Company shall be determined annually by the Board of Directors acting upon recommendation of the Compensation Committee, which may obtain the advice of such experts as the Committee deems appropriate. Compensation may be paid in the form of cash or equity interests in the Company or other such forms as the Board deems appropriate and shall be at levels that are consistent with those in effect for directors of similarly situated businesses. Separate compensation may be provided to members of Committees of the Board and additional compensation may be provided to the chairs of Committees and to any non-executive Chairman of the Board. Directors who are also employees of the Company shall not receive any additional compensation for their service as Directors." Tables 1.4 and 1.5 show compensation information cited from Yahoo Finance.

By comparing with Time Warner, one can see board members in this industry are normally extremely highly paid. Their compensation packages include annual compensation and stock options. Eisner, CEO of Disney, received compensation exceeding $700 million from 1996 to 2002. Table 1.6 lists some controversial compensation issues in Disney, which includes Eisner and other executives.

In 2004, the company's performance problems, following a resounding lack of confidence from shareholders and stakeholders, led these shareholders to strongly urge limits on the amount of options granted and performance assessment policies.

Interlocking directorate

Media corporations share members of the board of directors with a variety of other large corporations, including banks, investment companies, oil companies, health care and pharmaceutical companies, and technology companies.

Table 1.4 Executive compensation summary

Name	Total annual compensation	Long-term incentive plans	All other	Fiscal year total
Officers and directors (Disney) for fiscal year ending 9/30/2003 (not including stock options)				
Staggs, Thomas O.	$2,291,827	$0.00	$4,775	$2,296,602
Murphy, Peter E.	$2,291,827	$0.00	$4,775	$2,296,602
Eisner, Michael D.	$7,313,656	$0.00	$4,775	$7,318,431
Iger, Robert A.	$6,394,231	$0.00	$504,775	$6,899,006
Braverman, Alan	$1,385,291	$0.00	$579,403	$1,964,694
Officers and directors (Time Warner) for fiscal year ending 12/31/2003 (not including stock options)				
Kimmitt, Robert M.	$3,227,840	$0.00	$354,324	$3,582,164
Pace, Wayne H.	$4,191,411	$0.00	$822,219	$5,013,630
Logan, Don	$7,852,736	$0.00	$1,851,000	$9,703,736
Parsons, Richard D.	$9,767,715	$0.00	$2,114,250	$11,881,965
Bewkes, Jeffrey L.	$7,606,841	$0.00	$10,806,000	$18,412,841

Table 1.5 Stock options compensation

Name	Options	Value
Officers and directors (Disney) as of 3/4/2004		
Braverman, Alan	840,388	$463,140
Murphy, Peter E.	2,309,795	$187,273
Staggs, Thomas O.	2,436,095	$213,155
Iger, Robert A.	5,569,353	$0
Eisner, Michael D.	21,387,060	$0
Officers and directors(Time Warner) as of 4/2/2004		
Pace, Wayne H.	1,296,213	$1,879,150
Kimmitt, Robert M.	1,305,000	$805,350
Logan, Don	5,235,000	$8,999,141
Bewkes, Jeffrey L.	5,464,592	$10,009,360
Parsons, Richard D.	7,200,000	$7,327,000

When Disney entered television, it was part of a move that further diversified Disney's business interests. Disney agreed to produce the "Disneyland" television series for ABC, if the network's parent company would join Disney and Western Publishing as the major investors in the new Disneyland theme park. The television show, amusement park, publishing interests, and movies would all promote each other in a synergistic relationship. By establishing interlocking business relationships with allied companies, Disney was able to create interlocking systems of promotion among different media.

Table 1.6 Eisner's compensation history

Year	Compensation History
1995	Disney hires Michael Ovitz as company president. Ovitz leaves the company and quits the board, effective late 1996, despite a five-year contract. Ovitz is paid about $39 million, and 3 million stock options vested automatically on his departure.
1996	Eisner earns $750,000 in salary, the same as previous years, and a bonus of $7.9 million. He is granted 8 million stock options. The amount triples to 24 million after a three-for-one stock split.
1997	Shareholder lawsuits are filed against the board, alleging the multimillion-dollar severance package granted to Ovitz represents a breach of fiduciary duty and a waste of corporate assets.
1998	In the fiscal year ended September 30, 1998, Eisner acquires 22 million Disney shares through the exercise of options, worth $570 million. Eisner's bonus for the year is $5 million, down from $9.9 million in fiscal 1997.
1999	Eisner earns his usual $750,000 in salary and no bonus in fiscal 1999. He acquires 2 million shares through options, valued at nearly $50 million.
2000	Eisner earns $813,462 in salary and a bonus of $11.5 million, $3 million of it deferred until January 2004. In fiscal 2000, Eisner exercises options for 3 million shares worth $60.5 million.
2001	Eisner's base salary rises to $1 million. He is granted no bonus.
2002	In fiscal 2002, Eisner's pay is $1 million, and is awarded $5 million in "stock unit" awards valued at $16.735 per share. Half the units vest two years from the January 27, 2003 grant date, and the other half vests four years after the grant date.
2003	Eisner's base salary is again $1 million, and he is awarded $6.25 million in stock units.

Board interlocking members for Disney ABC Cable Networks Group, a subsidiary of The Walt Disney Company (by June 2001), include Boeing, Casella Waste Systems, CB Richard Ellis Services, City National Bank, Columbia/HCA Healthcare, Doubleclick, Edison International, FedEx, Jenny Craig, LM Institutional Fund Advisors, Lozano Communications, Northwest Airlines, On Command Corp., Pacific American Income Shares, Shamrock Holdings, Sotheby's N. America, Staples, Starwood Hotels & Resorts, Sun Microsystems, SunAmerica, Trefoil Investors, UNUM, Provident, Verdon-Cedric Productions, and Xerox.

Executive penalty

With the centric culture in place, Disney does not have very clear executive penalty policies to tie executives' performance with their future compensation or status in the company. Here are some rough ideas of the process in deciding board conduct reviews and management succession:

Board conduct and review

Members of the board of directors shall act at all times in accordance with the requirements of the company's *Code of Business Conduct and Ethics* for directors. This obligation shall at all times include, without limitation, strict adherence to the company's policies with respect to conflicts of interest, confidentiality, protection of the company's assets, ethical conduct in all business dealings and respect for and compliance with applicable law. Any waiver of the requirements of the *Code of Business Conduct and Ethics* for directors with respect to any individual director shall be reported to, and be subject to the approval of, the board of directors.

The board shall conduct an annual review and evaluation of its conduct and performance based upon completion by all directors of an evaluation form that includes, among other things, an assessment of:

1. the board's composition and independence;
2. the board's access to and review of information from management, and the quality of such information;
3. the board's responsiveness to shareholder concerns;
4. maintenance and implementation of the company's standards of conduct; and
5. maintenance and implementation of these guidelines.

The review shall seek to identify specific areas, if any, in need of improvement or strengthening and shall culminate in a discussion by the full board of the results and any actions to be taken. The Governance and Nominating Committee shall have responsibility for ensuring that the annual review and evaluation are carried out.

Management succession and review

At least once a year, the CEO of the company shall meet with the non-management directors to discuss potential successors as CEO. The non-management directors shall meet in executive session following such presentations to consider such discussions. The CEO shall also have in place at all times a confidential written procedure for the timely and efficient transfer of his or her responsibilities in the event of his or her sudden incapacitation or departure, including recommendations for longer-term succession arrangements. The CEO shall review this procedure periodically with the chairman of the board and the Governance and Nominating Committee.

The CEO shall also review periodically with the non-management directors the performance of other key members of the senior management of the company, as well as potential succession arrangements for such management members.

Any waiver of the requirements of the company's Standards of Business Conduct with respect to any such member of senior management shall be reported to, and be subject to the approval of, the board of directors. If any director ceases to be independent under the standards set forth herein while serving on any committee whose members must be independent, he or she shall promptly resign from that committee. In the worldwide level, executive compensation is the focus of activity: Australia now requires listed companies to disclose all details of executive pay including severance and termination payments; this code of practice is voluntary but could become statutory depending on compliance. The Netherlands is proposing to increase the tax on "excessive perks" for executives.

Conduct code/Ethics programs

Disney states that it is committed to conducting business in accordance with the highest standards of business ethics and complying with applicable laws, rules, and regulations. In furtherance of this commitment, the board of directors promotes ethical behavior, and has adopted a code of business conduct and ethics for directors. Every director is required to represent the interests of the shareholders of The Walt Disney Company, exhibit high standards of integrity, commitment and independence of thought and judgment, dedicate sufficient time, energy and attention to ensure the diligent performance of his or her duties, and comply with every conduct code.

According to Disney's code of business conduct, the company requires that directors must avoid conflicts of interest and be careful about business relationships with the company. In terms of protecting corporate information, opportunities and assets, directors are required to protect and hold confidential all non-public information. Also, the company requires strict compliance by all its directors to applicable laws, rules, and regulations. These include federal and other securities laws, including insider trading laws, and the company's insider trading compliance policies. In addition, directors must deal fairly with the company's employees, customers, suppliers, and competitors. No director may take unfair advantage of the company's employees, customers, suppliers, or competitors through manipulation, concealment, abuse of privileged information, misrepresentation of material facts, or any other unfair-dealing practice. Directors are at all times accountable for compliance with the code.

Disney's standards of business conduct specify various aspects of ethical issues and business-related legal considerations. For ethical standards, it spells out: (a) responsibility to guests and customers; (b) responsibility to cast members and employees; (c) responsibility to the company and shareholders; (d) responsibility to other businesses; and (e) responsibilities to communities. At the same time, Disney's legal standards impose more specific and limited obligations that everyone is required to obey, including:

- Antitrust laws: The company will compete fully and fairly in each of the markets in which it operates.
- Securities laws: The company, and each cast member and employee acting on its behalf, will comply with the securities laws of the United States.
- Relationships with local, state, and federal officials: The company, and each cast member and employee acting on its behalf, will make no improper payments to government officials.
- Foreign Corrupt Practices Act and related matters: The company, and each cast member and employee acting on its behalf, will comply with the Foreign Corrupt Practices Act, the anti-boycott laws, all United States restrictions on doing business with certain foreign countries and other organizations and all export controls.
- Tax laws: The company, and each cast member and employee acting on its behalf, will comply with the laws of all taxing authorities.
- Cash-related reporting requirements: The company, and each cast member and employee acting on its behalf, will comply with cash and monetary instrument transaction reporting requirements and the laws regarding proceeds of illegal activity.
- Environmental laws: The company, and each cast member and employee acting on its behalf, will comply with all environmental laws.
- Food and drug laws: The company, and each cast member and employee acting on its behalf, will comply with the food and drug laws.
- Intellectual property: The federal copyright laws have rules governing the use of books, movies, records, and other works. The federal trademark laws prohibit the use of another company's trademarks. The federal patent laws prohibit the unauthorized use of patented inventions. Cast members and employees should assist the company in protecting its copyrights, patents and trademarks.
- Relationships with other companies: The company, and each cast member and employee acting on its behalf, will respect the trade secrets of other companies. No improper or unethical payments will be made by the company, or by cast members or employees or agents of the company acting on its behalf.

(Source: The author prepared this case example based on the published information from the company's website and numerous articles from the ABI/Inform database.)

REFERENCES AND FURTHER READING

Baliga, B.R., Moyer, R.C., and Rao, R.S. (1996). CEO duality and firm performance: What's the fuss? *Strategic Management Journal*, **17**: 41–53.

Barney, J.B. and Hansen, M.H. (1994). Trustworthiness as a source of competitive advantage. *Strategic Management Journal*, **15**: 175–90.

Baysinger, B.D. and Butler, H. (1985). Corporate governance and the board of directors: Performance effects of changes in board composition. *Journal of Law, Economics, and Organizations*, **1**: 101–24.

Berle, A.A. and Means, G.C. (1932). *The Modern Corporation and Private Property*. New York.

Borokhovich, K., Parrino, R., and Trapani, T. (1996). Outside directors and CEO selection. *Journal of Financial and Quantitative Analysis*, **31**: 337–55.

Chaganti, R.S., Mahajan, V., and Sharma, S. (1985). Corporate board size, composition and corporate failures in retailing industry. *Journal of Management Studies*, **22**: 401–17.

Davis, J.H., Schoorman, F.D., and Donaldson, L. (1997). Toward a stewardship theory of management. *Academy of Management Review*, **22**: 20–47.

Donaldson, T. and Preston, L. (1995). The stakeholder theory of the corporation: Concepts, evidence and implications. *Academy of Management Review*, **20**: 65–91.

Eisenhardt, K.M. (1985). Control: Organizational and economic approaches. *Management Science*, **31**: 134–49.

Eisenhardt, K.M. (1989). Agency theory: An assessment and review. *Academy of Management Review*, **14**: 57–74.

Eisenhardt, K.M. and Bourgeois, L.J. (1988). Politics of strategic decision making in high-velocity environments: Toward a midrange theory. *Academy of Management Journal*, **31**: 737–70.

Ellstrand, A.E., Tihanyi, L., and Johnson, J.L. (2002). Board structure and international political risk. *Academy of Management Journal*, **45**: 769–77.

Fama, E.F. and Jensen, M.C. (1983). Separation of ownership and control. *Journal of Law and Economics*, **26**: 301–25.

Freeman, R. and Reed, D. (1983). Stockholders and stakeholders: A new perspective on corporate governance. *California Management Review*, **25**(3): 88–106.

Glenn-Hubbard, R. and Palia, D. (1995). Executive pay and performance: Evidence from the US banking industry. *Journal of Financial Economics*, **38**: 105–30.

Hedlund, G. (1986). The modern MNC – A heterarchy. *Human Resource Management*, **25**: 9–35.

Jensen, M. and Meckling, W. (1976). Theory of the firm: Managerial behavior, agency costs, and ownership structure. *Journal of Financial Economics*, **3**: 305–60.

Judge, W.O. Jr. and Zeithmal, C.P. (1992). Institutional and strategic choice perspectives on board involvement in the strategic decision process. *Academy of Management Journal*, **35**: 766–94.

Khanna, T., Kogan, J., and Palepu, K. (2002). Globalization and corporate governance convergence? A cross-country analysis. Working Paper 02-041, Harvard Business School.

Kim, K. and Limpaphayom, P. (1998). A test of the two-tier corporate governance structure: The case of Japanese keiretsu. *Journal of Financial Research*, **21**(1): 37–52.

Klapper, L.F. and Love, I. (2002). Corporate governance, investor protection, and performance in emerging markets. World Bank Working Paper, No. 2818.

Kriger, M.P. (1988). The increasing role of subsidiary boards in MNCs: An empirical study. *Strategic Management Journal*, **9**: 347–60.

LaPorta, R., Lopez-de-Silanes, F., Shleifer, A., and Vishny, R.W. (1998). Law and finance. *Journal of Political Economy*, **106**: 1113–55.

Lorsch, J. (1989). *Pawns and Potentates: The Reality of America's Corporate Boards*. Boston, MA: Harvard Business School Press.

Luo, Y. (2005). Corporate governance and accountability in multinational enterprises: Concepts and agenda. *Journal of International Management*, **11**(1): 1–18.

Mizruchi, M.S. (1983). Who controls whom? An experimentation of the relation between management and boards of directors in large American corporations. *Academy of Management Review*, **8**: 426–35.

Mizruchi, M.S. (1997). What do interlocks do? An analysis, critique, and assessment of research on interlocking directorates. *Annual Review of Sociology*, **22**: 271–98.

Nohria, N. and Ghoshal, S. (1994). Differentiated fit and shared values: Alternatives for managing headquarters–subsidiary relations. *Strategic Management Journal*, **15**: 491–502.

Organization for Economic Cooperation and Development (1999). OECD Principles of Corporate Governance (www.oecd.org/daf/governance).

O'Reilly, C.A., Caldwell, D., and Barnett, W. (1989). Work group demography, social integration, and turnover. *Administrative Science Quarterly*, **34**: 21–37.

Sanders, W.G. and Carpenter, M.A. (1998). Internationalization and firm governance: The roles of CEO compensation, top team composition, and board structure. *Academy of Management Journal*, **41**: 158–78.

Saravanamuthu, K. and Tinker, T. (2003). Politics of managing: The dialectic of control. *Accounting, Organizations and Society*, **28**(1): 37–54.

Shearer, T. (2002). Ethics and accountability: From the for-itself to the for-the-other. *Accounting, Organizations and Society*, **27**(6): 541–59.

Shleifer, A. and Vishny, R.W. (1997). A survey of corporate governance. *Journal of Finance*, **52**: 737–83.

Singh, J. and Harianto, F. (1989). Management–board relationships, takeover risk, and the adoption of golden parachutes. *Academy of Management Journal*, **32**: 7–24.

Tihanyi, L., Johnson, R.A., Hoskisson, R.E., and Hitt, M.A. (2003). Institutional ownership differences and international diversification: The effects of boards of directors and technological opportunity. *Academy of Management Journal*, **46**: 195–211.

Tosi, H.L. and Gomez-Mejia, L.R. (1989). The decoupling of CEO pay and performance: An agency theory perspective. *Administrative Science Quarterly*, **34**: 169–89.

Wild, J.J. (1994). Managerial accountability to shareholders: Audit committees and the explanatory power of earnings for returns. *British Accounting Review*, **26**(4): 353–70.

Williamson, O.E. (1984). Corporate governance, *Yale Law Journal*, **93**: 1197–230.

Williamson, O.E. (1988). Corporate finance and corporate governance. *Journal of Finance*, **43**: 78–93.

Williamson, O.E. (1991). Comparative economic organization: The analysis of discrete structural alternatives. *Administrative Science Quarterly*, **36**: 269–96.

Willman, P., Fenton-O'Creevy, P., Nicholson, N., and Soane, E. (2002). Traders, managers and loss aversion in investment banking. *Accounting, Organizations and Society*, **27**: 85–98.

Zahra, S.A. and Pearce, J.A. (1989). Boards of directors and corporate financial performance: A review and integrative model. *Journal of Management*, **15**: 291–334.

Zajac, E.J. (1988). Interlocking directorates as an interorganizational strategy: A test of critical assumptions. *Academy of Management Journal*, **31**: 428–38.

Chapter 2

Corporate Governance Across Borders: Comparison and Analysis

EXECUTIVE SUMMARY

Intensified international competition and the spread of globalization raise the question about corporate governance in different countries. Differences in corporate governance across countries affect not only the competitiveness of countries' institutions but more importantly MNCs' global competition and expansion (e.g., mergers and acquisitions) and the design of corporate governance for overseas subsidiaries listed on local exchanges. In the US, shareholders have a comparatively big say in the running of the company they own; workers have much less influence. In many European countries, shareholders have less say and workers have more. In Japan, managers have been left alone to run their companies as they see fit – namely for the benefit of employees and of allied companies, as much as for shareholders.

  In this chapter, I first explain why corporate governance varies across nations and how such differences impact MNCs' international expansion and management. In the following sections, I detail the Anglo-Saxon and the continental European corporate governance systems, followed by corporate governance systems in Japan and transitional economies. The Anglo-Saxon model is essentially an "outsider" governance system in which ownership stakes are dispersed and owners exercise indirect control on management by electing representatives (directors) to the monitoring boards. The continental European and Japanese models both belong to an "insider" system but their structures differ. In continental Europe, control is typically unidirectional. A family, bank, or Company A owns a substantial or controlling interest in Company B and has representatives on Company B's supervisory board. Company B, in turn, owns a controlling interest in Company C, which in turn controls Company D, and so on. Companies B, C, and D, on the other hand, do not own shares in the organizations that stand above them in the corporate pyramid. By contrast, in the Japanese form of an insider system, several companies are linked together through interlocking director-ships, which are backed by cross-holdings of one another's shares. Within these intertwined groups of firms, known as *keiretsu*, there is also a main bank and typically several other banks or financial institutions, which hold shares in the companies in the group. The main bank has representatives on the group companies' supervisory boards. Within a Japanese *keiretsu*, therefore, control is multidirectional, with each company able to exercise some control over the companies that control it.

Corporate governance in transitional economies, notably China and Russia, is rather weak and an essentially relationship-oriented system that blends some stock market-based mechanisms (e.g., board structure, special committees, and code of conduct) and their unique tradition of relationships maintained with family, governments, and banks. Some major causes of this weakness are the lack of transparency, limited protection of property rights, underdeveloped sup-porting institutions (e.g., independent auditing, accounting, law and arbitration services), the poor enforcement of laws, rules and verdicts, the lack of independ-ence in banks' loan decisions, and distorted stock markets. Governments serve not only as the dominant owners in listed state-owned enterprises but also as the regulators and interveners that often powerfully change the judiciary, institutional, and economic parameters that affect corporate governance. Cor-porate governance in other major emerging economies such as India, Brazil and Mexico is, or will be, moving closer to the Anglo-Saxon system than that in China and Russia. In these emerging economies, the economic sectors are more privatized; state ownership and government control are substantially reduced, political regimes are more accommodative to market force determination, and there is increasing systems trust in society (as opposed to personal trust in China and Russia).

2.1 Why Corporate Governance Varies Across Nations

When firms expand globally, they find that corporate governance in different coun-tries is very idiosyncratic and that they have to compete with firms that are governed very differently. Such idiosyncrasy affects corporate governance at the subunit level in specific host countries, corporate-level harmonization of managerial governance over all subunits around the world, and cost effectiveness in governing internally differ-entiated yet globally coordinated business structure. The idiosyncrasy also implies that a multinational corporation has to deal with many different local institutions that play very different roles in different countries in determining corporate governance. For example, in many parts of Asia, it is not the financial markets but various govern-ment ministries that monitor corporate performance and control financial allocation. Meanwhile, in many continental European countries such as Germany and Switzerland, and in some parts of Asia such as Japan, Korea, Taiwan and Singapore, the banking sector as institutional shareholders monitor corporate performance and investment decisions. Vital strategic decisions in international expansion such as new market entry and diversification can be significantly constrained by the differences of home market institutions and host market institutions and by the differences among institutions in different host countries.

Among countries in which an MNC operates, some local corporations are diffusely owned with managers firmly in control, other countries' corporations have concentrated ownership, and in still others, labor strongly influences the firm. It is true that there is a slowly increasing tendency that corporate governance systems used by firms in different countries are gradually converging, and these changes are partly the result of multinational firms operating in many different countries and attempting to develop a more global governance system (Hitt, Ireland, and Hoskisson, 2005). Corporate governance prevalent in different regions or nations still remains distinctive for several reasons.

First, philosophical differences underlying corporate governance are responsible for this distinction. Under the Anglo-Saxon system mostly adopted in the US, the UK, Canada and Australia, the corporate governance system has been dominated by the importance of shareholder-driven firms characterized by open, outsider-oriented systems with a high degree of liquidity in capital. However, this perspective is prone to agency problems because the long-term interests of the principals (the owners) often diverge from the short-term needs of the agents (the managers). Furthermore, the overdependence on financial measures could lead to managerial myopia as the CEO (with a relatively short-term tenure) would have little incentive to undertake a long-term endeavor if it adversely impacts on the short-term results of the firm. It is therefore incumbent on the board of directors to devise monitoring mechanisms and incentive schemes to more closely align the interests of the managers with those of the shareholders and to act swiftly and decisively in case of deficient managerial performance in an attempt to minimize agency costs and bridge the separation of ownership and control. The hallmark of the shareholders' model is that ownership should be the basis of power subject to laws to protect the rights of minority shareholders under the jurisdiction in which the firm operates. Under this jurisdiction, the board has a fiduciary duty to the shareholders – the duty of care and the duty of loyalty – to oversee managerial decisions via an arm's length interaction, but without undermining or infringing on management's ability to run its daily business activities. In short, under the Anglo-Saxon system, management is accountable to the board, and the board has to answer to the shareholders.

In contrast to the agency philosophy of corporate governance under the Anglo-Saxon system, the governance structure that has been adopted in Germany, France, and Japan is an insider-oriented arrangement based on a stakeholder-friendly policy. While the agency system of corporate governance considers financial measures and shareholders' value as the main criteria for the success of a firm, the stakeholders' framework encompasses a broader set of quantitative and qualitative data including financials, customer satisfaction, training and development of employees, and R&D development. The board commonly consists of cross-shareholdings and cross-representation of labor, banks, and other constituencies of directorates to sustain long-term relationships with stakeholder groups other than shareholders. The recognition of this broader view of the role of the firm is rooted in the theory of property rights based on the perspective of pluralistic notions of distributive justice. Under this system, it is widely believed that stakeholders' satisfaction is not necessarily incompatible with shareholders' value maximization based on the assumption that a business will better serve its current or potential shareholders by building long-term relationships with other key constituencies such as customers, employees, creditors, neighbors, and suppliers. The stakeholder philosophy is not a standardized framework applied uniformly across the board. There is a distinct difference in the application of the stakeholder approach from one country to another. Its connotation is a reflection of the idiosyncrasies and nuances of each culture, particularly as it relates to the interaction between the board and management. In Japan, for instance, most directors are company executives; a real controlling body of management is virtually nonexistent as the board tends to exert little authority over management. The corporate governance system is thus by definition a dependent structure based on a web of interpersonal relationships through cross-shareholdings by affiliated companies including customers and suppliers.

Second, corporate governance is, at least partly, path-dependent, requiring a systematic match with a unique institutional environment in which corporate governance is embedded. Firms may perform better when they match their strategic actions to their environmental setting. Thus, changes in corporate governance would require a better understanding of the culture and institutions of the environment and the creation of systems that better reflect the existing culture and institutions, as opposed to adopting corporate governance systems developed in places with very different cultures and institutional systems. In a worldwide setting, firms in different countries are socially and institutionally equipped to follow different competitive strategies. Path dependence is also attributed to societal culture. For instance, Australia's auditing requirements for corporate governance are generally permissive, reflecting the distrust of government power embedded in that country's individualistic, frontier culture. In a high uncertainty avoidance country, institutions will be organized in ways that minimize uncertainty. Rules and standards tend to be explicit, prescriptive, all-embracing, and rigid. Individualism affects preferences for transparency and disclosure practices, and influences the willingness to accept uniform corporate governance rules in preference to a more permissible system involving the use of professional discretion such as external auditing. Hence, it is not surprising that countries with low uncertainty avoidance cultures such as the UK, the US, and Sweden tend to have strong independent auditing professions that are an important part of the corporate governance system.

Third, corporate governance is influenced by the legal system in which corporate governance is embedded. The legal system determines the extent to which company law governs the separation of ownership and management. In countries such as France, Germany, and Argentina, in which codified Roman law dominates, the legal system associated with corporate governance tends to be concrete and comprehensive. This contrasts with countries using common law such as the US and the UK. Laws in codified Roman law countries are a series of "*thou shalts*" (you shall) that stipulate the minimum standard of behavior expected. In most countries with a legalistic orientation, corporate governance rules tend to be prescriptive, detailed, and procedural. By contrast, laws in countries with a nonlegalistic orientation are a series of "*thou shalt nots*" (you shall not) that establish the limits beyond which an activity or practice is unlawful. Generally, corporate governance is influenced not only directly by related laws in corporate governance but also by other laws that may impact corporate governance. For instance, tax laws and regulations enacted by the US Securities and Exchange Commission (SEC) represent the legalistic approach to corporate governance. Similarly, the major governance effect of the Foreign Corrupt Practice Act in the United States is that US multinational corporations must establish a system of internal control and an internal audit staff to ensure that bribes are not being offered.

Furthermore, legal institutions differ from one country to another with respect to the protections that they afford shareholders. In some countries, for example, shareholders can demand access to the names and addresses of all other shareholders for the purpose of calling a special meeting of the shareholders; in others, they cannot. In some countries, managers must publish their shareholdings and their compensation packages; in others, they do not have to do so. Provisions like these obviously strengthen the shareholders vis-à-vis the management, and help to align shareholder and managerial interests. For instance, the common law system in the Anglo-Saxon countries and former British colonies offer outside and minority shareholders greater protection against managerial abuse of their position than do civil law systems. Within the civil law systems, the French system offers the shareholder lower protection than does the Scandinavian system.

Finally, the political system is a critical determinant of the prevalent standard of corporate governance because the corporate governance system will reflect political philosophies and objectives. In the egalitarian-authoritarian system such as former centrally planned economies, all production and operations are owned and controlled by governmental institutions. Corporate governance serves two roles in this circumstance: to help in centralized planning and to help in controlling the economy. Profit is essentially retained by the government instead of the private owner. All executives are the "agents" of the government. Therefore, "owner's equity" in state-owned enterprises actually reflects "state equity" or "government equity". Virtually all corporate governance mechanisms used in the Anglo-Saxon system are meaningless in a centrally planned system.

Similarly, in social democracy nations committed to private property but whose governments play a large role in the economy, emphasize distributional considerations, and favor employees over capital owners when the two conflict, public policy emphasizes managers' natural agenda and demeans shareholders' agenda. The pressure on the firm for low-risk expansion is high, the pressure to avoid risky organizational change is substantial, and the tools that would induce managers to work in favor of invested capital – such as high incentive compensation, hostile takeovers, transparent accounting, and acculturation to shareholder-wealth maximization norms – are weak. Hence, managerial agency costs have been higher in social democracies than elsewhere, and there is a political explanation not only for the persistence of family ownership in France, Germany, Italy, and Scandinavia, but also for the rise of the public firm in the United States. Social democracies do not strongly control public firm agency costs because they do not want unbridled shareholder-wealth maximization, and, hence, by weakening shareholder-wealth maximization institutions, they widen the gap between managers and dispersed shareholders.

In conclusion, due to the increasing role of multinational corporations in using harmonized corporate governance systems in their global businesses, along with similar legislatures by different nations, parallel organizational or statutory decisions of firms, and standardized governance rules on international capital markets, international corporate governance tends to slowly or gradually converge as globalization progresses. However, due to economic, political, cultural, and legal reasons, corporate governance differences across regions and countries will always exist. National governance systems are also path dependent (Roe, 1996). They have developed over long time periods into consistent systems, i.e. combinations of complementary elements. Therefore, changing individual elements would, at least temporarily, lead to inconsistent, less efficient systems that are unable to stand competitive pressures from "pure" systems (Shleifer and Vishny, 1997). Gordon and Roe (2004) further define the two sources of path dependence that jointly influence a country's prevalent corporate governance: structure-driven path dependence and rule-driven path dependence. Structure-driven dependence concerns the direct effect of initial ownership structures on subsequent ownership structures. Rule-driven dependence arises from the effect that initial ownership structures have on subsequent structures through their effect on the legal rules that govern corporations. Corporate rules are all the legal rules that govern the relationship between the corporation and its investors, stakeholders, and managers and the relationships among these players – including not only corporate law as conventionally defined but also securities law and the relevant parts of the law governing insolvency, labor relations, and financial institutions. Corporate rules are generally path dependent.

Therefore, different international corporate governance systems, with advantages as well as disadvantages for each system, may continue to coexist. A continuation of different corporate governance systems preserves cultural diversity. Good corporate governance is not a one-size-fits-all proposition, and a wide diversity of approaches to corporate governance should be expected and is entirely appropriate. This is even more so for companies active in geographically dispersed worldwide businesses. Of course, acknowledging these differences does not mean that each system should not learn from one another. On the contrary, if some elements of one system are more efficient and compatible in the blending process, they should be incorporated in a new system. For instance, in 2003, Japan created a new voluntary structure for boards of directors and committees. In Japan, the management of the company has traditionally composed of the board of directors. That means that the system is first and foremost aiming to perpetuate itself, and avoid any shareholder pressure at the level of the board. It is hard to believe that the traditional Japanese model is aiming at enhancing shareholder value. The whole history of the Japanese market confirms that attention to the market and to market values has not been the core of the values defended by corporate Japan. This is why the new "Committee Board" structure open to Japanese companies as of April 1, 2003, which calls for independent directors and board committees, is so revolutionary and essential and was immediately adopted by progressive companies such as Sony, Hitachi, and Toshiba.

2.2 Corporate Governance under the Anglo-Saxon System

In an earlier section, I explained several specific corporate governance mechanisms such as ownership concentration, board composition, board committees, and executive compensation, among others. This introduction is largely a reflection of the Anglo-Saxon system because these mechanisms are designed under the philosophy of the Anglo-Saxon system, also known as stock-market capitalism or the shareholder governance system. The Anglo-Saxon system focuses on the separation of ownership from control, financing through the stock market, and the use of an independent board of directors. The common law countries such as the US, the UK, and Canada extensively use this system. In the common law countries, the courts were generally effective in protecting investors' rights against "monarchial" (or state) expropriation and against insider dealing. In contrast, the civil law countries offered much weaker protection of ownership rights, and hence the tendency toward concentrated ownership and control by the banks. Under the Anglo-Saxon system, boards are structured in such a way as to mitigate conflicts of interest between the agents and the principals. This model assumes that it is essential for the board to achieve a critical mass of outside and independent directors because such structure minimizes agency costs. The Anglo-Saxon model of corporate governance is characterized by a single board (unitary board) that is constituted of directors in top management positions in the company and outside directors who are not company employees. Directors with management positions are usually referred to as insiders or executive directors. The other directors, who are not members of management, are known as non-executive or outside directors. It is the prevailing practice under a unitary board that new directors are nominated by the board of directors (and in particular by the corporate governance committee) and then elected by shareholders at the annual shareholders' meeting. In general, the board has the freedom to adopt its own style of *modus operandi* such as deciding meeting frequencies.

The Anglo-Saxon system views the corporation as a nexus of contracts. Corporate executives would negotiate and administer contracts with all the stakeholders of the firm – employees, customers, creditors, suppliers, and shareholders. However, the executives would be writing these contracts as agents for the shareholders and in the interests of the shareholders. Thus, the self-seeking behavior of all stakeholders other than executives would be held in check by executives seeking to maximize the wealth of the owners. Because of this, transparency, investor protection laws, markets, and the efficient functioning of markets become critical for a contractual approach relying on shareholders to advance the societal objective of economic efficiency and growth. Shareholders need reliable and trustworthy information in order to monitor management. This information must be available to everyone and not subject to insider (managerial and inside control group) manipulation. A primary responsibility of the government, then, is to ensure that information is disclosed to investors and that insiders cannot manipulate markets. In the United States, the SEC, established in the 1930s, along with similar state agencies, serves this regulatory function. Additionally, investor protection laws protect the property rights of public investors. While some emerging economies are mimicking the Anglo-Saxon's corporate governance systems, I doubt their effectiveness precisely for this reason: they lack well-functioning markets and well-enforced investor protection systems, and transparent and trustworthy information is difficult to obtain and verify.

In sum, the key to the Anglo-Saxon model is to view the corporation as a nexus of contracts among individuals in which the explicit and implicit contracts control everyone's self-interest. The role of the shareholders is to monitor the performance of management in order to ensure that managers are acting in the shareholders' best interests, which are equated with economic efficiency at the societal level. Ultimately, the shareholders and their agents evaluate managerial performance by looking at the present value of the residual claims on the firm – otherwise known as the market value of the firm's common stock. The managerial objective of shareholder wealth maximization is more than an end in itself; it is the means to the end of efficient resource allocation and economic growth – at least within the context of the agency theory of effective corporate governance.

Unfortunately, the Anglo-Saxon system is not without deficiencies: board duality (CEOs are also board chairmen) is still common; outsider directors and auditors are not always independent nor professionally and ethically competent; corporate transparency is not always present and insider trading practices are still frequent; many executives are overly paid and their poor performance is not effectively penalized; long-term strategic interests for the firm are not always fostered; and shareholders' interests are sometimes fulfilled at the expense of other stakeholders' interests, to name a few. Fortunately, these deficiencies have already received attention from legislators, regulators, and the public. For example, the current reforms in the US, led by Sarbanes and Oxley reports, have put much emphasis on independent directors, even stricter rules for financial disclosure, and require CEOs and financial directors to swear to the accuracy of their financial reports. At the same time, in the UK, following the report by Higgs, the emphasis has been shifted toward professional qualities of the non-executive directors, and adopting voluntary codes of self-regulation, allowing corporations to adapt more gradually to changing stakeholder expectations.

2.3 Corporate Governance in Continental Europe

Most corporations in continental Europe (mainly Germany, Austria, Italy, the Netherlands, and to some extent France) have adopted a two-tier board system. Such a structure utilizes two separate boards, namely the supervisory board and the management board, rather than a single board. For example, all German public limited companies and most private limited companies have by law a supervisory board (*Aufsichtsrat*) and an executive board (*Vorstand*). French jurisdiction is unique in continental Europe in the sense that it permits the shareholders to choose their own framework of board of directors (*conseil d'administration*) whether it is a unitary board or a two-tier board system consisting of a supervisory board (*conseil de surveillance*) and a management board (*directoire*). An outside non-executive director chairs the supervisory board consisting of shareholders and other key constituencies such as employees and banks' representatives. The supervisory board's responsibility is to oversee management performance (akin to what takes place in the unitary board system) such as the appointment and removal of the management board, the development of the firm's policies, the establishment of management directors' remuneration levels, and the review and approval of financial reporting. The company's chief executive officer chairs the management board, with an inherent role of being the management spokesperson and the point of contact with the supervisory board. Basically, the two-tier board system utilizes three legal organs for decision making: the supervisory board; the management board; and the general meeting of the shareholders. The difference between Germany and France is that German law puts responsibilities for the accounts on the management board, the supervisory board and the auditors collectively, allowing the system to find a balance between the interests of investors sitting on the supervisory board, and the executive managers. In France, the government and the public administration take more direct or more active responsibilities to influence large French corporations through industrial policy measures.

2.3.1 Corporate governance in Germany

Compared to the Anglo-Saxon system, German corporate governance is characterized by a lesser reliance on capital markets and outside investors, and a stronger reliance on large inside investors and financial institutions to achieve efficiency in the corporate sector. In many private German firms, the owner and manager are the same individual. In publicly traded corporations, there is often a dominant shareholder. Accordingly, the ownership of German corporations is far more concentrated than the ownership of US corporations. In addition, more than 40 percent of the shares in German companies are owned by other German companies. Individuals as well as institutional investors own very few shares of public corporations. Overall, Germany does not have a shareholder culture. The market capitalization of listed stocks in Germany is about 30 percent of its GDP, compared to 152 percent in the UK, 122 percent in the US, and 103 percent in Sweden.

Banks have been at the center of the German corporate governance structure, as is also the case in many other European countries, such as Italy and France. As lenders, banks become major shareholders when companies they financed earlier seek funding on the stock market or default on loans. Although the stakes are usually under 10 percent, the only legal limit on how much of a firm's stock banks can hold is that a single ownership position cannot exceed 15 percent of the bank's capital. This sharply contrasts the Anglo-Saxon system where banks make loans to corporations but do not take ownership positions in those firms. Because of partial ownership, German banks place their representatives on the companies' governing (supervisory) boards. Through their shareholdings, placing representatives in the companies' supervisory boards, and casting "proxy votes" for individual shareholders who retain their shares with the banks, several powerful banks, including Deutsche, Dresdner and Commerzbank, are strongly influential in the design and functioning of corporate governance in Germany. "Proxy votes" exist when shareholders are allowed to name proxy agents as their representatives at the annual general meeting. Any organization, bank, or other agent of the shareholder may cast the proxy vote. The shareholder has the option to reveal his name, regardless of whether he provides explicit instructions on how to vote his shares or not. Because banks are generally more interested in the survival of the firm, rather than the stock price, they are likely to discourage firms from making risky but positive investments. This is even reinforced by the fact that over 40 percent of the stock in German firms is owned by other corporations, which themselves are more likely to be interested in the survival of the firm so as to retain the benefits of interfirm commercial contracts; the prospects for protecting the interests of public shareholders in German firms are weak.

German firms with more than 2000 employees are required to have a two-tiered board structure (supervisory and executive). Through this structure, the supervision of management is separated from other duties normally assigned to a board of directors, especially the nomination of new board members. Generally, the executive board is made up of 5–15 full-time employees of the company and is responsible for the operations of the company. The executive board is appointed by the supervisory board and reports to it (e.g., in June 1994, Jürgen Schrempp replaced Edzard Reuter as chief executive of Daimler Benz – a move initiated by major shareholder, Deutsche Bank). All major investment and financing decisions must be approved by the supervisory board. The supervisory board normally consists of 9–22 members. The supervisory board is required by law to have labor representatives as well as shareholder representatives. Supervisory board members are not liable for management decisions that are detrimental to shareholder interests, as they would be in the US under the "duty of care" rules. Thus, whatever the supervisory board is, it is not a creature representing or charged with representing the primacy of shareholder interests.

Increased globalization of business activities does create some pressure that has led to some changes in German corporate governance in recent years. Many German firms, especially those active in international markets, are beginning to strengthen some discipline- and culture-based governance mechanisms – introduced in Chapter 1 – to improve their governance effectiveness and corporate transparency. For instance, there is an increasingly stronger voice in corporate Germany against the practice of allowing retired or former CEOs to sit in a company's supervisory board chairmanship, as this practice often allows former CEOs to handpick their successors (the case in Siemens). Among the top 30 German firms listed on the blue-chip DAX index, 18, including Volkswagen, have now begun to disclose individual salaries of management and supervisory board members. Meanwhile, a government-sponsored body, the Cromme Commission, enacted a code of corporate governance in May 2003, requiring a maximum of two former executives be able to sit on a company's supervisory board. State legislators or prosecutors are also investigating why Volkswagen has kept a pair of parliamentarians on its payroll for years, while ruling that Deutsche Bank must disclose how much it pays to members of its elite executive committee.

2.3.2 Corporate governance in France

Generally, shareholdings in French companies are highly concentrated; that is, the total number of shares in a given company is generally owned by a small number of investors. This differs from shareholdings in the US and the UK, which are more diffusely held.

The French system of centralized shareholding may be an outgrowth of the national tradition of family ownership, with company founders retaining majority interests in companies, as is the case with Carrefour, a distribution company. Centralized shareholding may also be the result of the state's large ownership interests in private companies, such as oil giant Elf Acquitaine.

Concentrated shareholding is largely the result of the cross-shareholding structures (*noyaux durs*) that exist in France, whereby one "friendly company" holds a large percentage of stock in another company, and vice versa. It is estimated that such cross-shareholding owns 20–30 percent of equity in French companies. Of course, cross-shareholding is not unique to France; it also exists in other countries, such as Korea and Japan. In France, however, cross-shareholding structures consist of related companies, diminishing any one company's incentive to monitor the behavior of another participating company. By contrast, cross-shareholding in Korea and Japan consists of unrelated companies, giving each company greater incentive to monitor the other companies to prevent the rise of an absolute power in the group. From the corporate governance perspective, the French version of cross-shareholding is more likely to insulate managers from external monitoring and from market discipline. In the wake of corporate scandals, however, many French companies such as Crédit Lyonnais, Alcatel Alsthom, and Rhone-Poulenc have begun to extricate themselves from these cross-shareholding arrangements. Some companies are doing so in response to minority shareholder demands for a more efficient management structure and for greater shareholder value. Other companies have initiated corporate restructuring to attract more foreign investors. Ultimately, of course, a more effective way to reduce cross-shareholding relationships is through a more robust use of French capital markets. Until now, the French have relied little on equity markets to raise capital, resulting in increased concentration of shareholdings.

In addition to cross-shareholding, companies are often connected by interlocking boards, where a director of one company sits on the board of another company, and vice versa. For instance, in 1989, 57 people held 25 percent of all of the board seats of the 100 largest French companies. This system of interlocking boards encourages legitimate information sharing as well as illegitimate collusion among directors, since a manager of one company may be reluctant to criticize another company's manager when the two sit on each other's boards.

The Commercial Code of 1966 in France allows French companies to select either a unitary or a two-tier governance structure. A unitary structure resembles the Anglo-Saxon system, which relies on a board of directors elected by the General Meeting of Shareholders. The board of directors appoints a chairman/CEO of the company in charge of the day-to-day running of the company. The two-tier model closely resembles the German *Vorstand/Aufsichtsrat* structure, as introduced above: the executive board manages the company under the authority of the CEO, and the supervisory board monitors decisions and exercises control over the company under the authority of the chairperson. As in Germany, the two-tier structure has both advantages and disadvantages. On the positive side, the smaller size of the two-tier board allows for quick decision making. It also facilitates more non-traditional candidates to rise to the ranks of director, thus creating more diversity and more open discourse among directors.

Finally, the two-tier board generally engenders good publicity and allows companies to attract foreign capital more easily. On the negative side, the two-tier system may be too formal, particularly regarding the executive directors' obligations to report to the supervisory board. In addition, some fear that the supervisory board will exercise too much power over executives, which may result in poor business decisions if supervisory board members are not as involved in the business practices as executive board members.

State intervention and centralized government have long played an important role in French corporate governance. "Stay close to government" is the rule of thumb in the French business community, reflecting the idea that one benefits by working closely with a government that has traditionally exercised great power over the business community. In the 1990s, partially in response to pressure from the European Union and partially in response to criticism about the inefficient functioning of certain public enterprises, the state initiated a new privatization plan to transfer state companies into public hands and to let management – not government – direct the course of business. But still, state intervention and control remain, partially through stock ownership and partially through administrative interference. For example, in 1997, the French government "opened up" France Telecom by selling 38 percent of the company's stock in one of the world's largest initial public offerings. Despite the magnitude of this offering, the state still retained majority equity control over France Telecom, allowing it to continue to exercise a substantial degree of control over the company without openly disclosing such control to the public. Another example is that the state continued to exercise a similar degree of control over Elf Acquitaine after the company was privatized, as the state indirectly owned 13 percent of the company's shares as well as a special privilege that granted the state the right to approve any change of control of the company or sale of any of its significant subsidiaries.

2.3.3 Corporate governance in other continental European countries

In what follows I briefly describe corporate governance in Italy, Spain, and the Netherlands. These countries are discussed either because of the active roles played by multinational corporations in these countries or because of some peculiar governance systems worthy of mention.

2.3.3.1 Italy

The Italian corporate governance system has several differences compared to both the Anglo-Saxon and the continental systems. In comparison with the Anglo-Saxon model, public companies in Italy are still rare, and the separation between ownership and control is limited. Contrary to the continental systems, financial companies such as banks and insurance companies have played a limited role in ownership structures. In 1999, the largest shareholder in listed companies owned on average 44 percent of voting rights (weighted by market capitalization), and the three largest shareholders owned 50 percent. This suggests that ownership structure in Italy is rather concentrated. In Italy, the separation between ownership and management is mainly achieved via the pyramidal group structure. The majority of Italian manufacturing companies are actually organized in groups. As an illustrative example, Telecom Italia, the large Italian listed company that was privatized in 1997 from the former state ownership, was taken over by Olivetti in 1999. Olivetti in turn is controlled, through a complex chain of control systems, by a group of Italian entrepreneurs. Thus, the control chain over Telecom Italia currently includes Tecnost (55 percent of Telecom), Olivetti (70 percent of Tecnost), Bell SA (25 percent of Olivetti), which is a foreign company controlled by a group of companies, owned in turn by some Italian entrepreneurs. As a result, the degree of separation between ownership and control is extremely high, and is achieved by means of a complex pyramidal structure.

The Italian government is a strong actor in corporate governance. In 1996, the voting rights share of the state represented approximately 30 percent of the Italian stock market capitalization, although this share was reduced to 19 percent after massive privatizations in recent years. Banks in Italy were forbidden from owning shares in non-financial companies. However, they have played a more informal role, for instance, through interlocking directorates. Although this prohibition was removed in 1992, banks have not exploited the opportunity to participate in corporate ownerships to any great extent. Generally weak corporate governance in Italy is also attributed to the lack of independence of non-executive directors on the board, the lack of independent and competent auditors, the hindrance of family members and local cronies in governance, and the common duality of board chairmanship and chief executive. All of these factors were responsible for the collapse and bankruptcy of Parmalat, an Italian dairy-products group.

2.3.3.2 Spain

High concentration levels, important cross-shareholdings, and an increasing importance of foreign companies as investors characterize ownership structure in Spain. On average, the two largest shareholders hold around 50 percent of the equity in listed companies. Like in other continental countries, both control and ownership often fall into the hands of controlling shareholders in Spain. Thus, the predominance of controlling shareholders in Spanish corporations has greatly influenced corporate governance practices. The overwhelming presence of controlling shareholders in Spanish companies distinguishes Spanish companies from US companies, which have predominantly dispersed ownership structures. Of the largest non-financial firms, the majority had been state-owned companies in strategic sectors such as oil and telecommunications until such sectors were privatized in the 1990s. Privatization most often led to the state being replaced by large shareholders, many of which afforded managers important control rights or formed coalitions with managers to extract rents from small shareholders. Given the concentrated ownership structure of Spanish firms, an important focus of corporate governance is to overcome conflicts between small shareholders and controlling shareholders, or between coalitions of controlling shareholders and managers.

A significant difference of Spanish listed companies from other EU countries is the absence of pyramidal structures to concentrate voting power and the adoption of the unitary board structure (board of directors). Moreover, in most Spanish listed companies, board directors only own a small amount of shares. For instance, in Telefonica, the sum of all 20 directors' shareholdings is only about 0.01 percent. Furthermore, takeover activity in Spain seems more active compared to other continental European countries, though most takeovers are mergers or friendly acquisitions.

2.3.3.3 The Netherlands

The board structure of listed firms in the Netherlands is characterized by two-tier boards. However, this structure differs somewhat from that in Germany, where the supervisory board is appointed by the shareholders at the annual meeting and exerts substantial independent influence on management. The Dutch supervisory board instead is largely advisory, and the management board has a very large influence on appointments to the supervisory board. Hence, the close relations between management and supervisory boards make the Dutch two-tier system functionally somehow similar to those US firms in which executive managers (insiders) sit on the board of directors, chaired by CEOs. According to Dutch company law, the supervisory board is independent of the company, and its members, acting as representatives of banks, customers or suppliers of related firms, are responsible for the supervision of management policy and the company's general course of affairs. Labor is not allowed to have a representative on the supervisory board. Instead employees are represented by a workers' council that is voluntary but exists in virtually all large firms. The workers' council has the right to recommend individuals for a third of the seats on the supervisory board. However, the supervisory board has the exclusive and ultimate right to nominate board members. The position of the workers' council bears some resemblance to that played by organized labor in the United States, where union representatives frequently hold a seat on the board of directors. By contrast, legal statutes grant German workers more normal influence on corporate affairs, including between a third and half of the seats on the supervisory board.

In order to reinforce the independence of the board, Dutch corporate law explicitly requires that supervisory board members appoint and dismiss each other as a specific institution of Dutch board member selection, a practice called co-optation. On the one hand, co-optation may enhance board independence and expertise, which is favorable to two-tier board functions. On the other hand, co-optation affords a large amount of discretion to board members in fulfilling their board roles. Moreover, it assumes that board members are free from any interests. To the extent that board members share interests with particular stakeholder groups, co-optation tends to favor the control by these stakeholders (Ees and Postma, 2004).

Shareholders exercise control through voting at the annual meeting and, for large shareholders, by sitting on the supervisory board. Apart from investors, other key stakeholders in Dutch corporate governance are financial intermediaries and inter-firm directorate network members. In recent years, Dutch institutional investors such as pension funds and insurance companies have begun to hold substantial equity stakes, thus often holding seats on the supervisory board. The role of Dutch banks is similar to that in Germany. Dutch banks hold large positions in both debt and equity and actively serve on, and often chair, supervisory boards. Because Dutch corporate law prohibits insiders from holding positions on the supervisory board, interlocking directorate members also sit on the board. In sum, Dutch corporate governance is characterized by power top management, which holds the dominant control rights of the company. The absence of voting rights attached to shares and dense interfirm networks further support the managerial hegemony. In this institutional context, the role of co-optation is rather limited in ensuring the formal independence of board members. The emergence of large institutional investors and the popularization of equity ownership in the Netherlands additionally undercut the legitimacy of board member co-optation.

2.4 Corporate Governance in Japan

The Japanese governance system is usually characterized by long-term, cooperative relationships among managers, major shareholders, and business partners. It uses the relational-insider governance model. The strongest control device of this system is a strategic board that is composed of representatives from investors with the largest holdings of corporate assets engaged in collaborative decision making where dedicated ownership makes it difficult to conceive exit strategies. In the system, shares are also held by key customers, suppliers, and allied corporations on a reciprocal basis, a fact also known as "alliance capitalism". Culturally, the Japanese relational governance model partially ascribes to the tradition of mutual obligation, family, and consensus. In Japan, an obligation may be to return a service for one rendered or it may derive from a more general relationship, for example, to one's family or old alumni, or one's company.

Although there are two distinctive sets of Japanese firms which correspond to two different types of corporate governance systems, the first set, large firms affiliated with *keiretsu* industrial groups, still dominate the Japanese economy. These *keiretsu* firms have stable and cooperative relationships with shareholders and business partners. In contrast, there are large firms which are not affiliated by *keiretsu*. These independent firms have a more arm's-length type of relationship with shareholders and business partners. A typical *keiretsu* network is comprises close, long-term business relationships established by large corporations with selected groups of smaller firms, financial and trading institutions. They represent a web of overlapping financial, commercial, and governance relationships, initiated from a central core to pull in large segments of the Japanese economy. Present Japanese intercorporate *keiretsu* relationships are considered in terms of three different structural conditions to facilitate interactions: corporate groupings, financial centrality, and industrial interdependency through value-chain activities. These groups are not conglomerates as the central holding companies are illegal under Japan's post-war commercial law. The companies are independent and publicly owned. However, they are linked through cross-shareholding investment and the exchange of personnel, through shared debt and equity, and mutual strategic plans. The strategic leadership resides within the presidents' club *shacho-kai*, a regularly convening association, which comprises the presidents of the core *keiretsu* member firms. It represents the inner circle of the *keiretsu* as a clique of firms whose reciprocal commitments stem from long association and strong collective identity. These councils hold monthly meetings to discuss group strategy. They support group solidarity, mediate intra-group activities, and settle intra-group disagreements. *Keiretsu* members can thus develop plans based on activities that other *keiretsu* members are pursuing. Other direct linkages within the *keiretsu* are represented by the stable corporate cross-shareholdings, by dispatch of managers to insider director positions, and by director interlocking as control relations that are superimposed on the network of business dealings. These cooperative relations bring intrinsic value to the corporate network and smooth the internal negotiations between agents, units, and member firms.

The cross-shareholding is more a symbol of commitment and mutual obligation, rather than motivated by expectations of dividends and returns on investment. A typical *keiretsu* core company will have 20–40 percent of its stock owned by other companies within the *keiretsu*. Long-term shareholding agreements with other corporations create a situation whereby 60–80 percent of the *keiretsu* stock is never traded. Aside from the direct forms of influence, there are a number of other indirect ties that bond the commercial and investment activities within the *keiretsu*, such as: (i) the selection of *keiretsu* trading partners; (ii) the amount of borrowing from group banks; (iii) the extent of shareholding by group banks and corporations; and (iv) the selection of board members from the management of big leading firms. *Keiretsu* equalizes the fortunes of their members, smoothing inequality in financial returns across participating firms. Members are not able to maximize their benefits, i.e. extraction of profits and rents, but instead have been obliged to optimize output measures. *Keiretsu* networks are seen as clusters of large firms charging each other "efficient" prices (i.e., prices in line with their respective opportunity costs) while collectively extracting other market benefits through a collective action for maximizing the joint welfare of all member firms. In light of these reasons, *keiretsu* members have lower risk than independent companies in Japan, because the whole *keiretsu* group shares individual risks. *Keiretsu* companies obtain lower interest rates from both *keiretsu* banks and other financial institutions, and they tend to have higher debt ratios than independent Japanese companies.

Although the role of institutional investors has increased throughout the world, it is also taking different forms. In Japan the largest public pension funds that manage over US$1.6 trillion have formed the Council of Public Institutional Investors, and are collectively discussing portfolio investment strategies and administration, managers' evaluation techniques, new investment techniques, regulatory changes and fiduciary responsibilities, and cases of institutional investors in other countries. These collective efforts go far beyond the Council of Institutional Investors in the US, engaged primarily in monitoring and benchmarking corporate performance and lobbying. The Japanese institutional investors demonstrate willingness to share responsibilities both for shaping their institutional environment and moderating the risk of their portfolios – another example of optimizing behavior contrasted with maximizing the objective in a classical competitive environment.

In contrast to the US, which has a market-based financial and governance structure, Japan has a bank-based financial and corporate governance structure. Japanese
banks play a critical role in financing and monitoring large public firms. The bank
owning the largest share of stocks and the largest amount of debt has the closest
relationship with the company's top executives. The percentage of shares owned by
financial institutions, particularly banks, remained at around 40 percent until recent
years. Since 1987, Japanese commercial law has stated that a bank is allowed to hold
a maximum of five percent in a single non-financial institution. There is, however,
no restriction on total share holding. Due to recent mergers among large banks,
there are today four financial *keiretsu* groups: (i) Mitsubishi-Tokyo Financial Group;
(ii) Sumitomo-Mitsui Banking Corporation; (iii) Mizuho Financial Group; and (iv) the
United Financial of Japan.

The Japanese board of directors (often 20–30 people) is normally larger than in
the US or the UK. Although large Japanese multinationals have been trying to place
more outsider directors in the boards in recent years, outside directors in Japan
are generally fewer as opposed to those in the US. Most of the outside directors are,
naturally, the main bank officials or *keiretsu* members. As a result, most directors are
executive managers and employee representatives. This management forum in the boardroom is fortified by having few outside directors and by the typical role of the board
chairman in Japan. The chairman of the board, typically the ex-president, is expected
to be a guardian of the president. As a consequence of the concentration of power and
control among executive managers, Japanese companies essentially do not have a built-
in check and control device.

It is noteworthy that Japanese executives are generally less remunerated compared to their counterparts in other countries. In 1999, for instance, the average total
pay for Japanese executives was US$0.49 million, compared to US$1.35 in the US
(*The Economist*, November 27, 1999). The share of incentive-based benefits is also
low. Only one-third of the total pay is non-basic pay in Japan, while more than half of
the total pay is remunerated as incentive-based pay in the US. In Japan, the pay level
is predominantly determined by rank and seniority, and incentives are created for
the employees to achieve higher ranks. Three-quarters of the basic pay is generally
determined by the job title and the remaining quarter is determined by age.

In conclusion, Japanese corporate governance is largely characterized by the
keiretsu system and the main bank system. These two features imply that Japanese
firms have enjoyed less pressure from the capital market, due to intermediate finance
via banks, stable shareholding among a group of firms, and interlocking directorate
practices. The cross-shareholding has been a main instrument for protecting against
hostile takeovers. Management control in Japan, on the other hand, may be best described
by a contingent governance system. In this system, control is shifted to the main
bank if financial conditions of a firm deteriorate. Hence, the main bank, or the main
monitor, has incentives to replace the management of a low-performance firm, since
the bank is often one of the largest shareholders and wants to maintain a stable and
long-term customer relationship with the firm. This system of control demonstrates
quite different relationships among stakeholders than, for example, the Anglo-Saxon
or the continental European systems.

2.5 Family-Centered Corporate Governance in Asia

This section is designed to focus on how the Asian family-centered relationship model affects corporate governance of some large diversified conglomerates listed on stock exchanges in Asia. For instance, 644 firms out of the 1000 largest firms in Thailand are identified as affiliated companies belonging to 212 family-owned groups and their combined sales account for over 50 percent of grand total sales of the 1000 largest firms. These figures apparently evidence the prominent presence of family businesses in large-sized Thai firms.

The family-centered relationship model in corporate governance is even more evident in those countries or regions where ethnic Chinese play a dominant role in local economies (e.g., Hong Kong, Singapore, and Malaysia). Asia's traditional corporate model sits uneasily with modern practice. Families are a key source of capital, contacts, and customers. That is logical enough when uncertainties and risks are high and capital markets underdeveloped. Interlocking networks of subsidiaries and sister companies can allow funds to flow quickly into promising new businesses. But such networks are opaque, and discriminate against outside investors. Moreover, the ambiguous role of the state, as not only a regulator but also often a shareholder in Asian companies, creates conflicts of interest and gives too much power to politicians. To illustrate the above points, ethnic Chinese family businesses in Singapore are perhaps the best example.

2.5.1 Corporate governance in Singapore

Ethnic Chinese in Singapore have been estimated to control about 80 percent of Singapore's listed companies by market capitalization alone. Three of Singapore's "Big Four" banks can each trace its origins to financing trade among the Chinese community in both Singapore and the rest of the world. About half of all public-listed Chinese family firms in Singapore own controlling stakes of more than 50 percent. This implies that public-listed Chinese family firms in Singapore are still, to some extent, controlled and owned by families or their family members. For example, hotelier Tan Sri Khoo Teck Phuat owns two firms (Central Properties Ltd. and Hotel Malaysia) out of the 157 public-listed Chinese family firms. In the two instances, he accounts respectively for about 85 percent and 90 percent of the total substantial shareholdings.

The selection of personnel for such key positions as chairmen, chief executive officers, and managing directors is another way through which family control of the firm is maintained. Although as generational shifts continue, younger executives are seeking to adopt more managerial and organizational practices popular in the US and Europe, more than 90 percent of public-listed Chinese family firms in Singapore still have family members holding key positions and/or have family members on the board of directors. For these firms, however, the family in question normally owns a majority portion of the shares. This ensures that the authority and importance of the family in the firm is not compromised. To illustrate, 83.3 percent of Centrepoint Properties Ltd. is owned by Fraser & Neave Ltd., in which the Overseas-Chinese Banking Corporation has a substantial stake. Other examples include the Overseas-Chinese

Banking Corporation (owning 77.7 percent of Focal Finance Ltd.) and the United Overseas Bank (another ethnic Chinese family-based bank, which owns over 70 percent of Hotel Negara).

Of course, there are several forces that are pushing the above traditional model of corporate governance toward change and improvement. Some companies are hiring more outside managers. The modern heir may have not only an MBA degree from a prestigious university in the US or UK but also western notions of how to run a business. It is becoming clearer that opacity costs money, as untrusting foreign investors demand bigger returns. In the external environment, these Asian countries are also looking for ways to protect minority shareholders. These might include, for instance, allowing minority shareholders who have voted unsuccessfully against a large transaction to insist that the company buy out their shares at the value prevailing before the transaction took place.

2.5.2 Corporate governance in Hong Kong

While the preference in the United States is clearly for a broad-based diversified shareholding model, business leaders in Hong Kong make a case for the merits of the predominant family-owned structure when it comes to corporate governance. Of the top 50 companies in the Hang Seng Index, only HSBC and Giordano do not have a single, large influential shareholder. This number is in sharp inverse proportion to the London and New York markets. Dating back to the 1960s, the family-controlled model proved to be able to deliver long-term sustainable shareholder value. The direct personal interest of the major shareholder in the well-being of a company is a strong positive. Family interests also typically have a long-term commitment to the business and a strong incentive to maintain the trust of other shareholders.

However, connected transactions – or misdealings – between the family's private interests and those of its listed vehicles are a particular area of wrongdoing and of major concern to Hong Kong regulators and investors. Director remuneration is another potential area for abuse. Recently, Hong Kong business leaders believe fair enforcement of listing rules by regulators is key to preventing abuses within the family-owned structure. A strong cultural commitment to ethical behavior is also widely viewed as imperative. In order to maintain a free and attractive market, corporate governance needs to be fostered from the top down within companies and by regulators, professional bodies, and academics rather than by government.

There are concerns that increasing checks and balances at the board and committee levels, as is occurring in the United States, can extend to the point of eroding the major shareholder's power. This creates its own potential problems and will ultimately not find favor in an Asian context. If the controlling family is marginalized to the extent that it has the fewest rights and least involvement, families may come to prefer private vehicles to listed companies. Companies could de-list or move to jurisdictions that have preferential listing arrangements. In the simplest scenario, regulations would be honored in name only and not in practice. Ultimately, the effect on the market would be negative.

Two important measures that companies are paying increasing attention to are in the areas of improved disclosure and putting company boards in place that can monitor family behavior. The momentum is coming from within since the notion of shareholder activism is still in its infancy in Hong Kong. Comparatively, Hong Kong companies seeking to tap the US capital markets must comply with standards outlined in the Sarbanes–Oxley Act. Companies listed only in Hong Kong do not have to adhere to this legislation, although many have shown significant initiative in the area of corporate governance with varying results. For example, family-controlled Li & Fung, a global leader in the trading and export of consumer products, has in recent years formalized corporate governance initiatives which have had a significant impact on the functioning of its board. It appointed a compliance officer in 1996, followed by an audit committee in 1998, and risk management and nomination committees in 2001. Li & Fung restructured its family holdings in 1989 and relisted as a focused export-trading group in 1992 with net assets of HK$300 million. By the end of 2002, net assets had reached HK$3.8 billion. The company has been rewarded with a relatively high ratio of earnings per share, exceeding the Hang Seng Index weighted average since 1996/7, with earnings per share showing an increasing upward trend from 1995/6. By strengthening compliance, ethics and transparency, the company has improved risk management and lowered the costs of acquisition.

Under Hong Kong's listing rules, all non-executive directors must have a degree of independence from company management, with some having to fulfill stricter independence criteria. It is not uncommon for non-executive directors in Hong Kong to have more than 50 other directorships, and in extreme cases several hundred. Many multiple directorships can be attributed to wholly owned subsidiaries, making it difficult to lay down strict limits. In Hong Kong, listing rules are the primary tool for regulating overseas-incorporated listed companies. They are of greater significance than in other major markets as 80 percent of companies are incorporated offshore and are primarily governed by the laws of those jurisdictions. At present, the stock exchange does not have the power to investigate a suspected breach of its listing rules. If it discovers a company has violated the rules, it can issue public censure and private reprimands but has no enforcement powers. The only other option is to de-list the company, which is detrimental to minority investors.

Hong Kong is currently taking important steps to improve its corporate governance regime. In addition to legislative changes, reforms introduced by Hong Kong Exchanges and Clearing (HKEx) are also enhancing corporate governance. Corporate governance proposals sent to the Legislative Council in 2005 include the establishment of an independent board that would investigate accounting fraud by auditors of listed companies, and an increase of the penalty powers of the Market Misconduct Tribunal, a civil court. To improve the quality of listed companies, listing sponsors were required beginning January 1, 2005 to make "private" declarations to the exchange that they had completed due-diligence work on listing applicants in accordance with HKEx guidelines. The Exchange can penalize errant sponsors, and the Securities and Futures Commission (SFC) can prosecute those that intentionally release misleading information to the public. The SFC can also reprimand, fine, suspend, or revoke the licenses of errant sponsors. In addition, sponsors will be responsible for ensuring that listing candidates have adequate internal controls and procedures in place before they go to the market for funds. Also from January 1, 2005, listed companies and issuers of securities have been required to include a Corporate Governance Report in their annual reports containing prescribed information on their corporate governance practices. If they deviate from the provisions of the Code, issuers of securities must explain the reasons for the deviation.

2.6 Corporate Governance in Transition Economies

2.6.1 Overview

Commonly, corporate governance in transition economies is weak, leaving much to be desired. Some major causes of this weakness are the lack of transparency, limited protection of property rights, underdeveloped supporting institutions (e.g., independent auditing, accounting, law, and arbitration services), the poor enforcement of laws, rules and verdicts, the lack of independence in banks' loan decisions, and distorted stock markets. Under these circumstances, governmental roles are paradoxical. On the one hand, the "visible hand" is inevitable and important to redress deficiencies in the legal, regulatory, and institutional infrastructures. For instance, the improvement of corporate transparency and suppressing corruption still depends on governmental support and related regulations. Allowing stock markets to play a bigger role in corporate governance still necessitates governmental efforts to consummate trading rules, improve transparency, and foster the establishment of large block institutional shareholders. On the other hand, however, if improperly or overly used, the "visible hand" may further distort stock market functions and worsen regulatory transparency. How to facilitate the improvement of legal and institutional environments without direct interference of the roles and functions that ought to be played by market forces seems to be the future direction for these policy or law makers.

Likewise, the relationship-based corporate governance in transition economies also has a paradoxical effect. Such relationships are reflected not only in interlocking directorate but also in government–business (companies, banks, accounting firms, etc.) links. Due to the deficiency of markets (stock, capital, products, and factors) and institutions (auditing, law, arbitration, accounting, etc.), corporate governance is still largely influenced by or dependent upon a company's relationship with major stakeholders, especially regulators and creditors. Governance often has to yield to the maintenance of the relationship with such stakeholders if the company wants to survive and thrive. In the Anglo-Saxon and continental European systems, good relationships with organizational and market stakeholders are typically established only after good corporate governance has been built and is functioning in the first place. On the contrary, in transition economies, it is the opposite. That is, building relationships with market and regulatory stakeholders has to be the very first step before designing or improving corporate governance.

While westerners attach value to systems trust, business practices in transition economies emphasize personal trust. Systems trust, as in a financial institution, assumes that the system is functioning correctly; trust is placed in the system, not in specific individuals or officials. Agencies which form part of the system function to generate trust, reduce reliance on people, and make personal guarantees dispensable. Thus, systems trust is associated with professionalism and rationalism. It is within this context that stock market-based corporate governance works well in North America and Europe. Executives in transition economies, however, view interpersonal and inter-organizational relationships as more important than systems trust. Although transition economy governments such as Russia and China have enacted thousands of laws, rules and regulations, few are completely enforced since personal interpretations are often made in lieu of legal interpretations. Rather than depending on the abstract notion of impartial justice, executives in these economies traditionally prefer to rely on their contacts with those in power to get things done. Such ties, therefore, are very helpful in dealing with governments, banks, suppliers, and clients. The main reason behind this behavior has to do with high institutional uncertainties. When property rights are poorly defined and protected, information is always difficult to secure, verify and predict, and social and political chaos often occurs, companies have to depend on their relationships to avoid or reduce the hazards of turbulence on governance and operations. Such relationships, however, are a double-edged sword, especially with regard to their effect on corporate governance. Investment or transaction decisions in both firms and banks are often based on the relationships rather than economic analyses and rationality, causing deviations and distortions from economic legitimacy and strategic transparency. While relationships with governments are helpful in some respects, they may impair corporate governance in the corrupting society because close personal ties with officials may be portrayed by the public and stakeholders as the evidence of executive incompetence and collusion with government agencies.

Since some major problems noted above are imbedded in the political structure, social norms and tradition, they are thus extremely difficult to solve. I wish I could be more optimistic about the outlook of corporate governance in transition economies. For the same reason, it seems that none of the models of corporate governance we introduced above (Anglo-Saxon, continental Europe, and Japan) should, and will, completely apply to companies in transition economies. It is more likely, though, that companies listed in stock exchanges in transition economies will use a mixture of corporate governance that integrates less formal and more relationship-based governance mechanisms primarily from their tradition (e.g., reliance on external relationships, government, and banks) with more formal and more market-determined mechanisms largely from the Anglo-Saxon system (e.g., reliance on stock markets, board supervision, and internal control). This will be more salient as these economies continually improve their property right protection system, stock market development, independency of commercial banks, corporate law and transparency systems, and institutional supports such as independent accounting, auditing and legal services.

Lastly, it is worth noting some differences in corporate governance between transition economies such as China and Russia, the two leading ones in this kind and detailed in the following pages, and some major emerging economies such as India, Mexico and Brazil, as we often categorize China and Russia into emerging economies as well. My overall reading is that corporate governance in India, Brazil and Mexico is, or will be, moving closer to the Anglo-Saxon system than that in China and Russia. That is, there will be a greater and faster convergence of emerging economy corporate governance with the Anglo-Saxon paradigm compared to transition economy corporate governance. This is because, in emerging economies such as India, Brazil and Mexico, the economic sectors are more privatized, state ownership and government control are substantially reduced, political regimes are more accommodative to market force determination, and there is increasing systems trust (as opposed to personal trust) in the society.

In India, for instance, the Securities and Exchange Board recently provided a few key provisions in compliance with the Anglo-Saxon model. For example, if the chairman of the board is an executive director, at least one-half of the board must comprise independent directors. In addition, the independent audit committee must be established within the board, and this committee must have adequate power to review all major investments and transactions. In Brazil, where family used to control the boards and appoint family members to senior management positions, companies newly listed on the exchanges are increasingly opening their boards to independent directors and setting up compensation, nomination, and audit committees. For instance, most initial public offerings (IPOs) on the Sao Paulo Stock Exchanges in 2004 have voluntarily met higher standards of corporate governance than required by law. In Mexico, the corporate governance movement has taken its cue from the international community. The Committee for Better Business Practices issued a seminal document in 1999, the Code of Better Business Practices, which has served as the benchmark for corporate governance principles in Mexico. The Code established a series of recommendations for better corporate governance in local public and private companies. Meanwhile, the Mexican securities regulators have, as part of their efforts to match global regulatory standards, been focused on enacting far-reaching amendments to the securities regulations designed to govern the conduct of the various participants in the securities market, including issuers, insiders, broker-dealers, underwriters, independent auditors, and securities lawyers. In June 2001, the securities market law (LMV) was amended to adopt the standard corporate governance provisions of other leading markets in the world. The new regulations also enhance the reporting and disclosure requirements of issuers.

2.6.2 Corporate governance in China

Corporate governance in China is transitional. Since late 1978, China has gradually transformed itself from a centrally planned economy into a market-oriented economy. Beginning in 1990, China developed a nationwide equity market with stock exchanges located in Shanghai and Shenzhen. Although the time is not that long, the number of listed companies has increased drastically, rising from 14 in 1991 to 1223 in 2002, while the market capitalization rose to about US$500 billion in the same year, placing China in ninth place globally in market capitalization terms.

The ownership structure in China's listed companies is unique. Table 2.1 provides a snapshot of this ownership structure. About two-thirds of the shares are not listed and are presently not allowed to be traded in the markets. Among these non-tradable

Table 2.1   Ownership structure of stocks listed on China's stock markets (in billion shares)

Share type	1992		2000	
	Shares	%	Shares	%
I: Tradable shares	2.118	30.75	135.43	35.80
1. A-shares	1.093	15.87	107.82	28.50
2. B-shares	1.025	14.88	15.16	4.01
3. H-shares	0.00	0.00	12.45	3.29
II: Non-tradable shares	4.77	69.25	242.85	64.20
1. State-owned shares	4.04	58.59	216.54	57.24
2. Institutional shares	0.65	9.42	21.42	5.66
3. Employee shares	0.09	1.23	2.43	0.64
4. Other shares	0.00	0.00	2.46	0.65

shares, state-owned shares accounted for 57.24 percent of the total in 2000, institutional shares for 5.66 percent, and employee shares for 0.64 percent. Among tradable shares, common stock A-shares accounted for 28.50 percent of the total stocks listed, common stock B-shares accounted for 4.01 percent, and common stock H-shares accounted for 3.29 percent. Regardless of share types, shareholders' entitlement is the same in terms of dividends and voting rights. However, the methods of exchange differ among the types of shares. The floating A-shares are freely traded on the stock exchanges while state and legal person shares cannot be traded publicly. Overall, the body of institutional investors in China is relatively small due to the absence of large block institutional shareholders such as pension funds and mutual funds. Institutional investors also do not actively participate in the governance of firms even when they possess a significant proportion of shares.

Although the Chinese stock market has made significant achievements since its initiation in 1990, its function, service, transparency, and efficiency are all far from completion. One of the major problems that hampers the market function has to do with the weak corporate governance of Chinese enterprises, whether state-owned or not, listed on the exchanges. For state-owned companies, which constitute the majority of companies listed, the state, or government, is usually the dominant shareholder and hence plays a dominant role in the decision-making process of the board of directors. The chairperson of the board of directors and the CEO are often the same person, who is appointed by the state to "administer" the company as a representative of state ownership. Therefore, it is reasonable to expect that such CEOs are more responsible in protecting the interest of the state, the biggest shareholder. On average, fewer than 10 percent of listed companies actually distribute cash dividends to shareholders. Therefore, the minority shareholders have no choice but to obtain the capital gain from the trading spread. This is why the Chinese stock market is enveloped by a thick atmosphere of speculation through short-term trading. In the Chinese stock market, the trading turnover ratio is four to five times per year on average. The relatively high turnover ratio indicates that the total trading volume is much more than the total market value and in turn implies that investors tend to speculate more than to invest for the long term. This kind of behavior distorts the market, particularly the market price.

The Chinese stock market is also often called a "policy market", as it is influenced by government policies much more significantly than by market forces and economic factors. The phenomenon that the stock market dances so closely with the rhythms of political events reflects the significance of the government's interference in the market. Moreover, the government intervention is more influential than the market-oriented, socioeconomic factors. Investors who have contacts in or with the government and know the news ahead of time can benefit the most from the stock market. Under such an asymmetric information flow mechanism, insider trading and price manipulation are rampant. The consequence is that Chinese investors are "government policy watchers".

Due to the dominant ownership by the state, Chinese enterprises are largely financed by state bank loans under government influence. Close links among firms, their banks, and the government have been developed through a business system of state and political deal making. Both firms and banks within this relationship-based system feel little need to develop corporate governance mechanisms, since the former are able to rely on banks to continue to finance their projects and the latter feel comfortable under the explicit or implicit government guarantee. Government agencies tend to provide subsidized credit to firms in targeted industrial sectors and implicitly share their investment risk. In this sense, subsidies act against strategic transparency as long as subsidized firms do not have to face market mechanisms and competition which both require adequate disclosure to outside investors. Meanwhile, outside investors have little incentive to heavily invest in a new relationship given the weak legal infrastructure that protects their rights and the resulting lack of corporate transparency.

The state ownership is administered by the State Asset Supervision Administration Commission (SASAC), which has branch offices in each province and city. Thus, listed state-owned companies are essentially supervised and governed by this agency. Compounding the state dominance and interference in corporate governance is the fact that many strategic decisions, if not all, are influenced by the senior secretary of the Community Party committee imbedded in a state-owned company. When this political "boss" in the company is the same person as the chairman of the board, he or she becomes even more powerful in intervening in management decisions. When the chairman and the secretary are separated, it often creates more conflicts and collisions among executive, board, and party secretary offices since they represent very different groups inherently concerned with different sets of interests.

Executive compensation in Chinese companies is generally low. Although many enterprises have begun trying a more market-oriented approach to executive compensation since 2000, few have considered corporate governance in the design and implementation of executive compensation incentive plans. In fact, most enterprises have their executives (internal staff) formulate their own compensation. Before 2000, the annual cash compensation of executives in most state-owned companies was below US$25,000. Executive compensation in Chinese enterprises generally comprises basic salary, annual bonus, benefits (such as housing), and perks. A minority of enterprises implement long-term incentive plans, tying executive compensation to company performance.

In general, listed companies today have a greater degree of autonomy than before in formulating their executive compensation and are currently moving toward market-based compensation. But still, such practices must comply with the SASAC formulated compensation policies.

In general, executive directors play a dominant role in the board while non-executive directors have a limited role. China's regulatory authorities have recently reformed the structure of executive compensation and corporate governance. The China Securities Regulatory Commission requires independent non-executive directors to make up one-third of the number of directors. Parent companies are also restricted from concurrently engaging in key positions of companies limited by shares. Overall, executive compensation and corporate governance in China still fall short of the compliance standards and best practices of developed countries, marked by insufficient information disclosure and a lack of transparency in the design and management of executive compensation and long-term incentives. Self-designed executive compensation and incentive plans still exist in some companies.

Chinese firms have been actively seeking to become more globalized in recent years, as evidenced by growing cross-border mergers and acquisitions undertaken by Lenovo and TCL, among others. They know, however, truly successful globalization cannot be achieved unless they sharply improve their corporate governance and transparency. Prominent Chinese companies on the global scene include Haier (China's largest producer of consumer products), Tsingtao (China's largest brewer), and Huawei (telecommunication producer). Other global players include Shanghai Automotive, Ningbo Bird (mobile phone provider), Little Swan (consumer appliance maker), Chulang (AC provider), and Changhong (home appliances manufacturer). Improved corporate governance becomes a particular priority for these companies interested in cross-border mergers and acquisitions as a means of global expansion. Perceived lack of transparency and questionable integrity of management have imposed hidden costs of mergers and acquisitions, both overseas and in China, involving Chinese firms. It is an increasingly common view among Chinese executives that true and efficient corporate governance will lead their top firms to be very competitive in the world, but the only way to achieve this and change a corporate culture is to have a physical, practical, and direct relationship with an organization that is used to operating in the world outside China.

2.6.3 Corporate governance in Russia

Foreign direct investment (FDI) in Russia has been significantly lower than in other leading transition or emerging economies such as India, China, Mexico, and even some Eastern European countries. For instance, FDI in the country in 2002 was only US$4 billion. Concerns over property rights and corporate governance are portrayed as the two leading barriers to higher levels of inbound FDI. When Russian executives face major problems, they tend to solve them at the expense of investors. No wonder foreign investors have been particularly insistent that they should receive full information about company affairs and take part in real control over the governance process.

Overall, there have been three stages of corporate governance in Russia. In the earliest stages characterized by the centralized regime, corporate governance was entirely in the hands of the state – it handled all property claims, monitored and reacted to corruption charges, and oversaw all financial transactions. Since the mid-1990s, Russia moved to the second stage during which local companies sought the Anglo-Saxon form of governance where the state was minimally involved and the rule of law and external markets governed individual enterprises as they attempted to respond to market signals and opportunities. However, the lack of legal and institutional infrastructure significantly hindered the adoption of the Anglo-Saxon system, causing a failure in using this system. There were few laws to establish fair rules of the game, and, when the formal rules were established, they conflicted with the informal norms and practices that had guided Russia for centuries. Consequently, the formal rules and laws were routinely ignored and not enforced. Moreover, underdeveloped stock markets and factor markets, along with the state ownership in "strategic" sectors, further obstruct the adoption of the Anglo-Saxon system.

In the current stage, Russia seems to be at a crossroads, using governance that blends the Anglo-Saxon system with the continental European model. On the one hand, the Russian stock markets have significantly developed in recent years, playing a more active role in funding and affecting corporate investments. Russian corporate and securities laws, regulations and practices designed to address and remedy severe corporate governance abuses also improve the institutional environment in which the stock market-based governance regime can work better. On the other hand, the bank-led financial industrial groups (FIGs) built up their industrial holdings in the loans-for-shares transactions and later privatization auctions. In 1998, such FIGs accounted for 4.4 percent of Russia's GDP and 10 percent of industrial production. They united over 2000 legal entities. This approach seems more aligned with Russian culture and history, which combine paternalistic and hierarchical control with participative decision making. It is worthwhile noting that the Russian banking system is paradoxical. On the one hand, this system is rather fragmented, with over 1300 banks. On the other hand, it is extremely concentrated where the top five banks control over 50 percent of banking capital. The Central Bank's power has also been substantially escalated in recent years.

Like in China, minority shareholders' interests are not well protected in Russia. In Russia's past, because of unaccountable controlling both shareholders and management reaped the benefit of a company's business and assets for themselves rather than for their shareholders. Direct tactics to achieve this sordid goal included driving shareholders out of the company by refusing to recognize their ownership interests on the company's share registry. Other tactics were holding meetings in remote locations at inconvenient times without proper notice. Management often dramatically diluted the company's shareholders by issuing new shares to entities affiliated or controlled by management. Examples also abound of Russian managers seizing corporate assets and opportunities for their own benefit, often using companies related to them to provide services or products to the company on terms unfavorable to the company, or simply engaging in a straightforward theft of corporate assets. Particularly in the natural resource sector, managers and controlling shareholders had stolen state assets to quickly build vast private companies and accumulate huge private wealth. Generally, Russia has almost sufficient corporate and securities laws; the fundamental problem of corporate governance does not stem from a lack of laws but instead from the lack of effective enforcement of such laws and the limited enforcement power of the securities regulators. Simply put, Russian managers and controlling shareholders have enjoyed a tremendous advantage over minority shareholders, particularly foreign shareholders, in manipulating the judicial and regulatory process to their own self-interested ends. In so doing, managers of major companies often enjoy privileged relationships with local and regional politicians whose influence frequently extends to the local judiciary.

A number of Russian-oriented and Russian-style initiatives are already completed or underway that are contributing to greatly enhanced awareness of corporate governance in Russia and to changes in prevailing corporate governance practices. These include judicial reforms, amendments to existing corporate securities and criminal laws, and the introduction of new laws to define and regulate affiliate relationships and insider trading. An even more promising step is a bold and innovative one taken by the Federal Commission for Securities Market (FCSM), which has prepared a corporate governance code, implemented by Russian joint-stock companies since 2002. This code is a summation of recommendations on all the main components of good corporate governance, including shareholder general meeting, board of directors, management (executive) board, corporate secretary, major corporate actions, information disclosure, supervision of financial and business operations, dividend policy, and resolution of corporate conflicts. The code has already received the endorsement of the Russian government and strong positive reviews from participants in the Russian securities industry as well as the investor community. Although it is not a legislative or regulatory act, the code serves as the basis for modalities of implementing its core principle. This will be done through the systems for regulations issued by the appropriate ministries and agencies, professional organizations' standards, amending the relevant laws, and rooting them in the business community practices.

CASE EXAMPLE 2.1: EUROTUNNEL IN FRANCE

The ouster of the Eurotunnel board in April 2004 after a highly publicized legal dispute and proxy contest reflects a fundamental transformation of French corporate governance. Proxy contests in France are exceedingly rare, but recent episodes show that shareholder activism is on the rise. This change is largely the result of a shift in French market mentality, driven by increased investment in French stocks by non-French investment funds. Recent legal reforms in France have also bolstered shareholder democracy. The Eurotunnel affair itself is as remarkable for the novel legal principles involved as for the fact that well-established shareholder powers were actually exercised against an incumbent board.

On April 7, 2004, the board of Eurotunnel lost a proxy contest led by Nicolas Miguet, a minority shareholder activist. At the general assembly Miguet's slate of directors received 63.42 percent of the votes cast. This represented about 64,000, or 5 percent, of the company's 1.1 million shareholders, but 35 percent of the company's capital. The procedure used to call the general assembly is exceptional in France: this is the first time that minority shareholders have made use of recent legal reforms that allow shareholders representing at least 5 percent of a company's shares to request a court to convene a general assembly. In December, a judge ordered Eurotunnel to hold the general assembly, following a request made by Adacte, a French minority shareholder association. Prior to his involvement in the Eurotunnel dispute Miguet was primarily known not as a businessman but as a populist French politician. Until late in the process, his campaign against the Eurotunnel board was portrayed in the business press as having little chance of success against a board well connected with British and French financial leaders and supported by institutional investors. The replacement of the Eurotunnel British chairman and chief executive officer by two French businessmen reflects a groundswell of the company's disgruntled individual shareholders, most of whom are French.

The ouster of the Eurotunnel board at the general assembly has not ended the controversy surrounding the proxy contest. Miguet, who publishes a financial advisory newsletter, is facing both a criminal investigation and a regulatory inquiry by the Autorité des marchés financiers (AMF), the French stock exchange regulator, which suspects him of having disseminated false or misleading information concerning Eurotunnel in 2003 in an effort to manipulate its stock price. Unlike the US, where proxy solicitations are heavily regulated, France does not have separate securities regulations concerning the conduct of proxy contests. In France, a dissident shareholder or shareholder association is bound only by the general obligation to avoid disseminating false or misleading information concerning the company. There has as yet been no case law interpreting this requirement in the context of a proxy contest.

There is no special form that proxy solicitations must take, and there is no requirement that the AMF review the solicitation in advance. There is no legal limit on the number of proxies that may be held by a shareholder. There is no requirement that proxy holders have to have been shareholders for any extended period of time. General assemblies of shareholders in France also have greater flexibility and power than their American counterparts. Most importantly, they may dismiss board members at any time, without cause. Staggered boards, as found in many US companies, do not exist in France.

Over the past several years, the rules governing proxy contests in France have been modified by two legislative initiatives: the new economic regulations law, adopted on May 15, 2001 (NER law), and the financial security law, adopted on August 1, 2003 (FS law). The NER law and FS law instituted several changes. The NER law reduced the threshold for certain shareholder initiatives from 10 percent to 5 percent of the company's capital stock. One or more shareholders holding or representing 5 percent of the company's shares may now exercise the rights to: (i) demand the dismissal or resignation of the company's commissaire aux comptes;

(ii) ask a judge to order the convening of a general assembly; (iii) request that a court appoint an expert to evaluate management's activities; and (iv) propose resolutions that the company must place on the general assembly's agenda. Any shareholder, regardless of the number of shares held, may also pose written questions to the board, which must be answered during the company's annual general assembly.

The NER law relaxed rules on participation in general assemblies by video-conference, and prohibited the practice of limiting participation to shareholders holding a certain percentage of the shares. The NER law has also increased corporate information disclosure requirements, and in particular requires companies to publish the personal remuneration received by each of the directors, and the number of other directorships held by each board member. The FS law granted shareholder associations the procedural right to legally represent groups of shareholders who have suffered direct or indirect injury to their interests. This provision moves in the direction of American-style class action suits, and substantially increases the power of shareholder activists. Taken together, the NER law and FS law have significantly expanded the information available to shareholders and their control over the board, and will make it easier for shareholder groups to conduct proxy contests or bring legal challenges against management.

Foreign institutional investors now play a significant role in the French market. As of 1997, approximately 37 percent of French market capitalization was held by non-resident shareholders. According to the International Monetary Fund (IMF), foreign equity portfolio investment in France in 2002 grew to roughly $290 billion, of which roughly $120 billion originated in the US and Great Britain. Such investors will insist on active involvement in the governance of their portfolio companies. Institutional investors holding significant participations can expect to receive benefits from better management that will cover the costs of involvement in a proxy contest.

Corporate management has come under increased media and judicial scrutiny in recent years. Shareholders have become more aware of corporate governance problems in major corporations as a result of scandals such as Vivendi, Elf and Crédit Lyonnais, and high-profile corporate trials, such as the conviction for abuse of corporate assets of Bernard Tapie, former chief executive officer of the French corporation Testut.

Notwithstanding recent developments, a number of legal and practical obstacles to the success of French proxy contests remain. First, the capital of many French listed companies remains concentrated in the hands of a few large French shareholders, including the French state and industrial shareholders. Significant minority shareholders can effectively lock up the management of a company, as is the case of the family-controlled companies Auchan, Lagardère, and Michelin. Faced with these intransigent blocs, dissenting minority shareholders often cannot accumulate enough votes to force a change in management.

Second, shareholder participation is limited. Traditionally, French shareholders have been indifferent to annual general assemblies, and have either failed to vote altogether or have given unconditional proxies to the management. The rise of organized minority shareholder associations may reduce this tendency, by eliminating the direct costs to shareholders of organizing a proxy contest. Turnout among shareholders at annual meetings is generally quite low. The average for a listed company is approximately 30 percent participation, and even in the highly controversial Eurotunnel case, the winning dissident shareholders represented only 35 percent of the company's capital stock. In 2003, the French Assembly enacted a law requiring investment funds holding large blocs of shares to either vote their shares in their own name at annual general assemblies or to justify their abstention. However, the AMF has not yet issued the necessary implementing regulations, and so the rule is currently not in effect. Approximately two-thirds of investment funds currently participate in general assemblies, compared with only 41 percent in 2000. Their participation has already contributed to increased shareholder activism in France, and a mandatory participation requirement would intensify this trend.

Third, companies are required to publish a list of their shareholders two weeks prior to the annual general assembly. Professional minority shareholder activists or shareholder associations therefore have limited time in which to collect the necessary proxies. The media can play a determining role in the outcome of a proxy contest. In the Eurotunnel case, the conflict between minority shareholders and the incumbent board was highly publicized for months prior to the general assembly, which served to mobilize support for the dissident shareholders. In France, as in the United States, it is also becoming common for dissident shareholders to communicate among themselves over the Internet.

Lastly, shareholders are considered to be acting in concert if they have agreed to acquire or sell shares, or exercise voting rights to implement a common policy. Shareholders deemed to be acting in concert are required to publish a declaration if they cross certain ownership thresholds, and in certain cases may be required to make a public tender offer for the remaining shares. One commentator has noted that the issues raised by most proxy contests, such as the dismissal of the officers or the board, or the rejection of a merger proposal, are too limited to fall within the scope of concerted action. However, in certain cases, where dissident shareholders seek to replace board members to shift the strategic orientation of the business in a specific direction, they might be considered to be acting in concert, which would trigger additional reporting obligations or even require a tender offer.

(Excerpted from Anonymous (2004). "Will Eurotunnel inspire French proxy battles?", *International Financial Law Review*, July: 1–5.)

REFERENCES AND FURTHER READING

Aoki, M. and Sheard, P. (1991). *The Role of the Japanese Main Bank in the Economy*. Cambridge: Cambridge University Press.

Aste, L.J. (1999). Reforming French corporate goverance: A return to the two-tier board? *George Washington Journal of International Law and Economics*, **32**(1): 1–72.

Berle, A. and Means, G. (1965). *The Modern Corporation and Private Property*. New York: Macmillan.

Blair, M. (1995a). Corporate "ownership". *Brookings Review*, **13**(1): 16–20.

Blair, M. (1995b). Rethinking assumptions behind corporate governance. *Challenge*, November–December: 12–18.

Ees, Hans Van and Postma, T.J.B.M. (2004). Dutch boards and governance. *International Studies of Management and Organization*, **34**(2): 90–112.

Fama, E. and Jensen, M. (1983). Agency problems and residual claims. *Journal of Law and Economics*, **26**: 327–50.

Fligstein, N. and Freeland, R. (1995). Theoretical and comparative perspectives on corporate organization. *Annual Review of Sociology*, **21**: 21–44.

Fruin, W.M. (1992). *The Japanese Enterprise System*. New York: Oxford University Press.

Gerlach, M. (1992a). The Japanese corporate network: A block-model approach. *Administrative Science Quarterly*, **37**: 105–39.

Gerlach, M. (1992b). *Alliance Capitalism: The Social Organization of Japanese Business*. Berkeley, CA: University of California Press.

Gordon, J. and Roe, M. (2004). *Convergence and Persistence in Corporate Governance*. Cambridge: Cambridge University Press.

Gugler, K., Mueller, D.C., and Yurtoglu, B.B. (2004). Corporate governance and globalization. *Oxford Review of Economic Policy*, **20**(1): 129–56.

Guillen, M. (2000). Corporate governance and globalization: Is there convergence across countries? *Advances in International Comparative Management*, **13**: 175–204.

Hoshi, T., Kashyap, A., and Scharfstein, D. (1990). The role of banks in reducing the costs of financial distress in Japan. *Journal of Financial Economics*, **27**: 67–88.

Hitt, M.I.A., Ireland, R.D., and Hoskison, R.E. (2005). *Strategic management: Competitiveness and globalisation*. South-Western Thomson.

Imai, K. and Itami, H. (1984). Interpenetration of firm and market: Japan's firm and market in comparison with the US. *International Journal of Industrial Organization*, **2**: 285–310.

Jacoby, S. (2000). Corporate governance in comparative perspective: Prospects for convergence. *Comparative Labor Law and Policy Journal*, **22**(1).

Judge, W. and Naoumova, I. (2004). Corporate governance in Russia: What model will it follow. *Corporate Governance*, **12**(3): 302–13.

Kester, W.C. (1991). *Japanese Takeovers: The Global Contest for Corporate Control*. Boston, MA: Harvard University Press.

Kim, K. and Limpaphayom, P. (1998). A test of the two-tier corporate governance structure: The case of Japanese keiretsu. *Journal of Financial Research*, **21**(1): 37–52.

Nobum, D., Boyd, B.K., Fox, M., and Muth, M. (2000). International corporate governance reform. *European Business Journal*, **12**(3): 116–33.

Pettigrew, A. and McNulty, T. (1995). Power and influence in and around the boardroom. *Human Relations*, Special Issue: Corporate Governance and Control, **48**(8): 845–74.

Philips, M. (2002). New rules of engagement. *Global Investor*, October: 126.

Prowse, S.D. (1990). Institutional investment patterns and corporate financial behavior in the US and Japan. *Journal of Financial Economics*, **27**: 43–66.

Roe, M.J. (1996). *Strong Managers–Weak Owners: The Political Roots of American Corporate Finance*, 2nd edition, Princeton: Princeton University Press.

Shleifer, A. and Vishny, R.W. (1997). A survey of corporate governance. *Journal of Finance*, **52**: 737–83.

Tezuka, H. (1997). Success as the source of failure? Competition and cooperation in the Japanese economy. *Sloan Management Review*, **38**(2): 83–94.

Williamson, O. (1975). *Markets and Hierarchies*. New York: Free Press.

Williamson, O. (1985). *The Economic Institutions of Capitalism*. New York: Free Press.

Williamson, O. (1988). Corporate finance and corporate governance. *Journal of Finance*, **43**: 78–93.

Williamson, O. (1991). Comparative economic organization: The analysis of discrete structural alternatives. *Administrative Science Quarterly*, **36**: 269–96.

Zielinski, R. and Holloway, N. (1991). *Unequal Equities: Power and Risk in Japan's Stock Market*. Tokyo: Kodansha International.

Chapter 3

Corporate Governance in Global Operations: Design and Actions

EXECUTIVE SUMMARY

This chapter addresses how the global activities undertaken by multinational corporations (MNCs) in international settings determine or influence corporate governance design and actual mechanisms at both the corporate and subsidiary levels. It emphasizes how an MNC's globalization attributes such as globalization scale, foreign adaptation, global competition, and international experience influence the design of governance mechanisms such as board size, board composition, executive compensation, market discipline, interlocking directorate, ownership concentration, duality and inbreeding, as well as the design of accountability systems such as accounting information, auditing standards, and financial and non-financial disclosures.

Large corporate failures have often stimulated debate about corporate governance and accountability, leading to regulatory action and other reforms. However, corporate governance and accountability are largely corporate affairs in the first place, and their improvement requires that MNCs themselves seek internal solutions and organizational remedies. In this chapter, I explain how an MNC's corporate governance and accountability design at both parent and subsidiary levels hinge on international expansion features such as globalization scale, required foreign adaptation, global competition, and international experience. I reason that an MNC's corporate governance and accountability should be properly aligned with the above-mentioned features for information processing and agency cost reasons. Increased globalization, adaptation requirements, and global competition all increase an MNC's environmental and operational complexity. Heightened complexity increases information processing and agency demands, and MNCs manage such demands by instituting more efficient governance arrangements. Meanwhile, information processing and agency demands are partly determined by an MNC's international experience; such demands may become even stronger if the firm has little global experience. Globalization scale, adaptation requirements, foreign competition, and international experience are hence proposed to affect information processing and agency requirements, and, in turn, governance and accountability.

3.1 Corporate Governance in Global Operations: An Overview

3.1.1 Global operations influence corporate governance

In recent years, MNCs have extended their presence all over the globe, conducting a multitude of activities for a multitude of purposes. In doing so, MNCs have had to manage the various forces – geographic, product, market, and technology – that interact and become more complex on a global scale. Governing these activities with the appropriate balance of transparency and efficiency or accountability and growth requires a well-prepared plan that strategically plots which governance mechanisms and accountability systems ought to be employed and how they should be deployed. At the heart of total governance of international business activities is corporate governance, which is the set of market-based, culture-based, and discipline-based mechanisms that induce self-interested executives to make decisions that maximize the company's value to its main stakeholders (especially shareholders); and corporate accountability, which is the set of institutional and accounting systems that enhance transparent disclosure and responsive support in corporate activities, strategic decision making, and financial information.

In this chapter, I suggest that an international firm's corporate governance and accountability systems are influenced by its globalization scale, local responsiveness, foreign competition, and international experience. Normatively, the design of corporate governance and accountability should be properly aligned with these firm-level globalization characteristics. In presenting this premise and its related propositions, I use a perspective that combines information processing and agency logics. The complexity an MNC faces is directly related to its geographic dispersion for several reasons including (but not limited to) its dependence on foreign sales and value-creation inputs, the diverse institutional and task environments within which it operates, and increased competitive pressures for cooperation and coordination across geographically distributed operations. Operations are further complicated by national adaptation requirements and foreign competition. This complexity in turn increases information processing and agency demands; the MNC will manage such demands by instituting more efficient governance arrangements (in terms of information acquisition and monitoring). Meanwhile, information processing and agency demands are partly determined by an MNC's international experience in that such demands become even stronger when a firm is not globally experienced. Hence, I propose that globalization scale, adaptation requirements, foreign competition, and international experience affect information processing and agency demands and as a result, governance and accountability design as well. Overall, the convergent and complementary insights of information processing and agency theories provide a richer theoretical context for studying governance and accountability than would either perspective alone. Based on the conceptual foundation I laid out in Chapter 1, I will first illustrate information processing and agency theories to explain corporate governance and accountability associated with globalization. Then several sections will detail how globalization scale, adaptation requirements, foreign competition, and international experience influence corporate governance mechanisms and accountability systems. Finally, I will address the theoretical and practical implications of these discussions.

As defined in Chapter 1, corporate governance is the system by which business corporations are directed and controlled. The corporate governance structure specifies the distribution of rights and responsibilities among different corporate participants and spells out the rules and procedures for making decisions on corporate affairs. Corporate governance ensures that all major stakeholders receive reliable information about the value of the firm, and it motivates managers to maximize firm value instead of pursuing personal objectives. Corporate governance works through:

1. Market-based mechanisms such as board composition, board size, market discipline, board chairmanship, executive compensation, and interlocking directorate.
2. Culture-based mechanisms such as governance culture and corporate integrity.
3. Discipline-based mechanisms such as executive penalty, internal auditing, conduct codes, and ethics programs.

In the MNC context, there are two iterative and interactive tiers of corporate governance: parent and subsidiary. Corporate governance design for MNCs should integrate both levels because they mutually support each other in enhancing overall corporate governance.

In this chapter, I also try to explain how an MNC's global operations influence its corporate accountability. From the corporate design perspective, accountability is a critical part of overall or total corporate governance, and this accountability is presumably affected by global operations as well. While Chapter 6 will specifically detail corporate accountability for MNCs, here I intend to illuminate how an MNC's global activities influence its accountability design in the same framework that integrates these activities with corporate governance. Overall, accountability for global operations or overseas activities is crucial to an MNC's total corporate governance, and it is this accountability that largely differentiates MNCs from companies that purely focus on domestic operations.

Corporate accountability is concerned with the extent to which a company is transparent in its corporate activities and responsive to those it serves. It requires not only financial reporting accountability but also strategic decision transparency. Central to corporate accountability is the widespread availability of relevant, reliable, and accurate information about a firm's performance, financial position, investment opportunities, governance, value, and risk. Accountability affects the investments, productivity, and value of firms in three ways:

1. By identifying promising investment opportunities.
2. By guiding managers to direct resources toward "good" projects and away from those that primarily benefit them over shareholders and stakeholders.
3. By reducing information asymmetries among investors and among the various stakeholders.

For firms engaging in international business activities, the design of corporate accountability systems is mainly concerned with:

1. Which accounting and auditing standards an MNC should follow (home country, host country or international standards). To what extent an MNC's accounting information systems should be globally harmonized.
2. How data management and communication systems should be implemented by geographically dispersed subunits to effectively support corporate accountability configured for an MNC's particular global traits and behaviors.

3.1.2 Agency and information-processing logic

Jensen and Meckling (1976) apply agency theory to the modern corporation and model the agency costs of outside equity. They formalize the idea that when ownership and control of corporations do not fully coincide, there is a potential for conflicts of interest between owners and managers. However, there are also benefits to separating ownership and control, otherwise the prevailing corporate structure is unlikely to have persisted for as long as it has. The conflicts of interest, however, combined with an inability to write perfect contracts or costlessly monitor management, ultimately reduce firm value.

For MNCs, international expansion also makes monitoring executive performance more complex and costly (Zajac and Westphal, 1994). Dependence on foreign markets for customers and factors of production strengthen foreign executives' specialized knowledge and increases the ambiguity surrounding their actions (Sanders and Carpenter, 1998), thus creating a classic agency situation. Moreover, since global expansion can result in far-flung enterprises, each with its own localized and specific knowledge (Nohria and Ghoshal, 1994), information asymmetries between principals and agents can arise, which further compounds the agency problem. The complexity of global operations is also likely to cloud the identification of cause–effect relationships and provide more possible decision options; this results in greater agent discretion, which is considered a prime source of principal–agent discord (Roth and O'Donnell, 1996).

Agency theory is concerned with relationships that mirror a basic agency structure involving a principal and an agent who engage in cooperative behavior but have differing goals and attitudes toward risk (Eisenhardt, 1989). Two key constructs that crystallize agency costs in the eyes of capital suppliers are task programmability associated with external environments and behavior observability associated with moral hazards and adverse selection (Fama, 1980). As a firm becomes more globalized, agency costs increase because both task programmability and behavior verifiability are more difficult to measure and monitor. Solving the agency problem necessitates appropriate governance mechanisms that limit an agent's self-serving behavior. Such governance mechanisms should align agent and principal interest and enable the principal to better verify agent behavior (Fama and Jensen, 1983).

Globalization also increases information-processing demands due to increased managerial complexity and environmental uncertainty. Managing such demands requires selecting and instituting more efficient governance arrangements. Information-processing theory holds that firms are open social systems that interface with internal and environmental sources of complexity (Tushman and Nadler, 1978) and a firm must develop information-processing mechanisms capable of dealing with the resulting complexity. As a result of globalization, a firm faces a multitude of customers, competitors, suppliers, partners, and regulators that increase the volume, variety, and disunity of the information it must process. Information-processing demands are further exacerbated as interdependencies among globally dispersed subunits become more complex through resource sharing, joint development, and value-chain integration (Egelhoff, 1982). For corporate governance, the ability of the board to vigilantly monitor the CEO is a function of its access to information and its power to exert control.

Both information-processing and agency theory are ultimately concerned with the efficient organization and distribution of information, and thus with information reporting and decision-making accountability. Agency theory holds that organizations can invest in information systems in order to enhance accountability and hence control agent opportunism. Information-processing theory maintains that organizations will be more effective when there is harmony between their information-processing requirements and their information-processing capacity (Tushman and Nadler, 1978). Information-processing capacity is critical to accountability, which requires the development of a system for gathering, interpreting, and synthesizing information in the context of organizational decision making. Deploying such a system globally may initially increase information-processing and agency costs, but improved accountability will ultimately help reduce these costs by converging principal and agent attitudes toward outcome uncertainty and risk.

3.2 Globalization Scale and Corporate Governance

Globalization scale is defined herein as the level or quantity of an MNC's active foreign direct investments (FDI) over which the parent firm maintains control. As globalization scale increases, information processing and agency demands increase as well. As a result, both parent-level corporate board size and the number of subsidiary boards are expected to increase. Research on firm governance generally concurs that board size is a direct function of the environment's complexity. Pfeffer and Salancik (1978) posit that increases in the number of dependencies between a firm and its external environment are likely to lead to increased organizational ties. Sanders and Carpenter (1998) argue that international firms often handle increased and more varied dependencies by adding board members who increase the overall information-processing capacity of the group either because they have valuable experience with the international constituencies or some particular expertise that applies.

As previously mentioned, a larger globalization scale may also increase the number of subsidiary boards. Subsidiaries with their own boards of directors are either independently listed and traded on foreign stock exchanges (in this case with local public shareholding), or not listed on exchanges but do meet either a host country's legal requirements or a parent firm's strategic considerations for establishing such boards. A subsidiary-level board of directors presumably governs the subsidiary as a legal entity, although there is considerable variation in local and legal requirements and how parent and subsidiary management choose to structure the roles, responsibility, and use of such boards. Subsidiary board members advise both subsidiary management and the parent board about local market conditions and regulatory changes, they network with local leaders and institutions, and they appraise and minimize political risks (Leksell and Lindgren, 1982). In light of increased globalization, I believe that having more subsidiary boards enables an MNC to quickly anticipate or respond to changes and opportunities in host countries. Put alternatively, as an MNC's globalization scale increases, the size of its corporate board and the number of its subsidiary boards will increase.

In addition, corporate boards frequently establish various specialized committees to fulfill certain specific duties such as auditing, selecting top management, monitoring conducts and ethics, and deciding executive compensation, among others. Often these committees consist of board members who are particularly knowledgeable in the committee's specific area of responsibility. In governance literature, larger boards are generally believed to have more skills and capabilities for solving large and complex tasks, and consequently greater information-processing capacity. Furthermore, the capacity of teams or committees to deal with complex agency situations is often regarded as superior to that of individual board members (Gugler, Mueller, and Yurtoglu, 2004). Committee expertise buffers principal–agent conflicts that arise from knowledge gaps between top management and board members; it reduces principal–agent information asymmetry that stems from having different information-processing abilities (Denis, Denis, and Sarin, 1997). With increased globalization, the amount and quality of information processing needed to accomplish increasingly specialized tasks are significantly higher. The surge of specialized committees under the board structure has become a solution to meet this challenge. Therefore, I suspect that as an MNC's globalization scale increases, the number of specialized committees within the corporate board will also increase.

Board composition (i.e., proportion of insider vs. outsider members) at both the corporate and subsidiary levels may also be affected by globalization. As an MNC globalizes, there is a stronger need for directorate networking and for board experts to cope with operational complexity (Mizruchi, 1997). As noted earlier, a board's ability to vigilantly monitor executives is a function of its access to information and its power to exert control. Outside directors with strong network backgrounds and with demanded expertise are often a cost-effective solution (Demsetz and Lehn, 1985; La Porta, Lopez-de-Silanes, and Shleifer, 1999). At the corporate level, outside directors can contribute to the MNC by networking with global suppliers, buyers, and distributors; at the subsidiary level, outside directors can network with local regulators, politicians, competitors, and other business community members. Kriger's study (1988) empirically supports this view that the proactive use of subsidiary-level outside directors enables a firm to cope with local legal and political pressures and increases its access to information regarding local economic developments. His study also shows that host country governments often come to perceive MNCs as less hostile when MNCs more extensively utilize outside local directors on subsidiary boards. Thus, a greater use of outside directors in foreign subsidiaries can increase local acceptance and mitigate the liability of foreignness. Therefore, it is as if when an MNC's globalization scale increases, the proportion of outside directors at its corporate board and subsidiary boards will also increase.

As globalization increases, MNCs face an increasing variance in accounting and reporting standards across the countries in which they invest and operate. Which accounting standard a geographically diversified MNC follows is central to corporate accountability because varying standards allow firms to manipulate financial statements like the balance sheet, income statement, and cash flow statement. Internally, the heterogeneity of applicable accounting, auditing, and tax rules may also hamper an MNC's ability to prepare the reliable and transparent financial information necessary for effective strategic analysis. To lighten cross-country differences in accounting standards, the International Accounting Standards Committee (the most dominant player in setting harmonized global accounting standards, founded in 1973) has developed an array of international accounting standards (IAS), which are now widely recognized and accepted in both developing and developed countries. Some MNCs even use IAS at the corporate level, and others may use it as a benchmark against which to compare their home country's accounting practices. MNCs that adopt more than one set of accounting standards (home country standards, host country standards, or IAS) must often issue a separate set of reports for each accounting standard; this often results in enormous reporting, documenting, and reconciliation costs as well as confusion to shareholders and other stakeholders, thus tempering transparency. Because of this, globalization often leads to pressure to use a consistent, harmonized, and globally accepted accounting and auditing system. Much of MNCs' sales, profits, assets, and investments come from overseas operations. It is therefore logical to expect that as globalization increases, MNCs are more likely to choose and follow IAS to strengthen accounting transparency, reliability, and consistency. Choosing IAS helps enhance information-reporting reliability and strategic decision transparency, which in turn reduces risk for investors. Moreover, using IAS also helps reduce the costs of preparing financial statements and facilitates the task of investment analysts, investors, and others in assessing a business. This saves on both the time and money currently spent consolidating divergent financial information. Therefore, it is possible that as an MNC's globalization scale increases, the probability of using IAS as its primary accounting, auditing, and reporting standard will also increase.

An MNC's accounting information system is another important part of accountability. As MNCs act more globally, their accounting and financial reporting systems become increasingly critical. These systems are essential in large part because global coordination has shifted away from rigid control mechanisms such as budget and bureaucratic control to information-based coordination, necessitating better and more transparent financial reporting. International accounting information systems (IAIS) involve accounting-related reporting systems, data management, and communication among various units of the same MNC. Financial controllers at MNC headquarters find themselves under increasing pressure to bring information to the market more quickly and more transparently, deliver more extensive information than previously required, and proactively manage business risk at the corporate level. Globalization also necessitates the implementation of computerized accounting information systems with overseas affiliates to furnish the accounting information needed to plan, evaluate, and coordinate business activities around the world. These systems also augment the consolidation process at the home office. Many MNCs such as Microsoft now use an intranet-based IAIS that links all financial units into a single, coherent system that provides managers and employees with real-time access to information and financial reports through the Internet. An effective IAIS provides an MNC with a competitive advantage arising from operating flexibility, transnational coordination, and strategic transparency in this increasingly competitive and complex global environment. In this way, IAIS becomes essential to achieving global business transparency. Therefore, it is likely that as an MNC's globalization scale increases, use of IAIS to improve corporate accountability and transparency will also increase.

3.3 Foreign Responsiveness and Corporate Governance

Given the increasing globalization of the competitive environment, balancing the dual imperatives of global coordination and foreign adaptation is more critical than ever for many MNCs. Due to varying objectives, capabilities, environments, and strategies, different MNCs face different requirements for local responsiveness or adaptation. Required adaptation or responsiveness to foreign markets' unique demands or market conditions influences corporate governance and accountability in several ways. First, increased local responsiveness requirements lead to higher information-processing costs. When required adaptation is higher, MNCs become more vulnerable to overseas market volatilities, which also leads to greater coordination and control costs. In this situation, an MNC must often decentralize power and disperse it among subsidiary executives, which, *ceteris paribus*, increases corporate governance costs. Second, subsidiary executives are essentially agents of the parent; this agency cost increases when required local responsiveness rises (Roth and O'Donnell, 1996). The corporate-level board may manage this agency problem by relying more on subsidiary boards to monitor subsidiary-level agent behavior. Thus, as the necessary local responsiveness increases, the second-tier board system may become more important and more powerful. Third, local responsiveness may increase the difficulty of maintaining accountability. Subsidiaries become more strategically and organizationally independent when they must be more responsive to host country environments. When subunits are independent, managerial behavior is likely to be less accountable with respect to corporate governance. Thus, globally integrated accountability becomes more difficult to achieve unless the parent firm uses viable measures to efficiently affect subunit executive incentives.

Required local responsiveness may influence corporate-level board size. Higher required responsiveness is often associated with such MNCs that are:

- pursuing market share and competitive power in host countries;
- establishing presence in different foreign markets and seeking transnational market power;
- diversifying operational and financial risk by investing in foreign countries;
- exploring production factor advantages in various host countries;
- seizing preemptive opportunities in emerging markets;
- enhancing learning in partnerships with indigenous firms;
- improving host country-specific experience; and
- gaining footholds by actively participating in local environments.

(See Bartlett and Ghoshal, 1989; Doz and Prahalad, 1981; Egelhoff, 1982; Gupta, 1987; Hedlund, 1986; Nohria and Ghoshal, 1994; Roth and O'Donnell, 1996.) Because these initiatives involve overseas activities, they all require greater monitoring of heightened international diversification and adaptation by the board (Judge and Zeithmal, 1992). The I–R framework (global integration vs. local responsiveness) holds that required local responsiveness will be effectively fulfilled if an MNC has:

1. superior abilities to reduce risk and manage uncertainties;
2. rich international experience;
3. competency in local operations and the organizational expertise needed for such operations; and
4. interpersonal and interorganizational networking abilities with local business communities.

(See Bartlett and Ghoshal, 1989; Roth and Morrison, 1991; Roth, Schweiger, and Morrison, 1991). Having a larger board, especially one with directors who have international experience in managing risk and uncertainty and who have international market knowledge can significantly help an MNC accommodate the above needs without losing corporate governance effectiveness. Therefore, as required local responsiveness increases, corporate-level board size is likely to increase.

An increased need for local responsiveness may escalate the activity and independence of an MNC's subsidiary boards for several reasons. First, one of a subsidiary board's most active roles is fostering local responsiveness. Kriger's survey (1988) identifies the following common activities in achieving this goal:

1. Guiding and encouraging management in dealing with local legal conditions.
2. Advising management on local country developments.
3. Appraising and reviewing local subsidiary operations.
4. Helping subsidiary management anticipate necessary strategic changes.

In these ways, subsidiary boards help align subsidiary operations with the parent's needs while conforming to local demands. Second, subsidiary boards need to be more independent and have more discretionary power in order to more effectively monitor subsidiary executives' implementation of local responsiveness strategies. A great deal of tacit knowledge is needed for subsidiary boards to play these sensing, decision-making, and advising roles (Leksell and Lindgren, 1982). Subsidiary board members need to have adequate discretionary power to develop such tacit knowledge and apply it to their own judgment. Lastly, we believe that subsidiary boards play a more active role in governing the subsidiary executive decision-making process when greater national adaptation is needed. For instance, subsidiary boards should be active in approving budgets and short-term strategies, monitoring operating performance, implementing corrective measures, participating in developing the subsidiary's strategic plan, and appraising and mitigating the political and economic risks inherent to local projects. Therefore, as required local responsiveness increases, subsidiary-level boards will become more active and more independent.

The number of outside directors at each subsidiary board is also expected to increase when there is a stronger demand for local responsiveness. Increasing the number of outside directors, especially those who add balanced expertise and bring in additional networking, is another important step in localization. Having outside directors who have network ties with strategically related firms can contribute to firm performance in an uncertain environment (Carpenter and Westphal, 2001). Bringing in more outside directors through interlocking directorates may also facilitate information acquisition, alliance formation, and resource procurement (Gulati and Westphal, 1999; Mizruchi, 1997), all essential to establishing better local responsiveness (Gupta, 1987). Once a subsidiary brings in outside directors, subsidiary executives representing the parent must share information and key decision making with outside directors, especially strategic and investment plans of the parent corporation and the ways in which the subsidiary fits into the MNC's total strategy. Therefore, as required local responsiveness increases, there will be a higher proportion of outside directors at subsidiary boards.

Internal auditing of both financial and managerial affairs performed by subsidiaries is an indispensable means to minimize the information-processing costs and agency costs that arise at the subsidiary management level. It is useful to have an internal auditing team at headquarters that is independent, powerful, and authoritative in auditing all overseas subunits using the MNC's unified financial and managerial standards. Timely, effective, and independent internal auditing conducted on both a periodic and non-periodic basis often identifies subsidiary misconduct. Such an auditing department should also be an important arm of the corporate board and should form a nexus for the work of the internal auditors. Internal auditing not only monitors each subsidiary's financial statement integrity and assesses its internal financial control systems, but it also identifies financial and managerial misconduct in areas such as cash flow management, asset management, business ethics compliance, bribery and corruption resistance, book-keeping accuracy and completeness, documentation of business activities not recorded in accounting books, and documentation of internal funds and capital flows between the subsidiary and the parent or other corporate members. When required local responsiveness rises, country managers will typically be vested with greater local authority to deal with host country-unique commercial practices, some of which may not be legally permissible at home (e.g., gift giving, facilitation fees, or internal funds for the CEO's discretionary use). Thus, an MNC's internal auditing function becomes even more critical to these subsidiaries facing greater adaptation requirements, despite the extra costs involved in such auditing (e.g., international travel, documentation, labor, consulting, etc.). A recent survey showed that the average cost of compliance with the Sarbanes–Oxley Act for large US MNCs was $4.6 million, which includes 35,000 hours of internal staff time, $1.3 million for consulting and software, and $1.5 million in new audit fees (Ulfelder, 2004). However, such an effort is critical to an MNC's comprehensive compliance architecture and enables both the parent and its subsidiaries to receive higher long-term economic and social payoffs (Bushman and Smith, 2003). Therefore, as required local responsiveness increases, there will be more frequent and more rigorous internal auditing conducted by the headquarters of the subsidiary's financial, managerial, and ethical affairs.

If an MNC owns a large number of geographically dispersed subsidiaries that are strategically designed to target host markets – that is, if an MNC has so many subsidiaries that it must be nationally adaptive or locally responsive – then headquarters must emphasize incentive-based discipline to ensure these subsidiaries' corporate accountability. Incentive-based discipline (IBD) exists when the parent firm employs financial and non-financial measures such as bonuses, share holding, name recognition, merit adjustment, rewards, promotions, and penalties for senior subsidiary managers to improve subsidiary transparency and accountability. The IBD system links these measures with:

1. quality of subsidiary reporting, including measurement principles, timeliness, and credibility of disclosure;
2. quality of information dissemination to headquarters and regional headquarters as well as corporate members located in other countries and regions; and
3. quality of information reporting concerning the off-the-balance sheet activities such as pooled investment schemes, insider trading activities, executives' internal accounts, reinvoicing of intra-corporate transactions, transfer pricing practices, entertainment expenses for government officials, and facilitation fees for new projects, among others.

IBD becomes particularly essential to this type of MNC (multidomestic in nature) for two reasons. First, process and bureaucratic controls, two commonly used control schemes, are often difficult for very global MNCs. Process control requires direct personal surveillance and high levels of management direction and intervention. Bureaucratic control consists of an explicit set of codified rules and regulations that delineate desired norms, standards, and behaviors. These two types of controls cannot be used as primary control methods for locally responsive subunits since they do not corroborate the need for specific adaptation. Second, using them is not realistic for financial, temporal, or labor cost reasons. This type of MNC cannot efficiently dispatch internal teams to each individual subsidiary abroad to conduct frequent, thorough, and rigorous auditing. Instead, a more viable and effective approach is to enact and enforce a globally unified comprehensive IBD system to be followed by all subsidiary executives and other senior subsidiary managers. Since the IBD captures both material rewards and serious penalties, it sends a clear message about the importance of subsidiary accountability to all country managers because their own livelihoods are directly and significantly tied to their performance in achieving strategic transparency and information accountability. Therefore, when the majority of an MNC's subsidiaries are locally responsive to their respective host markets, there will be a greater need for the MNC to employ a unified incentive-based discipline to strengthen accountability.

3.4 Global Competition and Corporate Governance

Rapid technological development, reduction of cross-border trade and non-trade barriers, shortened industry life cycle, and increasingly sophisticated global consumption have considerably increased global competition. Global competition also increases as global rivals' competitive goals increasingly converge or overlap. This occurs as: (i) rivals use the same competitive strategies or place emphasis on the same competitive advantage building blocks or (ii) product, business, and market portfolios become more similar as MNCs globally compete in similar business lines, product domains, and common markets. As the industry's life cycle moves into maturity, industry-level competition among participating players intensifies. At this stage, global players compete heavily in order to maximize cash inflows from respective market positions.

Global competition influences corporate governance and accountability in several ways. First, as global competition increases, corporate governance needs to foster a more stimulating environment that motivates senior executives to strive to excel at global competition. Such governance should not undermine executives' discretion in processing external information to move quickly ahead of rivals. Executive compensation should be more flexible and more rewarding if the MNC does well in global competition. Second, global competition increases the pressure to separate the CEO position from the board chairmanship. Increased global competition makes corporate transparency and accountability even more critical in the eye of shareholders, consumers, creditors, suppliers, and partners. This separation promotes transparency and accountability in both the board and executive rooms. Third, when global competition is fierce, the mechanisms for monitoring the agency's global organizing and decision making should be largely output-based, rather than behavior-based. This is because the agencies at both the corporate and subsidiary levels need to have the autonomy to formulate and implement desired strategies and processes. Such autonomy requires operational flexibility and is best achieved through the aforementioned output-based monitoring mechanisms. Finally, global competition provokes a greater need for the coordination of the MNC's two-tiered governance system. Parent-level boards depend more on subsidiary-level boards for advice, governance sharing, information reporting, and directorate expansion.

An MNC's executive pay schemes are an important part of corporate governance. I posit that these schemes are affected by global competition. Pay schemes orient executives toward different aspects of their organization and environment, influence risk preferences, and can act as agency control devices (Gomez-Mejia, 1992; Zajac and Westphal, 1994). In particular, the degree of global competition may influence the level of executive compensation and types of long-term incentive plans such as stock options and dividends. Literature on corporate governance generally concurs that CEO pay is determined by the environmental and/or operational complexity he or she manages (Henderson and Fredrickson, 1996; Sanders and Carpenter, 1998). Increased global competition inevitably amplifies the environmental and operational complexity a firm faces, and thus increases the CEO's information-processing burden. Thus, the CEO should be paid more than other executives who do not manage such complexity arising from global competition because the agent's ability is a scarce and valuable resource (Henderson and Fredrickson, 1996). Additionally, since increased global competition increases the cost and difficulty of monitoring CEO behavior (Aggarwal and Samwick, 1999), the corporate board may implement a "long-term pay" schedule for the CEO to shape his or her commitment and behavior. Long-term pay for the CEO often works because it ameliorates the board's burden of gathering information in the face of such geographic dispersion of sales, assets, capital, investments, and personnel. Long-term incentive plans encourage CEOs to monitor themselves, converge their interests with the principals' interests, and streamline the implementation of long-haul business strategies for more effective global competition. Therefore, as an MNC grows in a highly competitive global market, the parent-level CEO's total compensation as well as the percentage of this compensation in the long term are both likely to increase.

The above logic applies to subsidiary executives as well. MNCs are increasingly reliant on their subsidiary-level executives to help them excel at global competition in geographically diversified markets. As previously discussed, parent firms face more difficulty in monitoring overseas operations as foreign competition intensifies. In order to align subsidiary executives' interests and actions with the MNC's, headquarters needs to furnish bigger and better incentives. Higher pay and greater long-term incentives offered to subsidiary executives should make it less likely for such executives to take personal advantage of the information asymmetry resulting from diversified global competition. Roth and O'Donnell (1996) demonstrate that when country managers have considerable control over local operations in competitive markets, their pay includes significantly greater performance incentives. These incentives favorably impact subsidiary performance and expansion (Lambert, Larcker, and Weigelt, 1993). Research in global human resources suggests that compensation programs should be geared toward retaining and motivating country managers, creating consistency and equity in compensation, and maintaining global competitiveness (Biscoe, 1995). These programs should reduce expenses while enhancing commitment to the employer, job satisfaction, and willingness to relocate internationally (Tung, 1987). In light of the above, parent headquarters should use compensation as an incentive alignment device that ultimately enables country managers to monitor themselves. Therefore, as a subsidiary grows in a highly competitive foreign market, the subsidiary CEO's total compensation as well as the percentage of this compensation in long-term forms are both likely to increase.

Global competition may also reduce duality and inbreeding in the parent-level governance system. Duality is the situation in which the CEO is also the board chairperson. Inbreeding occurs when a retired CEO joins the board. Duality may impair the information-processing capacity of both the board and executives by restricting the number of key people involved in the strategic decision-making process (Sanders and Carpenter, 1998). Furthermore, global competition increases the duty burden for both the CEO and board chairperson positions. If these two positions are occupied by the same person, he or she is less likely to perform as well in either post. In contrast, without duality, the CEO is able to concentrate on designing and monitoring viable strategies for global competition while the chairperson concentrates on designing and monitoring corporate governance. Thus, increased global competition tends to split duality because as global competition increases, splitting the roles of the CEO and board chairperson disperses power and transmits more of it into the organization; it also potentially adds an additional information conduit back to senior executives and the board. Inbreeding, on the other hand, may hinder the appropriate governance needed for effective global competition because it hampers the board's ability to detect and correct governance problems such as fraud and illicit activities. Inbreeding also increases emotional dependence and attitudinal dependence of some board members on key executives. This will further impair each board member's independence and in turn the entire board's accountability. As global competition increases, such independence and accountability is even more important because fundamental board decisions, such as approving critical global resource deployments, deciding on enormous new investments in strategic regions, and reorganizing the global business structure, rely on each director's independent judgment and the entire board's overall accountability. Therefore, as global competition increases, duality and inbreeding are likely to diminish.

When increased competition reduces agency costs and creates more peer comparison opportunities, board members may be able to hold the executive and senior management teams more accountable by comparing their performance with that of major peer competitors and building incentive plans based on the outcome of the comparison. In more competitive industries, information about rival companies is more readily available, which enables MNCs to have more precise performance comparisons and benchmarks for internally assessing management behavior (Defond and Park, 1999). This comparison can help the corporate board to reduce the agency costs associated with monitoring CEO behavior. We anticipate that global competition will affect corporate accountability at both the parent and foreign subsidiary levels. Thus, the parent-level board monitors the behavior and performance of the MNC's senior executives as compared to other same-level global players in the same industry. In the second tier, the MNC's senior executives monitor the behavior and performance of subsidiary-level executives by comparing them with local players at the same level in the same industry (i.e., other foreign investors or indigenous firms in the same host country). In both cases, the principal compares the agent's performance with respect to profitability, liquidity, leverage, asset management, sales growth, and market share. The principal also evaluates the agent's comparability with respect to commitment, productivity, transparency, strategy, and integrity. If these performance and behavior areas are comparable and effective at both the parent and subsidiary levels, an MNC's overall accountability will be enhanced and the firm will be able to better balance accountability and growth in competitive international markets. Therefore, as global competition increases, peer (global rivals) performance comparisons will be more likely to be used to enhance accountability at both the parent and subsidiary levels.

Financial information transparency is a backbone of accountability for all firms. However, accountability involves more than mere corporate reporting; it also entails non-financial information disclosure, which broadly includes material information regarding issues that concern shareholders, employees, and stakeholders. More specifically, such issues may involve an MNC's risk as well as any social, ethical or environmental policies, standards or programs that all constituents must follow. Such issues typically include major share ownership, voting rights, human resource management, labor relations, environmental concerns, health policies, safety issues, anti-corruption measures, integrity programs, transparency standards, and the like. Increased global competition underscores the role of non-financial disclosure in promoting corporate accountability because of an increased demand for such information by global stakeholders including consumers, regulators, suppliers, creditors, partners, environmental groups, and labor unions. All things being equal, highly demanding stakeholders will place a higher value on MNCs that more seriously consider the labor, social, ethical, and environmental consequences of their activities. Stakeholders may switch the provision of business opportunities to other global players if an MNC is perceived as being unresponsive to such ramifications. Finally, non-financial disclosure should be made not only to outside stakeholders but also to corporate members within the firm; it should be circulated, exchanged, and shared among various subunits, especially foreign subsidiaries. Non-financial information sharing among corporate members can foster inter-unit exchanges of experiences, feedback, best practices, and programs in ensuring compliance with labor, social, ethical, and environmental policies, hence further bolstering overall accountability. Therefore, as global competition increases, non-financial information disclosure and sharing become more important in enhancing accountability and complementing financial information disclosure and sharing.

3.5 International Experience and Corporate Governance

Globalization is a challenge that calls for extensive organizational learning to overcome the liability of foreignness. Experience is a prime source of learning; it leads to country-specific and/or international knowledge that helps MNCs to reduce transaction costs that arise during global expansion. Two types of experience are especially important for globalization: general international operations experience and country-specific experience. An MNC's knowledge about a particular country increases as its commitment to operations and its sales in that country increase. This knowledge encourages the firm to engage in further investment there. In contrast, general international operations experience, which is composed of many country-specific experiences as well as the experience gained from managing the entire network of operations, tends to encourage more international operations in several countries. General international experience both enhances an MNC's ability to expand internationally and enables it to evaluate global market opportunities more objectively. In this section, we concentrate on how general international operations experience influences corporate governance and accountability.

International experience affects corporate governance and accountability in several ways. First, corporate governance structure is likely to be more "internationalized," i.e., characterized by more culturally diverse boards and stronger connections between the two tiers of corporate governance. Second, richer international experience will enable the MNC to benefit more from its global reputation and attract more global share-holders (both institutional and individual), thus reducing ownership concentration or at least increasing the proportion of foreign shareholders. Third, international experience bolsters corporate accountability in offshore investments and operations through enhanced familiarity with foreign country-specific commercial practices and business cultures and through greater knowledge in managing overseas subsidiaries. Finally, international experience helps the MNC to better handle increasingly demanding global shareholders and stakeholders who seek greater disclosure and more transparent explanations for major decisions. From an information-processing perspective, remember that organizations are more effective when information-processing requirements match information-processing capacities (Tushman and Nadler, 1978). Thus, despite globalization increasing information-processing requirements, international experience enhances information-processing capacity, thus allowing a firm to better cope with and grow in uncertain markets. All things being equal, this experience reduces governance and accountability costs over the course of globalization.

Cultural diversity, in both top management and corporate boards, is a direct result of international experience and may also reduce the information-processing costs of globalization because more culturally diversified top management teams and corporate boards have greater processing capacity and can attend to more environmental cues and foreign liability problems (Andersen, 1993; Henderson and Fredrickson, 1996; Sanders and Carpenter, 1998). On one hand, international experience itself is reflected in management localization and cultural diversity in senior management teams. Firm-level experience is accumulated as senior management's and board members' experience increases. Foreign natives have natural advantages in processing information pertaining to their home countries and in finding solutions that improve information processing. On the other hand, a causal link exists such that increased cultural diversity further facilitates the development and utilization of firm-level international experience. Transforming accumulated international experience into fruitful returns requires having experts who are well-versed in global market potentials and perils. Having high caliber, culturally diversified executives or directors who understand foreign market opportunities and challenges is effective in achieving these goals. Thus, as globalization progresses, an MNC's greater international experience may result in a higher percentage of senior executives and board members who are non-natives of the MNC's home country. This may further boost the deployment, exploitation, and upgrading of the MNC's international experience. These dual effects improve the top team and board's ability to process international business information, thus enhancing their capability to make accountable strategic decisions and monitor managerial behavior and performance. More substantive contributions from a culturally diverse board can also help the principal reduce governance costs in evaluating and monitoring top management performance while more substantive contributions from a culturally diverse top team may reduce costs of evaluating and monitoring subsidiary-level management performance. Therefore, as an MNC's international experience increases, the corporate board and top management team are likely to become more culturally diverse.

International experience is also likely to be negatively related to ownership concentration and positively related to foreign ownership. Ownership concentration refers to the number of large-block shareholders such as mutual funds, pension funds, and trust funds and their proportion of ownership. Foreign ownership is the proportion of foreign shareholders (institutional and individual) with respect to the entire shareholder body. Ownership concentration by a small number of large-block shareholders can improve governance effectiveness because it strengthens shareholders' power in dealing with management (Mizruchi, 1997). However, an overly concentrated ownership structure has its drawbacks; the power or voice of small individual shareholders is weaker when equity ownership is concentrated with a few large-block institutions. Moreover, conflicts of interest between shareholders and other stakeholders may intensify since managers may be more likely to maximize shareholder value at the expense of other stakeholders' value. As previously mentioned, as an MNC's international experience increases, it becomes more globally well known for its organizational reputation, brand image, geographical coverage, and competitive advantages. These image-based strategic assets attract more global shareholders, including foreign institutions (governments, security investors, mutual funds, pension funds, trust funds, etc.) and individuals. These shareholders may perceive an internationally experienced MNC's systematic risk as being relatively low because international experience reduces operational instability and performance volatility. Global players who understand global environments and strategies are generally able to make the firms not only more profitable but also more stable (Pauly and Reich, 1997). As stated by Ellstrand, Tihanyi, and Johnson (2002), an MNC's international experience lures global shareholders; this is a natural response to the increasing demand for lower international political risks. As global institutional and individual shareholders join the shareholder body, ownership concentration will be inversely affected. The dominant share positions of large-block shareholders will weaken, or become more difficult to maintain, when a larger number of global shareholders participate in daily stock trading that occurs in numerous international locations (Bebchuk and Roe, 1999). Advanced information technology has virtually removed access barriers to such exchanges, allowing global investors to gain critical information about distant companies and make trades with a simple click of a mouse. By the same logic, it is more difficult for any institution or individual to become a large-block shareholder with the growing number of globally dispersed shareholders participating in the firm's share exchange on a daily basis. Therefore, as an MNC's international experience increases, ownership concentration may decrease and foreign ownership may increase.

International experience is also likely to encourage the harmonization of accounting standards, disclosure requirements, and auditing standards. One of the main causes of poor accountability in MNCs is the use of varying standards in accounting, disclosure, and auditing for subsidiaries in different countries. This creates too much leeway for manipulating accounting numbers and financial ratios and may even provide loopholes for firms to conduct off-balance sheet arrangements (Vishwanath and Kaufmann, 1999). While it is true that national accounting standards vary, an MNC's internal accounting, disclosure, and auditing norms and requirements should be the same for all subsidiaries to ensure the firm's overall accountability. In fact, highly accountable

MNCs not only develop harmonized internal accounting and auditing standards but also use the IAS to avoid national accounting practice differences that hinder corporate accountability and transparency (Leuz and Verrecchia, 2000). Comparable and transparent financial information enhances the reliability of foreign financial statements prepared by subsidiaries. It also helps in making informed decisions which, in turn, reduce risk for investors. In addition, employing harmonized internal standards reduces the cost of preparing financial statements and facilitates investment and risk analysis, thereby reducing the cost of maintaining accountability. With richer international experience, an MNC better comprehends the importance of intra-corporate harmonization of accounting and auditing standards and is also more likely to have policies in place that ensure compliance with such harmonization. Moreover, internationally experienced MNCs are more likely to adopt IAS because of their more widespread geographical expansion, longer history in competing in global markets, higher familiarity with and confidence in IAS or greater need for intra-organizational reconciliation of information recording, dissemination, and sharing. Therefore, as an MNC's international experience increases, its internal standards for accounting and auditing will be more globally harmonized, and, moreover, it will be more likely to report its financial statements using IAS.

Corporate accountability is not just concerned with the accuracy and reliability of financial information, it also involves its disclosure and timeliness. The disclosure of non-financial but material matters of the corporation is essential to global investors, shareholders, and stakeholders (Bushman and Smith, 2003). For instance, the Sarbanes–Oxley Act requires that US companies clearly disclose major share ownership and voting rights, material foreseeable risk factors, material issues regarding employees and other stakeholders, governance structures and policies, environmental policies, corruption resisting programs and corporate ethics and codes. Such information should be prepared, audited, and disclosed in accordance with high-quality standards of accounting, financial and non-financial disclosure, and audit. More importantly, an essential component of disclosure is timeliness. For instance, in many countries continuous and timely disclosure is mandated to ensure that security prices reflect as closely as possible their underlying value and that investors have equal access to information that materially impacts the prices of traded securities. With increased international experience, an MNC is in a better position to understand international standards concerning what a corporate accounting system should cover and when and how frequently financial and non-financial disclosures should be released. More experienced MNCs may also be aware of the importance and effect of timely disclosure on their global reputation and about how to transform this reputation into a competitive advantage. A recent survey by the OECD in 2004 finds that more internationally experienced MNCs have better disclosure on off-balance sheet arrangements and non-financial policies. We posit that international experience can lead to better coverage and timeliness in disclosing financial and non-financial information. Therefore, as an MNC's international experience increases, its financial and non-financial disclosures are likely to be more timely and more thorough. Figure 3.1 summarizes how an MNC's global activities and operations may influence the design and mechanisms of corporate governance and accountability.

1. As an MNC's globalization scale increases, the size of its corporate board and the number of its subsidiary boards may need to increase.
2. As an MNC's globalization scale increases, the number of specialized committees at its corporate board may need to increase.
3. As an MNC's globalization scale increases, the proportion of outside directors at its corporate board and subsidiary boards may need to increase.
4. As an MNC's globalization scale increases, the probability of using international accounting standards (IAS) as its primary accounting, auditing, and reporting standards may increase.
5. As an MNC's globalization scale increases, there will be a greater use of international accounting information systems (IAIS) to improve corporate accountability and transparency.
6. As required local responsiveness increases, corporate-level board size may need to increase.
7. As required local responsiveness increases, subsidiary-level boards will become more active and more independent.
8. As required local responsiveness increases, there is a greater need for a higher proportion of outside directors on subsidiary boards.
9. As required local responsiveness increases, there is a greater need for more frequent and more rigorous internal auditing conducted by headquarters over the subsidiary's financial, managerial, and ethical affairs.
10. When the majority of subsidiaries are locally responsive to their respective host markets, there will be a greater need for the MNC to employ a unified incentive-based discipline (IBD) to strengthen accountability.
11. As an MNC grows in a highly competitive global market, parent-level CEO's total compensation as well as the percentage of this compensation in long-term forms may both increase.
12. As a subsidiary grows in a highly competitive foreign market, subsidiary-level CEO's total compensation as well as the percentage of this compensation in long-term forms may both need to increase.
13. As global competition increases, duality and inbreeding become less likely.
14. As global competition increases, peer (global rivals) performance comparison will be more likely to be used to enhance accountability at both the parent and subsidiary levels.
15. As global competition increases, non-financial information disclosure and sharing become more important in enhancing accountability and complementing financial information disclosure and sharing.
16. As an MNC's international experience increases, the membership of corporate board and top management team may need to become more culturally diverse.
17. As an MNC's international experience increases, ownership concentration may need to decrease and foreign ownership may need to increase.
18. As an MNC's international experience increases: (a) its internal standards for accounting and auditing will be more globally harmonized and (b) it will be more likely to report its financial statements by reference to IAS.
19. As an MNC's international experience increases, its financial and non-financial disclosures are likely to be more timely and more richly covered.

Figure 3.1 Global operations and corporate governance

3.6 Evidence on the Effects of Global Operations on Corporate Governance

One of the major studies that empirically verifies how an MNC's corporate governance is impacted by its global operations is Sanders and Carpenter (1998), and overall, their findings corroborate well with some of the above discussions and propositions I have made. This study found that multinational corporations respond to the complex global operations through their choice of governance structure. Using data from 258 MNCs drawn from the 1992 Standard & Poor's 500, Sanders and Carpenter demonstrate that MNCs cope with the challenges of internationalization by increasing the complexity of their boards of directors and top management teams. For instance, the data from this research link a corporation's degree of internationalization to high levels of CEO pay, with a large portion of that pay coming from such long-term compensation as stock options. According to Sanders and Carpenter, higher pay is a recognition that the CEO's job is more formidable than it would be in a company without international activities. In addition, since the board of directors has greater difficulty overseeing the CEO of a company with international operations, the use of stock options in a compensation package encourages the CEO to be self-supervising. Long-term forms of pay effectively align the corporation's performance with the CEO's self-interest.

Sanders and Carpenter also found that as firms become more internationalized, they develop governance structures that maximize their ability to gather and process information. Firms are likely to increase the size of their top management teams as they become more internationalized. Although a small, lean executive suite is typically desirable, a company with extensive international activities may require a larger top management team to keep tabs on activities overseas. Large top management teams are also likely to make better decisions than smaller teams, since the combined abilities and talents of many individuals should lead to well-informed decision making.

The key findings from Sanders and Carpenter (1998) also suggest that MNCs are more likely to separate the positions of chairman of the board and CEO, rather than combine them into one position, as is common in many corporations. Separating the two positions in multinational corporations allows for greater breadth of expertise and information than would be possible if one person held both positions. In addition, there is a significant connection between a firm's level of internationalization and the composition of its board of directors. As MNCs expand their international operations, they are likely to have larger boards. A large board, like a large top management team, allows the board to take advantage of a greater number of individuals with expertise across many functional or geographic areas.

One of the most intriguing findings of this study concerned the proportion of insiders, rather than outsiders, that make up an MNC's board of directors. Generally, as internationalization increased, so did the proportion of outsiders on the boards. The researchers suggest that outsiders facilitate a board's ability to monitor the corporation's international activities. The diverse expertise of outside board members may also help them to better control the top management team. Furthermore, when boards become especially large, the proportion of insiders is likely to increase. They note that multinationals may need to balance large boards with insiders in order to maintain control and minimize the confusion that otherwise occurs in large groups. In essence, the inside directors serve as multiple liaisons between the board and the rest of the company. However, because an inside director is a board member who is simultaneously an executive, usually a vice president, of that same corporation, the heavy use of inside directors is generally frowned upon. Critics argue that it may lead to a conflict of interest when vice presidents, sitting as directors, are required to oversee the CEO, who is their boss on a day-to-day basis. Interestingly, the researchers found that multinational firms may balance a high proportion of inside directors with a CEO pay package that is heavily tilted toward long-term compensation. Therefore, while boards dominated by insiders may not be perfectly responsive to stockholders because they are composed of executives sitting in judgment of the CEO, the use of stock options to align the CEO's pay to the stock price should effectively focus the CEO's attention on firm performance.

In conclusion, large corporate failures have often stimulated debate about corporate governance and accountability, leading to regulatory action and other reforms. However, corporate governance and accountability is largely a corporate affair in the first place, and its improvement requires that MNCs themselves seek internal solutions and organizational remedies. In thinking about incidents of corporate failure, one clearly finds that bad business plans (even though *ex ante* they might have appeared visionary) and poor managerial decisions contribute to corporate failure. Moreover, weak boards and poor independent judgment have also led to various problems in corporate governance and accountability. In addition, some collapses have involved fraud, cover-ups, or management deceit, or all three. In sum, although financial and non-financial corporate failures are not all attributable to corporate governance and accountability deficiencies, they have certainly played a major role and contributed to the scale of the distress.

This chapter deals with how an MNC's corporate governance and accountability design at both parent and subsidiary levels hinges on international expansion features such as globalization scale, required foreign adaptation, global competition, and international experience. I reason that an MNC's corporate governance and accountability should be properly aligned with the above-mentioned features for information-processing and agency cost reasons. Increased globalization, adaptation requirements, and global competition all increase an MNC's environmental and operational complexity. Heightened complexity increases information-processing and agency demands, and MNCs manage such demands by instituting more efficient governance arrangements. Meanwhile, information-processing and agency demands are partly determined by an MNC's international experience; such demands may become even stronger if the firm has little global experience. Globalization scale, adaptation requirements, foreign competition, and international experience are hence proposed to affect information-processing and agency requirements, and in turn, governance and accountability.

International expansion creates a dependence on foreign markets for customers and factors of production; as such, it increases the ambiguity of executive actions and strengthens their specialized international market knowledge. This presents a classic agency situation in which the board's role of directly monitoring executive performance becomes more difficult. As globalization scale, required adaptation, or international competition increases, both agency costs and information asymmetry between the principal and agency also increase. As a corporate response, the MNC either increases corporate and/or subsidiary boards, creates more specialized committees within these boards, invites more outside directors to join corporate or subsidiary boards, promotes greater directorate interlocking at corporate or subsidiary levels, adjusts incentives of parent and subsidiary executives, or tightens its policies on duality and inbreeding. These efforts improve corporate and subsidiary board ability to process environmental and operational information, thus reducing information asymmetry vis-à-vis the agencies or enhancing the board's power to vigilantly monitor and control the behavior and performance of parent- or subsidiary-level agencies. Firms with richer international experience leverage this expertise by embracing a more culturally diverse board structure to support their information-processing ability or reduce the disadvantage of being "foreign" in governing offshore operations and investments.

With respect to accountability, MNCs respond to increased international expansion, global competition, and adaptation requirements by referencing IAS for accounting, auditing, and reporting. Global MNCs also adopt effective IAIS to build information templates for corporate transparency, performing more frequent and rigorous internal auditing over various units' financial, managerial, and ethical affairs, and appropriately rewarding those units and executives dedicated to improving accountability. As international expansion grows, it becomes more important to disclose non-financial information to shareholders and other related stakeholders, especially concerning share ownership, voting rights, labor relations, environment protection, employee safety, business ethics, organizational integrity, and corporate transparency.

Globalization can also provide MNCs with additional devices by which to improve both accountability and governance. For instance, as global competition intensifies, comparing executive performance with that of executives at competitor firms will attenuate agency problems and enhance accountability at both the corporate and subsidiary levels. International experience generated from globalization also enables MNCs to globally harmonize the internal accounting and auditing standards to be followed by all subsidiaries, thus reducing reconciliation costs and improving timely and accurate disclosure.

In summary, globalization provides MNCs with additional challenges and opportunities in the realm of corporate governance and accountability. The centerpiece in the design of corporate governance is to improve the ability of the board to monitor top management, which is then a function of its access to information and its power to exert control. The centerpiece in the design of corporate accountability is to improve the firm's financial and non-financial transparency, which is then a function of financial accounting disclosures, governance disclosures, timeliness of disclosures, accounting and auditing policies, credibility of disclosures, and information dissemination. As international expansion, foreign adaptation, global competition, and international experience all increase, a situation that typifies heightened globalization, MNCs must institute more efficient governance mechanisms to satisfy the increasing demand for solving information-processing and agency problems and employ more effective accountability measures to fulfill the increasing need for nourishing governance and transparency. This chapter is a rudimentary effort that explains the effect of globalization on governance and accountability, with only a conceptual piece that discusses the design of corporate governance and accountability systems in response to globalization.

CASE EXAMPLE 3.1: GLOBALIZATION AND GOVERNANCE AT SIEMENS

Background

Siemens is Germany's biggest electrical company and Europe's largest private employer. It exemplifies several features of the German model of corporate governance, such as long-term strategies, peaceful labor relations, diversified quality production, comparatively low profits, and a sales growth orientation. Unusually for a German firm, its shares are widely dispersed, the biggest shareholder being the Siemen family with 5.3 percent of the equity share. Siemens' relationship with the banks was never as close as one would expect from well-known accounts of the bank–firm relationship in Germany. The *Hausbank* relationship has two components: long-term credits and supervisory board representation. In terms of financing, Siemens has not been dependent on external finance. It has accumulated enormous reserves that help to keep its independence from credit as well as from the capital markets. Banks have seats on the supervisory board, but very limited influence due to the lack of need to obtain credits. Moreover, Siemens has handled most of its financial transactions itself. Traditionally, Siemens' business strategy was technology-centered and focused on high-quality products. Its broad product portfolio stems from the strategic goal, going back to its funding days, of covering as many areas of electronics as possible.

Internationalization

Siemens concentrated on the German market until the mid-1980s, although it was already then a highly internationalized firm. In 1985 it made 53 percent of its sales in Germany, 21 percent in the rest of Europe, and 10 percent in North America. Since then, Siemens has been pursuing a much more aggressive internationalization strategy with a focus on the US, which constitutes a third of the world electronics market, and to a lesser degree on western Europe, especially the UK. The motivation was the assumption that Siemens could only stay competitive if it was present in at least two of the three triad regions. Sales in the US doubled in the 1990s to 22 percent of total sales, with the number of employees increasing from 15,100 in 1985 to 76,000 in 2001. Nevertheless, Siemens' presence in the US has been associated with high losses and the US business was still unprofitable in 2000.

The strategic decision to grow internationally by acquisitions made Siemens the biggest German investor abroad. Expansion could only take place abroad as the German market was saturated. Moreover, the growing importance of electronics resulted in an explosion in R&D, while at the time product life cycles and innovation cycles shortened dramatically. Consequently, in terms of sales,

Siemens' home market has become relatively less important. Over the course of the 1990s, Germany's share of total sales decreased from roughly 50 percent to 22 percent in 2001.

Overall, Siemens internationalized much more vigorously over the 1990s. However, its style and strategies of internationalization followed its traditional trajectory. The strategic functions remain in Germany, the distribution of assets has a bias toward the home base, top management is not at all internationalized, and R&D as well as value-added activities are heavily concentrated in Germany. This path generally does not threaten domestic corporate governance arrangements. There are also no signs that Siemens is transforming itself into a network corporation without a clear center, with strong influence by subsidiaries, and with no discernible nationality. Thus Siemens' aggressive internationalization has not resulted in a loosening of ties to the home base, and Siemens is still embedded in the German system of corporate governance. However, it would be misleading to characterize Siemens as a slow globalizer, as German firms have sometimes been perceived to be in comparative perspective. It showed a high degree of active globalization during the 1990s, but this catching-up process has not been hindered by the institutions of corporate governance.

Corporate restructuring

Continuous restructuring efforts were the other main feature of Siemens' business policy in the course of the 1990s. The recession in the early part of the decade and the changing economic environment made restructuring efforts at Siemens unavoidable. At the end of 1998, Siemens came under severe pressure. Share price and profits were falling sharply. In response, the CEO presented a 10-point program that was intended to put the company back on track. Some of the 10 points were meant to amend the capital structure in order to reach the desired financial figures; others were cost-cutting or motivational measures. The main points included a focus on increasing the share price and setting clear goals for management, as well as the option of floating divisions and the decision to list on the New York Stock Exchange.

Financial restructuring

The most significant change took place in investor relations. In the 1990s, Siemens disclosed much more information to the capital markets than it had done previously, and it abolished several traditions that might have deterred investors, such as multiple voting rights of family shares. Other capital market-related moves were the conversion of the DM50 shares into DM5 shares, which made them more appealing to investors, and the move to named shares in 1999 in order to communicate more directly with shareholders. These moves aimed at minimizing transaction costs in acquiring Siemens shares and adjusting to the standards of the international capital markets.

New standards have also been introduced for transparency. The most decisive move was that Siemens published divisional results, which has given analysts a better understanding of Siemens' individual divisions, but has made cross-subsidization between divisions much more difficult, thereby putting more pressure on poorly performing businesses. The head of Siemens' investor relations department explained the shift this way:

> The financial landscape has internationalized through the globalization of financial markets; by this increase in transparency and the intensification of equity research, big companies have to adjust to a continuous dialogue with shareholders and financial analysts. . . . we have to formulate value-creating strategies and communicate these to the financial markets. If this doesn't work, even big companies are in danger of falling behind in the global competition for equity and external capital . . . investors have a natural interest in being informed exhaustively . . . and we have an interest that our strategies are understood and valued by investors.

Siemens also decided to get listed on the New York Stock Exchange, which was seen as the jewel in the crown of the 10-point program and a symbol for its more investor-friendly approach. This is a step with far-reaching consequences for corporate governance because by doing so foreign firms become subject to US legal standards and encounter pressure to adopt American business practices. Several steps were necessary in order to get a listing, the most important being the introduction of accounting according to US GAAP. In terms of transparency, Siemens had introduced most of the transparency requirements before the listing and independently from it.

Apart from being a symbolic step in the framework of the 10-point program, two factors influenced the listing. The US had become Siemens' most important single market after Germany and Siemens had become the biggest foreign employer in the US. Nevertheless, the company was not very well known in the US. Thus, the listing aimed to increase its name recognition, especially at a time when Siemens was eager to enter the US mobile phone market. In this sense the step followed the logic of the listing in London in the early 1990s, when a significantly increased sales volume led to a listing in that country in order to support its expansion strategy. Furthermore, Siemens could only introduce stock option schemes for its US employees if it was listed on the US stock exchange.

The second reason for seeking a US listing had to do with the growing importance of stocks as an acquisition currency. Most mergers and acquisitions in the late 1990s had been financed by share swaps. Stock has become an increasingly important acquisition currency in company takeovers and mergers. No capital was raised by the listing; the shares were made tradable by American Depository Rights. Therefore, it is unlikely that US shareholders will get a greater influence;

their ownership base has remained constant. In 2001, US and Canadian investors held 8 percent of Siemens' shares, whereas German investors held 52 percent, continental European investors 29 percent, and UK investors 10 percent.

Organizational restructuring

In order to meet the financial goals a new management set, a controlling instrument – the economic value-added (EVA) concept – was introduced in 1998. EVA measures the success of each business group and of the whole company by incorporating the cost of internal and external capital. In this perspective businesses are only profitable if they earn at least their cost of capital. The expectations of the financial markets are thus incorporated into corporate decision making because the costs of capital can be equalized with the profit requirements of all investors, shareholders, and creditors. The EVA emerges when more than the costs of capital are earned, which is then benchmarked against competitors.

EVA is the most far-reaching and systematic attempt to achieve the longstanding goal of a return on equity of 15 percent. However, the most important feature of the concept is how it is used. The logic of EVA decrees that business groups that underperform their capital costs should be fixed, closed, or sold, in very much the same way that General Electric handles its business. However, Siemens seems to be unwilling to follow the concept in this crucial regard, which would mean determined and fast disinvestments. When EVA was introduced, over half of the business groups earned less than their capital costs. In 2001 the biggest loss-makers were Information and Communications, and Automotive, but their profit goals have been postponed and the CEO has declared that no division as a whole will be sold, only minor parts at most. Siemens sees its broad portfolio as an asset; it makes it less vulnerable against downswings in certain markets because the "cash cows" and the loss-makers change and so the single divisions support each other over time. The prime example is medical equipment which had been run at a loss for a long time, but achieved a turnaround in the 1990s; it is now one of the most successful divisions. The "fix-it" option enjoys primacy; despite EVA, Siemens is committed to its divisions and markets.

Furthermore, much depends on the definition of capital costs. On the whole, Siemens is operating with a figure of 9 percent, but the definition differs for each business group. This is significantly lower than the figure that Siemens' competitors with a similar system try to achieve. For Ericsson, the figure is 16 percent, for General Electric 13 percent, Philips 12 percent and GEC 10 percent. Hence, Siemens has adjusted the concept to its own needs and its own environment, which ultimately means a soft version of the original concept. The works councils welcomed the introduction of EVA on the grounds that it provides higher transparency about goals and did not set uniform profit goals for the company as a whole; the latter had always been resisted by the works councils, but differentiated between the divisions.

In addition to EVA, a share option scheme has been introduced. The design of stock options is of crucial importance for a corporate governance system because stock options can alter the managers' incentives and are the prime vehicle for a capital market orientation. Stock options are seen as the most important explanatory factor for the transformation of the US corporate governance system from a managerial to a capital market-oriented system. Siemens' incentive scheme was introduced in 1999 and affected 500 top managers; later it was extended to 1500 managers. The stock option plan is part of a broader incentive scheme. For the 200 top managers, 40 percent of income is fixed, and the rest is variable; for the next tier of 300 managers, the ratio is 60:40. Thirty percent of the variable part is an annual bonus and is based on yearly results, and the remaining 70 percent is a long-term bonus and is based on three-year results, using EVA and accounting figures as a baseline. The long-term bonus has the aim of preventing short-term incentives. The stock options themselves are only a supplement to these incentives. In a best case scenario, they can add up to 25 percent of the annual income of top management. The whole incentive scheme shows a deliberate long-term orientation. The yearly bonus is not fully paid; two-thirds of it is retained and paid only when the three-year goals are reached.

Compared to US standards the program does not provide high-powered incentives to tie strategic decisions to share price. Between 1980 and 1994, equity-based compensation in the US increased from less than 20 percent of total CEO compensation to almost 50 percent. It is obvious that Siemens' stock option plan is quite different. As indicated, the incentive scheme stresses long-term performance, and in 1999 the market value of granted stock options for the management board was only 10 percent of total salary. Thus, the design of the stock option program can also be said to have been adjusted to Siemens' environment and provides comparatively low incentives to embrace the promotion of the share price as the main goal for management.

Portfolio restructuring

The most spectacular strategic decision of the 10-point program was to spin off the semiconductor division. Until then, only marginal businesses had been sold, but listing semiconductors meant giving up 60,000 jobs and DM17 billion in sales. Siemens had invested huge sums in semiconductors from the early 1980s onwards; they were seen as a technology that was crucial for all areas of Siemens' businesses and the company appeared willing to bear huge losses in this field. The division's previous net losses, despite large sales, were the main reason for this spin-off decision.

Faced with the acute crisis in the semiconductor industry, Siemens was no longer willing to bear the cycles in this business and to finance the enormous capital requirement of the division. This capital would have been used at the expense of the other businesses. Because of the extraordinarily capital intensive nature of the business, semiconductors had absorbed the lion's share of Siemens' investment resources, thereby jeopardizing the growth of other business groups. Furthermore, semiconductors should be able to engage in cooperation with other firms, which was seen to be easier for an independent company. The division was renamed Infineon Technologies and in 1999 listed on the New York and Frankfurt stock exchanges. Siemens gave Infineon a generous capital start-up and appointed the chairmen of the management and supervisory boards, both members of the Siemens management board.

However, the spin-off did not represent the whole story. At the IPO, only 29 percent of Infineon was floated, although Siemens wanted to float a more significant share soon afterwards. However, if Siemens had a share of less than 50 percent, it would lose important patent rights. Thus, it seems unlikely that Siemens was actively pushing to get rid of its stake. It recently decreased its stake to 51 percent; however, this stake was not floated, but instead transferred to Siemens' pension trust, leaving Siemens in control. Retaining a stake of more than 25 percent, Siemens would be able to control Infineon. The works councils supported the spin-off. Crucial for the decision was the agreement of the divisional works councils whose main concern was Infineon's better prospects as an independent firm. Furthermore, Infineon adopted the employment conditions of Siemens wholesale, joined the employers' association, and made sure that dismissals would be avoided. Although the spin-off marks a break in Siemens' traditions, it was nevertheless done in a very traditional way; jobs were not affected, the decision was taken in agreement with the works councils, and Siemens is still in control of a majority stake.

From a shareholder-value perspective, this was not a far-reaching move. The core of the shareholder value approach is that firms should concentrate on one or only a few businesses with the highest profitability and growth perspectives. Conglomerates are punished by the conglomerate discount, which results from lower transparency. Siemens, with a portfolio that covers many more areas of electronics than all of its competitors, is therefore under pressure. Criticism by financial analysts thus centered on its missing core competencies and the breadth of its businesses. The suggestion has been to split and divest Siemens completely in order to unlock shareholder value; as a minimum it is said that it should concentrate on one or two core businesses, the then fashionable telecommunications business among them, and continue restructuring. The *Financial Times* suggested dividing it into a high-tech side composed of telecommunications, semiconductors, computers, and medical equipment; and a low-tech side with power plants, rail systems, capital goods, and lighting. J.P. Morgan urged Siemens to concentrate on a few core businesses and to get rid of all underperforming business groups.

However, Siemens has remained firmly committed to its business groups. Even those that incurred heavy losses for a long time were kept, and an attempt was made to repair them. Moreover, there are no signs that Siemens intends to further restructure its portfolio on a large scale. After Infineon, there have been no other IPOs of divisions nor have significant parts of Siemens been sold. Siemens' broad portfolio is still seen by the management as one of the firm's key assets, enabling the company to weather economic crises and achieve long-term economic success for the benefit of customers, shareholders, and employees. Diversification means risk reduction for Siemens because it makes it more independent from the business cycles in different industries and helps to contribute to stability. Thus it is unlikely that Siemens' structure and portfolio will change significantly in the foreseeable future.

Restructuring outcomes

The restructuring measures managed to increase profits and share price significantly. In 1999 profits were €1.8 billion. In 2000 Siemens announced that profits had increased to €3.4 billion, with all business segments in the black, while EVA was positive to the tune of DM859 million. After the announcement of the 10-point program, Siemens' share price started to outperform the DAX-Index and has continued to do so quite significantly. Siemens' market capitalization increased, supported by the high-tech bubble on the stock markets, from €28 billion to €85 billion between 1998 and 2000. However, it is still a long way behind its main competitor, General Electric, which has had a five to six times higher market capitalization. Nonetheless, the restructuring program, with its target of boosting profits and share price accomplished its main goals.

The distribution of Siemens' all-time-high profits shows its continuing stakeholder orientation. The company significantly increased dividends, but also let the employees participate in the success of Germany's largest and most generous employee-share program to date. The idea was to give an equivalent of the dividends to the employees in order to satisfy Siemens' two most important groups of stakeholders. Siemens offered shares to its employees at a discount of 50 percent. This scheme involved a cost of €600 million for Siemens. Comparing these payments with General Electric's shareholder orientation, the differences become obvious. Between 1994 and 1998, General Electric increased dividend payments by 84 percent and spent US$14.6 billion on share buy-backs, which together meant an outflow of 74.4 percent of cash from operations.

The program also led to an increase in employees' shareholdings of 1.2 percent. Before this point, the employees were estimated to hold somewhere between 9 and 17 percent of Siemens' equity. Thus, the employees are the most important group of shareholders, which increases their bargaining position. In this regard, the plan also helps Siemens bolster its defenses against potential take-over attempts. However, it also shows that Siemens is not only focused on its shareholders, but that it is still investing in consensus with its employees.

Generally, restructuring did not negatively affect the cooperative and consensus-oriented character of industrial relations at Siemens. Indeed, the full support of the works councils enabled the restructuring, which was carried out without major resistance and strikes. In exchange for their cooperation, employees were compensated by the avoidance of operational dismissals and a share in the financial success of the restructuring. The works councils were also successful in preventing uniform profit goals for the company as a whole, which would not differentiate between the divisions. They generally welcomed the higher transparency of the company because it increased their access to information. Above all, the works councils have been included in the decision making from the beginning beyond the legal requirements, and a consensus was sought. Siemens has an extensive system of committees at which management and workers' representatives regularly meet and reconcile their positions to new developments, and where the works councils are informed about new management initiatives. Besides these committees, informal and socialized relationships between key players help to prevent serious conflicts.

(Source: Excerpted from Borsch, A. (2004). Globalization, shareholder value, and restructuring: The transformation of Siemens. *New Political Economy*, **9**(3): 365–87.)

REFERENCES AND FURTHER READING

Aggarwal, R. and Samwick, A. (1999). Executive compensation, strategic competition, and relative performance evaluation: Theory and evidence. *Journal of Finance*, **54**: 1999–2043.

Andersen, O. (1993). On the internationalization process of firms: A critical analysis. *Journal of International Business Studies*, **24**: 209–31.

Bartlett, C.A. and Ghoshal, S. (1989). *Managing Across Borders*. Boston, MA: Harvard Business School Press.

Bebchuk, L.A. and Roe, M.J. (1999). A theory of path dependence in corporate governance and ownership. *Stanford Law Review*, **52**: 127–44.

Biscoe, D.R. (1995). *International Human Resource Management*. Englewood Cliffs, NJ: Prentice-Hall.

Bushman, R. and Smith, A. (2001). Financial accounting information and corporate governance. *Journal of Accounting and Economics*, **32**: 237–333.

Bushman, R.M. and Smith, A.J. (2003). Transparency, financial accounting information, and corporate governance. *Economic Policy Review – Federal Reserve Bank of New York*, **9**(1): 65–87.

Carpenter, M. and Westphal, J. (2001). The strategic context of external network ties: Examining the impact of board appointments on board involvement in strategic decision making. *Academy of Management Journal*, **44**: 639–60.

Defond, M. and Park, C. (1999). The effect of competition on CEO turnover. *Journal of Accounting and Economics*, **27**: 35–56.

Demsetz, H. and Lehn, K. (1985). The structure of corporate ownership: Causes and consequences. *Journal of Political Economy*, **93**: 1155–77.

Denis, D.J., Denis, D.K., and Sarin, A. (1997). Agency problems, equity ownership, and corporate diversification. *Journal of Finance*, **52**: 135–60.

Denis, D.K. and McConnell, J.J. (2003). International corporate governance. *Journal of Financial and Quantitative Analysis*, **38**: 1–36.

Doz, Y.L. and Prahalad, C.K. (1981). Headquarters influence and strategic control in MNCs. *Sloan Management Review*, Fall: 15–29.

Egelhoff, W.G. (1982). Strategy and structure in MNCs: An information processing approach. *Administrative Science Quarterly*, **27**: 435–58.

Eisenhardt, K.M. (1989). Agency theory: An assessment and review. *Academy of Management Review*, **14**: 57–74.

Ellstrand, A.E., Tihanyi, L., and Johnson, J.L. (2002). Board structure and international political risk. *Academy of Management Journal*, **45**: 769–77.

Fama, E. (1980). Agency problems and the theory of the firm. *Journal of Political Economy*, **88**: 288–307.

Fama, E. and Jensen, M. (1983). Separation of ownership and control. *Journal of Law and Economics*, **26**: 301–25.

Gomez-Mejia, L. (1992). Structure and process of diversification, compensation strategy, and firm performance. *Strategic Management Journal*, **13**: 381–97.

Gugler, K., Mueller, D.C., and Yurtoglu, B.B. (2004). Corporate governance and globalization. *Oxford Review of Economic Policy*, **20**(1): 129–56.

Gulati, R. and Westphal, J. (1999). Cooperative or controlling? The effects of CEO–board relations and the content of interlocks on the formation of joint ventures. *Administrative Science Quarterly*, **44**: 473–506.

Gupta, A.K. (1987). SBU strategies, corporate–SBU relations and SBU effectiveness in strategy implementation. *Academy of Management Journal*, **30**(3): 477–500.

Hedlund, G. (1986). The modern MNC – A heterarchy. *Human Resource Management*, **25**: 9–35.

Henderson, A. and Fredrickson, J. (1996). Information processing demands as a determinant of CEO compensation. *Academy of Management Journal*, **39**: 575–606.

Jensen, M.C. and Meckling, W.H. (1976). Theory of the firm: Managerial behavior, agency costs and ownership structure. *Journal of Financial Economics*, **3**: 305–60.

Judge, W.O. Jr. and Zeithml, C.P. (1992). Institutional and strategic choice perspectives on board involvement in the strategic decision process. *Academy of Management Journal*, **35**: 766–94.

Kriger, M.P. (1988). The increasing role of subsidiary boards in MNCs: An empirical study. *Strategic Management Journal*, **9**: 347–60.

La Porta, R., Lopez-de-Silanes, F., and Shleifer, A. (1999). Corporate ownership around the world. *Journal of Finance*, **54**: 471–517.

Lambert, R., Larcker, D., and Weigelt, K. (1993). The structure of organizational incentives. *Administrative Science Quarterly*, September: 438–61.

Leksell, L. and Lindgren, U. (1982). The board of directors in foreign subsidiaries. *Journal of International Business Studies*, **13**: 27–38.

Leuz, C. and Verrecchia, R. (2000). The economic consequences of increased disclosure. *Journal of Accounting Research*, **38**: 91–124.

Luo, Y. (2005). Globalization and corporate governance and accountability. *Journal of International Management*, **11**(1): 19–41.

Mizruchi, M.S. (1997). What do interlocks do? An analysis, critique, and assessment of research on interlocking directorates. *Annual Review of Sociology*, **22**: 271–98.

Nohria, N. and Ghoshal, S. (1994). Differentiated fit and shared values: Alternatives for managing headquarters–subsidiary relations. *Strategic Management Journal*, **15**: 491–502.

Pauly, L.W. and Reich, S. (1997). National structures and multinational corporate behavior: Enduring differences in the age of globalization. *International Organization*, **51**: 1–30.

Pfeffer, J. and Salancik, G. (1978). *The External Control of Organizations: A Resource Dependence Perspective*. New York: Harper & Row.

Roth, K. and Morrison, A.J. (1991). An empirical analysis of the integration–responsiveness framework in global industries. *Journal of International Business Studies*, **21**: 541–64.

Roth, K. and O'Donnell, S. (1996). Foreign subsidiary compensation strategy: An agency theory perspective. *Academy of Management Journal*, **39**: 678–703.

Roth, K., Schweiger, D., and Morrison, A.J. (1991). Global strategy implementation at the business unit level: Operational capabilities and administrative mechanisms. *Journal of International Business Studies*, **22**: 369–402.

Sanders, W.G. and Carpenter, M.A. (1998). Internationalization and firm governance: The roles of CEO compensation, top team composition, and board structure. *Academy of Management Journal*, **41**: 158–78.

Shleifer, A. and Vishny, R.W. (1997). A survey of corporate governance. *Journal of Finance*, **52**: 737–83.

Tricker, R.I. (1994). *International Corporate Governance*. Englewood Cliffs, NJ: Prentice Hall.

Tung, R.L. (1987). Expatriate assignments: Enhancing success and minimizing failure. *Academy of Management Executives*, **1**: 117–26.

Tushman, M.L. and Nadler, D.A. (1978). Information processing as an integrating concept in organizational design. *Academy of Management Review*, **3**: 613–24.

Ulfelder, S. (2004). Building a compliance framework. *Computerworld*, **38**(27): 33–7.

Vishwanath, T. and Kaufmann, D. (1999). *Towards Transparency in Finance and Governance*. World Bank.

Zajac, E.J. and Westphal, J.W. (1994). The costs and benefits of managerial incentives and monitoring in large US corporations: When is more not better? *Strategic Management Journal*, **15**: 121–2.

Chapter 4

Corporate Governance at Multilevels: The Parent–Subsidiary Link

EXECUTIVE SUMMARY

Unlike domestic corporations, MNCs encompass two tiers of corporate governance: parent-level corporate governance (first tier) and subsidiary-level corporate governance (second tier). The second-tier corporate governance is designed to address how foreign subsidiaries that have their own board of directors deal with their shareholders and other local stakeholders while simultaneously answering to and integrating with the parent firm. The second-tier governance can provide strategic input in addition to what local management can offer, inject a good dose of national know-how and contacts into the operations, explain national attitudes and practices to corporate headquarters abroad, and convey corporate attitudes and practices to the local business scene.

In this chapter, I first define the two tiers of corporate governance in a typical MNC, explain the roles and functions of each tier, and illustrate how the two tiers of governance are interrelated and mutually reinforce an MNC's global corporate governance. In a general framework of the two tiers of corporate governance, I explain both strong cross-links between parent management and subsidiary board and between parent management and subsidiary management, and weak cross-links between parent board and subsidiary board and between parent board and subsidiary management. Since the specific links embedded in the two tiers of corporate governance vary according to the different roles played by individual subsidiaries, this chapter further reviews and discusses differing roles of foreign subsidiaries and how these roles actually affect the design and function of second-tier corporate governance. For instance, when a foreign subsidiary is more strategically important to the MNC's global expansion, this subsidiary's board and its management are expected to maintain a stronger tie and more frequent communication between the first and second tiers of corporate governance. Likewise, if a foreign subsidiary is designed to become a dominant player penetrating

> and emphasized in the host country market, the subsidiary-level corporate governance mechanisms will have to be more strongly tailored to the host country environments and practices. If a foreign subsidiary is more organizationally autonomous, then parent board and parent management need to encourage subsidiary board to play a bigger role in monitoring subsidiary management.

4.1 Multilevel Corporate Governance in MNCs

4.1.1 Defining multilevel corporate governance

As briefly noted in Chapter 1, corporate governance in an MNC is generally composed of two tiers: parent-level corporate governance (how the parent company's rights, power, and responsibilities are divided and monitored) and subsidiary-level corporate governance (how foreign subsidiaries that have their own board of directors deal with their shareholders and other local stakeholders while simultaneously answering to and integrating with the parent firm). Subsidiaries with their own board of directors are either independently listed on local stock exchanges (in this case with local public shareholders) or they are not listed on exchanges but do either meet a host country's legal requirements or a parent firm's strategic considerations for establishing such boards. This subsidiary-level board of directors governs the subsidiary as a legal entity although there is considerable variation in local and legal requirements as well as how parent and subsidiary choose to structure the role, responsibility, and use of such boards.

In the first case (when a subsidiary is listed on a host country's stock exchange), the corporate governance structure in this subsidiary is not much different from the governance structure in host country corporations traded in local stock exchanges. The subsidiary independently traded in an indigenous stock exchange is subject to the same judiciary, institutional, and regulatory constraints as are local corporations and must abide by the same securities law and company law as do local corporations. For this type of subsidiary, corporate governance mechanisms or practices such as board composition, executive compensation, board committees, interlocking directorate, ownership concentration, auditing practices, and ethical programs are deemed to resemble the prevalent mechanisms or practices used by local corporations. Note that this type of subsidiary is, legally and financially speaking, not wholly owned by the MNC but rather a joint stock company in which the MNC parent is only one of many shareholders, large and small as well as foreign and local, who have some ownership participation in the subsidiary. However, if an MNC participates in some ownership in a foreign enterprise but not to the extent that it actually controls the enterprise, then this foreign unit is not considered second-tier governance. The unique property of this subsidiary's corporate governance is twofold: the MNC parent must have adequate power to control the subsidiary's board as well as the top management team and must, accordingly, be responsible for the subsidiary's performance, governance, and accountability. To exercise its power and monitor the subsidiary's governance and performance, the MNC parent generally has three channels or means, often used simultaneously, to fulfill the goals: (i) having its own directors on the board; (ii) controlling the nomination and appointment of key personnel; and (iii) implementing codes of conducts, ethical standards, and transparency practices set by the parent. It is also often the case that the subsidiary board is chaired by the parent's representative when the parent has a dominant stake in the subsidiary. If the subsidiary CEO is dispatched by the MNC parent, it is likely that the CEO also occupies the chairmanship; if the CEO is a local talent, then this position is likely to be separated from the chairmanship. Partial acquisitions of some publicly traded companies in local stock exchanges that allow the MNC parent to control these companies are recent examples that involve second-tier corporate governance of this kind.

In the second case (when a subsidiary is not listed on a local exchange but has its own board to meet a host country's legal requirements), subsidiary boards are often established in foreign–local equity joint ventures that are legally registered as independent companies in a host country. Joint-venture law in many emerging economies, for instance, requires the establishment of a board of directors that is the highest authority governing joint-venture activities and monitoring joint-venture executives' behavior and performance. Although this type of board tends to be small and does not have specialized committees, it does hold routine meetings annually or semi-annually and/or non-routine meetings called by the majority of directors. The board's power, authority, and agenda are typically specified in the focal joint-venture's company charter. Naturally, this type of subsidiary board consists of members appointed by and representing all investing parties of the joint venture. This type of board is also largely composed of insider representatives for different parties, generally without outside professionals or outside doctorates for the interlocking purpose.

In the third case (when a subsidiary board is established to meet a parent firm's strategic considerations), subsidiary boards play an important part in an MNC's global coordination, accountability, and governance. MNCs can increase internal coordination between the parent and subsidiaries through greater use of these subsidiary boards. Subsidiary boards can also play valuable roles in helping the parent MNC and subsidiary management to understand local host country economic, political, and social conditions. Board members, especially indigenous natives, can also use their networks to help connect parent and subsidiary executives with top decision-makers in the business community. It is increasingly evident that MNC parent firms increase subsidiary boards' power to include an explicit duty to appraise the subsidiary's strategic plans and operations (of course it is also important to provide clear divisions of labor between board and executives so that subsidiary executives do not feel that their legitimate decision-making role is impinged upon). Japanese MNCs illustrate some specific roles played by subsidiary boards to meet their parents' strategic considerations. Their subsidiary boards are generally designed to

1. approve budgets and short-term plans of the subsidiary;
2. monitor operating performance and corrective measures in the subsidiary;
3. participate in drawing up the subsidiary's strategic plans;
4. ensure compliance with local legal requirements;
5. provide knowledge of local social, economic, and political conditions; and
6. appraise and attempt to minimize the subsidiary's political risk.

These roles are a combination of environmental sensing, decision-making, advising, and monitoring roles. Overall, when subsidiary boards are established to fulfill an MNC parent's strategic considerations, these boards are not merely supervisors watching and governing subsidiary executive behavior, but more importantly, they are advisors and helpers.

Kriger (1988) offers some interesting survey results showing some advantages as perceived by MNC executives. When they are asked "what do you see as the advantages or disadvantages of having a subsidiary with an active board?" Japanese MNCs replied:

1. An activated board can give more concrete instructions to officers concerning both responsibility and management.
2. A member of a board, who obtains a fair knowledge of the present situation of the company, can perform the function of a sincere advising agent.
3. An activated board can encourage officers to have a greater interest in the corporation and a strong sense of responsibility.

Meanwhile, Swedish MNCs responded that an active subsidiary board can:

1. Present an independent view on how the subsidiary's business should be conducted with the goal of making the subsidiary both a business success and a good corporate citizen in its host nation.
2. Counsel the subsidiary's management on its relations with personnel, financial institutions, governmental bodies, and the public.
3. Periodically appraise the performance of the subsidiary's management, primarily through review of its financial reports and statements.
4. Counsel the company regarding local compensation standards.

Aside from these results, Kriger (1988) also found some differences between Japanese and North American MNCs in using subsidiary boards (with European MNCs in between). He documented that Japanese parent companies saw active use of subsidiary boards as not only mandated by law, but also as mechanisms for understanding local country conditions and new channels for advice, information sharing, and performance monitoring. In contrast, North American parent companies tended to attach lower value in the past to the role of subsidiary boards. Essentially, Japanese MNCs appeared to have a strong desire to dig "deep roots" into the host countries in which they operate whereas North American MNCs, on the whole, were less likely to view a particular host country as requiring such "deep roots". This implies that, as North American MNCs progressively fortify local responsiveness and adaptive diversification, they will need to be more active in using subsidiary boards as well.

4.1.2 Understanding multilevel links

Despite some differences in actual functions of subsidiary boards among the above three scenarios, there are some common threads that describe the relationship between the

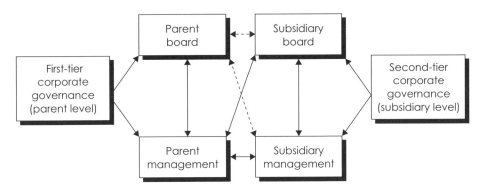

Figure 4.1 Two tiers of corporate governance in MNCs

first tier (parent governance) and the second tier (subsidiary governance). Overall, first-tier governance (including both parent board and management) influences the second-tier governance (including both subsidiary board and management) through ownership holding, organizational coordination, corporate support, and performance monitoring. Second-tier governance in turn channels back to the first-tier through advice provision, governance sharing, information reporting, and directorate expansion. Specifically, as illustrated in Figure 4.1, there are four links, whose strengths vary significantly, between the first and second tiers of corporate governance. While parent management maintains strong links (solid lines in Figure 4.1) with both subsidiary management and subsidiary board, parent board maintains weak links (dotted lines in Figure 4.1) with subsidiary management and subsidiary board.

More specifically, parent board maintains strong control over parent management, which in turn maintains strong control over subsidiary management and a strong link with subsidiary board. At the same time, the direct links between parent board and subsidiary board and between parent board and subsidiary management are weak. First, the link between parent board and subsidiary board is generally manifested in ownership participation in the subsidiary in question held by the parent. Parent board is often the utmost or final authority to approve large investments overseas, whether joint ventures or acquisitions. Board chairman and composition in critical subsidiaries may also need to be ratified by parent board. Although it is not common to have key foreign subsidiary board members sit in the parent board, it is viable to have one or a few board members from key domestic strategic business units (SBU) separately listed sitting in the corporate board. In addition, parent board and subsidiary board are also linked through information sharing. For instance, subsidiary board may inform parent board of ethical behaviors of subsidiary executives and advise parent board about how to improve ethical behaviors of overseas employees. In this sense, subsidiary board, to some extent, shares an MNC's total corporate governance with parent board.

As in all corporate governance, the shareholders have the last word. In subsidiary operations, the shareholders are corporate headquarters controlled by parent board. The subsidiary is, after all, a subsidiary. In any serious conflict, therefore, between local board members and the corporate representatives on the board, the corporate side wins.

This must be clearly understood by the local board members. By the same token, it would be a serious mistake if corporate board members did not listen very carefully to the local board members. Assuming that local board members have been selected on the basis of good personal and professional criteria, the case must be very strong if the corporate side decides to overrule the locals.

Obviously, an extensive professional background is a necessity for board members, as well as a high level of personal integrity. To do a good job, local board members must also have the full confidence of corporate top executives, who should make it a clear priority to get to know the board members on a personal and professional basis. This applies especially to cases where the chairperson of the subsidiary board is a local national. An important and yet often neglected element in maximizing the contributions of local board members is to keep them well updated on the overall strategies and concerns of corporate top management, through frequent phone contacts and formal/informal meetings.

Second, parent board and subsidiary management are linked, despite the very weak magnitude and infrequent manner, through information reporting and feedback. If parent board wants to find out how corporate executives are doing with respect to their ethical behaviors and global leadership during an MNC's internationalization, subsidiary managers in frontline companies are certainly an ideal channel from which to get related information and feedback for parent board. Global accountability and transparency for an MNC also depends in part on subsidiary management's timely disclosure and reporting of financial, accounting, and marketing information pertaining to individual subsidiaries dispersed in the world. Thus, some board committees in auditing and ethics may directly communicate with subsidiary management for the information they need. Unlike managers in wholly-owned foreign subsidiaries or those subunits not listed on local stock exchanges, where these managers are directly subordinated to parent management, executives in independently listed subsidiaries are primarily obligated and responsible to subsidiary board, rather than to parent management. Thus, if the first-tier board wants subsidiary management to report or provide feedback about the needed information relating to parent management behavior, subsidiary executives will not be reluctant to do so.

Third, parent management and subsidiary board, whose ties are stronger than those between parent board and subsidiary-level board and management, are linked via joint monitoring of subsidiary management, advice sharing, managerial governance sharing, and directorate expansion. While subsidiary board is the main body that monitors subsidiary managers' incentives and behaviors, parent management monitors subsidiary management's operational decisions that align with the MNC's corporate strategy and global integration. Subsidiary board also serves as an advising agent to parent management, providing the latter with various host country dynamics including both subsidiary activities and environmental conditions. Mutually, parent management may share advice with subsidiary board so that the latter knows better about the MNC's overall global strategy and the subsidiary's strategic position in the corporate portfolio. Together, subsidiary board and parent management also jointly govern strategic and operational activities in markets wherein the subsidiary participates. Because many of such activities are integrated, vertically or horizontally, with the rest of the MNC's global operations, parent management and subsidiary board must jointly oversee such subsidiary activities metrically. Lastly, subsidiary board is an additional channel to establish and extend business networking in foreign countries, and this networking helps parent management to improve local responsiveness and national adaptations. If managed properly, the relationship between subsidiary board members and host government can become a plus for both the MNC and the government. Through outside board members in the subsidiary, cultivating relationships with politicians, regulators and officials could be more effective, less cumbersome, and less sensitive than through subsidiary management.

The need for bridging gaps in business traditions and cultural patterns is not limited to situations where subsidiary management is an expatriate. With a locally recruited chief executive, the same risks of gaps and misunderstandings remain, but on a higher level, between the executive on the one hand, and corporate management on the other. In those cases, the local executive can benefit from the support of local board members in explaining to international board members and headquarters why recommendations and decisions have to be made in a special way. A good board and its individual members can serve as important catalysts between "here" and "there," between "them" and "us."

Finally, the relationship between parent management and subsidiary management, which is obviously stronger than all other links in Figure 4.1 as far as organizing and managing international expansion in host countries, will be further discussed in the second half of this chapter – sections on parent–subsidiary links and managerial govern- ance, which, respectively, deal with global coordination and organizational control over globally dispersed operations undertaken by various subunits in different nations. It is true that corporate governance does not include managerial governance. However, managerial governance can substantially foster corporate governance by improving an organizational infrastructure within the MNC so as to streamline internal control, strengthen transparency, coordinate interests of different stakeholders, and implement conduct codes and ethical standards for all employees.

It is also worthwhile to note the relationship between subsidiary management and subsidiary board. Usually, the local president, whether a national or an expatriate, feels he or she gets very valuable support from subsidiary board. There may, however, be occasions when the president and the board arrive at differences of opinion. The local directors, hopefully, had a chance to influence the choice of the local chief executive in the first place. Nevertheless, in most cases he or she is, in reality, a corporate appointee, with an employment contract made up or approved by corporate headquarters. In situations of conflict between the local board and the executive, and if compromises cannot be worked out, corporate headquarters must step in and take responsibility.

4.2 Corporate Governance and Subsidiary Roles

The above section explains the corporate governance link between parent firms (board and management) and foreign subsidiaries (board and management). This link, however, varies according to the different roles played by individual subsidiaries. For instance, when a foreign subsidiary is more strategically important to the MNC's global expansion, this subsidiary's board and its management are expected to maintain a stronger tie and more frequent communication between the first and second tiers of corporate governance. Likewise, if a foreign subsidiary is designed to become a dominant player penetrating and emphasized in the host country market, the subsidiary-level corporate governance mechanisms will have to be more strongly tailored to the host country environments and practices. If a foreign subsidiary is more organizationally autonomous, then parent board and parent management need to encourage subsidiary board to play a bigger role in monitoring subsidiary management.

4.2.1 Subsidiary roles and governance design

Subsidiary strategies are a critical mechanism for dealing with the parent–subsidiary relationship. As the strategy-oriented approach is emerging in lieu of the traditional control-centered approach, subsidiary strategies play an increasingly important part in corporate governance design for global operations and management. In general, subsidiary roles are categorized in different ways, and accordingly, the second-tier corporate governance should appropriately be in tune with various subsidiary roles.

First, in Jarillo and Martinez's (1990) scheme, the two basic dimensions underlying strategic choices are the geographic localization of activities (i.e., whether R&D, purchasing, manufacturing, marketing, etc. are performed in the same country), and the degree of integration of those activities with the same activities in other subsidiaries of the firm. These two dimensions are independent. A subsidiary that performs most activities of the value chain still has two very different options: it may either be highly autonomous from headquarters, selling most of its output in its local market, or very integrated with headquarters, exporting a large part of its production to the parent company or other subsidiaries, while importing from them many products or components. In light of these two dimensions, an *autonomous* role means that a subsidiary carries out most of the functions of the value chain in a manner that is relatively independent of its parent organization or other subsidiaries. It follows that in a *receptive* role, few of these functions are performed locally, and they are highly integrated with other business units. Lastly, in an *active* role, many activities are located locally, but they are carried out in close coordination with other subsidiaries, thus constituting an active node in a tightly knit network. The autonomous strategy is typical of subsidiaries in multinational firms competing in multidomestic industries. The receptive strategy is typical of subsidiaries in global firms competing in global industries. Finally, active strategies are used by subsidiaries in transnational firms, with strong mandates from headquarters. Only those subsidiaries which occupy important nodes in the MNC network will follow such active strategies.

Accordingly, corporate governance should cope with these three identities. For an autonomous subsidiary, subsidiary board should play a much bigger role in overseeing subsidiary management, evaluating subsidiary executives' performance, and governing the subsidiary's strategic directions. Subsidiary board can also be more proactive in directorate expansion, helping the autonomous subsidiary to network with local business stakeholders. More specialized committees under subsidiary board are also needed to direct and monitor the autonomous subsidiary in specific areas such as disclosure, auditing, and anti-corruption. It is also advisable to separate an autonomous subsidiary's CEO from the subsidiary's board chairmanship so as to fortify the governance effectiveness. For a receptive subsidiary, in contrast, subsidiary board becomes less important to an MNC's overall corporate governance, and the subsidiary CEO may also lead the subsidiary board so that the receptive strategy can be implemented in a more synchronized climate. It is parent management that becomes more important in governing a receptive subsidiary's corporate governance and accountability. Among corporate governance mechanisms, culture-based approaches, especially the code of conduct and ethical programs, are even more salient, requiring a receptive subsidiary to comply. Finally, for an active subsidiary which conducts many activities locally but carries them out in close coordination with the rest of the MNC, subsidiary board's advising role to parent board and parent management is heightened. Two-way communications between the two tiers of corporate governance systems also become more imperative. Some large investment decisions involving an active subsidiary may be made based on the inputs from both parent- and subsidiary-level governance bodies.

The second classification scheme of subsidiary roles is Gupta and Govindarajan's (1991) approach that focuses on knowledge/resource flow patterns. Intra-corporate knowledge (including resources, capabilities, and technologies) flow is defined as the transfer of either expertise (e.g., skills and capabilities) or external market data of strategic value. The type of expertise transferred could refer to input processes (e.g., purchasing skills), throughout processes (e.g., product, process, and packaging designs), or output processes (e.g., marketing knowledge and distribution expertise). Any MNC subsidiaries can be arrayed along the two dimensions involving knowledge flow, that is: (a) the extent to which the subsidiary receives knowledge *inflow* from the rest of the corporation and (b) the extent to which the subsidiary provides knowledge *outflow* to the rest of the corporation. As a result, four generic subsidiary roles can be defined: *global innovator* (high outflow and low inflow); *integrated player* (high outflow and high inflow); *implementer* (low outflow and high inflow); and *local innovator* (low outflow and low inflow). In the global innovator role, the subsidiary serves as the fountainhead of knowledge for other units. The integrated player role is similar to the global innovator role because it also implies a responsibility for creating knowledge that can be utilized by other subsidiaries. However, an integrated player is not self-sufficient in fulfillment of its own knowledge needs. In the implementer role, the subsidiary engages in little knowledge creation of its own and relies heavily on knowledge inflows from either the parent or peer subsidiaries. Lastly, the local innovator role implies that the subsidiary has almost complete local responsibility for the creation of relevant know-how in all key functional areas. However, this knowledge is seen as too idiosyncratic to be of much competitive use outside of the country in which the local innovator is located. Traditional MNCs have consisted almost entirely of subsidiaries with local innovator roles.

The subsidiary-level corporate governance should be properly configured with the above roles as well. When a subsidiary is a global innovator, it serves as an MNC's fountainhead of knowledge for other subsidiaries. As such, subsidiary executives must be provided with strong incentives to continuously develop new capabilities, especially those that have long-range and long-term implications for the MNC's global growth. A subsidiary's CEO compensation, therefore, should be higher than his or her peers', and his or her long-term benefits should be strongly tied to the subsidiary's perform- ance in developing knowledge that generates long-term returns for the entire MNC network. Because a global innovator is virtually a center of excellence in a specific knowledge area, this subsidiary is a role model for peer subsidiaries in other countries. Thus, despite the fact that subsidiary board is not extremely important to a global innovator, culture-based and discipline-based governance mechanisms are critical. Both governance culture and corporate integrity, which together constitute culture-based governance, are integral parts of role model, which can in turn foster knowledge development in a sustainable manner. Among discipline-based governance, internal auditing, a conduct code, and an ethics program are also essential elements of role model for other subsidiaries to follow.

When a subsidiary is an implementer who engages in little knowledge creation of its own and relies heavily on information and resources from parent or other subsidiaries, it is essentially a follower, receiving corporate governance guidance or guidelines from the first-tier governance body. Unless it is a judiciary mandate in a host country, subsidiary board is not very necessary; if established, this board's role is limited. Still, practices in corporate integrity, governance culture, information disclosure, and business ethics are important to implementers. In fact, good practices in knowledge transfer and sharing within an MNC should be such that knowledge transferred and shared encompasses not only "hard-side" technologies or capabilities but also "soft-side" culture and norms that underpin the greater use of "hard-side" knowledge. When a subsidiary is a local innovator who has all relevant knowledge and functions for the host country setting but too specific to be used elsewhere, subsidiary board becomes profusely important. In this situation, subsidiary board should be structured as a microcosm body responsible for the subsidiary's full range of corporate governance activities. Furthermore, a local innovator's governance system, particularly subsidiary board's structure, function, and committees and subsidiary managers' compensation and benefits, should be largely suited to a host country's prevalent corporate govern- ance practices. In this regard, a local innovator's market-based corporate governance is substantially differentiated to meet the local norm and yet its culture- and discipline- based governance mechanisms are still congruent with those used by the parent firm. As to an integrated player, its governance system is primarily a hybrid that blends the mechanisms used by a global innovator and an implementer.

The third scheme that classifies subsidiary roles is made by Bartlett and Ghoshal (1989). The strategic importance of the local environment and competence of local organization are two key considerations in determining subsidiary roles. The *strategic leader* role can be played by a highly competent national subsidiary located in a strategically important market. In this role, the subsidiary serves as a partner of head- quarters in developing and implementing strategy. *Contributor* subsidiaries refer to those operating in small or strategically unimportant markets but having distinctive capabilities. *Implementer* subsidiaries operate in less strategically important markets but have enough competence to maintain local operations. Their market potential is limited, as reflected by corporate resource commitment. The efficiency of an implementer is only as important as the creativity of its strategic leaders or contributors, for it is this group that provides the strategic leverage that affords MNCs their competitive advantage. The implementers produce opportunities to capture economies of scale and scope that are crucial to global strategies. Finally, *black hole* subsidiaries operate in important markets where they hardly make a dent, but their strong local presence is essential for maintaining an MNC's global position. Building a significant local presence in a national environment that is large, sophisticated, and competitive is extremely difficult, expensive, and time consuming. One common tactic has been to create a sensory outpost in the black hole environment so as to exploit its learning potential, even if the local business potential is beyond its reach. Establishing strategic alliances represents a way of managing the subsidiary out of the black hole.

The second-tier corporate governance should align with the above categories of subsidiary roles as well. When a subsidiary is a strategic leader who is highly competent in an important market and serves as a partner to headquarters in developing and implementing global strategy, the link between first and second tiers of corporate governance should be intense, strong, and frequent. Given the subsidiary's leading position in the MNC's network, this link should be two-way directional. That is, parent board and subsidiary board may mutually advise each other and exchange information regarding both corporate performance and subsidiary performance. Meanwhile, parent management and subsidiary board must maintain an even stronger link to jointly set the strategic goals for the subsidiary and evaluate subsidiary executives' performance based on these strategic targets. While parent management emphasizes the routine monitoring of a strategic leader's operations, subsidiary board has a greater responsibility to oversee this subsidiary's corporate governance. When a subsidiary plays a contributor and implementer role, the subsidiary-level corporate governance should resemble what I discussed above about governance systems for receptive or implementer subsidiaries. Nevertheless, when a subsidiary becomes black hole – it has few capabilities but operates in a very important market – parent management must figure out how to help the subsidiary develop needed capabilities to compete in this critical market, while subsidiary board must come up with a governance system that directs the subsidiary into a more capable and more transparent enterprise in the host setting.

The final scheme is Poynter and White's (1985) classification. The underlying factors affecting a subsidiary's strategic roles include organizational slack, the local environment, the values of key implementers, and organizational relationships affecting both the development and execution of strategy. Of these, organizational slack is of particular importance in the dynamic world of the MNC and its subsidiaries. Organizational slack plays a major role in determining an organization's ability to deal with environmental variations or buffer itself against environmental influences. The amount of organizational slack is related to the firm's ability to generate innovative strategies. If slack is not carefully managed, however, the resulting subsidiary strategies can conflict with those of the MNC parent and with those which would best fit the competitive environment. In light of the above factors, a subsidiary can be defined as one of five types: miniature replica, marketing satellite, rationalized manufacturer, product specialist, or strategic independent. A *miniature replica* produces and markets some of the parent's product line in the host country. Some low-volume products may be imported from the parent, but generally the business is a small-scale replica of the parent firm. A *marketing satellite* markets products manufactured centrally in the host market or trade region. Process and product development also occur centrally. These companies range from simple import firms to sophisticated marketers with extensive distribution, marketing, promotion, and customer support services. A *rationalized manufacturer* produces a designated set of component parts or products for a multinational or global market. Its product scope is limited. Marketing is usually performed by the MNC through marketing satellites. Generally, developmental activities are undertaken by the parent, but occasionally specific process improvements may be developed at the local plant. Major strategic decisions are made by the parent firm. A *product specialist* develops, produces, and markets a limited product line for global markets. Products, markets, or basic technologies are similar to those of the parent, but exchanges are rare. The subsidiary is generally self-sufficient in terms of applied R&D, production, and marketing. The subsidiary has strategic control over its established products, but not over other major strategic shifts. Lastly, a *strategic independent* has the freedom and resources to develop lines of business for either local, multinational, or global markets. It has unconstrained access to markets and the freedom to pursue new business opportunities. Administrative and financial relations are often the only links with the parent company. Of the above strategies, the miniature replica is most common, followed by MNC subsidiaries. Marketing satellite and rationalized manufacturer strategies are typically found only in highly integrated global MNCs. Although desired by host governments, the product specialist and strategic independent are uncommon.

When a subsidiary is a miniature replica, it serves as a pipeline to the host country by producing and marketing some of the parent's products. In this case, subsidiary board's role is limited. Instead, discipline-based governance such as executive penalty, internal auditing, information transparency, a code of conduct and ethics standards will constitute the major governance system. When a subsidiary is a rationalized manufacturer, it serves as an integrated player as explained above. This role propels a stronger tie between the first and second tiers of corporate governance, requiring more frequent information sharing and advice sharing between the two. Like corporate governance for global innovators, strategic leaders or integrated players, the governance for a rationalized manufacturer may be also established based on increased ownership concentration by the MNC's parent firm. Increased ownership allows the first-tier governance to have a stronger influence or power in subsidiary board. If a subsidiary becomes strategically independent, subsidiary board becomes more important, and the first-tier corporate governance depends more on subsidiary board to monitor subsidiary management. It is natural that as a subsidiary becomes more strategically independent, subsidiary management is more likely to be opportunistic unless corporate governance is effective. To this end, subsidiary executive remuneration, independent auditing, and executive penalty are important mechanisms to deter their possible opportunism.

Of course, here we emphasized corporate governance only and did not elaborate on how parent management and subsidiary management should be organizationally linked together. It should be pointed out that setting strategic roles for subsidiaries is insufficient for managing subunits abroad. Corporate management faces two other important challenges in guiding the dispersion of responsibilities and tasks. These include:

(a) building in differentiation, not only by designing diverse roles and distributing assignments but also by giving the managers responsibilities and the power to do the same and (b) directing the process to ensure that various roles are coordinated and that the distributed responsibilities are controlled.

Once subsidiary roles are allocated, the head office has to empower managers to ensure that they have an influence on the corporate decision-making process. This is not a trivial task, especially if strategic initiatives and decision-making powers have long been concentrated at headquarters. Often the most effective means of giving strategic access and influence to national units is to create entirely new channels and forums. This approach permits roles, responsibilities, and relationships to be defined and developed with far less constraint than would result from modifying existing communication patterns or shifting responsibility boundaries. When the roles of foreign subunits are differentiated and responsibility is more dispersed, headquarter executives must be prepared to de-emphasize their control over strategic content and develop the ability to manage the dispersed strategic process. In addition, the head office should adopt a flexible administrative stance that allows it to differentiate the way it manages each subsidiary and business within each unit.

Bartlett and Ghoshal (1989) have linked managerial approaches with different strategic roles of subsidiaries. In subunits with lead roles, the head office must ensure that developing business strategies fit the MNC's overall goals and priorities. Corporate management's major function is to support those with strategic leadership responsibility by giving them the resources and freedom needed for the innovative, entrepreneurial role they have been asked to play. Second, if the unit is placed in a contributory role, the head office should redirect local resources to programs outside the unit's control. In so doing, it must counter the natural hierarchy of loyalties that puts local interests above global ones. Head administrators must be careful not to discourage local managers so much that they stop contributing or leave in frustration. Third, if a unit is in an implementer role, the head office maintains tighter control. Such a unit represents an opportunity to capture the benefits of scale and learning. Therefore, the head office stresses economy and sales efficiency. Communication of strategies developed elsewhere and control of routine tasks can be carried out through systems that allow headquarters to manage these units efficiently. Finally, if a unit acts as a black hole, corporate management must develop its resources and capabilities to make it more responsive to the local environment. Managers of these units depend heavily on head offices for help and support, creating an urgent need for intensive training and transfer of skills and resources.

4.2.2 Corporate strategies and governance design

In brief, an MNC's corporate strategy for the purpose of global coordination and integration entails three options.

Multidomestic strategy: A multidomestic strategy is one in which strategic and operating decisions are decentralized to the strategic business unit in each country in order to tailor products to the local market. A multidomestic strategy focuses on competition within each country. It assumes that the markets differ and are therefore segmented by national boundaries. In other words, consumer needs and desires, industry conditions (e.g., number and type of competitors), political and legal structures, and social norms vary by country. Multidomestic strategies allow for the customization of products to meet the specific needs and preferences of local customers. Therefore, they should be able to maximize competitive response to the idiosyncratic requirements of each market. However, multidomestic strategies do not allow for the achievement of economies of scale and thus can be costly. As a result, firms employing a multidomestic strategy decentralize strategic and operating decisions to the strategic business units operating in each country. The multidomestic strategy has been more prominent among European multinational firms because of the varieties of cultures and markets found in Europe.

Global strategy: A global strategy assumes more standardization of products across country markets. As a result, the competitive strategy is centrally controlled by the home office. The strategic business units operating in each country are assumed to be interdependent, and the home office attempts to achieve integration among these businesses. Therefore, a global strategy is one in which standardized products are offered internationally while the competitive strategy is dictated by the home office. A global strategy emphasizes economies of scale and offers great opportunities for utilizing innovations developed at the home office or in one country in other markets. However, a global strategy often lacks responsiveness to local markets and is difficult to manage because of the need to coordinate strategies and operating decisions across national borders. Achieving efficient operations with a global strategy requires the sharing of resources as well as coordination and cooperation across national boundaries. The Japanese have often pursued this centralized strategy with success.

Transnational strategy: A transnational strategy is a corporate strategy that seeks to achieve both global efficiency and local responsiveness. Realizing the diverse goals of the transnational strategy is difficult because one goal requires close global coordination, while the other requires local flexibility. Thus, flexible coordination is required to implement the transnational strategy. It requires building a shared vision and individual commitment through an integrated network and provides an asymmetrical treatment in coordinating worldwide businesses within the MNC network.

The three global integration strategies have implications on the design of the global corporate governance as well. As the global integration strategy moves from the global to transnational and then to multidomestic, subsidiary board is becoming more important for an MNC's global corporate governance because required local responsiveness heightens with this shift. In particular, subsidiary board's roles in advising, local environment scanning, host country information sharing, and doctorate expansion become much more essential along these strategic moves. On the other hand, an MNC's global corporate governance may be more greatly harmonized and synchronized as its global integration strategy shifts from the multidomestic to transnational and then to global. This increased harmonization supports global integration and control by disseminating and sharing the unified corporate integrity, governance culture, internal auditing, and ethic codes that must be shared by all employees in various countries. This harmonization shift is also feasible as an MNC's dependence on and interaction with host countries reduces along the above strategic shifts, thus making it less susceptible to indigenous governance norms or peculiar practices. All else being equal, an MNC's ownership participation in foreign subsidiaries should be higher in the case of the global strategy than in the case of the transnational strategy, which in turn should be higher than with the multidomestic strategy. Increased ownership provides parent board and parent management with greater organizational control over subsidiary activities, thus facilitating global coordination, integration, and control. Finally, global interlocking directorate is expected to become more important as the global integration strategy shifts from global to transnational and then to multidomestic. Extended interlocking directorate with the foreign business community may not only enhance the company's international networking, but it may also improve the company's organizational legitimacy and redress certain deficiencies in host countries' underdeveloped institutional and investment infrastructures.

Lastly, I want to note that the advisory board at the subsidiary level can also play an important part in an MNC's global corporate governance. Subsidiary board discussed so far is only about the board of directors for subsidiaries. Unlike the board of directors established only for subsidiaries that are locally listed or to meet legal mandate, the advisory board can be established for any type of foreign subsidiary since this establishment is entirely an MNC's organizational choice. A wholly-owned foreign subsidiary may need independent advice from knowledgeable, well-informed local people serving as advisory board members. The advice could be on host country politics, regulations, networks, or new projects, among other issues. Moreover, well-known and respected local business leaders on advisory boards bring credibility, contacts, and the ability to facilitate business growth. These advisory board members may help the subsidiary to gain fresh insights and "outside the box" thinking on some fundamental issues. In addition, experience without the baggage of any controlling or judgmental aspect can be brought to bear on a broad array of situations and issues. Generally, advisory boards provide valuable advice at a much lower cost than that provided by external consultants. The format and structure of advisory boards are also much easier and more flexible than regular boards of directors. Management is not constrained by the requirements of a regular board of directors with full oversight responsibilities. The focus of advisory boards is on non-binding advice, not on control. To conclude, although building advisory boards for foreign subsidiaries is really an MNC's organizational decision that needs to be balanced between the advantages and disadvantages of using these boards, I expect that advisory boards for foreign subsidiaries will play some more positive roles in the evolution of global corporate governance, supplementing and complementing regular boards of directors for these subsidiaries.

4.3 Managerial Governance in Global Business

Managerial governance and corporate governance together comprise total governance or organizational governance. Corporate governance involves governance and control of corporate affairs, while managerial governance emphasizes those internal processes and structures that regulate operational decisions and business activities undertaken by an MNC's various subunits (departments, divisions, subsidiaries, and affiliates). Managerial governance includes the systems that bring about internal adherence within the corporation to a set of strategic goals designed by top management through using corporate power or authority. Unlike corporate governance that often uses ownership concentration, board composition, board leadership, and executive compensation, managerial governance is a more direct intervention involving output monitoring, bureaucratic monitoring, and cultural monitoring.

Although managerial governance is not the focus of this book, it does have a certain impact on corporate governance. Managerial governance directly impacts corporate transparency, accountability, and ethics, which in turn determine the effectiveness of corporate governance. Hence, managerial governance nurtures corporate governance by providing an improved organizational platform to perform internal control, information disclosure and financial or non-financial auditing and to bolster corporate integrity and ethical practices. Managerial governance is even more relevant in the global setting because it plays a bigger role in improving an MNC's accountability involving increasingly sophisticated global competition and foreign business activities.

Managerial governance is manifested in control, coordination, and orientation. Control is seen as the process which brings about adherence to a goal through the exercise of power or authority. Coordination is seen as more of an enabling process which provides the appropriate linkage between different task units within the organization. Coordination is associated with integrating activities dispersed across subsidiaries. Control is a more direct intervention into the operations of subsidiaries. It can be very specific and short term. It has a tendency to be more costly because it requires direct forms of communication. For instance, to agree upon a budget generally necessitates a great deal of communication and expense. Coordination is distinguished not by direct intervention but by situating the subsidiary in a network of responsibilities. The coordination pattern can be imposed, but the resulting responsibilities are rooted in coordination. Coordination is generally less costly because communications are minimal and routine. Compared to control, coordination is less direct, less costly, and has a longer time span.

MNC parents are often unable to use centralized decision-making processes to maintain global managerial governance and control for several reasons. First, the diversity of countries in which the firm operates, the differences in the extent of integration across functions, and the firm's evolving product diversification make a centralized way of managing trade-offs between responsiveness and integration impractical for large, complex MNCs. Second, maintaining the proper global integration–local responsiveness (I–R) balance is an ongoing process which requires occasional reassessment. Lastly, there may be no single vantage point within the firm from which to consider all of its needs. The perceived needs for responsiveness and integration are likely to come from different parts of the organization in distant geographical locations. Proximity to market conditions and the host country government, as well as awareness of the importance of success at the local level, make subsidiary managers sensitive to needs for responsiveness. In contrast, perceiving needs for integration usually requires a multinational view of the business, and its markets, technologies, and competitors. Such a view usually comes from headquarter executives.

Coordination's contribution to global managerial governance has two dimensions: breadth and diversity. Breadth of coordination refers to the number of other units with which a subsidiary coordinates. The more extensive the network of reciprocal obligations, the greater will be the burden of coordination, and the more integrated the subsidiary (thus making it easier to implement managerial governance). It will also have less room for independent maneuvering. Similarly, if the subsidiary coordinates a number of different functions with the other units, it will be more enmeshed in the network than if coordination was confined to a single function. The breadth of coordination (the number of units in the coordination network) and the diversity of coordination (the number of functions coordinated) are both important aspects of the degree to which a subsidiary is integrated into the MNC network.

The process of coordination requires mechanisms which can be divided roughly into two groups: formal and informal or subtle. The formal group contains four mechanisms comprising centralization, formalization, planning, and behavioral control. Centralization is the extent to which the locus of decision making lies in the higher levels of the chain of command. Formalization is the extent to which policies, rules, job descriptions, and the like are written down in manuals and other documents, generally leading to the establishment of standard routines. Planning refers to systems and processes like strategic planning, budgeting, scheduling, and goal setting. Finally, behavioral control is based on direct, personal surveillance of individual behavior.

The subtle group includes three kinds of managerial mechanisms, namely lateral relations, informal communication, and organizational culture. Lateral relations cut across the vertical structure and include direct contact between managers of different departments that share a problem, task force, team, integrating role, etc. Informal communication supplements formal communication by means of a network of informal, personal contacts among managers across different units of the company: corporate meetings, management trips, personal visits, transfers, and the like. Informal communication differs from lateral relations in that it is not structured around specific tasks, thus being even more indirect as a means of coordination. Finally, organizational culture can be developed through a process of socialization of individuals by communicating ways of doing things, decision-making styles, and the objectives and values of the company. Thus, a system of ideology is internalized by executives, generating identification with and loyalty to the organization. This process is performed by training corporate and subsidiary managers, transferring them to different units, managing their career paths, and evaluating and rewarding them appropriately.

Porter (1986) links network coordination with activity configuration. Faced with an industrial structure, each firm has to devise a strategy along two key dimensions: the configuration of activities in the firm's value chain (i.e., where they are carried out), and the coordination of those activities (i.e., how interdependent the different subsidiaries really are). When international activities are geographically dispersed, high coordination is needed if foreign direct investment is heavy. When international activities are geographically concentrated and coordination of activities is high, it is called a simple global strategy. When activities are geographically concentrated but coordination is low, it is then referred to as an export-based strategy.

MNCs are increasingly using strategic orientation in lieu of conventional controls to monitor the operation of foreign subsidiaries and to perform managerial governance. Strategic orientation is an efficient mid-range instrument linking global integration with local responsiveness. Compared to control and coordination, strategic orientation arrangement is the least direct, least costly, and has the longest or most sustained effect. The global strategy literature asserts that the alignment of an overseas subsidiary with its environment is critical for international expansion because competition in the global marketplace occurs at the business unit level. There is a linkage between a firm's strategic profile and its external context, and this linkage has significant implications for international performance in an uncertain context.

When confronting a heterogeneous-to-home external environment and a complex interorganizational structure, an MNC subsidiary needs a preformulated strategic posture which governs and facilitates its role accomplishment. This necessity seems reinforced when a subsidiary operates in a complex and dynamic environment because its strategic choice determines its exposure to uncertain environmental components that impact firm performance.

The strategic context of MNC subsidiaries within a diversified MNC network is substantially influenced by the role and corresponding orientation that the business is intended to play in the corporate portfolio. A foreign subsidiary can be prospector, analyzer, or defender. A prospector subsidiary concentrates on scanning, identifying, and capitalizing on emerging market opportunities beyond the MNC network, and it maintains and bears the costs and risks inherent in maintaining extensive capabilities for responding to market and contextual changes in the host setting. In contrast, a defensive subsidiary is rigid, shortsighted, nonadaptive, and risk-averse. It deliberately reduces innovative and adaptive costs and risks by selecting a stable, narrowly defined product or market domain, or by merely exploiting internalization benefits within an MNC network. As a hybrid orientation between proactiveness and defensiveness, the analysis strategy seeks both risk-adjusted efficiency and emerging market opportunities. A foreign business with this orientation defends existing product markets through efficiency-oriented strategies while cautiously penetrating new markets through intensified product/market innovation. From the ecological perspective, a subsidiary's orientation must be capable of accommodating variability in its task and institutional environments as well as internal differentiation.

The impact of a host country's task and institutional environments on a subsidiary's decision-making characteristics and organizational behavior is fairly vigorous and direct. In the task environment, customers, suppliers, and competitors all shape competition in the industry and influence the input and output dimensions of local operation. In the institutional environment, regulatory, sociocultural, economic, technological, and international sectors all potentially affect the survival and growth of MNC subsidiaries in a given country. The above sectors represent a societal profile of a host country which has an ongoing influence on the operation and management of MNC subsidiaries.

The alignment of a subsidiary's strategic orientation to its uncertain host environment is of paramount importance for business performance. A good coupling between strategic orientation and the local environment can facilitate the exploitation of firm-specific competitive advantages and host country-specific comparative advantages. When managerial discretion is constrained in a complex, dynamic setting, the environment-strategy fit significantly affects financial and market performance. A foreign subsidiary's survival and expansion in a local economy depend on its ability to understand the environment and react in time to permit necessary organizational adjustments. From the neo-contingency perspective, a good fit between strategic orientation and environment conditions in a turbulent context can enable an MNC subsidiary to maximize economic rents from the interface between the "societal effect" and the "organizational effect". A pre-arranged strategic orientation that is appropriate for both internal arrangements and external alignment can boost subsidiary incentives, reduce vulnerability to contextual changes, and spur the accomplishment of goals set for foreign direct investment.

Managerial control is further composed of output control, bureaucratic control, and cultural control. Put simply, output control concerns the measurement of outcomes. To apply output controls, an MNC estimates or sets appropriate targets or outcome indicators for its subunits abroad, and then monitors their performance relative to these targets. Often, the MNC's reward system is associated with performance so that output control also provides an incentive structure for motivating overseas managers. In general, output controls require very little managerial direction and intervention, and hence they are less likely to result in attempts to influence how individual activities are performed. Therefore, the relative amount of influence headquarter managers exert over how individual tasks are performed in the foreign market reflects a managerial control over monitoring outputs.

In contrast to output control, process control theoretically requires direct personal surveillance and high levels of management direction and intervention. In order to provide this, managers need to be involved in what and how activities are being carried out. Process control requires central managers to spend more time and effort monitoring foreign activities. Practically, such personal surveillance and direct intervention is neither appropriate nor realistic for global integration and control in large, complex multinational corporations. Instead, MNCs more often use bureaucratic and cultural control mechanisms to monitor and evaluate the performance of their subunits abroad.

Bureaucratic control is extensively employed by MNCs. It consists of a limited and explicit set of codified rules and regulations which delineate desired performance in terms of output and/or behavior. For an individual to become a functional member of a bureaucratic organization, he or she must accept the legitimacy of organizational authority and its rules and regulations so that he or she can follow them. The authority and power exercised in this system is through control over resources. That is, it is of the remunerative type, while personal involvement is relatively limited.

A bureaucratic control system has several implications for the selection, training, and monitoring of organizational members. People must be found who have the required technical skills or are trainable, who will accept organizational authority, and who can learn to perform in accordance with the organization's rules and regulations. The selection and training process is relatively straightforward since rules and regulations are explicit and written down. In addition, new members must learn whatever technical competence is required of their position. Monitoring in a bureaucratic system involves comparing an individual's behavior and output to the standards set forth in the rules and applying the rewards or sanctions prescribed therein.

Organizational culture is often defined as a pattern of beliefs and expectations shared by the organization's members. It generates a system of symbols, language, ideology, rituals, images, and myths that shapes the behavior of individuals and groups in the organization. In a culturally controlled organization, there exists an implied organizational code or "game", which is an important guide to behavior in addition to explicit rules.

A number of organizational practices facilitate the existence of a cultural control system. Most important are long-term employment guarantees, consensual decision making, and nonspecialized career paths. The consensual decision-making process forces interaction around organizational issues among organizational members. This interaction is one of the ways in which, through a process of repeated interactions over time, cultural values become systematized and shared. In addition, the fact that career paths in a culturally controlled organization are less than fully specialized means that people are rotated through the various functional areas of the organization, thus contributing to a greater organization-wide culture. A less than total commitment to a functional specialty on the part of organizational members reduces competition from outside professional groups for member loyalty, thus enhancing the potential strength of the corporate culture.

The use of a cultural control system has several implications for the selection, training, and monitoring of organizational members. Members of an organization with cultural control mechanisms must be integrated into the organizational culture in order to become functional members. Therefore, selection of members is of prime importance. In addition to having the requisite skills necessary for the job, a candidate for organizational membership must be sympathetic to the organizational culture and must be willing to learn and accept its norms, values, and behavioral prescriptions. Thus, the initial "zone of indifference" required of new members is fairly specific and extensive.

Compared to bureaucratic controls, training and socialization in a cultural control system are of greater importance. An organizational member must not only learn a set of explicit, codified rules and regulations, but he or she must also learn to become part of a subtle, complex control system which consists of a broad range of pivotal values. Training and socialization can be quite intense and extensive. The degree of socialization required is reduced if the broader societal culture approximates that of the organization.

Monitoring a pure cultural control system occurs through interpersonal interactions. All members of the culture are familiar with and share its expectations. Performance and compliance with the culture are observed during the course of interpersonal interactions. Feedback, often subtle, is given on a person-to-person basis. In addition, a culture is a very rich, broad guide to behavior; an individual and the people around him or her will always have an implicit sense of his or her performance in the context of that culture.

More specific tools of managerial governance are information systems, managerial mechanisms, human resource administration, communication systems, expatriate dispatching, entry mode selection, global business structures, corporate culture, and ethics programs. Data management and information system tools can be used to control the following: the kinds of information gathered systematically by members of the organization; how such information is aggregated, analyzed, and given a meaning; how, in which form, and to whom it circulates; and how it is used in major decisions. Information systems must have a dual focus. Accounting and strategic data must be aggregated both for analytical purposes and to support integration (a portfolio of countries within a business) and responsiveness (a portfolio of businesses within a country). Furthermore, the assumptions underlying how information is obtained, aggregated, structured, and presented must be understood and agreed upon so that differences between cognitive maps reflect the actual ambiguity of choices, rather than fuzziness in the information. Information transparency also forces differences to be resolved on the basis of improved problem definition rather than smoothed over or decided on the basis of leadership skills, intellectual acumen, personal savvy, or hierarchical position. The flow of information can also be structured with sufficient asymmetry that individual managers will be encouraged to identify strongly either with responsive or integrative strategies while others will develop more balanced perspectives.

Management tools can be used to set norms and standards of behavior as well as personal objectives that are consistent with a desired strategic direction. Such tools work both directly, through their actual impact on managers, and indirectly, through the precedents they set and the meanings they assign to specific situations and choices. Selecting key managers, for instance, has direct consequences on both responsibility and power, and indirect ones via signals sent to other members of the organization. Management tools also include more typical human resource management components, such as shaping careers, reward and punishment systems, and management development. Less formal tools can also help develop norms, standards, and personal objectives. Patterns of interaction between managers can be influenced by the nature of meetings, the way in which top managers spend their time and encourage or discourage dissent, the respect shown for analysis, and so on. Measurement systems can be used to orient managerial attention toward specific priorities, as can career paths and evaluation and reward criteria. Management tools, therefore, also ensure that relevant differentiated information will be brought to bear on decisions. Such tools help create an internal advocacy process which reflects the conflicting external needs for responsiveness and integration. Resource allocation procedures may also help ensure that checks and balances are introduced before resources are appropriated.

Several managerial mechanisms can be used integrally. Planning processes can catalyze the process of strategic convergence and consensus building among executives whose initial perceptions and priorities may differ widely. By imposing a framework requiring multiple steps in making decisions, time horizons, and deadlines, these processes create some pressure and the necessary channels for convergence to take place. Specific conflict resolution tools can also be linked to the planning process. Management tools may create a climate where managers will be encouraged to interact and will be motivated to undertake successful lateral relationships. Rewards may be based more on participation and contribution than on individual results. Managerial development activities may emphasize a corporate-wide perspective and flexible attitudes. Career paths may create alternations between geographic and product-oriented responsibilities for individual managers so that they develop an empathy for both responsiveness and integration priorities.

The alignment of relative power with decision outcomes can also be performed using multiple mechanisms. Observation shows that key managerial appointments, reward systems, apparent career tracks, and the interpretations these are given by other managers all play a central role in the allocation of power. Information and resource dependence are other well-known sources of power. The configuration of such tools as information systems and resource allocation procedures is also critical to the management of relative power.

Conflict resolution is also a part of managerial mechanisms. It provides the necessary channels for confronting perceived needs for integration and responsiveness. They provide the actual structure through which information is applied and behavior takes place. Beyond the more formal aspects (e.g., planning procedures), they structure how key processes actually work. Among such tools are the creation of specialized coordinator roles, the clear assignment of responsibilities in the decision processes, and the provision of specific channels for preparing decisions such as committees, task forces, study groups, business teams, and so forth.

Intensity of communication may be employed for the purpose of managerial governance. The intensity of communication between a focal subsidiary and the rest of the corporation can be treated as a positive function of the frequency, informality, openness, and density of communications between the subsidiary, the other units, and the head office. Highly frequent inter-unit communications help facilitate the diffusion of innovations across multinational subsidiaries. More intense communication patterns create higher information-processing capacity; these patterns become especially desirable in contexts where such capacities are necessary. Openness in the parent–subsidiary relationship is even more beneficial in the case of subunits that use differentiation strategies rather than harvest or cost-leadership business strategies. Effectiveness at adapting to environmental uncertainty requires unstructured decision-making processes involving highly open communication patterns. Overall, frequency, informality, openness, and density of communications between a focal subsidiary and the rest of the corporation should be higher for those subunits which play a greater part in global integration.

Informal interactions such as corporate socialization of subsidiary managers can be applied as an effective tool for managerial governance as well. This is defined as the processes through which subsidiary managers' values and norms become aligned with those of the parent corporation. Socialization of managers can be a powerful mechanism for building identification with and commitment to the organization as a whole, as distinct from the immediate subunit in which the manager is operating. Some of the key processes through which such socialization occurs are job rotation across foreign subsidiaries and management development programs involving participants from several subunits. Global corporate socialization of a subsidiary's top management team should vary across subsidiary strategic roles. Using Gupta and Govindarajan's (1991) scheme, socialization should be high for integrated players, medium for global innovators and implementers, and low for local innovators.

Dispatching expatriates to foreign subsidiaries and manipulating the ratio of expatriates in the top management team of subsidiaries are also important for maintaining global integration. Host country nationals are generally more familiar with the local environment, develop stronger rapport with local managers, and have a stronger identification with and commitment to the local subsidiary than to the parent MNC. Cognitively, host country nationals are likely to have a more nearly comprehensive understanding of the local sociocultural, political, and economic environments. By contrast, expatriate managers are likely to have a more nearly comprehensive understanding of the MNC's overall global strategy. Motivationally, the local commitment of host country nationals results from the fact that, in most cases, their career progression outside of the local subsidiary and into the hierarchy of the parent corporation tends to be a rarity. Expatriate managers do not operate under such a constraint. Therefore, the ratio of expatriates as a percentage of the top management team should be higher for those subsidiaries which play a bigger role in the MNC's global integration.

Entry mode selection is a fundamental investment strategy which affects the MNC's ability to control local operations and integrate these businesses into its global network during subsequent operational stages. Other things being equal, the umbrella investment, wholly-owned subsidiary, and dominant joint-venture modes enable the MNC to maintain greater control and integration than minority joint-venture or other cooperative arrangements in which the MNC is a minority owner. Among other entry modes, franchising and build–operate–transfer modes enable the MNC to control foreign operations more effectively than in licensing and leasing. Therefore, MNCs should align their entry mode selection with their needs for organizational control and global integration. In the case of joint ventures, the equity distribution between partners can make substantial differences in control and integration. Majority equity ownership helps the MNC not only to protect its proprietary knowledge and control joint-venture activities but also to mitigate the partner firm's possible opportunism while strategically orienting the joint venture to comply with the MNC's global mission.

A company embarks on a global strategy when it starts to locate manufacturing and other value-creation activities in the lowest-cost global location to increase efficiency, quality, and innovation. In seeking to obtain gains from global learning, a company must cope with greater coordination and integration problems. It has to find a structure that can coordinate resource transfers between corporate headquarters and foreign divisions while providing the centralized control that a global strategy requires. The answer for many companies is a global product group structure.

In this structure, a product group headquarters (similar to an SBU headquarters) is created to coordinate the activities of the domestic and foreign divisions within the product group. Product group managers in the home country are responsible for organizing all aspects of value creation on a global basis. The product group structure allows managers to decide how to best pursue a global strategy. For example, they decide which value-creation activities, such as manufacturing or product design, should be performed in which country to increase efficiency. Increasingly, US and Japanese companies are moving manufacturing to low-cost countries like China but establishing product design centers in Europe or the United States to take advantage of foreign skills and capabilities.

The main failing of the global product group structure is that while it allows a company to achieve superior efficiency and quality, it is weak when it comes to customer responsiveness because the focus is still on centralized control. Moreover, this structure makes it difficult for the different product groups to trade information and knowledge and thus obtain the benefits of cooperation. Sometimes the potential gains from sharing products, marketing, or research and development knowledge between product groups are very high, but when a company lacks a structure that can coordinate the group's activities, these gains cannot be achieved.

Recently, more companies are adopting global matrix structures which allow them to simultaneously reduce costs by increasing efficiency and differentiate their activities through superior innovation and customer responsiveness. On the vertical axis, instead of functions are product groups which provide specialist services such as R&D, product design, and marketing information to foreign divisions or SBUs. For example, they might be petroleum, plastics, drug, or fertilizer product groups. On the horizontal axis are the company's foreign divisions or SBUs, in the various countries or world regions in which they operate. Managers in the subsidiaries control foreign operations and report back to divisional personnel. They are also responsible, together with divisional personnel, for developing control and reward systems that promote the sharing of marketing or research and development information to achieve gains from synergies.

This structure both provides a great deal of local flexibility and gives divisional personnel at headquarters considerable access to information about local affairs. Additionally, the matrix form allows knowledge and experience to be transferred among geographic regions and divisions. Since it offers many opportunities for face-to-face contact between domestic and foreign managers, the matrix structure facilitates the transmission of company norms and values and hence the development of a global corporate culture. This is especially important for an international company, where lines of communication are longer and information is subject to distortion.

Corporate culture sets the moral tone for an organization. Corporate culture is defined as the statements, visions, customs, slogans, values, role models, and social rituals that are unique to, and used by, a focal organization to resist corrupt practices. The cornerstone of an organizational architecture combating corruption is the detailed anti-corruption statement, which guides managers in how to make day-to-day decisions. Such statements should be instrumental rather than principled in tone. They can suggest that there is no inconsistency between profitability and refusal to bribe, or they can state that the organization will not compete for business where bribery is a requirement. Organizations should have detailed procedures for disseminating their anti-corruption statements to employees in all hierarchical levels, subunits, and locations. An effective architecture for resisting illicit conduct necessitates a multifaceted anti-corruption effort that promotes a compliance culture within the entire organization.

Visions and commitments from leadership (e.g., board of directors, CEO, general counsel, CFO, chief internal auditing, regional or country manager) play a significant role in enhancing managerial governance for global operations. Ethical leadership sets the moral standards for an organization by focusing on the integrity of common purpose. These leaders should be champions and role models in efforts to improve managerial governance and ethics in global activities. Role models are important in setting a positive ethical climate because humans as social beings are influenced by other humans. Without sufficient commitment from the leadership, it is impossible for an organization to position itself as a good citizen that is concerned with honest business practices and the need to maintain a level playing field in domestic or global markets. Identifying corruption by these leaders as a threat to an organization's long-term health and growth serves important strategic interests. An organization should also take reasonable measures to communicate its anti-corruption culture and values in an open environment to encourage participation and feedback. Employees should be informed to whom they should report violations or ask questions.

Global managerial governance is incomplete unless an MNC has established and implemented conduct code and ethics programs for all global employees, together constituting an effective managerial governance that minimizes corporate illegalities. This control makes information and expectations about legal and ethical behaviors clear, increases the likelihood of detection, assures the punishment of transgressions, rewards desired behaviors, and disciplines those who engage in illegal behavior. This system begins with written commitments in areas of business ethics that are relevant to the firm's activities – that is, a code of corporate conduct that provides a set of legal and ethical guidelines for employees to follow. Such codes are voluntary expressions of commitment, made to influence or control business behavior for the benefit of the firm itself and the communities in which it operates. The codes seek to heighten employees' awareness of corporate policy and enlist their support in the fight against corrupt acts. They also draw a distinction between the acceptable quid pro quo and networking that are necessary to develop business relationships and avoid corrupt practices. Codes can contain general precepts and mandate specific practices, providing clearly stated provisions that deal with legalities and ethical concerns, and detail sanctions and enforcement including the methods of investigation and detection.

Compliance programs (e.g., training, due diligence, formalized procedures) ostensibly bring the behavior of organization members into conformity with a shared ethical standard. They constitute an organizational control system that encourages shared ethical aspirations and compliance with rules. Enhancing managerial governance within an MNC requires legal and ethics training at every level of an organization. Regular ethics and compliance training programs should be held for all company employees, including board members and senior management officials. It may also be necessary to educate overseas employees about host country's requirements for legitimate behavior and practices. Undertaking due diligence is vital to ensure that managerial governance processes are efficient and effective. Due diligence reviews are also important for preventing potential harm to the organization's reputation. It is important not to delegate substantial discretionary authority to individuals or subunits that the organization knows (through the exercise of due diligence) have a propensity to engage in wrongful acts. Additional ethical practices include formalized procedures or mechanisms for evaluating ethical and legal performance and for rewarding or punishing behavior. Examples include establishing a system for auditing and reporting legal–ethical violations, a formal ethics department for initiating, coordinating, and supervising an organization's anti-corruption process, and a cross-functional committee for setting and assessing ethics policies and procedures. Motivating employees to behave legally and ethically can be prompted by the incorporation of ethics into selection, performance appraisal, discipline, and job analysis procedures.

CASE EXAMPLE 4.1: PARENT AND SUBSIDIARY BOARDS AT VOLKSWAGEN

Volkswagen AG CEO Bernd Pischetsrieder got an earful last week from worried VW dealers in the United States. But VW's group boss also brought word of change on the way for the struggling US sales arm during a two-hour meeting with dealers. Pischetsrieder met with the brand's National Dealer Advisory Council on October 11, 2004 in Los Angeles. He announced changes that would include a new Volkswagen of America Inc. CEO to replace Gerd Klauss, who retires December 31, 2004 and a revamped US board of directors less dominated by German executives.

US dealers long have complained about product decisions made at VW's Wolfsburg, Germany, headquarters. Lately they have been up in arms about poor quality too. "We have to have quality products," says Al Gossett of Gossett Motor Cars, a VW dealer in Memphis, Tennessee, and a member of the Volkswagen National Dealer Council. "The bacon there has not been delivered, and it has to be. Without product quality, we get killed." The VW dealers told Pischetsrieder that VW must improve product quality, shorten product life cycles, and maintain a strong presence in the $16,000–$18,000 price segment. Dealers are worried that VW's recent trend toward moving its models more upscale will leave the heart of the market uncovered.

Over the years, Volkswagen of America has had to lobby hard for everything from more automatic transmissions to better cup-holders. This year dealers demanded better incentives to help them move aging products and keep pace with competitors' deals. The automaker finally succumbed to zero percent financing last spring and offered some competitive lease deals. However, sales continued to slide in 2004. VW sales of 195,530 through September in 2004 were off 15.7 percent from the year-ago period. Audi sales of 57,299 for the first nine months were down 9.9 percent.

Dealers say the problem is that VW's German executives do not always understand or recognize US tastes and are not savvy enough about US market conditions. But VW is shaking things up. The company will add four US executives to its North American executive board to try to give the US sales arm more clout in Wolfsburg. Klauss, Volkswagen of America's top executive since 1999, has been the lone US executive with a seat on the subsidiary's board of directors. The 59-year-old German will be replaced as CEO by Frank Witter, 45, Volkswagen of America's CFO. Witter and four other US Volkswagen executives will become board members. They will join three executives from the parent company on the Volkswagen of America board. "Volkswagen of America will have more influence, we believe, with this structure," says Tony Fouladpour, a Volkswagen of America spokesman. "You now have all the key players on the board of directors." Other Volkswagen of America executives joining the board are Len Hunt, VW brand chief; Axel Mees, head of the Audi brand; Kevin Kelly, chief of Volkswagen Credit and Audi Financial Services; and vice president Volker Steinwascher.

They will join Jens Neumann, a Volkswagen AG management board member in charge of North American strategy; George Flandorfer, VW sales chief; and Ralph Weyler, an Audi AG management board member in charge of sales. Witter joined Volkswagen of America in 1998 as treasurer for the US and Canada operations. He left the company for SAirGroup in Zurich, Switzerland, from July 2001 to May 2002, when he rejoined Volkswagen of America.

Volkswagen of America will launch a new convertible in 2006 based on the Concept C show car. Also on the drawing board for Volkswagen of America, but not yet approved, are an SUV smaller and less expensive than the Touareg and a seven-seat SUV similar in size to next year's Audi Q7. The still-unnamed front-wheel-drive convertible will have a retractable folding hard top, similar to those on expensive roadsters such as the Mercedes-Benz SLK. VW's car will be positioned between the upscale Phaeton and the mid-sized Passat sedan. VW wants to sell the car in the $30,000 range in the United States. But final pricing is subject to the relationship between the dollar and the euro.

At the parent level, the corporate board is undergoing change as well. The appointment to the Volkswagen corporate board in October 2004 of Wolfgang Bernhard (former chief operating officer at Chrysler) has signaled that the car-maker is determined to cut costs and improve efficiency. The announcement came as GM said it may slash up to one-sixth of its European workforce. Shares in Europe's largest automaker jumped more than 6 percent with the news, and the appoint-ment prompted analysts to up their ratings for the company. Bernhard is expected to take control of the VW division by 2006. That would put him in charge of not only the eponymous badge, but also of Skoda, Bentley, and Bugatti. Placing a cost slasher atop two of the company's three luxury units – Lamborghini falls under the Audi division – indicates Pischetsrieder may be ready to unravel some of the high-end projects created by his predecessor, Ferdinand Piech.

Pointing to Bernhard's background in cost cutting and efficiency improve-ment, Pieper said the manager is "exactly what VW needs." Bernhard faces a corporate culture that has little in common with Chrysler, where he slashed more than 20,000 jobs and closed plants. The manager and VW are "a good fit on paper," Pieper said, but he cautioned that Wolfsburg is not Detroit. Bernhard's ability to institute cuts at Chrysler may not translate to this side of the Atlantic. One of the biggest obstacles to serious restructuring at VW is the right of the state of Lower Saxony to block decisions. The state, which is the largest shareholder in VW, has a stake of just over 20 percent and controls 20 percent of voting rights; all big decisions require more than 80 percent of votes.

The European Union is examining the legality of the investor rules, but this "golden share" has provided state politicians and their proxies with seats on the supervisory board, half of which are controlled by labor representatives. German politicians, including former supervisory board member and current German Chancellor Gerhard Schroeder, have promised to fight to retain the golden share. The composition of the board has made the subject of job cuts anathema at VW:

workers' representatives are likely never to approve them. As for state officials, sacking voters is political suicide. VW management is asking for a wage freeze over the next two years, but most analysts say the company is overstaffed. While outright redundancies are a non-starter, the company has threatened to shift up to 5000 workers into a subsidiary, where they will receive less pay.

Representatives from IG Metal are ignoring the pressure. The union is demanding a pay hike of 4 percent, above most wage agreements in Germany this year, and pushing for job guarantees for the 103,000 workers at plants in western Germany. VW's selection of a manager who has tangled with unions in the past spells more confrontation in the German car industry. Not only is the European giant demanding a wage freeze, General Motors says it may also axe 10,000 or more workers in Europe. The world's largest carmaker has been losing money in Europe for years, and it is thus believed to be finalizing plans for cost cuts.

GM chief executive Rick Wagoner told the magazine *Stern* that the Adam Opel factory in Russelsheim is not competitive when measured on productivity. Workers' representatives are pushing for an extraordinary meeting of the company's supervisory board. Opel has long been a sore spot for GM. The German company has often been at loggerheads with Detroit, and after years of complaining about American meddling, a German was assigned to run the company. But cost-cutting steps have failed to improve results; the German unit is expected to report a loss.

(Sources: Anonymous (2004). Volkswagen new cost-cutter and unions rev up for battle. *Knight Ridder Tribune Business News*, October 10: 1; Anonymous (2004). Volkswagen gives US arm more clout. *Automotive News*, October 18, **79**(6117): 3; Anonymous (2004). Former Chrysler maverick to become chairman at Volkswagen. *Knight Ridder Tribune Business News*, October 7: 1.)

REFERENCES AND FURTHER READING

Bartlett, C.A. and Ghoshal, S. (1989). *Managing across Borders*. Boston, MA: Harvard Business School Press.

Bjoorkman, I. (1994). Managing Swedish and Finish multinational corporations: The role of the board of directors in French and Norwegian subsidiaries. *International Business Review*, **3**(1): 47–59.

Blumberg, P.I. (1993). *The Multinational Challenge to Corporate Law: The Search for a New Corporate Personality*. New York: Oxford University Press.

Doz, Y.L., Bartlett, C.A., and Prahalad, C.K. (1981). Global competitive pressures and host country demands: Managing tensions in MNCs. *California Management Review*, **23**(3): 63–74.

Doz, Y.L. and Prahalad, C.K. (1980). How MNCs cope with host government intervention. *Harvard Business Review*, **58**(2): 149–57.

Ellstrand, A.E., Tihanyi, L., and Johnson, J.L. (2002). Board structure and international political risk. *Academy of Management Journal*, **45**: 769–77.

Gupta, A.K. and Govindarajan, V. (1991). Knowledge flows and the structure of control within multinational corporations. *Academy of Management Review*, **16**(4): 768–92.

Hedlund, G. (1980). The role of foreign subsidiaries in strategic decision making in Swedish multinational corporations. *Strategic Management Journal*, **1**(1): 23–36.

Jarillo, J.C. and Martinez, J.I. (1990). Different roles for subsidiaries: The case of multinational corporations in Spain. *Strategic Management Journal*, **11**(7): 501–12.

Johnson, S.C. and Thomson, R.M. (1974). An active role for outside directors of foreign subsidiaries. *Harvard Business Review*, **52**(5): 13–14.

Kim, K. and Limpaphayom, P. (1998). A test of the two-tier corporate governance structure: The case of Japanese keiretsu. *Journal of Financial Research*, **21**(1): 37–52.

Kriger, M.P. (1988). The increasing role of subsidiary boards in MNCs: An empirical study. *Strategic Management Journal*, **9**: 347–60.

Kriger, M.P. (1991). The importance of the role of subsidiary boards in MNCs: Comparative parent and subsidiary perceptions. *Management International Review*, **31**(4): 317–22.

Kriger, M.P. and Rich, P.J.J. (1987). Strategic governance: Why and how MNCs are using boards of directors in foreign subsidiaries. *Columbia Journal of World Business*, Winter: 39–45.

Leksell, L. and Lindgren, U. (1982). The board of directors in foreign subsidiaries. *Journal of International Business Studies*, **13**(2): 27–38.

Nohria, N. and Ghoshal, S. (1994). Differentiated fit and shared values: Alternatives for managing headquarters–subsidiary relations. *Strategic Management Journal*, **15**: 491–502.

Porter, M.E. (1986). Competition in global industries: A conceptual framework. In M.E. Porter (ed.), *Competition in Global Industries*, pp. 15–60. Boston, MA: Harvard Business School Press.

Poynter, T.A. and White, R.E. (1985). The strategies of foreign subsidiaries: Responses to organizational slack. *International Studies of Management and Organization*, **14**(4): 91–106.

Saravanamuthu, K. and Tinker, T. (2003). Politics of managing: The dialectic of control. *Accounting, Organizations and Society*, **28**(1): 37–54.

Stopford, J.M. and Wells, L.T. (1972). *Managing the Multinational Enterprise*. New York: Basic Books.

Strikwerda, J. (2003). An entrepreneurial model of corporate governance: Developing powers to subsidiary boards. *Corporate Governance*, **3**(2): 38–57.

Tashakori, A. and Boulton, W. (1982). A look at the board 's role in planning. *Journal of Business Strategy*, **3**(1): 64–70.

Tricker, R.I. (1994). *International Corporate Governance*. New Jersey: Prentice Hall.

Zahra, S.A. and Pearce, J.A. (1989). Boards of directors and corporate financial performance: A review and integrative model. *Journal of Management*, **15**: 291–334.

Zajac, E.J. (1988). Interlocking directorates as an interorganizational strategy: A test of critical assumptions. *Academy of Management Journal*, **31**: 428–38.

Chapter 5

Corporate Governance and Accountability in MNCs

EXECUTIVE SUMMARY

Corporate governance is fundamentally supported by corporate accountability. Governance cannot go far unless accountability is in place. Corporate accountability helps investors and managers to identify promising investment opportunities, improve corporate control mechanisms that discipline managers to direct resources toward projects identified as good and away from projects identified as bad, and reduce asymmetries among investors and between investors and other stakeholders. Superior accountability functions as a credible information variable that supports the existence of enforceable contracts, such as compensation contracts with payoffs to managers contingent on realized measures of performance, the monitoring of managers by boards of directors and outside investors and regulators, and the exercise of investor rights granted by existing securities laws. This chapter conceptualizes corporate accountability as the construct encompassing two interrelated components: financial reporting accountability and governance system transparency.

   This chapter explains why international expansion of companies makes corporate accountability more difficult on the one hand and yet more important on the other. In contrast with domestic firms, MNCs encounter heterogeneous accounting, disclosure and auditing standards when they operate in different countries, not to mention their extremely sophisticated economic activities in investments, production, financing, risk management, and beyond. At the same time, MNCs face a much larger number of demanding stakeholders in various countries who intend to keep managers and directors accountable. Specifically, Section 5.1 discusses the importance of and approaches to corporate accountability for MNCs. Section 5.2 spells out the interrelationships between corporate governance and corporate accountability. In particular, it details how governance and accountability mutually reinforce each other for firms active in international business activities. Section 5.3 then articulates the first component of accountability – financial reporting accountability with a particular emphasis on how an MNC's financial reporting accountability is influenced by its globalization attributes and how it can improve financial accountability in an effective way. The following section illustrates the second component of accountability – governance system transparency with a focus on how governance transparency should be properly aligned with an MNC's global competition and strategies and on how MNCs can strengthen governance system transparency to meet the needs of global stakeholders. This chapter ends with a tale of corporate accountability problems or practices in several companies in Japan, North America, and Europe.

5.1 Corporate Accountability in MNCs

Corporate accountability is the extent to which a company is transparent in its corporate activities and responsive to those it serves. Broadly, corporate accountability consists of: (i) financial reporting accountability and (ii) governance system transparency. Accountability is essentially a matter of disclosure, transparency, and of explaining corporate policies and actions to those to whom the company is beholden (Shearer, 2002; Wild, 1994). A firm should be accountable not only to shareholders but also to all major stakeholders such as regulators, customers, employees, creditors, suppliers, and the local community (Shearer, 2002). A company functions most effectively when all these stakeholders – providers of capital, financing, skills, labor, services, and context – work together toward the long-term good of the undertaking. A central requirement for corporate accountability is the firm's ability to signal or provide relevant information quickly, accurately, and effectively to its shareholders, stakeholders, or other principal parties such as regulators who motivate and constrain the firm to behave in both the principals' and society's best interests.

Transparency about a company's governance policies is a critical aspect of corporate accountability. As long as investors, shareholders, and other stakeholders have clear and accessible information about these policies, the market does the rest, assigning appropriate risk premiums to companies that have too few independent directors or an overly aggressive compensation policy; it can also cut the cost of capital for companies that adhere to conservative accounting policies (Saravanamuthu and Tinker, 2003). Some recent practices, such as dramatically gearing up the balance sheet, switching the portfolio of assets from low to high risk, or engaging in off-balance sheet financial transactions that inherently alter the volatility of the business and increase its exposure to uncertainty, severely impair corporate accountability.

Compared to domestic firms, MNC corporate accountability is even more important and more complex. MNCs serve a larger number of stakeholders in numerous countries whose accounting systems are typically varied. A particular disclosure practice may comply with one country's financial reporting standards but not with another's. In general, a country's accounting system is shaped by institutions (economic system, legal system, taxation system, and professional system), societal culture, and external relations. These factors jointly determine a national accounting framework that includes accounting objectives, regulation mode, and regulation strictness; this framework in turn affects firm decisions on a variety of issues such as R&D expenditures, fixed assets, inventory valuation, accounting for income taxes, and foreign currency translation. The more diverse global stakeholders a firm has, the greater the differences in standards of corporate accountability. Without international harmonization of corporate accountability practices, conflicts and incompatibility of financial information from different countries will arise. In addition, global expansion makes it more difficult to offer transparent information about contingent liabilities and off-balance sheet arrangements, especially for the consolidation of entities that facilitate such arrangements.

Moreover, each MNC must consolidate its worldwide units' financial statements into a single currency. Foreign currency translation is necessary not only for reporting and disclosure purposes but also to achieve corporate governance objectives. Without foreign currency translation, MNC headquarters cannot properly plan, evaluate, integrate, and control overseas activities that should be coordinated within the network. The expanded scale of international investment activities also necessitates foreign currency translation, particularly when a subsidiary wishes to list its shares on a foreign stock exchange, contemplates a foreign acquisition or joint venture, or wants to communicate its operating results and financial position to its foreign shareholders or other stakeholders. Since countries have different financial statement consolidation requirements (for instance, it has long been a common practice in the Netherlands, the UK and the US, while it is a relatively recent phenomenon in other European and Asian countries), foreign currency translation methods vary across nations, further complicating accountability for firms engaging in multiple global operations.

Proper accountability calls for both voluntary and mandatory disclosure, bound by both competitive and legal constraints. Such accountability in the long run helps to create competitive advantages in the marketplace. Superior accountability enables the firm to receive a better rating or evaluation by certain market intermediaries who disseminate this information to the market, thus improving the firm's trustworthiness, credibility, and reputation. Barney and Hansen (1994) suggest that trustworthiness as perceived by market intermediaries is a critical source of competitive advantage, especially in a volatile and complex market. Voluntary transparency is especially valuable; it involves preparing, auditing, and disclosing information using high-quality standards of accounting, financial and non-financial disclosure. Moreover, the firm should have an annual independent audit conducted in order to provide an external and objective assurance on the accuracy and reliability of the financial statements the firm has prepared. Because this sort of voluntary transparency is not always present, mandatory transparency is imperative. Strict legal requirements for mandatory transparency are essential to a well-developed stock, especially to protect minority shareholder rights against insider self-dealing; it also provides shareholders with good information about the value of the firm's business.

To achieve all of the above, an MNC must have a harmonized accounting system throughout the firm. Establishing one comprehensive international accounting standard is beyond the scope of MNCs (key players in setting international accounting standards include the International Accounting Standards Committee, International Organization of Securities Commissions, International Federation of Accountants, and International Standards of Accounting and Reporting), but building a harmonized accounting system within the MNC is the responsibility of the firm itself. The MNC must therefore set a globally harmonized accounting information reporting system, adopt consistent company-wide accounting standards, and use parent-designed software to report financial and non-financial information. Every foreign subsidiary must then follow the aforementioned guidelines in order to achieve firm-wide accountability.

5.2 The Link between Governance and Accountability in MNCs

Corporate governance and corporate accountability are mutually facilitative, inclusive, and interdependent. Corporate governance involves corporate fairness, transparency, and accountability. Thus, accountability is both a key element of as well as a requirement for corporate governance, fortifying it by providing a transparent template governing critical decision making, procedures, and activities. Because corporate directors and executives are often perceived as being accountable for corporate performance and for firms' legal and ethical behavior, their accountability is also an integral part of corporate governance. Furthermore, boards of directors represent shareholders' interests and as such monitor and control the opportunistic behavior of managers; thus in the presence of superior accountability, agency costs can be reduced. All told, boardroom accountability spurs shareholder confidence and executive-room accountability bolsters the confidence of directors and other stakeholders in their managers.

Accountability improves governance not only by improving market functions as noted earlier but also by reducing monitoring costs. Monitoring the behavior of an MNC's stewards is a major aspect of governance and governance effectiveness is essentially a positive function of monitoring effectiveness. With high accountability, the principals – directors, shareholders, and other stakeholders – will find it easier, more effective, and less expensive to monitor and evaluate agent behavior for opportunism. When the executive room is accountable and transparent, principals are better able to tell if agents are making and executing strategic decisions in the principals' best interests; they can also gauge agent performance more accurately and motivate them to direct the company in the way the principals desire. Thus, high accountability reduces the monitoring, directing, and controlling costs of keeping agent behavior consistent with the principals' interests.

Accountability in an MNC's globally dispersed subunits also reinforces overall governance in several ways. First, an MNC as a whole cannot be accountable if its subunits are not accountable. Improving an MNC's overall accountability requires that every subunit has transparent processes for decision making, financial reporting, independent auditing, and internal control. Second, subunit accountability promotes information sharing and communication within an MNC. Effective governance is unlikely if an MNC cannot establish effective information-sharing and communication systems. Corporate governance needs to aggregate both accounting and strategic data for the purpose of organizational control. Thus, transparency also forces differences between subunits and headquarters and among subunits to be resolved on the basis of improved problem definition rather than smoothed over. Third, subunit accountability is a prerequisite for any MNC to build and execute "global wheels" such as corporate culture, global vision, corporate R&D, global branding, code of conduct, and business ethics (Nohria and Ghoshal, 1994). Although such subunits are legally and financially independent – hence responsible for their own behavior and performance – the parent company needs to establish such common tenets to protect its global reputation and foster global integration and control. Subunit accountability also helps headquarters balance global control with national responsiveness, as detailed in Chapter 4. Finally, because subunit CEO remuneration is partly decided by headquarters, subunit account-ability enables the parent company to more effectively evaluate and reward subunit management performance.

Effective governance further promotes accountability. An effective market-based governance system motivates managers to productively, transparently, and efficiently fulfill the tasks and roles that directors set. Superior working relationships between directors and managers, owners and directors, and shareholders and stakeholders reduce the managerial hazards and organizational complexities inherent in global management (Sanders and Carpenter, 1998). This reduction facilitates managerial control and the decision-making process when dealing with various stakeholders, ultimately bolstering corporate accountability. Second, when culture-based govern-ance is effective, accountability is likely to be more entrenched and more sustainable. Culture is what determines how people behave when they are not being watched. If an MNC successfully instills its corporate governance structure with the right culture, various strategic decisions across the entire company – from stock options and risk management tools to the board of directors composition and the decentralization of decision-making powers – will become more transparent, consistent, justified, and accessible to the organization's inside members and outside stakeholders. Third, an effective discipline-based governance system is likely to result in better-behaved agents. For instance, penalties can effectively stimulate more effort from management because of "loss aversion" (Willman *et al.*, 2002). Such penalties should be tied to transparency and accountability and specified in manager remuneration contracts so that managers will be more committed to enhancing accountability.

In sum, corporate accountability is becoming a critical part of corporate governance. Thus, it is not surprising that new laws and roles arise to address this issue. For instance, the Public Company Accounting Reform and Investor Protection Act of 2002 (Public Law 107–240), better known as the Sarbanes–Oxley Act in the US and other regula-tory changes now require much greater accountability for the boards of for-profit, publicly traded companies. While these standards do not yet fully apply to the boards of not-for-profit healthcare organizations, they are steadily and inexorably migrating into our world. The Internal Revenue Service (IRS) is also increasing its scrutiny of boards of not-for-profit, tax-exempt organizations through review of excess benefit trans-actions and is tending more often to hold board members personally and financially responsible for them. The IRS is also aggressively heightening its scrutiny of board overseeing of compensation of the CEO. Furthermore, it has begun to express interest in board composition in terms of board member independence and freedom from conflicts of interest. At the same time, the New York Stock Exchange (NYSE) has reviewed its corporate governance listings standards with the goal of enhancing the accountability, integrity, and transparency of listed companies. New rules mandate shareholder approval of stock option plans in which officers and directors participate, narrow the definition of independence, require approval by the audit committee of related party transactions and require market notification of going concern qualifications in audit opinions. Like other exchanges, the NYSE has permitted listed non-US companies to follow home country practices with respect to a number of corporate governance matters (based on a submission of an opinion of local counsel). While the new standards do not apply to such companies, they would be required to disclose the significant ways in which their corporate governance practices differ from the NYSE standards.

From the internal lens, corporate accountability is also crucial to overall corporate governance. Within a multinational organization, effective corporate governance comes down to the issue of accountability as well. It is a factor influenced by the leadership and composition of the board, by the means of compensating the directors, and by the process of communications with shareholders. Accountability starts with competent directors. The trend in the corporate governance movement is for greater influence from well-informed, independent directors. Open, honest, and frequent communication is vital to effective corporate governance. Achieving accountability leads to outside directors who are active and informed, frequent communication with shareholders, and compensation tied to performance.

Figure 5.1 schematically highlights an integrated conceptual model that contains various elements and arguments discussed above.

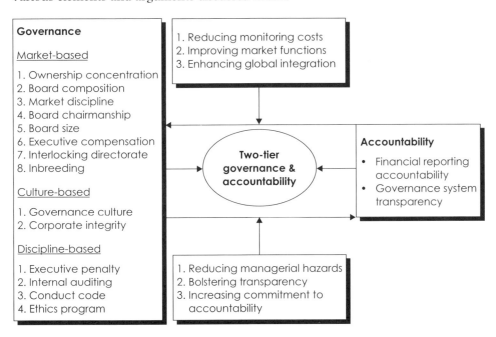

Figure 5.1 A conceptual model of corporate governance and accountability in MNCs

5.3 Financial Reporting Accountability and International Expansion

The very first impact of international expansion on corporate accountability is global reporting and disclosure of financial and non-financial information to various stakeholders both at home and abroad. As globalization increases, MNCs face an increasing variance in accounting and reporting standards across the countries in which they invest and operate. Consequently, MNCs face increasing challenges in global reporting and accountability as their international expansion increases. The unprecedented explosion of modern and efficient telecommunication and transportation infrastructures are making it easy to engage in global financial transactions. Specifically, the use of virtual stock markets that are interconnected via real-time electronic media (e.g., electronic communication networks) has greatly facilitated the exchange of securities among buyers and sellers. Corporations now could secure capital from outside their own borders. Multinationals who wish to have access to the capital markets in different countries must comply with the reporting and listing requirements of each jurisdiction. For listing in the US, for example, the Securities and Exchange Commission (SEC) is now mandating that multinationals publish their annual reports, executive compensation, and other financial and non-financial disclosures on the web – what has been referred to as the electronic data gathering, analysis and retrieval (EDGAR) system. Foreign firms would also have to satisfy the new SEC requirements of accelerated reporting schedule that are probably motivated by the need to reduce the flexibility and the time of financial statements' manipulation. Under the new regulations, the disclosure of the 10-K reports should be within 60 days of year end (in lieu of 90 days) and the 10-K report should be within 35 days of quarter end (in lieu of 45 days), thus adding to the pressure of foreign firms to satisfy both domestic and international reporting requirements.

Regulatory hurdles may often be a deterrent for cross-border listings. In particular, it is expensive and time consuming for many firms to convert their local accounting standards or to reconcile their financial reporting with those of another country. As an example, multinationals who wish to be listed in US exchanges should prepare audited financial reports that predominantly conform to the US generally accepted accounting principles (GAAP) standards or, at the very least, provide an audited reconciliation to US GAAP. Basically, US GAAP standards are akin to prescriptive specifications that describe the means to achieve an end result through the utilization of detailed and specific rules. As such, the US GAAP tends to have complex and detailed accounting compliance rules with relatively limited room for individual judgment and reporting flexibility, although it does allow the utilization of different depreciation schedules for long-term fixed assets, inventory reporting (FIFO and LIFO), and various assumptions for estimating the cost of employees' future benefits. The firms that fail to comply with the "letter of the law" would be in violation of the Financial Accounting Standards Board (FASB) regulations. Conversely, the International Financial Reporting Standards (IFRS), promulgated by the International Accounting Standards Board (IASB), are equivalent to performance-based specifications that specify the end result with a relatively significant degree of financial reporting discretion on the means by which the end result is achieved. As such, IFRS standards tend to rely on relatively broader concepts and principles than their counterpart US GAAP accounting standards. The firms that fail to comply with the "spirit" or "intent" of the IASB would be in violation of IFRS standards. An illustrative example pertains to lease accounting. US GAAP recognizes capital lease if more than 75 percent of the estimated economic life is assumed by the lessee and if the start of the lease does not fall in the last 25 percent portion of the total economic life of the leased property, along with other requirements. Conversely, the IFRS leaves it to the discretion of the managers and the auditors to decide whether or not the relevant risks and rewards incident to ownership have indeed substantially taken place to warrant the use of a capital lease. The development of a global and standardized financial framework of accounting standards would facilitate cross-border financial transactions and minimize their costs. The EU legislation now requires all companies wishing to be listed in European exchanges to adopt the IASB promulgated standards in their financial reporting by the year 2005.

Which accounting standard a geographically diversified MNC follows is central to corporate accountability because varying standards allow firms to manipulate financial statements like the balance sheet, income statement, and cash flow statement. Internally, the heterogeneity of applicable accounting, auditing, and tax rules may also hamper an MNC's ability to prepare the reliable and transparent financial information necessary for effective strategic analysis. To negate cross-country differences in accounting standards, the International Accounting Standards Committee (the most dominant player in setting harmonized global accounting standards, founded in 1973) has developed an array of international accounting standards (IAS), which are now widely recognized and accepted in both developing and developed countries. Some MNCs even use IAS at the corporate level, and others may use it as a benchmark against which to compare their home country accounting practices. MNCs that adopt more than one set of accounting standards (home country standards, host country standards, or IAS) must often issue a separate set of reports for each accounting standard; this often results in enormous reporting, documenting, and reconciliation costs as well as confusion to shareholders and other stakeholders, thus tempering transparency. Because of this, globalization often leads to pressure to use a consistent, harmonized, and globally accepted accounting and auditing system. As international expansion heightens, the use of IAS can help enhance information-reporting reliability, which in turn reduces risk for investors. Moreover, using IAS also helps reduce the costs of preparing financial statements and facilitates the task of investment analysts, investors, and others in assessing a business. This saves on both the time and money currently spent consolidating divergent financial information.

The inadequacy of financial reporting accountability arises due to several other factors in addition to the reporting standards. In many countries, including the US and the UK, recent problems have cast doubt on the accuracy of financial information given to boards and released to the markets as financial statements. Concerns about lack of integrity of the financial markets were reflected, for instance, in the record number of account restatements in the US during 2002. Criticism included internal and external audit procedures, accountancy standards, and the potential for conflict of interest on the part of both auditors and financial analysts who are employed by financial conglomerates. Rules covering whether external auditors should be restricted in their ability to perform non-audit work (such restrictions are already in force in Japan, the US, the Netherlands and France), arrangements covering activities by analysts, and arrangements covering company overseeing of external audits and the internal accounting system are also areas requiring attention.

At the firm level, MNCs vary in their experience in international expansion and such experience may encourage the harmonization of accounting standards, disclosure requirements, and auditing standards. One of the main causes of poor accountability in MNCs is the use of varying standards in accounting, disclosure, and auditing for subsidiaries in different countries. This creates too much leeway for manipulating accounting numbers and financial ratios and may even provide loopholes for firms to conduct off-balance sheet arrangements. While it is true that national accounting standards vary, an MNC's internal accounting, disclosure, and auditing norms and requirements should be the same for all subsidiaries to ensure the firm's overall accountability. In fact, highly accountable MNCs not only develop harmonized internal accounting and auditing standards but also use the international accounting standards stipulated by the IAS Committee to avoid national accounting practice differences that hinder corporate accountability and transparency. Comparable and transparent financial information enhances the reliability of foreign financial statements prepared by subsidiaries. It also helps in making informed decisions which, in turn, reduce risk for investors. In addition, employing harmonized internal standards reduces the cost of preparing financial statements and facilitates investment and risk analysis, thereby reducing the cost of maintaining accountability. With richer international experience, an MNC better comprehends the importance of intra-corporate harmonization of accounting and auditing standards and is also more likely to have policies in place that ensure compliance with such harmonization. Moreover, internationally experienced MNCs are more likely to adopt IAS because of their more widespread geographical expansion, longer history in competing in global markets, higher familiarity with and confidence in IAS, or greater need for intra-organizational reconciliation of information recording, dissemination, and sharing.

An MNC's financial reporting accountability depends in part on the effectiveness of its international accounting information system (IAIS). IAIS involves accounting-related reporting systems, data management, and communication among various units of the same MNC. Financial controllers at MNC headquarters find themselves under increasing pressure to bring information to the market more quickly and more transparently, deliver more extensive information than previously required, and proactively manage business risk at the corporate level. Globalization also necessitates implementing computerized accounting information systems with overseas affiliates to furnish the accounting information needed to plan, evaluate, and coordinate business activities around the world. These systems also augment the consolidation process at the home office. Many MNCs now use an intranet-based IAIS that links all financial units into a single, coherent system that provides managers and employees with real-time access to information and financial reports through the Internet. An effective IAIS provides an MNC with a competitive advantage arising from operating flexibility, transnational coordination, and strategic transparency in this increasingly competitive and complex global environment.

An accounting information system is a part of the information technology (IT) infrastructure that supports an MNC's global reporting, auditing, and control. Essentially, no MNC can go far in the process of improving corporate accountability (financial reporting and governance transparencies) unless it has successfully built and implemented IT governance. Therefore, IT systems have become the backbone of almost every organization. Good IT-based audits are essential to ensure proper controls, security, and efficient functioning. One company that achieved benefits by implementing IT governance is the Charles Schwab Corporation, one of the largest US financial services firms engaged, through its subsidiaries at home and abroad, in providing securities brokerage and related financial services for more than eight million active accounts. Charles Schwab's diverse and complex technology environment became even more complicated after it acquired US Trust and became a financial holding company. Because of the increased regulatory oversight resulting from this acquisition, senior management sought an improved IT governance control framework. The internal audit team recommended COBIT (control objectives for information and related technology) and mentioned that many regulatory bodies use COBIT during examinations, and therefore the framework would serve as a valuable tool to increase preparedness and facilitate communications. Schwab implemented COBIT, which helped establish an IT governance program, maintain consistency in risk management and IS audits, ensure that its audit approach was consistent with regulatory guidelines, enhance IT and business processes, and educate internal clients on risk and control concepts. As a consequence, implementing COBIT as part of its audit process has significantly enhanced Schwab's risk assessment process and has provided confidence that its audit strategy covers industry best practices and control objectives. The US Federal Reserve Board examiners have confirmed that Schwab's implementation of a COBIT-based audit approach is an appropriate method for assessing IT risks. Other benefits include increased client participation in audits and positive impacts on relationships with clients. Involved parties now believe the internal audit's approach is effective and a beneficial situation for all stakeholders.

According to DiPiazza and Eccles (2002), a good framework of financial reporting transparency is based on the three tiers of corporate reporting underpinned by the spirit of transparency, the culture of accountability, and the ethical base of integrity. This framework encompasses a set of principles-based (not rules-based), globally applicable, generally accepted accounting standards; industry-specific standards for measuring and reporting; and company-specific items such as strategy, plans, risk management practices, compensation policies, corporate governance, and other performance measures. In tier one, accounting standards vary widely from country to country. Even the best instances rely on historical cost models. Today's business reality also incorporates a market-to-market method, particularly in the case of certain complex financial transactions such as derivatives. If global GAAP ruled, comparative economic performance and investment choices could be more readily and equitably evaluated. Tier two extends beyond required GAAP financial reporting. Other financial and non-financial information about past performance and future prospects have value such as pro forma earnings, free cash flow, and information concerning intangibles, brands, customers, and innovation. How does the company's performance compare to its industry's peers along the lines of the unique critical values drivers in that industry? For instance, the airline industry values passenger load whereas the hotel industry values revenues-per-available-room figures. Finally, tier three concerns reporting of company-specific information such as management's views of the business and the competition, the company's strategies, their self-professed value drivers, their existing commitments to the various stakeholders, and value platform information (e.g., information on products, customers, people, innovation, supply chain, and corporate reputation).

Those MNCs that are particularly deficient in financial reporting accountability or sensitive to global financial reporting difficulties may need to formalize their organizational structures to improve such accountability. This structure is often manifested in the sponsoring committee, the implementation team, and the formal written plan. The success of an MNC's corporate accountability depends upon the endorsement and ongoing support of senior management and the board of directors. The sponsoring committee, composed of a company's CEO, CFO, in-house legal counsel, and the members of the audit committee of the board, is charged with defining the requirements for the implementation team. The sponsoring committee will also supervise the implementation team and be responsible for seeing that the team's duties and responsibilities are executed. The implementation team for improving corporate accountability is then responsible for developing the implementation plan and executing it. The team must generate all supporting documentation, including a new policy and procedure manual. The team must represent the company's disciplines and may include individuals such as the chief accounting officer, accounting department representatives, members of the internal audit department, the chief information officer, members of the information technology department, representatives of foreign subsidiaries, representatives of key business units, and members of the treasurer's department.

The next step to improving financial reporting accountability is documenting the financial cycles. Documenting financial cycles allows the company to assess the effectiveness of internal controls at an acceptable level of errors or omissions. The documentation process should reflect the internal control objectives and identify any internal control deficiencies that may exist. Three common methods of documenting the understanding of internal control are narratives, flowcharts, and internal control questionnaires. These can be used separately or in combination. While a narrative is a written description of a company's internal controls and financial cycles, a flowchart is a symbolic representation of a company's flow of documents and processes. The flowchart can be a better representation of document workflow and separation of duties as the documents and processes go through the financial cycle. Flowcharts have the advantage of being easily updated on a periodic or as-needed basis. An internal control questionnaire can be obtained from outside-audit firms. These questionnaires are very generic and can be difficult to customize if the questionnaire is not received in an electronic format. Software companies, such as SAP, PeopleSoft, and Oracle, have developed software evaluation tools that help users to automate the documentation of their internal control structure. Although technology has made the documentation process easy, a well-trained user of the software must be able to correctly understand the computer-generated documentation and evaluate its findings and conclusions.

The final step is to ensure that all transactions or global business activities are properly recorded and reported via the computer and manual processes so that all transactions reach an MNC's consolidated financial statements. If internal control deficiencies are identified, plans to remedy these internal controls should be documented and implemented as soon as possible. A company must take corrective actions to remedy an internal control deficiency as soon as it is noted. The corrected internal control procedure must be in place and in operation for a period of time prior to the reporting date for management to be able to evaluate the corrected control and conclude that the control is operating effectively as of the reporting date. A review of prior years' audit management letters should be conducted to ensure that all past identified weaknesses are addressed. A company may decide to upgrade existing computer systems, purchase a new accounting software system, or improve the integration of computer processes with the manual processes. In this process, it is important to have management's assessment of the effectiveness of the company's internal controls over financial reporting as of the end of the company's most recent fiscal year, including a statement as to whether the company's internal control over financial reporting is effective. The assessment must disclose any material weaknesses in the company's internal controls over financial reporting identified by management. Management is not permitted to conclude that the company's internal controls over financial reporting are effective if there are one or more material weaknesses in the company's internal controls over financial reporting.

5.4 Governance System Transparency and International Expansion

"Governance system transparency" (or governance transparency) is defined here as an MNC's ability to provide adequate and relevant information timely and openly about the firm's fundamental governance issues that highly impact the interests of the major stakeholders or other principal parties who have the rights to motivate and constrain the firm to behave within these parties' interests and in an acceptable way to the society. While financial reporting accountability captures the intensity, availability, and timeliness of financial disclosure, governance system transparency captures the intensity, availability, and openness of governance disclosures used by outside investors and other major stakeholders to hold officers and directors accountable. Governance transparency emphasizes those fundamental governance issues (e.g., executive compensation, auditing standards, investment decision procedures, corporate social responsibilities, rights and responsibilities of executives and directors, and compliance programs) that will considerably affect the interests of stakeholders who have the right to know how such governance issues affect their interests. Of course, the need for, and emphasis of, governance transparency varies according to different stakeholders and even different market positions of the firm. For instance, shareholders are more concerned with the dividend and investment policies, employees are more concerned with corporate integrity and organizational justice, and creditors (banks) are more concerned with internal auditing and financial control. Governance transparency is associated with the extent to which information disclosure will affect a firm's market position. On one hand, lenders prefer less information dissemination as long as it protects firms when in a weak competitive position. On the other hand, when the firm is in a strong market position, equity holders prefer more disclosure to maximize their profitability and capital gains. While the governing lenders discourage transparency, as this would endogenously undermine the value of their claims, firms governed by shareholders' interests prefer greater transparency, as information disclosure on average increases profitability as well as risk.

A critical part of governance transparency is accountability of non-financial but high-impacting material information regarding issues that concern shareholders, employees, and stakeholders. More specifically, such issues may involve an MNC's risk as well as any social, ethical or environmental policies, standards or programs that all constituents must follow. Such issues typically include major share ownership, voting rights, human resource management, labor relations, environmental concerns, health policies, safety issues, anti-corruption measures, integrity programs, transparency standards, and the like.

Governance transparency is interrelated with financial reporting accountability in such a fashion that strategic information would not be able to be transparent unless financial reporting accountability is already in place. In this sense, financial reporting accountability serves as a foundation that underpins and supports governance transparency. On the other hand, governance transparency accentuates corporate accountability much beyond financial disclosure transparency. To many stakeholders such as shareholders, employees, regulators and the community, knowing the rationale and expected gains or losses of those strategic decisions that influence the principal interests is often more important than financial figures. Thus, financial reporting accountability is a basic foundation for corporate accountability, but corporate accountability is certainly incomplete and insufficient if governance transparency is absent. It is only when both financial reporting accountability and governance transparency concurrently come into play that an MNC becomes accountable.

Improved governance transparency, or more broadly, enhanced overall corporate accountability, is more than just a mandate to meet various stakeholders' (including regulators) needs and demands. It is beneficial to the company as well. Transparency encourages employees to take a closer look and discover new ways to improve their efficiency and ultimately become a more capable workforce. A thoroughly cross-trained workforce that is knowledgeable about its job functions and corporate transparency standards and how they affect the company may promote its commitment, loyalty, and ethical behaviors. In addition, by documenting procedures for governance transparency, companies will expand awareness, allowing them to become more efficient in reducing operating costs, eliminating pointless or redundant processes, and maintaining correct staffing levels. Human capital makes the critical difference; assigning the right personnel to the right task and department enables companies to be most effective. For example, efficiencies allow a company to reduce the number of days needed to close its books. Documenting and testing the financial transaction cycles enables a company to develop or update its policy and procedure manual, and leads to more effective accounting and governance practices. A company with foreign operations or

multiple subsidiaries can become streamlined, with one unified financial accounting reporting system and one policy and procedure manual. Moreover, many recent
corporate accounting failures are traceable to members of the board of directors or audit
committee, who have been criticized for poor supervision of company senior executives
at home and overseas. The US Sarbanes–Oxley Act, for instance, mandates that audit
committees designate a board member as a "financial expert" as a way of improving the
quality of members of the board of directors and audit committee. Finally, corporate
transparency efforts may lead to some surprises, discovery of weaknesses in the internal
control system, or even revelation of past or present fraud. Companies should prepare by deciding in advance how to manage such a finding, bearing in mind that for
a company to find its own flaws is preferable to others finding them.

Increased global competition underscores the role of governance transparency in promoting corporate accountability because of an increased demand for such information
by global stakeholders including consumers, regulators, suppliers, creditors, partners,
environmental groups, and labor unions. All things being equal, highly demanding
stakeholders will place a higher value on MNCs that more seriously consider the labor,
social, ethical, and environmental consequences of their activities. Stakeholders may
switch the provision of business opportunities to other global players if an MNC is
perceived as being unresponsive to such ramifications. Finally, strategic information
disclosure should be made not only to outside stakeholders but also to corporate
members within the firm; it should be circulated, exchanged, and shared among various
subunits, especially foreign subsidiaries. Strategic information sharing among corporate
members can foster inter-unit exchanges of experiences, feedback, best practices, and
programs in ensuring compliance with labor, social, ethical, and environmental policies,
hence further bolstering overall accountability.

Governance transparency also requires the timeliness of strategic information
disclosure. The disclosure of such strategic information is essential to global investors,
shareholders, and stakeholders. For instance, the Sarbanes–Oxley Act requires that
US companies clearly disclose major share ownership and voting rights, material
foreseeable risk factors, material issues regarding employees and other stakeholders,
governance structures and policies, environmental policies, corruption-resisting programs, and corporate ethics and codes. Such information should be prepared, audited,
and disclosed in accordance with high-quality standards of accounting, financial
and non-financial disclosure, and audit. More importantly, an essential component
of disclosure is timeliness. For instance, in many countries continuous and timely
disclosure is mandated to ensure that security prices reflect as closely as possible their
underlying value and that investors have equal access to information that materially
impacts the prices of traded securities. With increased international experience, an
MNC is in a better position to understand international standards concerning what a
corporate accounting system should cover and when and how frequently financial
and non-financial disclosures should be released. More experienced MNCs may also be
more aware of the importance and effect of timely disclosure on their global reputation and how to transform this reputation into a competitive advantage. A survey by
the OECD in 2004 found that more internationally experienced MNCs have better
disclosure on off-balance sheet arrangements and strategic policies.

It must be stated that an MNC's governance transparency includes not only corporate- or parent-level governance transparency but also subsidiary-level governance transparency. The subsidiary-level governance transparency is even more important to an MNC's overall corporate accountability when this MNC's global activities are predominantly performed by a large number of frontline subsidiaries in different countries. Since these frontline subsidiaries are decision-makers of numerous activities in the frontline fields, their decision-making transparency is critical to the MNC's overall accountability. One way to strengthen the subsidiary-level governance transparency is to formulate and implement an incentive-based discipline to ensure these subsidiaries' corporate accountability. Incentive-based discipline exists when the parent firm employs financial and non-financial measures such as bonuses, shareholding, name recognition, merit adjustment, rewards, promotions, and penalties for senior subsidiary managers to improve subsidiary transparency and accountability. The incentive-based discipline system links these measures with: (i) quality of subsidiary reporting, including measurement principles, timeliness, and creditability of disclosure; (ii) quality of information dissemination to headquarters and regional headquarters as well as corporate members located in other countries and regions; and (iii) quality of information reporting concerning the off-the-balance sheet activities such as pooled investment schemes, insider trading activities, executives' internal accounts, reinvoicing of intra-corporate transactions, transfer pricing practices, entertainment expenses for government officials, facilitation fees for new projects, among others. Incentive-based discipline becomes particularly essential to this type of MNC (multidomestic in nature) for two reasons. First, process and bureaucratic controls, two commonly used control schemes, are often difficult for very global MNCs. Process control requires direct personal surveillance and high levels of management direction and intervention. Bureaucratic control consists of an explicit set of codified rules and regulations that delineate desired norms, standards, and behaviours. These two types of controls cannot be used as primary control approaches for locally responsive subunits since they do not corroborate the need for specific adaptation. Second, using them is not realistic for financial, temporal, or labour cost reasons. This type of MNC cannot efficiently dispatch internal teams to each individual subsidiary abroad to conduct frequent, thorough, and rigorous auditing. Instead, a more viable and effective approach is to enact and enforce a globally unified comprehensive incentive-based discipline system to be followed by all subsidiary executives and other senior subsidiary managers. Since the incentive-based discipline captures both material rewards and serious penalties, it sends a clear message about the importance of subsidiary accountability to all country managers because their own livelihoods are directly and significantly tied to their performance in achieving strategic transparency.

Internal auditing of financial and non-financial information is one of the prerequisites for both financial reporting accountability and governance transparency. An effective auditing system helps ensure that the strategic and financial information released is accurate, reliable, and accountable. This auditing system also serves as a filter that sorts out what strategic and financial information should be disclosed and to whom. Hence, internal auditing of both financial and managerial affairs performed by subsidiaries is an indispensable means to minimizing the information-processing costs and agency costs that arise at the subsidiary management level. It is useful to have an internal auditing team at headquarters that is independent, powerful, and authoritative in auditing all overseas subunits using the MNC's unified financial and managerial standards. Timely, effective, and independent internal auditing conducted on both a periodic and non-periodic basis often identifies subsidiary misconduct. Such an auditing department should also be an important arm of the corporate board for it to form a nexus for the work of the internal auditors. Internal auditing not only monitors each subsidiary's financial statement integrity and assesses its internal financial control systems, but it also identifies managerial and organizational misconducts in areas such as cash flow management, asset management, business ethics compliance, bribery and corruption resistance, book-keeping accuracy and completeness, documentation of business activities not recorded in accounting books, and documentation of internal funds and capital flows between the subsidiary and the parent or other corporate members. These measures are all essential to the improvement of governance transparency in the eyes of shareholders and other stakeholders at home and abroad. In fact, the US Sarbanes–Oxley Section 404 clearly requires internal control and auditing as the key step in improving financial reporting and strategic information transparencies. Section 404 specifies: "The Commission shall prescribe rules requiring each annual report required by Section 13 (a) or 15 (d) of the Securities Exchange Act of 1934 (15 U.S.C. 78m or 78o(d)) to contain an internal control report, which shall (1) State the responsibility of management for establishing and maintaining an adequate internal control structure and procedures for financial reporting; and (2) Contain an assessment, as of the end of the most recent fiscal year of the issuer, of the effectiveness of the internal control structure and procedures of the issuer for financial reporting."

In addition to incentive-based disciplines, peer performance comparison can be used to improve parent- and subsidiary-level accountability as well. This performance comparison can be both financial and non-financial, allowing the firm to identify the areas that can be further developed to sharpen its financial and strategic transparencies. This comparison takes place at either corporate or subsidiary level. At the corporate level, shareholders and other stakeholders can contrast company performance with the leading global rivals in the same or similar businesses. At the subsidiary level, parent management can benchmark its subsidiaries' performance with a rival's subsidiaries in the same country and/or with corporate members or peer subsidiaries in other countries. At the corporate level, when increased competition reduces agency costs and creates more peer comparison opportunities, board members may be able to hold the executive and senior management teams more accountable by comparing their performance with that of major peer competitors and building incentive plans based on the outcome of the comparison. In more competitive industries, comparing with rival companies is more readily available, which enables MNCs to have more precise performance comparisons and benchmarks for internally assessing management behavior. This comparison can help the corporate board to reduce the agency costs associated with monitoring CEO behavior. Thus, the parent-level board monitors the behavior and performance of the MNC's senior executives as compared to other same-level global players in the same industry. In the second tier, the MNC's senior executives monitor the behavior and performance of subsidiary-level executives by comparing them with local players at the same level in the same industry (i.e., other foreign investors or indigenous firms in the same host country). In both cases, the principal compares the agent's performance with respect to profitability, liquidity, leverage, asset management, sales growth, and market share. The principal also evaluates the agent's comparability with respect to commitment, productivity, transparency, strategy, and integrity. If these performance and behavior areas are comparable and effective at both the parent and subsidiary levels, an MNC's overall accountability will be enhanced and the firm will be able to better balance accountability and growth in competitive international markets.

Governance transparency cannot be effectively materialized unless the company has built and enforced codes of conduct and reporting of which all managers and employees are aware. For instance, the Internal Revenue Code in the US requires businesses that receive more than US$10,000 in cash or certain monetary instruments in a single transaction or related transactions to file reports with the IRS and the state. These reports must be filed by the company: (a) whenever it receives more than US$10,000 in cash or (b) upon receipt of a cashier's check, bank draft, traveler's check, or money order with a face value of less than US$10,000, if when combined with another monetary instrument and/or cash, the value of the transaction totals over US$10,000. Severe criminal and civil penalties can be imposed against the company and its employees for failure to file these reports or for structuring transactions to evade the requirements. Disney, for instance, clearly states that it is the policy of the company to comply fully with all cash and monetary instrument reporting requirements and to file timely and accurate reports for all reportable transactions. Cast members and employees are prohibited from providing any advice or help to customers on how to structure transactions to evade the reporting requirements. Any cast member or employee who has reason to believe that a transaction may be reportable or is being conducted to evade the requirements must notify his or her supervisor immediately and, if required, file a report. In addition, the cast member or employee must report the transaction to the guideline or to the corporate legal department.

Another way to improve governance transparency is an MNC's sustainability reporting. Many MNCs are today taking a long-term view and turning to the wide-ranging "sustainability" approach to amplify their governance transparency. Sustainability reporting aims to provide internal and external stakeholders with a clear picture of company values and principles, governance and management practice. Guidelines on sustainability reporting have been developed by the Global Reporting Initiative (www.globalreporting.org). For example, a European energy group, Shell, has now produced a corporate sustainability report (www.shell.com/shellreport) for the past five years. Holcim, a global cement manufacturer with headquarters in Switzerland, is another European company that has adopted the sustainability approach to corporate transparency reporting. The company makes it clear that it sees this reporting as one way in which the firm can take control of the burgeoning corporate accountability agenda. Although sustainability reporting is not required by external reporting rules, it certainly help promotes a company's transparency, integrity, and citizenship in the perceptions of internal and external stakeholders.

Here, to conclude this section, let us see some examples of governance transparency statements regarding business ethics policies and internal control:

Johnson & Johnson: It has always been the policy and practice of the Company to conduct its affairs ethically and in a socially responsible manner. This responsibility is characterized and reflected in the Company's Credo and Policy on Business Conduct which are distributed throughout the Company. Management maintains a systematic program to ensure compliance with these policies.

Campbell Soup: The company believes that its long-standing emphasis on the highest standards of conduct and business ethics, set forth in extensive written policy statements, serves to reinforce its system of internal accounting control.

DuPont: The company's business ethics policy is the cornerstone of our internal control system. This policy sets forth management's commitment to conduct business worldwide with the highest ethical standards and in conformity with applicable laws. The business ethics policy also requires that the documents supporting all transactions clearly describe their true nature and that all transactions be properly reported and classified in the financial records.

IBM: We believe that it is essential for the company to conduct its business affairs in accordance with the highest ethical standards, as set forth in the IBM Business Conduct Guidelines. These guidelines, translated into numerous languages, are distributed to employees throughout the world, and reemphasized through internal programs to assure that they are understood and followed.

Texaco: It is Texaco's long-established corporate policy to maintain a control conscious environment and an effective internal control system throughout its world-wide operations. Included in this system are Corporate Conduct Guidelines which require that all employees maintain the highest level of ethical standards.

Sears: The Company's formally stated and communicated policies demand of employees high ethical standards in their conduct of its business. These policies address, among other things, potential conflicts of interest; compliance with all domestic and foreign laws, including those related to financial disclosure; and the confidentiality of information.

Overall, discipline, structure, integrity, ethical values, employee competence, management's philosophy and operating style, and the leadership provided by senior management and the board of directors are all important components used to improve governance transparency and overall corporate accountability. To achieve this end, the information and communication system within an MNC is crucial. Information must be identified, captured, and communicated in a form and time frame that enables people to carry out their responsibilities. Personnel must understand their own role in internal control, as well as how individual activities relate to others. Employees must have the means to communicate information upstream, with customers, suppliers, regulators, and shareholders.

CASE EXAMPLE 5.1: CORPORATE ACCOUNTABILITY IN HOYA AND TEIJIN OF JAPAN

Hiroshi Suzuki's first day on the job as president of Hoya Corp. differed from most senior management appointments. The company's board of directors asked him to sit down and write the name of his successor. "What they were telling me is if I screw up, I'll be out," says Suzuki with smile. With an eye toward creating shareholder value – and protecting their shareholdings after they retired – Suzuki's father and uncle, before handing over the reins, took the unusual step of installing not one, but three, outside directors to the board to oversee management activities. "It's a way to make sure that shareholders feel more comfortable that the company is being run in their interest," says Suzuki. "And to prevent the management team from detouring the company in the wrong direction and destroying its value."

For now, Hoya's commitment to shareholders remains the exception rather than the rule in Japan. Captains of industry nod their heads in understanding when talking about creating shareholder value, but most like the status quo, which leaves their power base intact. However, as the economy enters its fourth recession in a decade and the Nikkei 225-stock average tests 17-year lows, Japan Inc. is paying closer attention to long-term shareholder value. It has little choice. The dwindling ability of banks to provide support and fresh capital means that companies have to make themselves more attractive to investors interested in the bottom line.

For decades, Japanese management has not needed to woo capital providers. The once-booming economy meant profits continued to grow, while cozy relationships with their banks ensured the docility of shareholders. Upper echelons of management could do as they pleased, with little accountability to the company's shareholders no matter how the company performed. "In some countries, it's taken very seriously when leaders mismanage state wealth," says one observer. "But in Japan, what has happened to the directors? Nothing."

In coming years, however, good companies will be global companies, willing to open their accounts and their boardrooms. With trendsetters such as Sony and NEC implementing corporate governance reforms and increasing attention in the local media to shareholders' rights, it is widely believed that it will only be a matter of time before others follow. Teijin, a textile maker, decided to strengthen its communications with shareholders after its share price plummeted to below book value during the Asian crisis. Upon speculation that Teijin's Southeast Asian subsidiaries would be badly hit, investors sold their shares, driving the stock down a harrowing 55 percent from Y400 to Y220 ($3.70 to $1.80) per share. At that point, its then-new president, Shosaku Yasui, went on the offensive, establishing an investor-relations office, implementing standard rules for disclosure, and holding regular meetings with investors. Teijin now employs half of its auditing officers from outside the company and has formed an advisory board to discuss Yasui's successor as president. The share price has since recovered to around Y550 per share.

As companies tentatively open up, their shareholder base is also changing. Faced with a shortage of funds to cover their bad loans, banks have been unwinding their huge portfolios of shares. According to the Japan Investor Relations Association, foreign investors have stepped in to pick up about 50 percent of the shares on offer. Overall, there has been a steady increase of shares held by non-Japanese investors, rising to almost 14 percent from 4 percent a decade ago.

Attracting foreign investors is considered key to boosting share price, as along with their investment comes some forthright feedback on how the company is doing and where it should be headed. "Foreigners tend to tell you what they think," says Hoya's Suzuki. "Japanese investors will be more polite but don't tell you what they think. The next morning, you wake up to find that they've sold all your shares". In 1999, foreign investor shareholders accounted for 12.4 percent, while individual investors, financial institutions, and corporations accounted for 26.4 percent, 36.1 percent, and 23.7 percent, respectively.

Foreigners are also less inclined to blindly cast "yes" votes on company resolutions. Earlier this year, Institutional Shareholder Services (ISS) opened its first sales office in Japan. The US research firm analyzes resolutions drawn up by Japanese firms for shareholder meetings and advises US institutional investors on how they should vote on them. As US institutional shareholdings grow, it is likely that their interest in management decisions will increase as well.

While foreign investors have not had the critical mass to influence the outcome of a vote, they have been able to force improvements in disclosure. The next step is to ensure that companies do not ram through proposals that are not in shareholders' interests, such as the transfers of assets that benefit a controlling shareholder at the expense of minority shareholders, according to Marc Goldstein, senior analyst at ISS.

But, for fundamental change to take root, traditionally pliant Japanese institutional investors have to play a larger role in exercising their voting rights as shareholders. Corporate and public pension funds own about 10 percent of listed shares and that number is expected to grow as the amount of pension assets increases. The Pension Fund Association says it plans to give new guidelines to its fund managers by the end of the year to help push company management to focus on shareholder value. "Pension funds should raise their voice," says Kazutaka Nakazawa, general manager of investment research at the Pension Fund Association. "They have to." As Japan's population ages, the number of workers supporting retirees will shrink, creating desperate needs to improve returns on pension-fund assets. In the meantime, once-taboo shareholder lawsuits are helping to entrench the concept of accountability. In a landmark case last September, the Osaka District Court ordered the current and former directors of Daiwa Bank – including bank president Takashi Kaiho – to pay the bank a total of $775 million in compensation for failing to maintain checks on unauthorized bond activities in the US. It was the first major lawsuit to recognize directors' responsibility to shareholders, and more are jumping on the bandwagon: According to data compiled by Japanese courts, the number of shareholder suits pending rose from 31 in 1992 to more than 280 in 1999.

An increasing number of Japanese companies are focusing on investor relations, hiring IR advisory firms, using the Internet to transmit information, publishing annual reports in English, and holding more meetings with shareholders. The nonprofit group, Japan Investor Relations Association, now has 500 members who account for nearly 66 percent of total market capitalization. Some firms have gone a full step further. About 40 percent of listed companies now have one or more directors recruited from outside the firm. Many have reduced the size of their boards and a total of 55 companies last year sought to reduce the director's term in office from two years to one, according to ISS. Still, adoption of IR policies can be merely cosmetic. A few company heads have gotten more than they bargained for when they arranged overseas meetings with foreign shareholders, according to Tetsu Yoneyama, general manager of business development at Daiwa Investor Relations. Instead of being greeted with applause like they are at annual shareholder meetings, they are met with difficult questions about company performance. "It's a shock to them", he says.

The Tokyo Stock Exchange needs to tighten up its listing requirements for companies. At the recent International Corporate Governance Network conference in Tokyo, a representative of the Shanghai Stock Exchange said it plans to require listed companies to have audit committees and independent directors. In contrast, Tokyo Stock Exchange president Masaaki Tsuchida said it was not exchange policy to impose listing standards and that it trusted companies to change of their own volition. "The exchange isn't aggressive enough," says Taiji Okusu, vice-chairman at UBS Warburg Japan. "They will realize that they are going to have to compete with other exchanges."

So, for now, any requirements that companies appoint outside directors and board committees will have to come through comprehensive reforms of Japan's commercial code, which are currently being debated. But the basic nuts and bolts are in place to foster change, says Ross Kerely, managing director of PricewaterhouseCoopers in Tokyo. New accounting rules, which put the spotlight on unprofitable subsidiaries, will force management to acknowledge when a unit is losing money. More dirty linen will be aired with the introduction of mark-to-market accounting, which will require firms to record the actual value of their shareholdings, rather than the value at the time of purchase. But the real push will have to come from the market, says ISS's Goldstein. "If companies find investors willing to pay more for shares of companies with good corporate governance, that will put pressure on them to do just that."

(Sources: Schultz, J. (2004). Day of the shareholder. *Far Eastern Economic Review*, Hong Kong, **164**(36): 53–6; Hayashi, Y. and Morse, A. (2005). At Japan Inc., shareholders grow restless. *Wall Street Journal* (Eastern edition), June 21: C1; Morse, A. (2005). Regulatory heat drives Japan Inc. to clear up act. *Wall Street Journal* (Eastern edition), New York, May 27: A11.)

CASE EXAMPLE 5.2: CORPORATE ACCOUNTABILITY IN EUROPEAN MNCS

Europe's new generation of CEOs – who have taken power during one of the worst economic downturns in years, a jittery stock market, and a post-Enron fear of corporate scandals – say that their biggest challenge today is restoring investor confidence. After the debacles of the bubble era, shareholders want corporate chieftains with proven records who can master retrenchment as well as expansion and who value high profits over high profiles. Their performance could prove crucial to restoring the battered image of the CEO, dented by the spate of corporate scandals.

CEOs of companies ranging from Dutch consumer electronics company Philips Electronics NV to scandal-hit food retailer Ahold NV, German media group Bertelsmann AG, and Swedish–Swiss engineering concern ABB Ltd. inherited companies with heavy debt loads, battered share prices, and unprofitable units. Some are trying to execute rescue plans during an unrelenting downturn, while others face demanding shareholders.

"During the late 1990s, when you had 20- and 30-something CEOs, the premium was on youth, vigor and risk-taking and experience wasn't as important," says Iain McNeil, chief of staff at London-based Odgers Ray & Berndtson, an international executive search firm. "Now, when companies are under greater scrutiny than ever before, shareholders want a CEO who will help them sleep well at night."

Anders C. Moberg, the 53-year-old Swedish chief executive of Ahold, says the demands on CEOs have become much tougher since he was a 35-year-old chief executive of Swedish furniture retailer Ikea International in 1986. In May of this year, he took the top job at Ahold as it was mired in one of the continent's biggest accounting scandals. The company's US food service unit had inflated rebates from vendors, forcing it to restate profits over several years, prompting a US Securities and Exchange Commission (SEC) investigation.

Mr. Moberg says his challenges – calming shareholders, dealing with creditors, and handling corporate governance issues – mean that he is forced to spend 80 percent of his time on just about everything except running the business. He says it is a stark contrast to his days at Ikea, from 1986 to 1999, when he presided over the expansion of a closely held company that did not need to worry about explaining its results and strategy to outside shareholders, as Ahold does. "Instant information these days means you can't hide in the executive suite," he says. "Sometimes you ask yourself if it is possible to fulfill all the demands on you and whether you have the right balance".

When Gerard Kleisterlee took over the top job at Philips about three years ago, he inherited a conglomerate that made everything from semiconductors to maternity-ward beds. The global economic downturn had shrunk demand for its high-end consumer electronics gear. Investors regarded the company as a chronic restructurer with little growth potential.

Mr. Kleisterlee has reduced the number of employees by 50,000 to 170,000, cut the number of divisions to five from seven, and shut down unprofitable units, such as Philips's components division. He says that rather than spending a lot of his time thinking about aggressive expansion plans, he has focused on cutting costs and generating the $1 billion in annual cost savings that he had promised to deliver by the end of this year. "During the downturn, when profit margins are hit, you have to mind the shop first", the 57 year old says.

Executive recruiters say veteran CEOs are in such demand in Europe that once-nationalistic companies in recent years have been forced to look beyond their borders in search of talent. ABB's Mr. Dormann is a German who runs a Swedish–Swiss company. Belgian brewer Interbrew SA recently chose American John Brock as CEO, hoping the former Cadbury Schweppes executive could help restore investor confidence in the brewer following a series of controversial acquisitions, and pharmaceutical firm GlaxoSmithKline PLC tapped a Frenchman, Jean-Pierre Garnier, when it was looking to improve its performance.

However, hooking a turnaround specialist with decades of experience does not come cheap. Richard Lamptey, an executive-remuneration specialist at Mercer Human Resource Consulting in London, says the ascent of the old-timer CEO has contributed to ever-bigger pay packages at a time when shareholders are complaining about excessive executive pay, fueling fights over compensation.

In November 2002, GlaxoSmithKline shareholders protested a 26.2 million euro ($31.2 million) total benefits package, including share options and bonuses, that board members considered giving Mr. Garnier, who in 2001 received about £3.4 million ($5.8 million) in salary and bonus. The company told shareholders that Mr. Garnier should be measured against his higher paid US peers, but it was forced to back down and Mr. Garnier was paid a £2.4 million salary and bonus in 2002. The company says it is reviewing its remuneration policy.

Some company insiders complain that leaders brought in to succeed ousted executives are overcautious. After becoming Bertelsmann CEO in August 2002, Gunter Thielen, 61, wasted little time in reversing many of the policies championed by his predecessor, Thomas Middelhoff. He restored Bertelsmann's traditional decentralized structure and had the company divest itself of most of its e-commerce activities.

While Bertelsmann says Mr. Thielen has concentrated on selling and restructuring unprofitable businesses, some executives say Bertelsmann has remained too much on the sidelines at a time when media valuations have hovered near all-time lows. (Earlier this month, however, Bertelsmann and Sony Corp. announced a deal to merge Bertelsmann's music division with Sony Corp.'s music division.)

Francisco Gonzalez, the 59-year-old chairman and CEO of Spanish banking powerhouse Banco Bilbao Vizcaya Argentaria (BBVA), says being risk-averse in today's economic environment can be a virtue as CEOs eschew some of the risk they were willing to embrace in the 1990s. In the case of BBVA, he has reined in the bank's expansion in South America and avoided some of the higher risk products.

"Today's CEOs just can't look at how a decision will affect the share price in the next few days," Mr. Gonzalez says. "You have to look four, five years ahead and weigh short-term risk against long-term results because that's what you will ultimately be judged on."

(Sources: Bilefsky, D. (2003). CEOs in Europe try to regain trust and shareholders are demanding greater accountability from business leaders. *Wall Street Journal* (Eastern edition), November 24: A10; Capell, K. et al. (2004). Europe's old ways die fast; in scandal's wake, boards are embracing the holy trinity: shareholder rights, transparency, and accountability. *Business Week*, May 17: 54; Anonymous (2003). Europe company: Talking up corporate accountability, *EIU ViewsWire*, July 16: 1.)

CASE EXAMPLE 5.3: CORPORATE ACCOUNTABILITY IN GENERAL ELECTRIC

Aristotle said the most hated form of wealth getting was usury, which makes a gain out of money itself. The Koran decrees, ". . . let there be amongst you traffic and trade by mutual good will. . . ." These philosophical and religious principles have long been a basis for commercial activities throughout the world. In the last 10 years, however, business has seemed to reach beyond ancient wisdom, using these principles as a base for ethical standards that have subsequently been codified, hand-booked, adopted, and enshrined by corporations all over the industrialized world.

Because of the rise of laws and watchdog bodies, the ethics business in the US, including private and nonprofit consultants who conduct what are known as ethical audits of corporations, has become an industry that estimates its own worth at over $1 billion a year. As regulatory measures appear in other countries, companies with a global presence now distribute their ethical manifestos by parcel and by email, although many are finding that what works fine in Indianapolis may have to be altered in Indonesia.

What is happening in the corporate world represents an evolution in the public perception of who the guardians of ethical behavior are, a job that through most of history was entrusted to philosophers, clergy, and government officials. It seems that business leaders have come a long way from the Confucian doctrine that held the merchant at the bottom rung of society and from Dickens's depictions of cruel workhouse masters.

Take the case of General Electric. Following a series of pricing scandals that rocked the defense industry in the 1980s, General Electric became representative of American corporations in need of an image overhaul. In response, the company created a corporate ombudsman's office 10 years ago, originally for the purpose of examining its government defense contracts. The company also drew up a summary of in-house rules on ethical concerns, called *Integrity: The Spirit & the Letter of Our Commitment*, which runs to 80 pages and is available in Arabic, Urdu, and most other languages that are spoken in the General Electric world-wide network. In early 1993, the office started a network of toll-free helplines for each business unit in the US. Employees can call the hotlines anonymously to ask questions about the guidelines and to report suspected violations. The infrastructure is solid. "GE now has one of the best ethics compliance programs in existence", says Larry Ponemon, national director of business ethics services at KPMG, the accounting and consulting firm.

Other US companies began to set up ethical programs as well. One motiva-tion was to comply with Chapter Eight of the United States Federal Sentencing Guidelines passed in 1991 in the wake of the defense industry pricing scandals. Applicable to all US businesses, the guidelines stipulate that if a company's senior management is aware that a staff member has committed an illegal act, the company can be held liable for fines that, as Ponemon puts it, "can be stiff enough to put them out of business". However, if the company can prove it is making a serious effort to clean up its act, the penalties may be substantially reduced.

Companies often created compliance systems as a public demonstration of an effort to clean up their own ranks before the courts did it for them. Nynex, for instance, set up an ethics office and hotline in 1990, before the federal guidelines were in place, because of a company scandal in the late 1980s. Eight purchas-ing managers at Materiel Enterprises Company, Nynex's purchasing subsidiary, attended wild parties thrown by vendors. Although the managers did not accept money or gifts, Nynex instituted the code of conduct to protect against future conflict-of-interest situations.

While the long arm of the law is a factor in business decision making, some-times the arm of ethics is longer still. Margaret Somerville, a McGill University professor of law and medicine who has been a consultant on ethics to executives, politicians, doctors, and scientists for more than 20 years, says, "We moved to asking the question, this is legal, but is it ethical? More recently we have turned around the order of analysis to ask first, what is ethical, then, does this coincide with the law, and if not, what should we do about it?"

Still, the Federal Sentencing Guidelines have been a powerful incentive to American companies to establish comprehensive compliance systems. These come complete with training programs in corporate ethics and hotlines for reporting violations (for the very purpose of avoiding court appearances for transgressions). Codes of conduct, spelling out a corporate ethical credo and explaining exactly what acts will not be tolerated, have also been part of an attempt to show that a company wishes to comply with existing laws and avoid being a lightning rod for a government crackdown.

The Conference Board, a research organization in New York City, estimates that at least 95 percent of the Fortune 500 companies had codes of conduct in the mid-1990s and about 90 percent of those firms said that they had them for compliance reasons. Among the first companies to establish codes of conduct were General Electric, General Dynamics, Martin Marietta (now Lockheed Martin), and other defense contractors. All had been caught up in procurement scandals (although General Dynamics and Martin Marietta were not charged), but now the defense sector is actively policing itself. In 1986, 17 contractors signed the Defense Industry Initiative on Business Ethics and Conduct, which declares that each of the companies will review its ethical practices annually.

The push for ethical standards has spread worldwide. The World Bank is involved in a certification of ethical standards that will serve as criteria in granting loans. South Africa recently set up the King Commission, which established standards for ethical conduct and issued a report listing companies that live up to the standards. In the UK, Stanley Kiaer – director of the Institute of Business Ethics, founded by a group of businessmen and supported by corporate and private funds – says 47 percent of the country's 500 largest companies have codes of conduct. Kiaer says that companies are trying to stay ahead of the government in enacting compliance measures. "Massive privatization here has created more media interest in business, and there is a feeling that we should give self-regulation of newly privatized industries a chance", he says.

The Chinese government is also trying to address corruption through various new regulations and disciplinary measures prohibiting a wide range of practices, including giving and accepting gifts, hosting excessive banquets, accepting kickbacks, and charging illicit fees. Clifford Chance, a law firm in Hong Kong, cites the statistic that in the first five months of 1996, 26,667 corruption cases were handled by Chinese prosecutors.

In Hong Kong, the Independent Commission Against Corruption (ICAC) has shifted its emphasis from government malfeasance to corruption in the private sector. As a result, many publicly traded companies have adopted codes of conduct, according to Sally Stewart, director of the Center for the Study of Business Values, launched in 1994 at the University of Hong Kong. Stewart, however, does not have a great deal of faith in codes of conduct alone. "Many just post a code on the bulletin board to pay lip service", she says. "Worse still are those that feel pressured by the government and the ICAC to show a gesture of ethical conduct and crack down in the wrong places. We've seen some cases, for instance, of an office abandoning the tradition of giving tips to the cleaning women at Chinese New Year on the grounds that this could be bribery. Companies that are ethical are going to be ethical with or without a formal policy". Due more to public sentiment than to law, the corporate world has been under increasing pressure to contribute something to society. The buzz words of the 1970s (corporate social responsibility) and of the 1980s (employee empowerment and total quality management) have given way in the 1990s and 2000s to the concept of responsibility to a body politic known as stakeholders, who include not only investors and creditors but also employees, suppliers, customers, and the community. How much consideration do these stakeholders merit?

The idea of social accountability has gained the most credence in Europe. According to a Conference Board survey of large firms in Canada, Europe, Mexico, and the United States, 55 percent of the European firms said their code of conduct was a social compact, worked out with management and employee representatives. Only 13 percent of US firms had drafted their code this way.

Robert E. Allinson, a lecturer and author on business ethics, writing in the book *Whose Business Values? Some Asian and Cross-cultural Perspectives*, absolves corporations of any sting of original sin: "One might require a definition of business such as the following: the ownership or use of capital investment, labor or land to produce a product, or to provide a service that fills some existent social need, or creates a new need to be filled or some social value in order to generate revenue for the owner. The point is, one cannot have a business enterprise in the first place unless one takes social needs into account".

For some, that is a selling point. A whole sector of ethical corporations has arisen in recent years, with such well-known companies as The Body Shop, Ben & Jerry's, and Working Assets making social consciousness their raison d'être. Levi Strauss has become almost synonymous with the "good guy" image because of its refusal to use subcontractors that exploit workers in developing countries.

Ethical is a particularly resonant word in the pharmaceutical industry, signifying not only moral choice but also "drugs that are available only by prescription". Astra AB of Sweden is an ethical company in both senses of the word. In fact, Astra's Canadian subsidiary has turned to the clean image to hold its own against competition from the generic drug industry. Under Canada's socialized healthcare system, the government pays for drugs prescribed to many citizens and tends to favor generic drugs, which may cost 15 to 50 percent less than an original product.

"The government has the key to our market access", says Gerald McDole, president and chief executive officer of the subsidiary, Astra Pharma, Inc., in Mississauga, Ontario. "If the government doesn't approve of a company, its products aren't distributed and customers aren't reimbursed for it". In 1993, Canadian manufacturers of brand-name pharmaceuticals received a boost from a law that extended the life of a patent from 17 to 20 years and changed licensing regulations. As a result, generic drugs had less market access. Opponents of the measure said the brand-name sector, in return for the privileges granted, should engage in more research and development in Canada, which has the lowest research and development rate of any industrialized nation.

Although there was no legal requirement to do so, Astra Pharma set up a $225 million research facility in Quebec, employing about 50 researchers. It helps the company to be known as an ethical company when government panels review pharmaceutical products. "Generic prices are clearly lower than ours, but that doesn't take into account . . . the fact that we help find cures for diseases," says McDole. Through its advertising campaigns, Astra Pharma has let the public know of its ethical policies. The company discontinued making chlorofluorocarbon aerosol inhalers, even though it wasn't required to by law until 1996. It compensates its sales staff by salary rather than commission, to eliminate any temptation to sell customers something they don't need. Amid the debate, corporations that choose to meet any of the definitions of good are finding that at least a degree of so-called empowerment seems to go hand in hand with a comprehensive ethics policy. Employees need to feel that they have the authority to do the right thing and to communicate concerns to the top brass.

Those at the lower rungs of the corporate ladder may be more likely to observe misconduct, or at least to acknowledge it, says a recent survey by the nonprofit Ethics Resource Center in Washington. The survey found that the pressure to engage in misconduct increases as one moves down the organization. Frontline supervisors were significantly more likely to spot ethical violations – and feel pressure to engage in misconduct – than senior managers, who reported observing 20 to 35 percent less misconduct than staff at other levels. And while senior managers were most likely to have confidence in their knowledge of the law, they were no more or less likely than those at other levels to select clearly acceptable responses to hypothetical scenarios.

AES Corporation, an independent power producer based in Arlington, Virginia, has taken the empowerment concept to previously unheard of heights at its seven US plants. Duties are rotated so that no one feels pigeonholed: Control-room operators arrange multimillion-dollar financial deals, storeroom operators plan budgets, and everyone on staff is held responsible for ethical decisions. AES has recently begun an ambitious global expansion and now has 27 plants open or under construction in countries including Argentina, Brazil, Hungary, Kazakhstan, Pakistan, and the UK. All of the foreign plants operate with a strong degree of autonomy.

"People often make the assumption that the more controls you have at the top, the fewer mistakes will be made", says Dennis Bakke, president and chief executive officer of AES. Before the start-up phase of each new plant, everyone at every level of the organization participates in a three- to four-month training program at which values and culture are important topics of discussion. Bakke says that the company does not like to do a great deal of checking for ethical transgressions before the fact because "that keeps people from taking responsibility".

AES, which reported profits of $100 million on sales of $533 million in 1995, has been a darling of both Wall Street and the ethics industry for some time, yet the system has not been foolproof. In 1992, AES officials publicly disclosed employee fraud at a large plant in Oklahoma. The plant's assistant manager had discovered several employees falsifying federally required reports on the quality of the facility's waste-water discharge.

Bakke does not believe that tighter controls would be any guarantee against this kind of incident, especially in plants that are an ocean away from the home office. "We'll assume people will follow the principles, but when they don't, we'll deal with it", he says. So far the biggest scandal the company has uncovered abroad was a dilemma over what to do about 50 workers at the newly acquired Kazakhstan plant who repeatedly came to work drunk. The manager there fired them, choosing not to practice cultural relativism and shrug the problem off as a local custom. Although some companies are simply posting their codes in every far-flung office, those most likely to succeed at a global ethics program try to find more innovative and visible ways to make their standards as harmonized as possible, says Michael G. Daigneault, president of the Ethics Resource Center. He likes the idea of communicating over the Internet. "A whole code of conduct could be put online, for employees all over the world to view and comment on. You could also post questions people ask and solicit answers from all over," says Daigneault.

General Electric, Motorola, and Levi Strauss are among the major multinationals that bestow a great deal of responsibility for ethical decisions on managers in each country. Local managers and ethics ombudsmen are trained through rigorous discussion of situations that might present a need for an ethical decision. Hewlett-Packard conducts an annual review of its 20-page code with its employees around the world. General Electric took its ethics program global. Gene Mensching, deputy ombudsman at General Electric corporate headquarters in Fairfield, Connecticut, and his boss, Jay Ireland, vice president of corporate audit staff, spend a great deal of time these days traveling to train ethics ombudsmen in divisions worldwide. They often find that they have to address an ethical dilemma themselves: Should they advocate cultural absolutism, i.e., the letter of the company law must be identical all over, or cultural relativism, allowing local ethics officers to interpret certain practices according to local custom? Where local customs are not in violation of US law, they try to take the second approach.

The very idea of reporting to an ombudsman is problematic in countries – such as China, Germany, and Russia – that still bear scars of totalitarianism. "We explain this as a resource and assist line, not as a way to turn in a friend," says Mensching. In Eastern Europe, the mention of sexual harassment tends to elicit guffaws instead of concern. "When we go there, we'll fold sexual harassment into training focused on respecting the individual", says Mensching. Nor can General Electric go into India and say unequivocally that nepotism is unethical. It is standard practice for Indian companies to hire the relatives of valued personnel, reflecting a belief that business opportunities should not break up the family. "We ask managers there to try to mitigate a conflict of interest through the way responsibilities are assigned, so that members of the same family aren't controlling a division", says Mensching.

Because people will have to make judgment calls about ethics, especially when juggling different cultural norms, Thomas Donaldson, a professor of legal studies who teaches business ethics at the Wharton School of the University of Pennsylvania, says that a code should give clear direction but also clarify when individual judgment will be necessary. Gift giving in Japan and South Korea, for instance, is such standard practice that it might seem rude under certain circumstances to refuse a gift. Motorola says in its code of conduct that in some situations a gift "may be accepted so long as the gift inures to the benefit of Motorola" and not to the benefit of the employee. It is also important to exercise moral imagination, says Donaldson, as Coca-Cola did when it turned down requests for bribes from Egyptian officials, but gained political support there by sponsoring a project to plant fruit trees.

(Sources: Jan, A. (1997). On the right side. *Worldbusiness*, **3**(1): 38042; Woods, M. (2003). The global reporting initiative. *CPA Journal*, **73**(6): 60; Clieaf, M.V. (2004). Are boards and CEOs accountable for the right level of work? *Ivey Business Journal Online*, May/June: 1; Svendsen A. and Wheeler, D. (2003). A model relationship. *CA Magazine*, **136**(6): 33.)

REFERENCES AND FURTHER READING

Alford, A., Jones, J., Leftwich, R., and Zmijewski, M. (1993). Relative informativeness of accounting disclosure in different countries. *Journal of Accounting Research* (supplement): 183–223.

Barney, J.B. and Hansen, M.H. (1994). Trustworthiness as a source of competitive advantage. *Strategic Management Journal*, **15**: 175–90.

Bebchuk, L.A. and Roe, M.J. (1999). A theory of path dependence in corporate ownership and governance. *Stanford Law Review*, **52**: 127–70.

Biddle, G. and Saudagaran, S. (1995). Foreign listing location: A study of MNCs and stock exchanges in eight countries. *Journal of International Business Studies*, **26**: 319–41.

Bushman, R.M., Piotroski, J.D., and Smith, A.J. (2004). What determines corporate transparency. *Journal of Accounting Research*, **42**(2): 207–48.

Bushman, R.M. and Smith, A.J. (2001). Financial accounting information and corporate governance. *Journal of Accounting and Economies*, **31**: 237–333.

Bushman, R.M. and Smith, A.J. (2003). Transparency, financial accounting information, and corporate governance. *Economic Policy Review – Federal Reserve Bank of New York*, **19**(1): 65–82.

Charkham, J.P. (1995). *Keeping Good Company: A Study of Corporate Governance in Five Countries*. Oxford: Oxford University Press.

Damianides, M. (2004). Sarbanes–Oxley and IT governance: New guidance on IT control and compliance. *EDPACS*, **31**(10): 1–14.

DiPiazza, S.A. and Eccles, R.G. (2002). *Building Public Trust: The Future of Corporate Reporting*. New York: Wiley.

Jaggi, B. and Low, P. (2000). Impact of culture, market forces and legal system on financial disclosures. *International Journal of Accounting*, **35**: 495–519.

Judge, W.O. Jr. and Zeithmal, C.P. (1992). Institutional and strategic choice perspectives on board involvement in the strategic decision process. *Academy of Management Journal*, **35**: 766–94.

Khanna, T., Palepu, K.G., and Srinivasan, S. (2004). Disclosure practices of foreign companies interacting with US markets. *Journal of Accounting Research*, **42**(2): 475–508.

Lang, M. and Lundholm, R. (1996). Corporate disclosure policy and analyst behavior. *The Accounting Review*, **71**: 467–92.

LaPorta, R., Lopez-de-Silanes, F., Shleifer, A., and Vishny, R.W. (1998). Law and finance. *Journal of Political Economy*, **106**: 1113–55.

LaPorta, R., Lopez-de-Silanes, F., Shleifer, A., and Vishny, R.W. (1999). Corporate ownership around the world. *Journal of Finance*, **54**: 471–517.

Nobum, D., Boyd, B.K., Fox, M., and Muth, M. (2000). International corporate governance reform. *European Business Journal*, **12**(3): 116–33.

Nohria, N. and Ghoshal, S. (1994). Differentiated fit and shared values: Alternatives for managing headquarters–subsidiary relations. *Strategic Management Journal*, **15**(6): 491–511.

North, D. (1990). *Institutions, Institutional Change, and Economic Performance*. Cambridge: Cambridge University Press.

Ptel, S.A., Balic, A., and Bwakira, L. (2002). Measuring transparency and disclosure at firm level in emerging markets. *Emerging Markets Review*, **3**: 325–37.

Quall, J.C. (2004). Implementing Section 404: A practical approach to the Sarbanes–Oxley Act. *CPA Journal*, **74**(8): 52–9.

Sanders, W.G. and Carpenter, M.A. (1998). Internationalization and firm governance: The roles of CEO compensation, top team composition, and board structure. *Academy of Management Journal*, **41**: 158–78.

Saravanamuthu, K. and Tinker, T. (2003). Politics of managing: The dialectic of control. *Accounting, Organizations and Society*, **28**(1): 37–54.

Shearer, T. (2002). Ethics and accountability: From the for-itself to the for-the-other. *Accounting, Organizations and Society*, **27**(6): 541–59.

Verrecchia, R. (2001). Essays on disclosure. *Journal of Accounting and Economics*, **31**: 97–180.

Wagenhofer, A. (1990). Voluntary disclosure with a strategic opponent. *Journal of Accounting and Economics*, **22**: 341–63.

Wild, J.J. (1994). Managerial accountability to shareholders: Audit committees and the explanatory power of earnings for returns. *British Accounting Review*, **26**(4): 353–70.

Willman, P., Fenton-O'Creevy, P., Nicholson, N., and Soane, E. (2002). Traders, managers and loss aversion in investment banking. *Accounting, Organizations and Society*, **27**: 85–98.

Williamson, O.E. (1988). Corporate finance and corporate governance. *Journal of Finance*, **43**: 78–93.

Chapter 6

Corporate Governance and Anti-Corruption in Global Business

EXECUTIVE SUMMARY

This chapter addresses anti-corruption from the corporate and organizational governance perspective. Although fighting corruption is a system project requiring the efforts of everyone (e.g., legislators, politicians, educators, officials), in individual societies as well as in the coordinated efforts of international organizations, MNCs themselves cannot escape responsibility for corrupt practices, and anti-corruption cannot succeed if these MNCs do not actively fight. In this chapter, I seek to provide a holistic view that addresses six sequential issues:

1. What is the nature of corruption in international business activities?
2. How do MNCs differ themselves in corrupt acts? Is there a workable taxonomy that identifies them?
3. What are the task and institutional environments that present pressures for corruption? How do such environments influence corrupt practices?
4. What are the malfeasant behaviors demonstrated by corrupt organizations?
5. What are the major consequences of corruption? How do overall organizational consequences differ from transaction-specific consequences?
6. How should MNCs resist corruption? What are the common distinctive approaches each MNC can use for this purpose?

I used metaphors to illustrate the organizational perspective of corruption. I explained the logic that: (i) a mad fox metaphor presents the system malfeasant behavior, uses positioning to align with the task environments and control to align with the institutional environments, and needs a structural surgery to heal the corruption disease; (ii) an errant rabbit metaphor presents procedural malfeasance, uses bridging to cope with the task environments and acquiescence to cope with the institutional environments, and needs a partial medication to alleviate corrupt acts; (iii) a wild puppy metaphor presents categorical malfeasance, uses interpenetration to respond to the task environments and selection to respond to the institutional environments, and needs a specialized operation to cure serious malfeasance; and (iv) a sick bulldog metaphor presents structural malfeasance, uses leveling to configure with the task environments and pacification to configure with the institutional environments, and needs a decoupled injection to eradicate corruption. I develop the framework which presents that: (i) corruption increases when task pressures (uncertainty, oligopoly, and regulation) and institutional pressures (opaqueness, injustice, and complexity) heighten; (ii) moral consciousness is a modifier of transmitting these pressures into malfeasant behaviors and corrupt acts; (iii) organizational architecture, which is crafted by culture, structure, and system, ultimately determines how morally conscious the MNC is and how effective its initiatives are to cut off corruption's supply side; and (iv) without this architecture, the MNC would suffer from organizational deficiency, strategic impediment, competitive disadvantage, and evolutionary hazards, all caused by corruption.

6.1 Corporate Governance and Anti-Corruption

Corruption has drawn the enormous attention of executives, directors, legislators, politicians, and scholars around the world. Recent debacles of many well-known companies, from the US's Enron and WorldCom to China's GITIC and Yuanhua Group, have further raised the profile of corrupt practices and their organizational repercussions. Anti-corruption is crucial to corporate governance because bribery and corruption damage the governance of corporations and impede efforts to develop corporate integrity. Corruption, or any illicit behavior, conducted by executives, managers, and employees can fundamentally deter the legitimate and long-term interests of internal and external stakeholders. On the other hand, good governance practices are important to prevent companies from being asked to pay bribes. In general, corruption is the conspicuous consequence of poor corporate governance, along with weak internal systems, non-existent controls, and bad management, although poor corporate governance does not solely result in corruption.

In the international business context, anti-corruption becomes even more important to global corporate governance because MNCs confront significantly varying norms, laws, and standards pertaining to business practices in general and corruption practices in particular. For instance, bribery is culturally ingrained as an acceptable business practice in some countries, such as some regions of Mexico, and kickbacks are common in selling activities in many parts of China. To cope with increasingly stringent anti-corruption law and, more importantly, to enhance the effectiveness and transparency of global corporate governance, more MNCs are voluntarily disclosing potential violations of federal anti-corruption laws. Not only can such public announcements minimize liability for nondisclosure, which was at the heart of many recent corporate governance scandals, but they may also reduce the reputational risk of being caught engaging in potentially illegal activities outside the home country.

Surely it is true that anti-corruption necessitates efforts and commitments from various institutions, especially legislators, regulators, and government officials. Transparency in both the public and private domains is key in the fight against bribery and extortion. The business community, non-governmental organizations, and governments and inter-governmental organizations all need to cooperate to strengthen public support for anti-corruption measures and to enhance transparency and public awareness of the problems of corruption and bribery. The adoption of appropriate corporate governance practices is a complementary element in fostering a culture of ethics within the multinational enterprise.

Still, however, companies or business organizations have an inescapable liability from such efforts and commitments. First, an organization is a basic unit of corruption practice. Most corruption activities take place between profit-driven organizations (bribers or donors) and government officials or legislators (corruptors or recipients) (The Conference Board, 2000). Second, organizations that are motivated to bribe for transaction-specific gains are partly responsible for the reason why corruption is difficult to eradicate. Unlike individuals, corrupt organizations cannot be "arrested" and thus only face legally prescribed economic sanctions. Unless organizations are fully determined to resist corrupt practices, it is very difficult to fight corruption in a society. Third, an organization is a window through which to see a nation's corruption climate. Corruption may be a passive reaction to cumbersome regulatory environments that impose a hurdle to business development or an active seeking of economic rents from corruption-generating opportunities. Lastly, knowing organizational implications of corruption is imperative. Those emphasizing the satisfaction of corporate utility functions for specific transactions generally believe that corruption gains outweigh corruption costs (e.g., Schleifer and Vishny, 1993). Organizational-level, rather than transaction-level, consequences need to be addressed.

Anti-corruption is also critical to corporate accountability. The Foreign Corrupt Practices Act (FCPA) in the US, passed in 1977, revised in 1988 and further amended in 1998, clearly states the importance of anti-corruption in fortifying MNCs' global corporate governance and accountability. In fact, record keeping and accounting constitute the main part of the Act and mutually reinforce anti-corruption. Accountability of foreign transactions can significantly help MNCs to detect and resist foreign corruption practices. Under the law, public companies are required to: (i) make and keep books, records, and accounts, which, in reasonable detail, accurately and fairly reflect the transactions and dispositions of assets of the company; and (ii) devise and maintain a system of internal accounting controls sufficient to provide reasonable assurances that all transactions are executed in accordance with management's general or specific authorization. Poor accountability often causes more bribery and corruption. For instance, some transactions associated with bribery may not be recorded at all, or some records may be falsified to disguise a certain aspect of the transaction. The books may show a payment to "X" when the payment was actually made to "Y". This presents the problem of mislabeling, which can arise if one company makes a legal but embarrassing payment and changes the records to mask the nature of that payment. In other cases, some records may be entered correctly but with a qualitative misrepresentation. For example, a payment of $100,000 to agent "X" may be entered when in reality there is an understanding that agent "X" will pay $20,000 to foreign official "Y". This problem is by far the most difficult to detect on audit, and it also represents one of the principal devices that the FCPA is supposed to eliminate.

6.2 Corruption Practices and Properties

Corruption is a complex and multifaceted phenomenon with multiple causes and effects, occurring as it takes on various forms and functions in differing contexts. Here I define corruption as an illegitimate exchange of resources involving the use or abuse of public or collective responsibility for private ends (i.e., gains, benefits, profits, or privileges). This definition includes corruption between organizations and political agencies (when public power is misused) and between organizations and other organizations (when collective responsibility is abused). In a narrow sense, corruption involves a bureaucratic behavior that deviates from the norm or violates rules specified by a given political context and is motivated by private gains that can be accrued from the public role. In a broad sense, corruption involves a behavior in any institution (not just government or public service) that violates formally defined role obligations in search of private gain. Organizations in this study refer to profit-driven business organizations. Much of the argument herein applies to nonprofit organizations as well, but arguably profit-seeking organizations have greater obligations for curbing corruption. The majority of corruption takes place between business organizations and political agencies, both domestically and internationally (US Department of State, 2001).

Corruption practices generally include bribery, fraud, extortion, and favoritism. As the primary form of corruption, bribery is the payment (in money or kind) given or taken in a corrupt relationship. Equivalent terms to bribery include kickbacks, red envelopes, gratuities, baksheesh, grease money, facilitation payment, and expediting fees. To most companies, bribery of public officials is the most prevalent form of a corrupt act. Fraud is an economic crime that involves some kind of trickery, swindle, or deceit. Extortions involve corrupt transactions where money or other resources are violently extracted by those who have the power to do so. Lastly, favoritism is a mechanism of power that privatizes public resources, or a highly biased distribution of state resources no matter how the resources were accumulated in the first place. Favoritism is the human proclivity to favor friends, family, and anybody close and trusted at the expense of public interests. It is a misuse of public responsibilities and implies a corrupted distribution of public resources. It must be noted that the definition of corrupt acts varies across nations. For instance, the US Foreign Corrupt Practices Act (FCPA) defines bribery as the offer, promise, or gift of undue pecuniary or other advantage, whether made directly or through intermediaries, to a person holding public office for that person to commit an act or refrain from acting in relation to the performance of official duties. This definition has not been effective outside the US, nor with non-US companies (The Conference Board, 2000).

By focusing on organization-level corruption, I am not implying that individual-level corruption is unimportant. In fact, organization-level corruption is performed by executives or employees at various levels who do so, partially or entirely, on behalf of the organization. This is analogous to a system illness activated by a few virosis cells. Most of the logic I discuss below may also apply to business–business corruption. Nonetheless, I view business–government corruption as being especially responsible for the corruption that is rampant in most economies. Corruption has a market in all countries that lack transparency in all areas of government practice and that also lack strong and independent institutions to combat corruption. As such, corruption is global in both its subject matter and origin. Because corruption is particularly rampant in emerging and transitional economies, I focus more on these types of economies. The basic logic, however, applies to other types of economies as well.

It is necessary to understand the nature of corruption. First, *corruption is context-based.* Depending on the individual, ideology, culture, or other context, the term "corruption" can mean different things to different people. It is particularly important to take into consideration the impact that a changing political environment may have on the term. Politics not only affects the understanding and explanation of corruption, but it also produces and identifies certain social behaviors as corrupt. Therefore, it is necessary to examine not only corrupt practices per se, but also the attitude and performance of the political system toward corruption – such as the exposure of corruption by the press, by the party in power, and by different factions – as well as the reaction of government to corruption, whether administrative or judiciary.

Second, *corruption is norm-deviated.* Although corrupt behavior can arise in a number of different contexts, its essential aspect is an illegal or unauthorized transfer of money or an in-kind substitute. Although there may be a situation where certain behavior is generally considered corrupt but no legal precedent has been established for it (in this case, the legalist definition lags behind the moralist definition), legality-based norms are the most widely used. This is because the legalist definition of corruption is generally more operational, clear-cut, consistent, and precise than the moralist definition. Moreover, it usually does not take long for judiciary rules or institutional stipulations in a given political context to "catch up" through the modification of the legal framework. The person bribed must necessarily be acting as an agent for another individual or organization since the purpose of the bribe is to induce him to place his own interests ahead of the objectives of the organization for which he works. In general, corruption leads the corruptor to secure private gains at significant public expense. Although not all corruption will definitely be detrimental to social welfare, it violates legal codes and institutional rules stipulated in a given political context. Without this essence, corruption cannot be distinguished from gift-giving and interpersonal links. In fact, the FCPA treats the norm-deviation in a host country as the key condition to determine violations of the Act. A US company accused of making a prohibited payment can avoid liability under the FCPA by showing that the payment was: (i) lawful under the written laws of the foreign official's country and such practice is the norm of business and social cultures in the host country; or (ii) was made as a reasonable expenditure directly related to promotional activities. An example of a reasonable expenditure would be covering travel and lodging expenses of an official coming to the United States for a demonstration of your product.

Third, *corruption is power-related*. In order to be eligible as a corrupt transaction, a corruptor or briber must necessarily be in a position of power, created either by market imperfections or an institutional position that grants him discretionary authority. Corruption always depends on power; power, however, does not necessarily spring from the law. People in public service such as physicians in Taiwan, customs clerks in the Philippines, and low-level staff who process bank loans in mainland China gain power not from the law but from the actual influence they exert on procedural costs afforded by businesses. Nevertheless, bureaucratic corruption (involving governmental officials) constitutes the most corruptible and corrupted part in many societies. Because of this, the FCPA is particularly stringent against bribery of foreign officials. Keep in mind that most companies have been charged with FCPA violations for paying excessively lavish expenses for foreign officials. The FCPA makes a rather curious distinction between a foreign official and a private person. It is illegal to bribe a "foreign official" but, at least under the FCPA, it is not illegal to bribe a private procurement agent of a private foreign company.

Fourth, *corruption is virtually covert*. Because of the nature of the operation, corruption is hidden in the underground informal arena. No formal written contract is delivered. Contact is made through oral communication so that it cannot be documented and used to prosecute a responsible entity. Maneuvers are carried out to conceal the identity of the actors. Overall, corruption is an informal, veiled system transforming benefits derived from one's public roles and power to personal gain. On the other hand, corruption is partly provoked by the incompleteness of the formal system. It fills the interstices of the formal system, causes its decomposition, and provides new impetus for its recomposition. The incompleteness of the formal system causes actors to bring their corruption schemes into the underground where they are protected by secrecy and where they can flourish and reproduce themselves in the shadow of the formal system.

Fifth, *corruption is intentional*. The motivation of personal gain conveys the very connotation of corruption. Illegal misconduct may not necessarily be corruption if there is no personal gain. Economists generally treat corruption as another means by which to maximize profits or seek optimal economic resources. Addressing its sensitivity to the rationality underlying corruption enables us to differentiate purposive dereliction of duty for personal gain from other careless maladministrative behaviors. The penalties specified in the FCPA clearly state such intentions. The penalties for violation of the bribery are quite severe – the company can be fined up to $2 million, and an officer or director who commits a *willful* violation can be fined $100,000 or imprisoned for up to five years. This fine cannot be indemnified by the company. Civil penalties may also be imposed.

Sixth, *corruption is ex post opportunistic*. Unlike normal transactions, corrupt practices are not codified in any explicit way nor written in any documented form. Parties participating in these practices are also not protected by any legal system. Corrupt transactions are therefore particularly endangered by ex post opportunism posed by the other party. Since corruption payments are a form of investment, which have no value outside the transaction, the payer places himself in the potential hold of the receiver who can later demand additional payment or who may not (or insufficiently) perform the agreed service without fears of counter measures from the payer. Due to this opportunism, ex post uncertainty associated with a corrupt transaction is formidable, especially for the bribing party.

Finally, *corruption is perceptual*. It relates to individual behavior as perceived by public as well as political authorities. Since it is a perceptual term judged by others, the concept becomes dynamic, subject to changes in social attitudes and political ideologies. As such, corruption can be further classified as "white," "black," or "gray". Although all violate legal codes or institutional rules, each of these has different moral implications. "White" corruption (i.e., some types of misconduct) can be tolerated by mass opinion. However, "black" corruption is clearly condemned. In between falls "gray" corruption, which is often ambiguous. Accordingly, the legal definition of corruption remains important for "black" and "gray" corruptions, but is not as important for "white" corruption. Under certain circumstances, the public may reasonably feel that an act legally defined as corruption is a necessary tool to survive. This explains in part why anti-corruption laws and rules in many transition economies, such as China, have been changing so rapidly. The nature of "perception" is even more prominent when one considers the dynamic nature of "norms," "duties," and "rules".

6.3 Taxonomy of Corruption in International Business

MNCs engaging in corrupt activities differ in the intensity scale and hierarchical scale of corruption, resulting in varying organizational identities, which display different levels of seriousness regarding the corruption involved. The *intensity scale* of corruption concerns the multitude (quantity) as well as the magnitude (gravity) of the corrupt activities. The *hierarchical scale* concerns the number of hierarchical levels (e.g., group/team level, function/department level, division/subsidiary level, and corporate/head office level) that are directly involved in corrupt acts. When a firm engages in large-scale and geographically diversified international businesses, especially in countries with rampant corruption, it runs the risk of heightened intensity scale as well as hierarchical scale of corruption. Unless an MNC has established and implemented an effective organizational system to combat and resist corrupt activities involving its employees, more foreign subsidiaries that are organizationally decentralized and operationally localized may increase the quantity of corrupt activities and involve more levels of hierarchies. Together, these two dimensions (intensity scale and hierarchical scale) jointly mirror the seriousness of organizational corruption. Specifically, intensity scale manifests the seriousness of the incidence of corrupt events while hierarchical scale reveals the hierarchical involvement of corruption within an organization. Organizational disease stemming from corruption is more severe along such incidence and extensiveness. The more hierarchical levels involved, the more severe the disease of corporate-wide corruption. These two dimensions are interrelated, yet distinct. They may reinforce each other such that the more hierarchies that are involved, the greater the intensity of the corruption that is likely to occur. Yet they describe differing aspects of organizational engagement. Most frauds within a large organization take place in a low level of the hierarchy, meaning

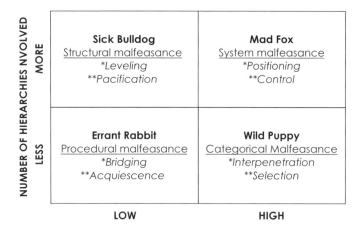

Figure 6.1   Taxonomy of corrupt organizations

that managers on the bottom of the organizational structure are responsible for the organizational corruption. Likewise, there are organizations whose corruption is small in scale, but that involves top-ranked senior executives. Using the intensity scale and the hierarchical scale as two axes, four metaphorical identities emerge (see Figure 6.1):

1.   *mad fox* (high intensity and more hierarchies);
2.   *errant rabbit* (low intensity and few hierarchies);
3.   *sick bulldog* (low intensity and more hierarchies);
4.   *wild puppy* (high intensity and few hierarchies).

As I will explain later, organizations with differing identities may live in different environments, act with different behaviors, bear different consequences, and require different architectures. Note that below I define and explain these taxonomical metaphors for the entire organization of an MNC. Nevertheless, the classification scheme of these metaphors equally applies to the subsidiary level; that is, they can be used to categorize different subunits within an MNC along these dimensions.

A mad fox is a metaphor for an MNC where a large number of the managers and employees at many hierarchical levels or in various subunits perform corrupt practices, resulting in very serious illegalities. The mad fox metaphor thus infers the illness of a whole MNC in which both the intensity scale and hierarchical involvement have reached very high levels. Within an organizational structure, managers at function, business, and corporate levels actively and extensively participate in corrupt activities or collude with external stakeholders to achieve certain objectives that are, as they perceive, in the interest of the MNC. The worst scenario among the four identities, this type of MNC often holds some rationalizations that lead to misconduct, including: (i) a belief that the activity is within reasonable ethical and legal limits; (ii) a belief that the activity is in the subunit's or corporation's best interests; (iii) a belief that the activity is "safe" because it will never be known or publicized; and (iv) a belief that because the activity helps the MNC, the MNC will condone the activity and even protect the person or people involved. Although some of these beliefs may also occur in other scenarios, the magnitude of these beliefs is strongest in the mad fox.

An errant rabbit is a metaphor for an MNC in which intensity and hierarchical scales of corruption are both very low, implying fewer instances of misconduct, narrower hierarchical involvement, and a weaker plague from corruption compared to other metaphors. It is nonetheless errant, involving illicit practices that MNCs with good business ethics would not perform. Misconduct in this type of MNC is not structurally systematic but is occasional or spontaneous, typically performed by a few employees at lower level hierarchies. Even with programs to resist corruption, some companies may still engage in errant rabbit behaviors because of difficulties in governing the implementation of these programs at business and function levels. For most companies undergoing pyramidal politics (i.e., decentralizing power to every lower hierarchy), errant rabbit behavior is likely to arise unless the system of enforcing counter-corruption policies is effectively and endurably functioning.

A sick bulldog is a metaphor for an MNC whose corrupt activities are not intensive but are nonetheless the practice of executives, managers, or employees at many different levels. In spite of low intensity, organizational breadth is high and many levels of the hierarchical structure are involved. This type of MNC is "sick" because corrupt practices spread to so many hierarchies that the entire body of the MNC is contaminated. It is true that many large corporations today consist of a conglomerate of subunits, each with its own management. It is ultimately the individuals within each unit or department that make decisions and compromises or that react to external environments. However, this conglomerate system is an integrated moral and social entity responsible for business-related misconduct by individuals who represent the company. Although it does not produce a large number of corruption events, the sick bulldog behavior massively harms the entire organizational morality. Misconduct is typically caused by two connected structural mechanisms – corporate structure (tasks, responsibilities, rules, and procedures for individual members) and corporate culture (ideas, expectations, values, visions, and customs shared among individual members). The roots of a sick bulldog reside in the malfunctioning of both structural mechanisms.

Lastly, a wild puppy is a metaphor for an MNC in which most corruption is narrowly concentrated at one or a few levels of the hierarchy. This metaphor is characterized by large-scale corrupt practices that are primarily performed by employees at one or few narrow levels of the MNC. The adjective "wild" is used to symbolize a rampant situation of bribery, fraud, or other illicit activities occurring at one level or in one sub-unit. The majority of these activities are localized in a level of the hierarchy that lacks moral conscience. It is natural that responsibility increasingly diffuses and fragments when an MNC decentralizes its complex operations and deploys distinctive resources to subunits. Accordingly, it is possible that one subunit, which can work independently to produce harm, may be responsible for most of the corporate-wide wrongdoing. In this instance, if evidence of potential harm is unassembled and fragmented and if corporate- or parent-level executives do not strive to suppress and exterminate subunit behaviors through integrated codes of conduct, a wild puppy may transform into a mad dog, dwarfing the healthy growth of an entire MNC.

6.4 Corruption and Organizational Environment

Organizational corruption is attributable to both corporate and environmental factors in individual countries wherein an MNC conducts businesses. The impact of country-level environmental dynamics – whether economic, political, legal, or cultural – on national-level corruption has been rigorously studied. Corruption derives from numerous environmental factors, notably distorted or opaque governmental behavior and decisions, weak counter-corruption institutions, cultures that intertwine gift-giving with bribery, ambiguous business–government relations, subtle networking practices, shortage of independent and well-functioning market mechanisms and institutions, poor quality of public service, low salaries in the public sector, influence of an underground economy, strong linkage between officials and family businesses, deficiency in democratic power-sharing formulas, weak media functions, and inadequate openness in trade and market access (e.g., Ackerman, 1975, 1999, 2001; Doig and Theobald, 2000; Goldsmith, 1999; Husted, 1999; Johnson, Kaufmann, and Lobaton, 1998; Kaufmann, Kraay, and Lobaton, 1999; Lambsdorff, 1999; LaPalombra, 1994; Mauro, 1995; Tanzi, 1998; Treisman, 2000; Wei, 2000).

Here I intend to emphasize how the organizational environment facing an MNC's various units, whether divisions or subsidiaries and whether at home or overseas, influences organizational corruption. Organizational theorists suggest that a firm's behavior, strategy, and response are shaped by its organizational environment, which is composed of both task and institutional constituents (Lawrence and Lorsch, 1967; Meyer and Scott, 1983). The task environment pertains to external resources, information, or conditions that may immediately affect goal setting and goal attainment. The institutional environment pertains to the external needs and requirements to which individual units of an MNC must conform in order to receive legitimacy and support. Here I focus on three traits of the task environment in which a specific unit of an MNC operates, namely: (i) oligopolistic intensity; (ii) regulatory control; and (iii) structural uncertainty, and three traits of the institutional environment, namely: (i) institutional transparency; (ii) institutional fairness; and (iii) institutional complexity. In my view, organizational corruption increases or decreases when conditions in these environments change. It is true that firms may also be able to shape, at least to some extent, these task and institutional environments (corruption itself may be one of the means for this purpose). Here I intend to illustrate how corruption is influenced by these task and institutional conditions that already exist, the argument being consistent with the above organizational theorists.

Specifically, I suggest that, all else being equal, oligopoly, regulation, and uncertainty, together with institutional opaqueness, injustice, and complexity escalate pressure for corruption and increase the probability of its incidence for an MNC's individual units that operate in this type of environment. Whether or not this pressure will eventually transform into real corruption, however, depends in large part on an MNC's moral consciousness and related programs combating corruption. Moral consciousness concerns the extent to which an MNC's leaders and employees are aware of the moral goodness or blameworthiness of their own behavior, together with a feeling of obligation to do the right thing. In my view, moral consciousness is a prerequisite for moral behavior.

Although a corporation is a juristic and not a real person, society has the right to look at its moral consciousness to see to what degree its moral behavior conforms to a social standard of what is right. Moral consciousness and related anti-corruption programs are thereby likely to be either a conditioning factor or a moderating factor, affecting the form or strength of the link between corruption and the environment.

6.4.1 Task environments

Although they may not be completely inclusive, oligopolistic intensity, regulatory control, and structural uncertainty are proposed as the ingredients constituting the task environments of corruption. Task environments include the elements that actively and directly cooperate and compete with the focal units of an MNC (Dess and Beard, 1984). They interact with the MNC units through resource dependency (Pfeffer and Salancik, 1978) and information uncertainty (Lawrence and Lorsch, 1967). Task environments affect MNCs through the process of making available or withholding resources and information. Oligopolistic intensity and regulatory control reflect a focal unit's resource dependency on competitors and regulators while structural uncertainty indicates the variability of industry structural information that drives up the costs of transactions and coordination for the MNC units. Both dependency and uncertainty are viewed as salient parameters affecting business strategy and corporate response. The way an MNC reduces such dependency or uncertainty in order to cope with these conditions will affect that MNC's outcomes (Child, 1972; March and Simon, 1958).

Oligopolistic intensity describes the extent to which a small group of firms in the focal industry have dominant control and market power in the industry. If a corrupt MNC subsidiary is a member of this group, it will be motivated to continually bribe officials in power or collude with other members of the group in order to retain its advantageous position. It also has a monopolistic power to distort, withhold, or hide the industry's structural information needed by other business stakeholders (suppliers, buyers, new entrants, small rivals). In this case, abnormal economic returns are not created from building blocks of competitive advantages but from a corruption-based monopoly. If an oligopoly is threatened to be reduced by governments, the company may even fortify its corruption. Competitive pressure arising from deregulation or privatization will challenge the sustainability of market power and the advantageous position already occupied by the oligopolistic firms. From the perspective of a corrupt government agency, oligopoly motivates public servants to seize parts of economic rents obtained by oligopolistic firms using extortion and corruption. For a morally unconscious company not belonging to this oligopolistic group, the incentive to bribe is also present. Because of the liabilities of newness, smallness, or remoteness (i.e., not close to political authorities), a firm outside this group spends more in accessing the focal industry, confronts pressure to follow oligopolistic firms' pricing and policy, and encounters greater difficulty in utilizing upstream inputs or downstream resources controlled by oligopolistic players. Morally unconscious executives may think that corruption with political or bureaucratic authorities can help the company secure a foothold or privileges (financing, taxation, distribution channel, or procurement) so as to neutralize its foregoing liabilities. A weak outsider may also bribe decision-makers in a monopolistic firm to obtain a subcontract, which provides some specialized services needed for the latter's value-chain activities.

Regulatory control is concerned with the extent to which government authorities regulate and intervene in various industrial policies such as market access, capital investment, technological standard, distribution channels, and environment protection, which may significantly impact business operations in a focal industry. Executives at subsidiaries participating in an overly or poorly regulated industry may use more corruption to countervail changing and uncertain regulations. From the information uncertainty viewpoint, excessive or poor regulatory control, which is often nontransparent and unstable in most emerging economies, increases the costs of information scanning and processing. From the resource dependence viewpoint, excessive or poor regulatory control, often conducted by controlling key production inputs such as land, natural resources, and capital, increases the costs of strategic planning and creates difficulties in maintaining flexibility. In the mind of ethically questionable managers, bribing officials can help the company reduce information costs, lighten the regulation's hindrance, or obtain institutional privileges. Under this presumption, there may be a positive link between excessive, poor, or uncertain regulatory control and corruption intensity for companies lacking business ethics. The practice of "getting in by the back door" used by many Chinese companies, especially those in a weak market position, illustrates this link. In the past four decades, whenever regulatory control heightens, "back door" activities intensify.

Structural uncertainty describes the extent to which an industry's structural attributes such as demand and supply are volatile and unpredictable. This uncertainty implies an absence of sufficient information about industry structure and its changes. It also implies executives' inability to predict these changes and their impact on organizational decision alternatives (Dess and Beard, 1984). Since this uncertainty is largely caused by changes in government policies, ethically questionable executives at subsidiaries operating in this type of industry may aggressively bribe officials in power to obtain insightful information and a lead on unreleased new policies. Such "insights" may transform into short-term privileges, which enable the corrupting firm to occupy a superior position in the market or grasp some early mover opportunities. Institutional economics holds that structural uncertainty propelled by industrial policy is significantly more difficult for firms to predict, respond to, and cope with than structural changes caused by market disequilibrium itself (Tool, 1993). In this situation, executives are apt to emphasize personnel interlocks with officials to trade upon ambiguity. For morally unconscious executives, such interlocks may become acts of corruption. In a society lacking organizational morality and anti-corruption systems, corruption may be portrayed as more prompt, direct, and effective than socialization-based interlocks in the eyes of ethically ill-behaved executives.

6.4.2 Institutional environments

Institutional environments serve as conditioning factors that either undercut or entice organizational corruption. This study proposes that institutional transparency, institutional fairness, and institutional complexity are important components of these environments. Both task and institutional environments simultaneously place pressures on an MNC's units in such environments, to which they are forced to respond. But the types of pressures vary between the two (Scott, 1992). Task environments affect business operations through structural forces, which impact input and output. Institutional environments affect business operations through legal, regulatory, sociocultural, and professional requirements that impact the costs of maintaining organizational legitimacy. Institutional theorists emphasize that institutional rules and requirements themselves are important types of resources and that those who shape them (e.g., state, regulatory bodies, or professions) possess a valuable form of power (Burns and Flam, 1986). Institutional requirements affect organizational arrangements through both cognitive and normative mechanisms. In most emerging markets where MNCs are increasingly active, professional organizations (e.g., auditing, arbitration, taxation) and trade associations or unions are virtually state-instituted. As a result, they are parts of broadly defined regulatory institutions. Institutional transparency and fairness essentially describe the transparency and impartiality of the regulatory system. While transparency and fairness reflect the degree of openness and nondiscrimination of institutional rules and requirements, complexity displays the level of difficulty in coping and adapting to regulatory systems and sociocultural environments.

To most MNCs, the institutional environment may exert a relatively stronger effect on the incidence of their corrupt activities than the task environment mentioned above. Institutional hurdles and barriers amplify the liabilities of foreignness. To curtail such liabilities, morally conscious MNCs with rich resources and capabilities may use their competitive advantages to compensate for their disadvantageous positions in the wake of foreignness liabilities. Morally unconscious firms, especially when they do not possess competitive advantages suitable to host country operations or when their possessed competitive advantages cannot be effectively exploited due to the poor infrastructure for investments and operations in a host country, are likely to use bribery or other illicit methods to overcome their liabilities of foreignness arising from institutional hurdles, particularly discriminatory treatments against foreign companies.

More specifically, institutional transparency describes the extent to which regulatory systems (political, bureaucratic, industrial, and professional) are open, clear, and easy to understand in a particular country in which an MNC's unit invests and operates. This transparency is especially low in regulated industries in most emerging economies (e.g., telecom, automobile, insurance, media, retailing, banking) and with respect to issues such as project approval, market access, environmental standards, and requirements for gaining taxation exemptions or holidays (Luo, 2002). The lack of experience by regulatory bodies in administering many experiment-type practices is a main reason for this opaqueness. In turn, this opaqueness provides regulatory authorities and individual bureaucrats with the exclusive right to explain and interpret ambiguous rules and requirements, which leads in part to business–regulatory body corruption. In this circumstance, corrupt officials realize that the opaqueness propels the dependence of some businesses on the officials, thus facilitating the transformation of regulatory power into monetary gains. Morally unconscious executives, especially in companies more prone to these regulations, may realize that bribery is the only way to acquire regulatory insights or to skew new rules toward a direction that agrees with the firm's interests. Corruption is indeed found to be an increasing function of institutional opaqueness (Goldsmith, 1999; Johnson, Kaufman, and Lobaton, 1998).

Institutional fairness describes the extent to which various regulatory treatments (political, bureaucratic, industrial, and professional) are impartial, just, and nondiscriminatory to every business, including foreign business, within the institutional reach. During structural reforms, most transition economies are characterized by regulatory heterogeneity across regions, locations, sectors, industries, ownerships, and often between domestic and foreign firms. Previously controlled policies are increasingly becoming idiosyncratic and discriminatory according to these parameters in a bid to redress structural distortions or regional disparities caused by a long period of a centrally planned economy (Luo, 2002). As a negative derivative of this change, many businesses, especially those close to government authorities, are able to receive institutional privileges that other businesses do not have. Institutional privileges include, but are not limited to, tax relief, favored financing, fiscal subsidy, exclusive rights in using certain resources, government protection, ensured early mover position, special rights in using governmentally instituted distribution or export channels, and heightened entry barriers against new rivals. Granting these privileges can directly foster business–government corruption and business–business collusion. Privileged group members, by exploiting their monopoly power and institutional advantages, are able to seize more economic rents than non-group members. This motivates morally unconscious executives, including those working at MNC subsidiaries, to bribe bureaucrats who have the power to decide this membership in exchange for institutional privileges that are considered of high value. With more unfairness, firms encounter a stronger pressure to bribe in order to remain in this institutional environment.

Finally, institutional complexity describes the extent to which the institutional environments (regulatory systems and sociocultural environments) that an MNC or its units must relate to are complicated and difficult to verify, analyze, comply, and cope with. The information-processing view holds that complexity increases the information processing and agency demands facing the firm and its top executives (Tushman and Nadler, 1978). The firm must develop information-processing mechanisms capable of dealing with this complexity. Executive interlocks with bureaucrats and leaders in other stakeholder groups are one such mechanism (Geletkanycz and Hambrick, 1997). It is generally harder to internally absorb and process required information in emerging economies than in advanced market economies because of opaque and uncertain regulatory systems, diverse and peculiar sociocultural environments, and lack of market-supporting institutions. When facing such complexity in an advanced economy, executives can go to the market to find agencies or persons (e.g., experts at consulting companies or law offices) who can interpret and deal with these regulations. Such services, however, are virtually lacking in most emerging markets and developing economies due to the facts that the market service sector has not yet been developed and that institutional complexity itself is difficult to analyze by organizations and professionals. In this context, when executives of MNC subsidiaries cannot find a professional agency or are unable to process complex information by themselves, they are more likely to bribe those bureaucrats or leaders in various segments of institutional environments who can provide authoritative insights and creditworthy information. They may expect that such insights will help dispel the threat of institutional complexity on business development. In markets in which corruption persists and there is a failure to punish corporate illegalities, this likelihood increases.

In conclusion, this section defines task environments (oligopolistic intensity, regulatory control, and structural uncertainty) and institutional environments (transparency, fairness, and complexity) that partly explain organizational malfeasance in corruption involving an MNC's various units in these environments. I illustrate the logic that corruption may increase along degrees of oligopoly, regulation, and uncertainty and decrease along degrees of transparency, fairness, and simplicity. These testable propositions, however, should be viewed in a larger context wherein political, legal, economic, historical, and sociocultural causes of corruption are also taken into account. In fact, the task and institutional environments that this study emphasized are intertwined with these causes. For instance, institutional transparency reflects the superiority of political and legal systems while oligopolistic intensity is a product of economic, political, and legal conditions, which affect industrial structure. The extent to which these task and institutional environments will actually provoke corruption depends largely on an MNC's moral consciousness and support programs that combat corruption. Different organizational metaphors may use varying tactics to respond to different task and institutional environments, thus presenting different MNC behaviors associated with illicit acts.

6.5 Corruption and Organizational Behavior

This section emphasizes an MNC's malfeasant behaviors in its corrupt practices. Specifically, it attempts to use a typology to elucidate which deviant behaviors will be used by organizations with differing metaphors to align with the above task and institutional environments. A typology of malfeasant behaviors is useful for a better understanding of organizational corruption and giving parsimony and order to the diverse set of behaviors that comprise organizational deviance or corruption. Malfeasant behaviors are opposed to ethical behaviors in that the former focuses on behaviors that violate rules specified by a given political, social, and legal context whereas the latter focuses on behaviors that are considered right as judged in terms of justice, law, or other societal guidelines determining organizational morality. I conjecture that a mad fox metaphor is accompanied with *system malfeasance*, an errant rabbit with *procedural malfeasance*, a wild puppy with *categorical malfeasance*, and a sick bulldog with *structural malfeasance*.

6.5.1 System malfeasance

System malfeasance exists when an entire organizational system is contaminated with corrupt acts and corporate illegalities. The mad fox metaphor applies well here because it involves system-wide fraud characterized by a great magnitude of corrupt activities carried out by many hierarchies. Here, malfeasance is both intensive and extensive, plaguing the whole system tantamount to a cancer. A mad fox metaphor assumes that the benefits of corruption outweigh the costs of corruption, thus permitting senior executives and board members to be involved in bribery and tolerating managers and employees at lower levels with such deviant behavior despite the risks of legal sanctions and reputational damage.

Corresponding to system malfeasance, a mad fox metaphor may emphasize *positioning* to align with structural uncertainty, regulatory control, and oligopolistic intensity and focus on *control* to align with institutional opaqueness, injustice, and complexity. Positioning is a tactic that seeks a strong position in oligopoly, bargaining with regulatory bodies and reducing uncertainty through corruption. Among the four metaphors, a mad fox is the most aggressive in corruption, attempting to secure an advantageous position for maximizing possible gains from task environments via illegitimate means. Control is a tactic that seeks to influence, shape, and dominate institutional environments through corruption. A mad fox metaphor intends to establish power and dominance over institutional constituents, which apply pressure on the MNC. To this end, it uses corruption to manipulate institutional processes such that institutional opaqueness, injustice, and complexity may hamper other MNCs but not itself, or provide it with new benefits, via exceptions, concessions, secrecies, or privileges.

6.5.2 Procedural malfeasance

Procedural malfeasance exists in the errant rabbit metaphor whose formalized procedures on business ethics are not strictly followed by some employees at one or few levels or in one or few subunits, resulting in a low scale and a narrow scope of illicit acts. In a highly decentralized system, one or a few subunits may face explicit normative or coercive pressures in a particular task and institutional environment that require bribery under threat of losing deals, concessions, or privileges by corrupt officials. Employees in a subunit may assert that if they do not make payoffs, a less competent rival will win such deals, concessions, or privileges. In other cases, some employees in a remote location or subunit (e.g., foreign subsidiary) may believe that payoffs are a routine part of doing business there and are indigenously acceptable. If the implementation of corporate programs alleviating illegalities is not strictly monitored, some individuals may find leeway to escape blame and punishment. Under these circumstances, low intensive corruption with few hierarchies involved occurs, despite the existence of MNC-wide procedures for resisting corruption.

In conformity with procedural malfeasance, an errant rabbit may consider *bridging* to configure with task environments and use *acquiescence* to configure with institutional environments. Bridging is a tactic that seeks connection with relevant stakeholders in task environments such as regulators, competitors, suppliers, buyers, and distributors. An errant rabbit metaphor involves low-scale corruption on a sporadic or occasional basis in an effort to cultivate, through corruption, relationships with the task environment community. Managers in some new firms may think that bridging through corruption is a shortcut to connect with outsiders who control input and output resources on which the firm depends. Acquiescence is a tactic that unwillingly accepts, follows, and mimics corrupt acts already conducted by other firms to deal with the same institutional environments. An errant rabbit metaphor tolerates some employees' illicit behaviors that are necessary for coping with institutional hazards. In this case, the pressure for corruption comes from institutional requirements rather than from an organizational intention for corporate illegality.

6.5.3 Categorical malfeasance

Categorical malfeasance exists in a wild puppy metaphor in which many corrupt practices are concentrated in one or few categorical levels (team level, functional level, business level, or corporate level), categorical units (group, department, division, branch, or subsidiary), or categorical locations (domestic vs. foreign; developing vs. developed countries; within vs. beyond the regional bloc). This type of malfeasance is not systematic and extensive throughout the entire MNC, but instead it ascribes mainly to a few managers in one or a few of these categories that conduct a great deal of serious corruption. In a highly diversified structure, various categories face idiosyncratic task and institutional environments relating to corruption. Because this structure is also decentralized and provides categorical managers with adequate decision power, it becomes possible that corruption varies across categories. Malfeasance may increase when: (i) one category or unit confronts strong bribery pressure from its task and institutional environments; (ii) it has difficulty in fulfilling short-term financial goals set by its parent; (iii) it is dysfunctional and mismanaged; and (iv) senior managers in this category despise or overlook illicit behaviors.

Categorical malfeasance is further revealed in the way a wild puppy metaphor deals with its task and institutional environments. It may emphasize *interpenetration* to deal with task environments and use *selection* to deal with institutional environments. Interpenetration is a tactic that seeks to influence task environment constituents, which affect a focal categorical level, subunit, or location. In doing so, it bribes those with decision power in order to create favorable task environments that will permit the problem puppy to grow. As a malfeasant behavior, interpenetration may confer a strong position in oligopoly, infiltrate industrial regulation, and yield confidential insights into industrial environments. Selection is a tactic that seeks to manipulate institutional environments facing the categorical level, location, or unit that is heavily involved in corruption. It thus emphasizes corrupt acts in selected areas. Because it is impossible for any organization to manipulate the entire institutional environment due to the latter's exogenism and residualism (Oliver, 1991; Scott, 1992), selection is a reasonable behavior consistent with categorical malfeasance.

6.5.4 Structural malfeasance

Structural malfeasance exists in the sick bulldog metaphor where corruption acts are structural in nature and most levels of the hierarchy, if not all, are involved, despite the fact that the latter are small scale in terms of quantity and gravity. When an MNC is highly integrated (vertically or horizontally) or centralized (along functions or areas), it increases the probability that corruption practices are collectively performed by, or jointly involved with, multiple levels of the hierarchy. This is the case of corruption sharing. When an MNC is structurally decentralized but each hierarchical level or subunit faces strong pressure to perform illicit acts and lacks clear codes of business conduct enacted on its own or by the head office, it increases the probability that corrupt acts will simultaneously yet independently take place at multiple levels or in multiple subunits. This is the case of corruption multilocation. In either case, malfeasance is structural not only because it occurs at many hierarchical levels but also because it marks the MNC's failure to correct this system-wide defect through structural measures such as harmonized anti-corruption programs and responsibility-sharing systems across hierarchical levels. Although structural malfeasance involves less intensive corruption than system malfeasance, the former can transform into the latter if the MNC allows the illness to remain.

A sick bulldog may focus on *leveling* to align with task environments and on *pacification* to align with institutional environments. Leveling is a tactic that seeks to smooth the impact of the task environments' fluctuations on business operations. Under structural malfeasance, leveling is achieved through bribing or colluding with decision-makers in task environments to motivate suppliers of inputs, stimulate demand for outputs, or influence bureaucrats of regulatory authorities. Unlike a mad fox metaphor that relies on aggressive positioning in order to dominate in the task environment, a sick bulldog attempts to reach out into the task environment through corruption-bolstered smoothing in order to reduce fluctuations in its input or output environments. Pacification is a tactic that seeks to appease institutional constituents for the entire MNC. Corroborating structural malfeasance, pacification mounts a low intensity of corruption but devotes most of the corruption resources to placating institutional pressures encountered by the whole MNC. Corruption is performed to accommodate demands for bribery, gratuities, or payoffs from politicians and bureaucrats who have the power to manipulate institutional transparency, fairness, and complexity which influence the entire company's business activities.

In conclusion, this section discusses the organizational behavior of different metaphors and how this behavior may be configured with the task and institutional environments identified in the preceding section. I suggest that a mad fox may respond to task parameters through positioning and to institutional parameters through control, together presenting systematic malfeasance. An errant rabbit may respond to task environments through bridging and to institutional environments through acquiescence, together presenting procedural malfeasance. A wild puppy may respond to task constituents through interpenetration and to institutional constituents through selection, together presenting categorical malfeasance. Lastly, a sick bulldog may respond to task pressures through leveling and to institutional pressures through pacification, together presenting structural malfeasance (see Figure 6.1). All these behaviors and underlying methods in response to task and institutional environments are illicit, immoral, unethical, and illegal. Case studies are needed in the future to substantiate this line of discussion and advance our understanding of illicit tactics in different scenarios. MNCs with these deviant behaviors fail to fully realize their serious consequences, both visible and invisible.

6.6 Corruption and Organizational Consequences

Because corruption must be hidden from the public, transaction costs arising from corruption can be significantly higher than those incurred for legal exchanges. Because of the ever-present threat of mutual denunciation, partners of a corrupt agreement are locked in to each other even after an exchange has materialized. Thus, corruption can involve high costs and great uncertainties about payoffs. Although it is possible that returns from corruption may outweigh costs incurred for a specific deal in the short term, it is unlikely, if not impossible, that a firm can build on corruption to achieve a sustainable competitive advantage or abnormal profitability in the long run. In fact, what differentiates the organizational view and the microeconomics view is that the former addresses the corruption effect at the organizational level whereas the latter assesses this effect at the transaction level. From a short-term economic perspective, one may argue that corruption can help reduce costs of a specific transaction from increased institutional privileges or reduced regulatory barriers (see Bunker and Cohen, 1983; Schleifer and Vishny, 1993). However, when one looks at an overall, long-term organizational effect of corruption, the combined organizational losses may outweigh the gains from a specific transaction or deal. In some cases, corruption can make the MNC suffer enormously from many visible or invisible damages that are so enduring and far-reaching that no single transactional gain can compensate. I explain below that corruption may create evolutionary hazard, strategic impediment, competitive disadvantage, and organizational deficiency.

Of course, one can always find some exceptional or historical cases to counter-argue the above premise. That is, some firms may achieve some short-run as well as long-run net financial gains. This likelihood is precisely one of the principal origins of rampant corporate corruption – they want these gains by a fluke. The degree of trusting luck (not being caught) is determined by both external environments (e.g., anti-corruption laws, stringency of law enforcement, political transparency, and media freedom) and internal environments (e.g., code of conduct, consciousness of senior management, myopia of executives, and relationship with politicians or regulators in power). When these external and internal anti-corruption measures are absent, the above net financial gains are more likely to accrue. As the climate of anti-corruption improves, the net gains in the eyes of corrupting executives are expected to differ from those as perceived by the public. The image effect in the eyes of the public is enduring, far reaching, and more significant than the financial figures. Even if the corruption is permanently unknown by the public (surely rare), it still deters corporate confidence, managerial morale, and the organizational culture necessary for the healthy growth of the firm, particularly in the long run. These invisible and imprinted effects are often ignored, and the image punishment is sometimes more profound than the justice punishment. One may escape from the justice conviction, but it is difficult to do so from the image punishment forever.

6.6.1 Evolutionary hazard

As an evolutionary hazard in the long term, corruption obstructs firm growth and business development through four interrelated channels, namely risk effect, punishment effect, image effect, and cost effect. First, all corrupt activities are highly risky for all actors because of their illicit nature. Such activities are always based on oral agreements that are covert, hidden, and nontransparent (Lambsdorff, 2002). The degree of risk is a function of the bureaucratic corruptor's willingness, power, position, experience, and network. Since many corrupt activities are associated with many people, including officials, businessmen, and others who may not even know each other, the discovery of a criminal fraud in any stage of the corruption process or any person in the corruption web could quickly impose high risks to everyone else linked to the network. When a firm uses bribery to achieve its business goals, an entire MNC is thus involved with the risky and unpredictable process. Any person, whether top or middle management, can risk the whole company's reputation if he is found to be engaged in corruption for organizational purposes.

Second, when a criminal fraud of corruption for an organizational purpose is found, both the individual and the MNC will be punished legally, institutionally, and disciplinarily. During the anti-corruption campaign, judiciary punishment is particularly harsh and includes criminal sanctions as well as economic fines. Institutional punishment includes the reorganization of an entire firm led by the upper level government authority, removing the top managers involved in bribery, and rectifying a series of operational and financial policies. Generally, it will take several years for a company to restore its normal business after reorganization by the government. The firm has to rebuild business connections and its reputation. Institutional punishment may also include the cancellation of institutional membership in industrial associations, elimination of preferential policies previously provided by the government, and placement of quasi-governmental auditors in top management decisions or board meetings. Although disciplinary punishment is relatively parochial and affects only those middle managers who are directly involved as well as those senior managers who are indirectly engaged, its impact on business operations can be crucial. Disciplinary punishment against those important managers of a firm by governmental authorities demotes or freezes their business posts. This substantially deters their future commitment to the firm. When they quit their jobs after punishment, most of their customers and networks go with them. As explained below, the punishment also sabotages the firm's reputation or legitimacy, which further deters organizational evolution.

Third, the image effect mainly lies in the stereotypical loss that either increases costs or reduces the income stream for the company. Many consumers around the world purchase products according to the stereotype or image of a company. When a company's engagement in corruption is publicized, consumers will quickly form a stereotype that this company is poorly managed, produces defective products, and is incapable of ensuring customer service. Once a company is perceived as fitting this stereotype by the market, it is difficult for it to survive and grow. Previous research suggests that organizational image is positively associated with organizational performance (Hogg and Terry, 2000) and that social image and organizational identity are reciprocally interchanged (Gioia, Schultz, and Corley, 2000). Indeed, the corruption–performance relationship is often a vicious cycle: corruption hurts firm performance, ill-performing firms tend to use more bribery as the prescription to cure their illness, and more bribery further increases costs and plagues their reputation, thereby deteriorating performance.

Finally, all transactions entailing some element of corruption inevitably involve financial costs. Corporate bribery itself is a monetary investment aimed at organizational payoffs through suborning bureaucratic or collective power, which is otherwise not legally achievable. Unlike social networking that essentially builds on favor exchanges, bribery is a fully monetary transaction between power and illegal private gains. Although the price of these transactions varies among different deals depending upon the clearing equilibrium between "demand" and "supply," the marginal revenue of bribery is generally low due to a high level of visible costs and invisible risks as mentioned above. A bureaucratic corruptor will usually "charge" more (i.e., "risk premium") when this risk is perceived to be higher. As a result, a company must not only pay more but also assume more risk when corruption risk is high. This cost effect directly arrests a firm's growth potential.

6.6.2 Strategic impediment

Corruption as a strategic impediment is mainly manifested in resource misallocation, capability-building deterrence, and lack of confidence and predictability. According to the resource-based view of firms, resources that can generate a sustainable competitive advantage in every firm are limited. Facing this constraint, the strategy to allocate these resources is essential to the growth and evolution of the firm. This allocation could have an even deeper impact on firm performance than resources themselves, since the former affects a firm's dynamic capability, whereas the latter influences only a firm's static capability (Barney, 1991). All bribery activities, no matter whom they target, have to invest financial resources, human resources, and time. Financial resources may not be strategic in advanced market economies, but are still distinctive in many emerging economies. This is because bribery money mostly comes from a firm's internal discretionary funds that are not exposed in the open accounting book (some new private entrepreneurs may pay from their own pockets). In all nations' accounting laws or standards, bribery expenditures cannot be recorded as production costs (direct or indirect) or as operational expenses (overhead). For most firms in emerging or transition economies, accumulated internal funds are very limited given the high risk of exposure.

In a competitive environment, firm growth depends on its dynamic capabilities such as organizational learning, knowledge upgrading, continuous innovation, and innovative corporate culture. In a bribery culture and corruption atmosphere, none of these dynamic capability mechanisms can be fostered and nourished. Instead, corruption obstructs organizational movement in such directions. A firm relying on bribery generally perceives corrupt acts as a substitute for innovative technological and organizational skills. It may expect bribery to be a quicker, and perhaps more effective, strategic instrument by which it may accomplish its organizational goals, rather than focusing on building and upgrading its dynamic capabilities. When top managers attach high value to corrupt acts, firms may experience greater organizational inertia and less commitment to the development of new organizational capabilities.

Lack of predictability and confidence always accompanies corrupt deals, which in turn impede business development. In all corrupt deals, whether within task environments or institutional environments, terms and conditions are never sufficiently specified at the beginning. Partners in this deal may avoid precision to preserve the chance of finding better excuses later, and to suggest that their deal is merely an exchange of gifts between friends. This non-specification and related uncertainty create additional costs and difficulties in strategic planning, flexibility maintenance, and strategy implementation. A confidence loss can be portrayed from two lenses – confidence of outside stakeholders, especially investors and creditors, is adversely affected by a focal firm's corruption, and confidence of internal managers is undermined by fears of leakage of the illegal activities. Both types of confidence loss undercut business evolution.

6.6.3 Competitive disadvantage

Corruption as a competitive disadvantage is reflected by dishonesty and untrustworthiness which can hurt a firm's competitive position in the market. An exchange partner worthy of trust is one who will not exploit the other's exchange vulnerabilities. While trust is an attribute of a relationship between exchange partners, trustworthiness is an attribute of individual exchange partners. According to the resource-based view, credibility is an important resource that creates competitive advantage and distinguishes a firm from its rivals. Corrupt acts, however, precipitate dishonesty and dissipate credibility. When a firm is involved in corruption and bribery, other firms will perceive it as unreliable and will avoid conducting business with it. Dishonesty and unreliability thus destroy, rather than stimulate, business networks.

The illicit nature of corruption mirrors organizational untrustworthiness. Adherence to the law is a prerequisite element for corporate reputation and trustworthiness. Because organizational trustworthiness is in large part embedded in top managers' credibility and honesty, corruption has an enduring impact on the firm unless these managers are removed from the MNC. In an increasingly competitive environment, long-term relationships with suppliers, buyers, distributors, and other firms affecting a firm's backward or forward value chain become fundamental. A break in such long-term relationships as a result of corrupt activities longitudinally and fundamentally hampers a firm's market reputation and competitive advantages. Restoring old relationships and initiating new networks may take years if an incidence of corruption or bribery occurs. Moreover, unreliability and untrustworthiness arising from corruption practices reduce consumer loyalty in a firm's service. This further inflates a firm's competitive disadvantage in the market. In the perception of most consumers, corporate illegalities imply organizational illness and operational deficiency.

The hazard of untrustworthiness arising from corrupt acts goes further. Trustworthiness is particularly important in facilitating implicit long-lasting contractual ties to employees, suppliers, and customers. If a firm does not have a reputation for trustworthiness, implicit contracts will be tenuous and limited. The costs of writing and monitoring contracts and supervising employees, suppliers, or buyers will be much higher. On the contrary, a moral reputation can attract superior suppliers, employees, distributors, and customers to do business with the firm, which reduces transaction costs in the longer term through repeated exchanges. From the population perspective, if all firms are untrustworthy due to corruption involvement, such widespread unscrupulous behaviors can erode public confidence in the market and seriously hinder the ability of honest businesses to carry out their activities. In this case, the entire market system leaves itself open to charges of immorality and illegitimacy, which eventually undermines market efficiency and organizational efficiency.

6.6.4 Organizational deficiency

Corruption is often the product of mismanagement. It violates business ethics and arms-length business principles. Since top managers are more or less involved with corrupt activities, corruption implies problematic organizational leadership and ill business morality. Under such leadership, it is realistically impossible for a firm to have an innovative culture, efficient administration, transparent communication, effective information flow, and productive collaboration across departments or divisions within a firm. Corruption is an organizational pathology that results from impediments created by the bureaucratic structure (Ackerman, 2001). Its essential theme is the inability of bureaucratic organizations to accomplish public purposes because there are certain inherent characteristics in every administrative system, which are detrimental to honest behavior. Bureaucratic managers have, in general, a complex set of goals. Some goals are manifestations of pure self-interest and some are altruistic. Other goals may stand in the middle as mixed motives. Thus, every manager acts at least partly in his or her own self-interest, while some officials are motivated completely by their self-interest.

This view agrees with March and Simon's observation (1958) that most members within an MNC are motivated indirectly by organizational objectives and directly by the incentive structure. It is clear that the bureaucracy is not pure from the inside. It is also not surprising to find that organizational officials are motivated to create informational networks of friends, favor recipients, contracts, and communication links based upon primarily personal, rather than official relationships. Nor is it unusual that MNCs that cannot charge money for their services must develop non-monetary costs to impose on their clients as means of rationing their outputs. Anthony Downs calls this "the law of non-money pricing" (1967: 188). Some scholars explicitly illustrate the linkage between bureaucratic corruption and characteristics of bureaucratic MNCs. Banfield (1975) compares the main structural features of the "typical" business (a competitive MNC) with those of a government organization and concludes that corruption can be readily seen as a feature of the latter. Robert Williams (1987: 63) expresses the same concern: opportunities for bribery and nepotism may increase as the scope and size of government expand because of the impossibility of framing rules and regulations to meet every circumstance or contingency. Susan Ackerman (1999) has a more refined analysis of the relationship between bureaucratic structures and corrupt bureaucratic behavior. By examining how alternative bureaucratic structures affect the incidence and level of corruption, she stresses the necessity for reformers to "move on to propose more particularized structures – closer monitoring, higher pay, nonvested pension, rights, and so forth – that will increase the expected costs of peculation at the critical soft spots".

In conclusion, this section distinguishes between deal-specific outcomes and overall organizational outcomes of corruption. Many executives active in corruption see some gains from a short-term economic perspective, which emphasizes a specific transaction and ignores hazardous consequences from an overall, long-term organizational perspective. Organizational consequences of corruption are four-fold:

1. evolutionary hazards, including risk effect, image effect, punishment effect, and cost effect;
2. strategic impediments, including resource misallocation, capability-building deterrence, and lack of predictability and confidence;
3. competitive disadvantage, including dishonesty, untrustworthiness, and inefficiency in repeated ties; and
4. organizational deficiency, including problematic leadership, ill business morality, and mismanagement.

To avoid these negative consequences, firms must have an organizational architecture in place, which monitors and rectifies all illicit behaviors.

6.7 Corruption and Organizational Architecture

Corruption is a durable and adaptable virus. Combating corruption requires a set of measures at various levels including addressing poverty and inequity (social aspect), enacting and enforcing anti-corruption law (legal aspect), improving democracy, media freedom, and civil service (political aspect), and reforming dysfunctional governments (regulatory aspect), among others (see Ackerman, 1999; Lambsdorff, 1999; LaPalombra, 1994; Scott, 1972; Tanzi, 1998; Treisman, 2000). Aiming at presenting an organizational logic of corruption, this study suggests that, in addition to the above legal, social, political, and regulatory measures, the corporate community is also an important force in combating corruption. Anti-corruption in any society cannot succeed unless it is addressed by individual organizations. Anti-corruption at the organizational level is institutionalized through an organizational architecture, which is composed of: (i) culture; (ii) structure; and (iii) system. An effective organizational architecture is one that ultimately yields intended results, namely, education, detection, and deterrence, through an interlaced corporate culture, organizational structure, and compliance system.

Institutional theorists hold that pressures for legitimacy may reside in the explicit demands of task and institutional environments or in the fact that certain forms of organizational commitment and action become taken for granted, or infused with intrinsic value (DiMaggio and Powell, 1983; Oliver, 1991; Scott, 1992). Treating anti-corruption efforts merely as legitimacy-preserving responses to external pressures from task and institutional constituents offers an unrealistically constrained view of their origin (Weaver, Trevino, and Cochran, 1999). Such a view ignores the role of managerial choice in organizational decisions. Research on strategic choice suggests that organizational endeavors at various levels, from executive leadership to corporate culture or from individual employees' responsibility sharing to each subunit's business conduct, play an important role in affecting organizational actions and performances (Child, 1972; Hitt and Tyler, 1991). In line with this view, this study holds that organizational architecture designed to counter corruption is built not merely for preserving legitimacy but also for enhancing organizational performance. This architecture improves firm performance because it brings an MNC's decisions and actions more into conformity with societal expectations, sharpens an MNC's governance, transparency, and accountability, boosts employee morale, business confidence, and corporate reputation, and enables the firm to secure the stronger support of key institutional actors. Since not all MNCs' needs for combating corruption are the same, organizational architecture should be tailored to fit a specific MNC's needs and circumstances. Different metaphors therefore should have different emphases and different programs in fighting corruption. This section discusses common architecture first, followed by special architecture to different metaphors.

6.7.1 Corporate culture

Corporate culture sets the moral tone for an MNC. Corporate culture is defined here as the statements, visions, customs, slogans, values, role models, and social rituals that are unique to, and used by, a focal MNC to resist corrupt practices. The cornerstone of an organizational architecture combating corruption is the detailed anti-corruption statement, which guides managers in how to make day-to-day decisions. Such statements should be instrumental rather than principle in tone. They can suggest that there is no inconsistency between profitability and refusing to bribe. Or they can state that the MNC will not compete for business where bribery is a requirement. MNCs should have detailed procedures for disseminating their anti-corruption statements to employees in all hierarchical levels, subunits, and locations. An effective architecture for resisting illicit conducts necessitates a multifaceted anti-corruption effort that promotes a compliance culture within the entire MNC.

Visions and commitments from leadership (e.g., board of directors, CEO, general counsel, CFO, chief internal auditing, regional or country manager) play a significant role in squashing corruption. Ethical leadership sets the moral standards for an MNC by focusing on the integrity of common purpose. These leaders should be champions and role models who lead anti-corruption efforts. Role models are important in setting a positive ethical climate because humans as social beings are influenced by other humans. Without sufficient commitment from the leadership, it is impossible for an MNC to position itself as a good citizen that is concerned with honest business practices and the need to maintain a level playing field in domestic or global markets. Identifying corruption by these leaders as a threat to an MNC's long-term health and growth serves important strategic interests. An MNC should also take reasonable measures to communicate its anti-corruption culture and values in an open environment to encourage participation and feedback. Employees should be informed as to whom they should report violations or ask questions.

Anti-corruption is widely incorporated in many MNCs' corporate culture statements and/or ethical codes. A typical example from a US MNC would be: "The Company has had a longstanding policy forbidding bribery of government officials in the conduct of its business in the United States and abroad. The Company also expects its employees to comply with the Foreign Corrupt Practices Act which prohibits the making or offering of any payment to any foreign official to induce that official to affect any governmental act or decision or to assist the Company in obtaining or retaining business. No Company employee anywhere in the world may make a bribe, payment, or gift to any government official whether or not there is an intent to influence. The Company takes this position not only because such bribe, payment, or gift would be in violation of the law, but also because of the Company's commitment to good government and the fair and impartial administration of the law".

Another general statement example for a US-based MNC would be: "It is the Company's policy to comply with the FCPA in the US and in every jurisdiction in which we operate . . . It is the Company's policy to follow both the literal terms of the FCPA and the spirit behind the law . . . This policy applies worldwide."

A more specifically stated example would be: "Bribery, or the giving of money or anything else of value in an attempt to influence the action of a public official, is unlawful. All employees are not authorized to pay any bribe or make any other illegal payment on behalf of the Company, no matter how small the amount. This prohibition extends to payments to consultants, agents or other intermediaries when you have reason to believe that some part of the payment or 'fee' will be used for a bribe or otherwise to influence government action". Appendix D illustrates some more examples of company policies and statements resisting corruption.

6.7.2 Organizational structure

Misconduct can be detected and corrected through organizational structure since this structure establishes the content of the jobs, specifies a monitoring process, and regulates ways to fulfill tasks and responsibilities. Because many corrupt acts are actually performed by individual employees on behalf of the MNC, which is often defined as an autonomous moral entity, it is critical to maintain corporate integrity. Integrity is the disposition and behavior directed at realizing the wholeness of the MNC. Formal structure is a necessary mechanism to maintain this integrity and realize legitimate moral expectations in a coherent manner. When an MNC is highly decentralized and globalized, corporate or headquarters' control of anti-corruption policies and procedures through integrated structure is imperative for integrity. Apart from structural formalization to educate, detect, and rectify illicit behaviors, an MNC may also establish an anti-corruption committee and appoint a corporate compliance officer within an existing structure to better deter corrupt activities. This committee or officer can play a key role in drafting codes of conduct and educating and training employees on compliance procedures. Committee members may include senior vice presidents for marketing and sales, auditing, operations, human resources, and other key officers. Empowering compliance officers with access to senior members of management and with the capacity to influence overall company policy on integrity issues is of utmost importance.

Transparency throughout the entire organizational structure is a necessary condition for reducing the potential for illicit dealings. Record keeping and reporting are procedures that the MNC can use to document key aspects of its compliance effort and to monitor its program for effectiveness. Even the reporting of minor incidents within the MNC can serve a useful purpose in underscoring a zero tolerance policy for questionable behaviors. The failure to report such occurrences may lead to the perception that such irregularities will be tolerated. Auditing and monitoring of systems of internal accounting controls also contribute to building an effective system by detecting corporate malfeasance early on. MNCs should have a clear and concise accounting policy that prohibits off-the-books accounts or inadequately identified transactions. They should monitor their accounts for deceptive book-keeping entries that may disguise illegal bribery.

Structural mechanisms that enforce anti-corruption programs and policies must be in play. Creating reporting mechanisms with adequate policies on confidentiality and non-retaliation as well as other safeguards related to reporting is extremely important. Despite best efforts, no MNC can be certain that the necessary element of trust is present in all formal reporting relationships. Whistle-blowing systems can help to achieve open communications when ordinary channels fail. An MNC should ensure that all employees understand that failure to comply with its anti-corruption policy and procedures will result in disciplinary action, ranging from minor sanctions to more severe punishment, including termination of employment. A good communications effort (e.g., hotlines or helplines) can build employee confidence that the MNC will not tolerate either retaliation against whistle-blowers or false reporting.

6.7.3 Compliance system

The compliance system that suppresses corruption consists of *conduct codes* and *ethics programs*, together constituting an effective organizational control that minimizes corporate illegalities. This control makes information and expectations about legal and ethical behaviors clear, increases the likelihood of detection, assures the punishment of transgressions, rewards desired behaviors, and disciplines those who engage in illegal behavior (Baucus, 1994; Weaver, Trevino, and Cochran, 1999).

6.7.3.1 Conduct code

This system begins with written commitments in areas of business ethics that are relevant to the firm's activities – that is, a code of corporate conduct that provides a set of legal and ethical guidelines for employees to follow. Such codes are voluntary expressions of commitment, made to influence or control business behavior for the benefit of the firm itself and the communities in which it operates. A corporate code of conduct generally consists of a clearly written set of legal and ethical guidelines for employees to follow. A comprehensive and clearly articulated code of conduct, as well as clear policies and procedures relative to seeking guidance and making disclosures may reduce the likelihood of actionable misconduct by employees. The codes seek to heighten employees' awareness of corporate policy and enlist their support in the fight against corruption acts. They also draw a distinction between the acceptable quid quo pro and networking that are necessary to develop business relationships and corrupt practices. Codes can contain general precepts and mandate specific practices, providing clearly stated provisions that deal with legalities and ethical concerns and detail sanctions and enforcement including the methods of investigation and detection. It is important that a company's code of conduct be distributed to everyone in the company, and, if necessary, translated into the languages of the countries abroad where an MNC invests. Finally, developing a code of conduct should not be the final act. The code must be effectively implemented and enforced at all times.

To ensure the effective enforcement of a company's code of conduct, compliance officers should be accessible so that employees will feel comfortable discussing any of their compliance questions or concerns. In this regard, creating reporting mechanisms with adequate policies on confidentiality and non-retaliation as well as other safeguards related to reporting is extremely important. Whistle-blowing protections or helplines facilitating detection and reporting of questionable conduct will further help.

Here are two examples illustrating such codes. The first one concerns a code that specifies how to deal with a foreign country's consultants and intermediaries, the approach often used by western MNCs. The second example illustrates a general statement of a code regarding the resistance of corruption in international business activities.

> Commission or fee arrangements shall be made only with firms or persons serving as bona fide commercial representatives, agents, or consultants. Such arrangements may not be entered into with any firm in which a government official or associate is known to have an interest unless the arrangement is permitted by applicable law and has been specifically approved by the company's general counsel. All commission and fee arrangements shall be by written contract. Any commission or fee must be reasonable and consistent with normal practice for the industry, the merchandise involved, and the services to be rendered. Payments shall not be made in cash. An associate may not take any action or authorize any action which involves any illegal, unethical, or otherwise improper payment of money or anything else of value.

> When conducting business in other countries, laws and local customs and practices will be encountered that differ from those in the United States. The Company's policy is to comply with all laws that apply in the countries where we do business. In countries where common customs and practices might indicate acceptance of standards of conduct different from those to which we aspire, employees should continue to follow the more stringent code of conduct, subject to reasonable business judgment. The Company's policy prohibits the making of any payment in violation of the US Foreign Corrupt Practices Act. Except as provided in this section, all payments are forbidden to officials or employees of governments or government-owned or related agencies. In some areas of the world, timely action by low-ranking government employees can be obtained only by generally accepted payment of modest gratuities. Payment of modest gratuities to

induce a person to do only what he or she is required to do and to which the Company is legally entitled is permissible if it clearly conforms to local custom. However, such payments should not be made as a matter of course; they should be the exception and not the rule, and should be considered only in circumstances where proper alternatives are not meaningfully available. Such payments must be properly recorded on the books of accounts. In no circumstances are any such payments to be made to any official or employee of any governmental entity or government-related entity of any US jurisdiction. While it is difficult to monetize "modest gratuities", local practice and good judgment should always be applied. In one country, the expediting of customs clearance for a product sample may require payment of a nominal sum, while a commercial shipment of a perishable or urgently needed item might require payment of a greater amount. In any event, should it appear that significant payments are required under conditions that would make failure to deliver extremely expensive, the Chief Financial Officer of the Company should be contacted promptly for resolution. Such disbursements should be recorded as "facilitating payments".

6.7.3.2 Compliance program

Compliance programs (e.g., training, due diligence, and formalized procedures) ostensibly bring the behavior of MNC members into conformity with a shared ethical standard. They constitute an organizational control system that encourages shared ethical aspirations and compliance with rules. Combating corruption requires legal and ethics training at every level of an MNC. Regular ethics and compliance training programs should be held for all company employees, including board members and senior management officials. It may also be necessary to educate overseas employees about host country's anti-corruption laws. For instance, foreign employees may often be confused with respect to the use of "facilitating" fees (payments to obtain such items as licenses, permits, or police protection), which are legal and customary in some developing countries. In this case, the company's well-defined policy as to how to handle such facilitation fees should be included in the training program of expatriates who are about to be dispatched. According to the FCPA, companies are allowed on occasion to make a minor payment to a foreign government employee whose duties are essentially ministerial or clerical in nature. This minor payment is usually for the purpose of expediting rather than influencing a particular decision. It is made simply to expedite some matter in a more timely or efficient manner. Facilitating payments (sometimes called "grease payments") may not be illegal under the FCPA or foreign government law enforcement policies and customs; however, in certain instances, such payments may violate local law enforcement policies or other federal statutes, particularly if they involve substantial amounts. If they involve large amounts or if otherwise material, public disclosure under SEC regulations, as noted above, may also be required. Facilitating payments must be strictly controlled and every effort must be made to eliminate or minimize such payments. Facilitating payments, if required, will be made only in accordance with local custom and practice. Recognizing that some confusion may exist as to the propriety of making facilitating payments, such payments should not be made except under the guidance of the company's legal department.

In addition, more specific legal and ethical training may be necessary for employees in high-risk and high-corruptive areas. A company should also take reasonable measures to communicate its values and procedures in an open environment to encourage participation and feedback. Furthermore, employees should be informed as to whom they should contact to report violations or ask questions. Companies should provide guidance to assist employees and agents on how to cope with and resolve difficult situations. Such counseling not only protects the person in the field, it also protect the company. More importantly, compliance issues should not be limited to training classes and the compliance team. Corporate compliance should be stressed as an integral part of the company's way of doing business.

Undertaking due diligence is vital for ensuring that anti-corruption processes are efficient and effective. Due diligence reviews are also important for preventing potential harm to the MNC's reputation. It is important not to delegate substantial discretionary authority to individuals or subunits that the MNC knows (through the exercise of due diligence) have a propensity to engage in corrupt acts. Additional ethical practices include formalized procedures or mechanisms for evaluating ethical and legal performance and for rewarding or punishing behavior. Examples include establishing a system for auditing and reporting legal–ethical violations, a formal ethics department for initiating, coordinating, and supervising an MNC's anti-corruption process, and a cross-functional committee for setting and assessing ethics policies and procedures. Motivating employees to behave legally and ethically can be prompted by the incorporation of ethics into selection, performance appraisal, discipline, and job analysis procedures. In addition, self-monitoring, monitoring of suppliers, and reports to the board of directors are all good tools for ensuring that a compliance program is being followed. Moreover, from vetting new hires, agents, or business partners to assessing risks in international business dealings (e.g., mergers, acquisitions or joint ventures), due diligence reviews can uncover questionable conduct and limit liability.

It is also crucial that all of the elements of an MNC's corporate compliance program receive the full support of upper management. If upper level management does not take efforts to combat corruption seriously, then neither will employees. The corporate compliance program must be enforced at all levels with a diversified MNC. In instances of noncompliance, a company should take the necessary preventive steps to ensure that the questionable conduct does not recur in the future.

The above elements of an organizational architecture are common to all MNCs that are active in eliminating corruption. However, MNCs differ themselves in the extent to which they emphasize each of these elements because of different organizational needs and different effectiveness of these elements in curing organization-specific illness. A compliance program therefore should be tailored to fit an individual MNC's needs and circumstances. MNCs vary in their task and institutional pressures for corruption, susceptibility to corrupt environments, motives for corrupt practices, and malfeasant behaviors. In my view, a mad fox metaphor needs a *structural surgery* to effect a radical, thorough, and drastic cure seeking a permanent removal of the corruption disease. A wild puppy needs a *specialized operation* to heal a specific part (level of hierarchy, subunit, or location within an organization body) that is substantially contaminated by corrupt practices. A sick bulldog needs a *decoupled injection* that seeps throughout an organization body in order to treat unserious but whole body affected malfeasance. Lastly, an errant rabbit needs a *partial medication* to alleviate some early-phase corruption symptoms plagued in a small part of an organization body.

Corresponding to a mad fox metaphor's system malfeasance, a structural surgery requires an entire MNC's systematic efforts to obviate rampant illicit acts permeated throughout the whole MNC. Regular codes of conduct, compliance programs, and control systems may not be sufficient to redress corporate illegalities for the mad fox. Instead, it necessitates a series of structural changes, including: (i) dismissing ill-behaved board members, senior managers, and subunit executives; (ii) restructuring the malfeasant subunits and replacing their leaderships; (iii) formalizing and routinizing anti-corruption procedures, actions, and norms into everyday organizational activities; (iv) linking ethics to personal consequences to fortify each employee's compliance and encourage salience in each individual's minds; and (v) establishing an anti-corruption office which initiates, mandates, coordinates, and supervises all corruption resistance activities. For a mad fox metaphor, it is especially essential that all elements of the anti-corruption programs receive the full support of upper management and the board of directors. More importantly, these programs must be enforced at all levels within the organization. It is important that codes of conduct be distributed to everyone in the MNC and, if necessary, translated into the languages of foreign countries where the MNC operates.

To address a wild puppy metaphor's categorical malfeasance, a specialized operation requires an area surgery which focuses on the treatment of a specific level of hierarchy, subunit, or location in which corruption is so severe and grave that the area accounts for a majority of the entire MNC's corruption. In this case, the MNC can devote most of the anti-corruption resources to suppress corruption in the area. The MNC may adopt prompt-impacting approaches and take specialized stopgap measures to quickly correct wrongdoing in this area. These measures include: (i) special training and educational seminars on resisting corruption for all employees in the area; (ii) more specific legal and ethical training for senior managers in high-risk areas or functions such as sales, promotions, procurement, public relations, and international business; (iii) change or rotation of senior managers in the area if these managers are involved in major illegalities; (iv) formation of a special workforce or committee composed of cross-functional managers in the area, role models from other areas, and officers specialized in business ethics and legal norms, in a bid to find an effective prescription; (v) enhancement of internal auditing, recording, and control over various activities conducted by the focal unit that are especially prone to corruption; (vi) stringent disciplinary punishment for failure by anyone in the area to meet ethical expectations; and (vii) requiring chief managers or directors in the area to bear or share responsibility for anti-corruption activities and tying their performance appraisal with the anti-corruption fulfillment in the area.

To rectify a sick bulldog metaphor's structural malfeasance, a decoupled injection is designed to curb system-wide corrupt practices using a series of anti-corruption policies and procedures that are standardized within an MNC and separated from its everyday workings. Unlike structural surgery that integrates anti-corruption policies and processes with other organizational policies and programs (e.g., human resource management), thus affecting the MNC's everyday decisions and actions, decoupled injection proceeds through an independent package of special rules, standards, norms, and procedures to be followed by all-level employees. The reason why this package is nonintegrated with other organizational programs and disconnected from the firm's everyday actions is the fact that the sick bulldog's corruption is not severe and its illness is at the early stage. Structural surgery may be too costly and excessive for this metaphor. Formalization and communication are especially essential to decoupled injection. Formalized rules on business ethics and conduct norms minimize leeway and opportunities that encourage corrupt acts by morally unconscious units and employees. Effective channels (e.g., memos, manuals, newsletters, and policy documents) should be established to communicate an ethics message to everyone. Singling out role models is another way of communicating explicitly what the anti-corruption efforts entail. Ethics-focused memos or newsletters may include articles highlighting recent actions undertaken by particular units or employees. These concrete examples increase the credibility of the MNC's decoupled policies, add an important texture to the definition of the organizational architecture, and communicate these policies in an accessible manner.

Finally, to redress an errant rabbit metaphor's procedural malfeasance, a partial medication is used to rectify a small scale of corrupt practices engaged by a small number of employees. Since these practices are sporadic, infant, and unserious, the errant rabbit metaphor particularly needs to sharpen employees' awareness of the importance and procedure of resisting corruption. It is possible that some employees in this metaphor face a definitional problem with bribery, and thus need special guidelines clarifying differences between legitimate activities in cultivating interpersonal connections and illicit actions that deviate from legal, ethical, and moral norms. In particular, these guidelines should specify under what circumstances certain culturally embedded practices such as gift giving and entertainment are legitimate and what formalities (approval, signature, procedure, etc.) should be conducted. Drawing the line between acceptable relationship building and corruption practices is especially crucial for employees working in a sensitive area or location in which transactions depend largely on personal links. An MNC should take steps, including compliance rewards, responsibility sharing, and an auditing system, to ensure that these guidelines and related codes of conduct are strictly carried out.

We must note, however, that ethical or compliance codes alone are not enough to combat company-level corruption for several reasons. First, codes focus primarily on company processes and employee behavior. Understandably, the key objective of a code is to establish an MNC's own business conduct standards. Companies do not consider themselves responsible for the behavior of those parties with whom they deal. It is up to each company to set and monitor standards for its own performance. This asymmetry between acceptance and giving policies suggests a less than full understanding of the most effective ethical strategy for deterring corruption. This becomes even more evident when an MNC must deal with outside business partners in a host country or from a third nation. For instance, it is difficult for an MNC to control a foreign supplier or subcontractor's bribery of governmental officials. Second, code principles are not always binding on suppliers, vendors, and joint-venture partners. Many MNC executives, especially their country managers in developing countries, believe that their host country suppliers and vendors do not necessarily subscribe to the company's anti-bribery provisions. Thus, the demand for agent and partner compliance needs to be more common for codes to be a significant factor in deterring corruption. Third, code effectiveness depends in large measure on whether or not they are introduced in an environment of trust. Absent a system that encourages employees to expose inappropriate conduct, codes will never achieve their full potential to deter wrongdoing. For most employees outside of the United States, for instance, the concept of whistle-blowing has a pejorative connotation or not much real meaning. For example, US operations in western Europe report little employee use of the company's "hotline" to report abusive practices. The picture is similar elsewhere and is sometimes complicated by other conditions such as the fear of reprisal and reported shortages of workplace telephones in certain regions.

Lastly, MNCs need to strengthen code compliance verification procedures. Precatory words are insufficient weapons for effective action. Recognizing this principle, Shell has undertaken an initiative that relies on its code as a major tool in combating corruption. Shell country managers are required to certify that "neither the company nor its authorized representatives has been party to the offering, paying or receiving of bribes" and that "no payments have been made which knowingly violate the laws of the country in which the company has operated." Where such assurances are not possible, a discussion of the reasons why and a description of specific incidents must be noted. Follow-up reports that document actions taken are also required. After all, internal procedures that demand greater disclosure and accountability are key elements in a code's rule-making authority. Corporate codes have a potentially vital role in the fight against corruption but, for the most part, MNCs have yet to acknowledge and to rise to the challenge of these new possibilities. Ultimately, global companies need to recognize that if they are serious about deterring corruption, a properly formulated, implemented, and monitored code is essential.

To sum up, this section delineates an organizational architecture designed to fight corruption. This architecture, which aims to generate three intended results, namely education, detection, and deterrence, comprised three interrelated components – culture, structure, and system. Culture addresses anti-corruption from a moral perspective while structure and system address anti-corruption from the power-related control and ethics-related compliance perspective, respectively. Because MNCs differ in task and institutional pressures for corruption, opportunity and motive for corruption, and intensity and hierarchical scales of corruption involvement, different metaphors should emphasize different treatments to rectify various illicit acts. I suggest that a mad fox metaphor needs a structural surgery to curb rampant corrupt practices permeated throughout the entire organization; a wild puppy needs a specialized operation to heal serious corruption diseases concentrated in a specific unit, area, or location; a sick bulldog needs a decoupled injection to cure its small-scale, early-phase, but whole body-plagued corruption illness; and finally, an errant rabbit needs a partial medication to exterminate a small number of corrupt symptoms residing in a small part of an MNC.

CASE EXAMPLE 6.1: RIGA CORPORATION: COLLECTION OR CORRUPTION?

In 1989, Riga Corporation was a closely held New Jersey corporation with one stockholder, Watson Riga. Riga had 15 employees and engaged in buying and selling commodities both domestically and internationally. Watson Riga had met Ricardo Logo of Verticales, a commodities broker in the Dominican Republic (DR), through a series of introductions of business acquaintances.

Logo proposed a sale of milk powder between Riga and the DR government in which Logo would receive the industry standard broker's commission. Watson Riga, on behalf of his corporation, entered into a contract to sell milk powder to the government of the DR. This was his first foray into this Caribbean nation, and he was unfamiliar with the country and its history. Riga had been warned about the Foreign Corrupt Practices Act by his lawyer, Darlene Trump, but this deal seemed straightforward.

Specifically, Riga agreed to sell 1500 tons (metric) of milk powder to the DR government for $2200 a metric ton, bringing the contract price to $3.3 million (US). Logo would get a commission of $102 per metric ton or $153,000. This was a standard clause and comparable to contracts around the world. Riga was to release the milk powder after payment was wired and received by his bank in New Jersey. Alternatively, Riga could choose to release the powder, and the government would be obligated to pay within 60 days of delivery of the powder. They would pay an interest rate of prime rate plus one percent and after 60 days there would be late fees and additional penalties.

In October 1989 and January 1990, Riga shipped 870 tons of powder to the Dominican Republic pursuant to the contract. It was placed in a warehouse there until Riga received a wire transfer of funds at his designated bank in New Jersey. The government made full payment.

Riga shipped the final 630 tons of powder to the Dominican Republic warehouse between March and May of 1990. Riga did not plan to release the powder until he was paid in New Jersey. In May of 1990, just prior to an election in the Dominican Republic, government officials asked Riga for a favor. Before the election and without prepayment (as was done previously), they wanted him to release the remaining powder, which was in the local warehouse.

Riga discussed this with his wife. He understood that if he did release the powder giving the DR time to pay, there would no doubt be more business. If he did not release it, he might as well say goodbye to this new market. His wife asked him, "Doesn't the contract protect you? If you give the DR the powder, don't they have to pay you? And if they are late, you will get even more money in penalties? So what's the problem?"

He wondered. After all, the DR had made the first payment with no problem. There had been no squawking about the quality of the powder; they seemed very satisfied. The contract supposedly protected him. If they were late in paying him, he would collect interest on the unpaid balance. It seemed like a win–win proposition. Logo had encouraged him to accede to the government's request too.

His lawyer, Darlene Trump, had not been as sanguine about the whole idea. She reminded him, "Riga, you can be legally correct and still not have the money in your pocket. It can cost you money to collect, and everyone knows that, especially in international transactions. They can squeeze you by offering less money up front in settlement of the debt. They know it could take years to collect the full amount, and then it is usually a victory because you have spent so much in legal fees trying to collect. That doesn't factor in the time value of money either. Think about it before you release that powder without money in your hand. But only you can gauge the value of the unspoken promise of future business in return for these delayed payment terms."

Riga was annoyed. Lawyers always seemed to be covering their backsides. Never a clear answer. But business involved risk, and he was ready to move forward.

Riga gave the go ahead to release the powder in May 1990. Two months passed and there was no payment from the DR. By November 1990, the DR had made a payment, but still the DR owed Riga one million dollars in principal and interest. Riga was a small company and its customer, albeit a government, owed it a million dollars. This account had been due for seven months. Riga believed the account receivable was an intolerable drain on the cash flow of the business.

Riga began a campaign to collect the money. Riga called and wrote DR government officials. Nothing changed. By January 1991, Riga began focusing on US officials – trying congressmen, the ambassador and the American Chamber of Commerce in the Dominican Republic. Finally in September 1991, over one year after Riga had completed his performance under the contract, the DR paid him $400,000. During this time, the DR government never disputed that it owed the money or that there was any problem with the powder delivered.

For the next year, Riga continued to write letters to assorted officials of both countries, trying to get some attention to this problem of his uncollected contract payment. He even wrote to the president of the DR, Dr. Joaquin Belaguer. By June of 1992, a full two years after delivery, Riga had received a few interim payments, but $163,000 was still due.

Riga's frustration was palpable. He regularly talked to Logo about what he could do to get paid. At some point in June 1992, Logo related that he had had a conversation with an unnamed Dominican official who said that for a "service fee" he could personally arrange the payment of what was owed on the contract. Reluctantly but anxious to secure payment, Riga agreed to Logo's proposal. He made arrangements with a Dominican bank on August 11, 1992 to transfer a portion of the money to be paid to a New Jersey bank and the rest to Logo's account. On August 12, the Dominican government deposited $100,000 in the DR bank which followed Riga's instructions transferring $70,000 to New Jersey and $30,000 to Logo's local account.

On August 17, 1992, Riga spoke with Robert Jenks, a foreign service officer in the US Embassy in Santo Domingo. Riga was recounting the two-year horror show of trying to collect his money, and Jenks commiserated with him. Riga mentioned the "service fee" request, and Jenks audibly gasped. Jenks said very loudly, "Don't do it. Just say no. It ain't worth it, you know. What are you owed – $60,000 now? What, are you crazy?"

Riga tried to get off the phone. He mumbled, "Don't worry – I am not crazy. I have been around and can smell trouble. Oh. . . . O.K. Say Jenks, I have got a call on the other line about a deal in Nigeria. From the frying pan into the fire, eh? So I'll talk to you later – Okay? Take care and stay out of those hurricanes' paths". Jenks replied, "Right. Take care man. Stay out of trouble." Riga heard the dial tone and cradled the receiver. He placed the phone down uttering softly, "They owe me, damn it. Why should I give up what amounts to years of college tuition when I don't have to?"

The next day Riga received a fax from Jenks. The fax stated:

[. . . This will confirm our phone conversation of August 17, 1992. Any payment of a "service fee" to a "foreign official" will be deemed a violation of the Foreign Corrupt Practices Act. You are warned that any payment hereafter will be deemed a "knowing" violation of the law.]

Five days later Riga responded by fax to Jenks:

[August 23 Dear Robert: Thanks for your concern. As my contact in Jamaica always says – no problem – not to worry. I don't plan on setting myself up for a vacation at Lompoc Federal Prison. There are better ways to get the rest. Perhaps I will see you in DC this fall. Best, Watson]

Riga wanted Jenks to forget they ever had a conversation in which the words "service fee" surfaced. For that matter, Riga wanted to forget he had ever heard the words and he wanted to erase this two-year nightmare collection process from his memory. Riga consoled himself. How different was this from collecting delinquent accounts in the United States? He had allowed a middleman to take a percentage of money collected on overdue accounts. Isn't that what Logo was – a middleman? How did he really know or control what Logo was doing thousands of miles away? Riga had on file a form which Logo had signed which acknowledged that Logo would follow the FCPA. Riga knew he would never have paid a bribe to get the business in the DR. This was murky though. He did not agree with Jenks but he just was sick of the whole matter and wanted it to be over. After he was paid, he would have plenty of time to decide if he wanted to do business in the DR again.

On September 3, 1992, the Dominican government made the last payment of $63,905 to the DR bank and following Riga's instructions transferred $20,000 to Logo's account and wired the remaining amount to Riga's New Jersey account. A smile inched across Riga's face. Two years and it was over. He exhaled loudly. Riga felt he could finally close the book on the DR milk powder deal. He had learned some lessons. Business school had not fully prepared him for the dilemmas he had faced in his career. Everything seemed more clear-cut when he was analyzing those cases in Philadelphia. But he was 40 years old and still learning. He thought that was a good sign.

Three months later, Watson Riga was indicted for violations of the Foreign Corrupt Practices Act and faced a trial in New Jersey Federal District Court.

(Source: Excerpted from Shenkar, O. and Luo, Y. (2004). *International Business*. New York: Wiley. The original case was written by Beverley Earle, Bentley College.)

REFERENCES AND FURTHER READING

Ackerman, S.R. (1975). The economics of corruption. *Journal of Public Economics*, **4**: 187–203.

Ackerman, S.R. (1999). *Corruption and Government: Causes, Consequences, and Reform*. Cambridge: Cambridge University Press.

Ackerman, S.R. (2001). Trust and honesty in post-socialist societies. *KYKLOS*, **54**: 415–44.

Banfield, E.C. (1975). Corruption as a feature of government organization. *Journal of Law and Economics*, **18**: 587–605.

Barney, J. (1991). Firm resources and sustained competitive advantages. *Journal of Management*, **17**: 99–120.

Baucus, M. (1994). Pressure, opportunity, and predisposition: A multivariate model of corporate illegality. *Journal of Management*, **10**: 699–721.

Bunker, S.G. and Cohen, L.E. (1983). Collaboration and competition in two colonization projects: Toward a general theory of official corruption. *Human Organization*, **42**: 106–14.

Burns, T. and Flam, H. (1986). *The Shaping of Social Organization: Social Rule System Theory and its Applications*. London: Sage.

Child, J. (1972). Organizational structure, environment and performance. The role of strategic choice. *Sociology*, **6**: 1–22.

The Conference Board (2000). Company programs for resisting corrupt practices: A global study. *Research Report 1279-00-RR*, New York: The Conference Board.

Dess, G.G. and Beard, D.W. (1984). Dimensions of organizational task environments. *Administrative Science Quarterly*, **29**: 52–73.

DiMaggio, P.J. and Powell, W.W. (1983). The iron cage revisited: Institutional isomorphism and collective rationality in organization fields. *American Sociological Review*, **48**: 147–60.

Doig, A. and Theobald, R. (2000). *Corruption and Democratization*. London: Frank Cass.

Downs, A. (1967). *Inside Bureaucracy*. Boston: Little, Brown.

Geletkanycz, M.A. and Hambrick, D.C. (1997). The external ties of top executives: Implications for strategic choice and performance. *Administrative Science Quarterly*, **42**: 654–81.

Gioia, D.A., Schultz, M., and Corley, K.G. (2000). Organizational identity, image, and adaptive instability. *Academy of Management Review*, **25**(1): 63–81.

Global Corruption Report (2001). Transparency International, Berlin, Germany.

Goldsmith, A.A. (1999). Slapping the grasping hand: Correlates of political corruption in emerging markets. *American Journal of Economics and Sociology*, **58**(4): 866–83.

Hitt, M.A. and Tyler, B. (1991). Strategic decision models: Integrating different perspectives. *Strategic Management Journal*, **12**: 327–51.

Hogg, M.A. and Terry, D.J. (2000). Social identity and self-categorization processes in organizational contexts. *Academy of Management Review*, **25**(1): 121–40.

Husted, B.W. (1999). Wealth, culture, and corruption. *Journal of International Business Studies*, **30**(2): 339–60.

Johnson, S., Kaufman, D., and Lobaton, P.Z. (1998). Regulatory discretion and the unofficial economy. *American Economic Review*, **88**(2): 387–92.

Kaufmann, D., Kraay, A., and Lobaton, P.Z. (1999). Governance matters. World Bank Policy Research Paper, no. 2196, Washington, DC: World Bank.

Lambsdorff, J.G. (1999). Corruption in international research: A review. Transparency International Working Paper, Berlin. www.transparency.de [10.11.00].

Lambsdorff, J.G. (2002). Making corrupt deals: Contracting in the shadow of the law. *Journal of Economic Behavior and Organization*, **48**: 221–41.

LaPalombra, J. (1994). Structural and institutional aspects of corruption. *Social Research*, **LXI**: 325–50.

Lawrence, P.R. and Lorsch, J.W. (1967). *Organization and Environment: Managing Differentiation and Integration*. Boston: Harvard Business Press.

Luo, Y. (2002). *Multinational Enterprises in Emerging Markets*. Copenhagen: Copenhagen Business School Press.

March, J.G. and Simon, H.A. (1958). *Organization*. New York: Wiley.

Mauro, P. (1995). Corruption and growth. *Quarterly Journal of Economics*, **110**: 681–712.

Meyer, J.W. and Scott, W.R. (1983). *Organizational Environments: Ritual and Rationality*. Beverly Hills, CA: Sage.

Oliver, C. (1991). Strategic responses to institutional processes. *Academy of Management Review*, **16**: 145–79.

Pfeffer, J. and Salancik, G. (1978). *The External Control of Organizations: A Resource Dependence Perspective*. New York: Harper & Row.

Provan, K.G. 1983. The federation as an interorganizational linkage network. Academy of Management Review, **8**: 79–89.

Schleifer, A. and Vishny, R.W. (1993). Corruption. *Quarterly Journal of Economics*, **108**(3): 599–617.

Scott, J.C. (1972). *Comparative Political Corruption*. Englewood Cliffs, NJ: Prentice Hall.

Scott, W.R. (1992). *Organizations: Rational, Natural, and Open Systems*. Englewood Cliffs, NJ: Prentice Hall.

Tanzi, V. (1998). Corruption around the world: Causes, consequences, scope, and cures. IMF Working Paper 98/63. Washington, DC: IMF.

Tool, M.R. (1993). *Institutional Economics: Theory, Method, and Policy*. Boston: Kluwer Academic.

Treisman, D. (2000). The causes of corruption: A cross-national study. *Journal of Public Economics*, **76**: 399–457.

Tushman, M. and Nadler, D. (1978). Information processing as an integrating concept in organizational design. *Academy of Management Review*, **3**: 613–24.

US Department of State (2001). *Fighting Global Corruption: Business Risk Management*. Washington, DC: Department of State Publication 10731.

Wei, S-J. (2000). Natural openness and good government. NBER Working Paper 7765, www.nber.org.

Weaver, G., Trevino, L., and Cochran, P. (1999). Integrated and decoupled corporate social performance: Managerial commitments, external pressures, and corporate ethical practices. *Academy of Management Journal*, **42**: 539–52.

Williams, R. (1987). *Political Corruption in Africa*. Aldershott, UK: Gower.

Chapter 7

Corporate Governance and Social Responsibilities in International Business

EXECUTIVE SUMMARY

Corporate social responsibility (CSR) is a growing trend that reflects changing social attitudes about the obligations that firms hold with respect to the societies in which they operate. More then ever before, MNCs are now expected to account explicitly for all aspects of their performance – not just their financial results, but their social and environmental performance as well. This chapter illuminates four interrelated issues: (i) defining and understanding the importance of CSR; (ii) explaining global CSR's principles, elements, standards, and practices for MNCs; (iii) discussing the relationship between global CSR and global corporate governance; and (iv) offering managerial guidelines for improving MNCs' global CSR.

CSR refers to a business organization's configuration of social responsibility processes of social responsiveness, and policies, programs and observable outcomes as they relate to the firm's societal relationship. As explained in this chapter, CSR has various dimensions, one of which is ethics, but CSR is distinct from business ethics. In general, CSR encompasses four dimensions, namely, economic, legal, ethical, and philanthropic. An MNC's global CSR encompasses four categories: (i) internal aspects that address the relationships with employees and unions; (ii) external aspects that address the relationships with foreign suppliers, local community, and indigenous people; (iii) accountability and transparency; and (iv) corporate citizenship.

Global CSR is an important part of global corporate governance because it helps satisfy the needs of all major stakeholders. MNCs must address social, environmental, and economic demands from stakeholders, as well as financial demands from shareholders. It becomes clear that CSR is a governance issue, which means it belongs squarely on the board's agenda. A typically structured approach to CSR development consists of six sequential steps:

1. List the expectations and demands of the stakeholders.
2. Formulate a vision and a mission with regard to corporate social responsibility and, if desired, a code of conduct.
3. Develop a set of short- and longer-term strategies with regard to corporate social responsibility.
4. Set up a monitoring and reporting system.
5. Embed the process by rooting it in the organization's culture, quality, and management systems.
6. Communicate internally and externally about the approach and the results obtained.

The later part of this chapter emphasizes how MNCs can practically improve and strengthen their global CSR performance. To this end, my discussion focuses on the following eight areas:

1. Following global guidelines and mandates.
2. Redefining corporate values in global business.
3. Implementing corporate ethics programs by directors, executives, managers, and employees around the world.
4. Understanding the global stakeholders' needs.
5. Fortifying organizational credibility and legitimacy in host countries.
6. Reformulating the key roles of both corporate and subsidiary boards.
7. Formulating a viable sustainability program that addresses global stakeholders' long-term concerns.
8. Undertaking CSR auditing and assessment.

7.1 Concept and Importance of Corporate Social Responsibility

7.1.1 Concept of corporate social responsibility

Corporate social responsibility (CSR) is fundamentally an ethical concept. It involves changing notions of human welfare and emphasizes a concern about the social dimensions of business activity that have a direct impact on quality of life in the society. Thus, CSR is about an organization's obligation to conduct business in a way that safeguards the welfare of society while pursuing its own interest. The concept provides a way for a business to concern itself with social dimensions and pay attention to its social impacts. The basic idea of CSR is that business and society are interwoven rather than distinct entities; therefore, society has certain expectations for appropriate business behavior and outcomes. The word "responsibility" implies that business organizations have certain obligations towards the society in which they function to deal with social problems and contribute more than just economic services. CSR involves a balanced approach for organizations to address economic, social, and environmental issues in a way that aims to benefit people, community, and society. Recent crises have certainly highlighted the importance of corporate social responsibility along with corporate governance. The failings of Enron, WorldCom, and Global Crossing, the dubious accounting practices of countless more firms, and the charges of poor governance practices of publicly held firms have shaken the confidence of every investor.

CSR is related to but different from business ethics. CSR has various dimensions, one of which is ethics. In general, CSR encompasses four dimensions, namely, economic, legal, ethical, and philanthropic. In Carroll's definitional framework (1999), economic responsibilities are placed at the foundation of the pyramid; moving up the pyramid are legal, ethical, and philanthropic responsibilities, respectively. Society requires business to discharge its economic and legal responsibilities, it expects business to fulfill its ethical responsibilities and it desires that business meet its philanthropic responsibilities. Ethics is a part of corporate values and shapes decisions concerning social responsibility with respect to internal and external stakeholders or environments. Business ethics comprises principles and standards that guide behavior in the world of business. Whether a specific required behavior is right or wrong, ethical or unethical, is often determined by stakeholders. Again, ethics is one of the dimensions of CSR, and relatedly, ethic codes or programs are one of the means to develop and improve a company's corporate social performance.

CSR must be seen in conjunction with the basic functioning of the company in a broader sense. It must radiate outwards to the society from within the core efficiencies of the firm. CSR, thus, self-consciously raises the stakes for itself, and, in doing so, sets new targets and challenges that eventually impact the industry as a whole. For example, Bill Gates' efforts in raising computer literacy will eventually help the software industry all around the world in general and Microsoft in particular. Pharmaceutical concerns can set up public health clinics to better understand how people react to illness and then factor that knowledge into research and development. Similarly, R&D activities by the business may be outsourced to academic and research institutions to a greater extent, in the pattern of advanced economies such as the US and Europe, the benefit of which can jointly be enjoyed by larger segments of society. As major users of nature, society, and environment, companies should, and could, play an important role in the protection of nature and the environment and promote social objectives. To achieve these objectives they can work in partnership with government, with other interest groups, or on their own. For example, an informal partnership between Exxon Mobil, the Government of Zimbabwe, and some local groups in the design of exploration for oil in the Zambezi River Valley is a positive step towards the growth and development of a sense of joint social responsibility.

Wood (1991) offers an integrated framework on the principles of corporate social responsibility, which is reproduced in Table 7.1. First, legitimacy is the institutional principle of CSR. Society grants legitimacy and power to business. In the long run, those who do not use power in a manner which society considers responsible will tend to lose it (Davis, 1973: 314). This principle, which is Davis's (1973) iron law of responsibility, expresses legitimacy as a societal-level concept and describes the responsibility of business as a social institution that must avoid abusing its power.

Table 7.1 Principles of corporate social responsibility

The principle of legitimacy: Society grants legitimacy and power to business. In the long run, those who do not use power in a manner which society considers responsible will tend to lose it.

Level of application	Institutional, based on a firm's generic obligations as a business organization.
Focus	Obligations and sanction.
Value	Defines the institutional relationship between business and society and specifies what is expected of any business.

The principle of public responsibility: Businesses are responsible for outcomes related to their primary and secondary areas of involvement with society.

Level of application	Organizational, based on a firm's specific circumstances and relationships to the environment.
Focus	Behavioral parameters for organizations.
Value	Confines a business's responsibility to those problems related to the firm's activities and interests, without specifying a too-narrow domain of possible action.

The principle of managerial discretion: Managers are moral actors. Within every domain of corporate social responsibility, they are obliged to exercise such discretion as is available to them, toward socially responsible outcomes.

Level of application	Individual, based on people as actors within organizations.
Focus	Choice, opportunity, personal responsibility.
Value	Defines managers' responsibility to be moral actors and to perceive and exercise choice in the service of social responsibility.

Thus, this principle expresses a prohibition rather than an affirmative duty, and it applies equally to all companies, regardless of their particular circumstances. Second, public responsibility is the organizational principle of CSR. Under this principle, businesses are responsible for outcomes related to their primary and secondary areas of involvement with society. Public responsibility refers to the functions of organizational management within the specific context of public policy. This principle eliminates the convenient hiding place that was temporarily available to executives who would rather not take on duties that were so vaguely defined. Businesses are not responsible for solving all social problems, but they are responsible for solving problems that they have caused, and they are responsible for helping to solve problems and social issues related to their business operations and interests. This principle brings CSR down to earth for specific firms. It also leaves substantial room for managerial discretion in determining what social problems and issues are relevant and how they should be addressed. The third principle, which is at the individual level, addresses managerial discretion. Under the principle of managerial discretion, managers are moral actors. Within every domain of corporate social responsibility, they are obligated to exercise such discretion as is available to them toward socially responsible outcomes. Ackerman (1975: 32–3) wrote about corporate social responsibility as "the management of discretion," referring not to philanthropy or community involvement programs, but to the discretion extant in the total realm of managerial actions and choices. Hence, the principle of managerial discretion is premised on the following ideas: (i) managers exist in an organizational and societal environment that is full of choices; (ii) managers' actions are not totally prescribed by corporate procedures, formal job definitions, resource availabilities or technologies; and (iii) management contains moral actions. Because managers possess discretion and choices, they are personally responsible for exercising it and cannot avoid this responsibility through reference to rules, policies, or procedures.

CSR encompasses several common elements. KLD (Kinder, Lydenberg and Domini & Co. Inc.) provides multifaceted scores that rate the entire Standard & Poor's 500 companies. KLD is an independent rating service that focuses exclusively on assessment of corporate social performance across a range of dimensions related to stakeholder concerns. KLD's CSR performance entails (i) community; (ii) diversity (treatment of women and minorities); (iii) employee relations; (iv) environment; (v) product; and (vi) negative screens. The first five items are really about relationship management with different groups of stakeholders while the last item deals with some very special social issues such as military involvement (e.g., weapon-manufacturing contract from the Department of Defense) and nuclear power involvement (e.g., construction or ownership participation in nuclear power projects).

A more recent global survey (Welford, 2005) included a total of 20 items constituting a company's overall CSR. This new approach is a better fit for MNCs' CSR in the international business environment. These 20 items are grouped into four categories: (i) internal aspects that address the relationships with employees and unions (six items); (ii) external aspects that address the relationships with foreign suppliers, local community, and indigenous people (nine items); (iii) accountability and transparency (two items); and (iv) corporate citizenship (three items). These items include:

A. Internal aspects

1. Written policies on non-discrimination in the workplace (non-discrimination).
2. Equal opportunities statements and implementation plans (equal opportunity).
3. Statement on normal working hours, maximum overtime, and fair wage structure (fair wages).
4. Staff development, in-house education, and vocational training (vocational education).
5. The right of freedom of association, collective bargaining, and complaints procedures (association or union).
6. The protection of human rights within the company's own operations (human rights within the firm).

B. External aspects

7. Policy on labor standards adopted by suppliers in developing countries (labor standard).
8. Policy on restrictions on the use of child labor by suppliers (child labor).
9. Commitment to the protection of human rights in the company's sphere of influence (human rights in the supplier firm).
10. Inspection of suppliers' facilities for health, safety, and environmental aspects (supplier environment).
11. Commitment to local community protection and engagement (community).
12. Policy on responding to stakeholders including procedures for the resolution of complaints (stakeholder responsiveness).
13. Policies on fair trade, equitable trade, and end-price auditing (fair trade).
14. Policies on the protection of indigenous populations and their rights (indigenous people).
15. Code of ethics (including bribery and corruption) (ethics).

C. Accountability

16. Commitment to reporting on corporate social responsibility and/or sustainable development (reporting).
17. Policies and procedures for engaging in wide range of stakeholders in two-way dialogue (openness).

D. Citizenship

18. Direct support for third-party social and sustainable development-related initiatives (third parties).
19. Educational programs for the promotion of corporate citizenship (education).
20. External campaign programs for raising social and sustainable development issues (campaigns).

Each of the above items is not static. The CSR system is instead a dynamic process that requires the company to properly assess environment first, then undertake stakeholder management, and finally perform issues management. CSR is essentially about responsiveness, an ecological concept suggesting organizational survival through adaptation to environmental conditions. To translate CSO into managerial action, executives must first know the norms and requirements of the social, political, and legal environments at home and abroad. In the process of stakeholder management, companies must know the different interests and changing demands of varying stakeholders in order to build and maintain a solid and healthy relationship with them. Issues management refers to policies developed to address social issues, which are often further classified into issues of identification, issues of analysis, and response development. These three facets of responsiveness – environmental assessment (context), stakeholder management (actors), and issues management (interests) – are pragmatically and sequentially interlocked. Stakeholders are involved in issues; issues involve stakeholders and their interests; and information about the environment is necessary for responses to be made. Responsiveness provides a link among these facets and, thus, can help to map how managers and firms act regarding environmental and stakeholder conditions and expectations.

7.1.2 Importance of corporate social responsibility

A central assumption underlying CSR is that organizations are social entities whose responsibilities far exceed maximizing shareholders' wealth. Organizations are expected to disperse value to primary stakeholders. Primary stakeholders include shareholders, creditors, employees, customers, and suppliers, together with the public stakeholder group consisting of community residents, the natural environment, and governments that provide natural resources, infrastructures, and other supports necessary to nourish business development. Stakeholder theorists propose that building better relations with primary stakeholders like employees, customers, suppliers, and communities could lead to increased shareholder wealth by helping firms develop and exploit intangible, valuable assets which can be resources of competitive advantages. The relationship between CSR and corporate performance is often reciprocal. Companies that perform well usually support CSR, and those companies that pursue CSR perform well financially (Berman *et al.*, 1999). Recent studies have reaffirmed the positive effects of CSR on a firm's financial performance (Johnson and Greening, 1999; Berman *et al.*, 1999; Hillman and Keim, 2001). Morgan Stanley also recently conducted a study using data from the Oekom Research, a German agency that rates environmental and social performance. Morgan Stanley found that companies with higher sustainability ratings outperform their counterparts who score lower on sustainability practices. The study examined the 602 companies in the Morgan Stanley Capital International World Index that have received Oekom's Corporate Responsibility Ratings and found that, between January 2000 and October 2003, the 186 highest-ranked companies in terms of sustainability outperformed the remaining 416 companies by 23.4 percent.

It is a widespread consensus that investing in stakeholder relations can lead to customer or supplier loyalty, reduced turnover among employees, or improved firm reputation (Hillman and Keim, 2001). These valuable assets in turn lead to a positive relationship between a firm's investment in relationships with primary stakeholders and shareholder value wherein effective stakeholder management leads to improved financial performance. The resource-based view of the firm (Barney, 1991; Wernerfelt, 1984) suggests that a firm's ability to perform better than competitors depends on the unique interplay of human, organizational, and physical resources over time. Resources that often lead to competitive advantages include socially complex and causally ambiguous resources such as reputation, corporate culture, knowledge assets, and long-term relationships with suppliers, customers, and other major stakeholders. By developing longer term sustainable relationships with primary stakeholders, especially customers, suppliers, employees, and communities, firms expand the set of value-creating exchanges with these groups beyond that which would be possible with interactions limited to market transactions. Because of the relational aspects that underscore these activities, the time dimension will constitute an important, intangible, path-dependent quality of the relationship with that stakeholder group. These relationships will be difficult for other firms to duplicate at least in the short run. For these reasons, managing relationships with primary stakeholders can result in much more than just their continued participation in the firm. Effective stakeholder relationship investment can constitute intangible, socially complex capabilities that may enhance a firm's ability and probability to outperform competitors in terms of long-term value creation.

Reputation is also a key factor explaining the positive link between CSR and long-term performance. With enhanced CSR, a firm's organizational reputation improves in the eyes of its stakeholders. As a strategic asset of the firm, reputation is valuable, rare, and inimitable, thus creating a competitive advantage for the firm. Sustained commitment to and development in CSR may sharpen a firm's organizational legitimacy as perceived by its investors and creditors, improve a firm's organizational citizenship as portrayed by its public community stakeholders, strengthen a firm's corporate image as perceived by product-related stakeholders such as customers, suppliers, and distributors, and finally, fortify trust and confidence in the mind of organizational stakeholders such as present and future employees and shareholders. These reputation-based advantages can significantly help the firm to fulfil its economic and social objective, which is to create and distribute wealth or value sufficient to ensure that each primary stakeholder group continues as part of the firm's stakeholder system. To many companies, an increasing percentage of their corporate value today is made up of reputation, goodwill, or benevolence – assets easy to lose and difficult to regain. In consequence, companies that recognize this fact are increasingly seeing the need to take appropriate steps to minimize their negative impact on stakeholders and thereby protect their valuable reputations and goodwill. Above all, business partners always look forward to doing business with socially responsible companies.

7.2 Corporate Social Responsibility in International Business

Recall that CSR encompasses the economic, legal, ethical, and philanthropic (discretionary) expectations that society has of organizations at a given point of time. In general, an MNC's global CSR consists of four components: (i) economic responsibility (do what is required by global capitalism); (ii) legal responsibility (do what is required by global stakeholders); (iii) ethical responsibility (do what is expected by global stakeholders); and (iv) philanthropic responsibility (do what is desired by global stakeholders). An MNC's economic responsibilities remain the bedrock foundation for business. Sound strategic management offers guidelines as to how and where profit may be achieved in a global setting. At the same time, just as countries have sanctioned economic systems, they also sanction legal systems. The social contract between business firms and host countries varies by country and thus, legal systems and expectations vary as well. For example, Chinese labor laws often are not enforced and foreign investors there are finding that China's legal system resolves few disputes. Because laws are not adequate and companies and executives must care deeply about their reputations, as well as about "doing the right thing", ethical responsibilities, the third component, are essential. Ethical responsibilities embrace those activities and practices that are expected or prohibited by society even though they may not be codified into law. Ethical responsibilities encompass the full scope of norms, standards, and expectations that reflect a belief in what employees, consumers, shareholders, and the global community regard as fair, just, and consistent with the respect for and protection of stakeholders' moral rights.

The ethical category is where divergent views traceable to different cultures are likely to be most significant. Global business ethics are essentially about the reconciliation of home- and host- country ethical standards and the identification of norms that will satisfy both. The practice of *moral relativism*, wherein companies simply adapt to local norms, creates an often untenable situation because many countries, especially those with emerging and developing economies, do not have articulated ethical standards that protect vulnerable stakeholders. *Moral universalism*, a response or remedy to this deficiency, involves the identification of a particular set of ethical standards that has broad, international support, such as the UN Global Compact or the Global Reporting Initiatives.

The last component, philanthropic responsibilities, reflects global society's expectations that business will engage in social activities that are neither mandated by law nor generally expected of business in an ethical sense. Philanthropy today is more often than not strategic in nature, with businesses expected to play an active role in global corporate citizenship. As in the case of law and ethics, philanthropic expectations vary widely by country, and savvy executives will carefully research expectations of the host countries in this category.

As firms go global, their CSR concerning economic, legal, ethical, and philanthropic responsibilities are all heightened. Thus, it is a common view that international companies bear greater CSR than their domestic counterparts. Globalization has increased calls for MNCs to use their resources to help alleviate a wide variety of social problems. The pharmaceutical industry, for example, is asked to donate free drugs and vaccines to third-world nations where the afflicted cannot pay. MNCs engaged in manufacturing are encouraged to apply developed nations' laws and norms to issues such as child labor and environmental pollution in less developed countries, regardless of local laws and customs. Globalization has resulted in the proliferation of new laws and regulations that direct business activities to address diverse social problems. The long-term impact of these social policies is a sea change in the "rules of thumb" by which businesses are expected to operate in harmony with the social environment. The firm's external environment, manifested in public policies and expectations, is becoming a key factor in major strategic business decisions. In addition, changes in social values and ideologies have tremendous implications for the role that business is expected to play in society. It is no wonder that the attention of top management, government, and society is being directed toward corporate governance and corporate accountability.

As MNCs diversify into more foreign countries, they face not only more social and environmental responsibilities, but, more importantly, greater heterogeneity or differences in these responsibilities, which further raise their required commitment to meet such disparate standards. Also, in an international setting, stakeholders from country

B may be able to significantly impact an MNC's decision in country A. As will be seen in the Shell case in the last section of this chapter, Shell-UK complied with the pressure of the Shell consumers in continental Europe, and, although it was Greenpeace-UK who started the opposition to the deep-sea disposal of the Spar, it was the public from Germany, the Netherlands, and Denmark who finally made Shell change its policy.

In the foregoing section, I mentioned the importance of reputation, which links CSR and corporate performance. This is even more striking for MNCs. An MNC's organizational reputation and corporate image transcend national boundaries so quickly in today's information world. This reputation effect can act as an international enforcement mechanism in matters of social and environmental responsibility. Quite often, corporations act in ways which are considered to be socially responsible by important constituents out of concern for their reputation, which is one of the most significant intangible resources a business firm can have. Let us assume a given subsidiary of an MNC functioning in Jamaica, which engages in a series of actions that do not have a negative impact in the firm's reputation in that country, but because the firm is a multinational and its reputation extends across national boundaries, the actions of its subsidiary in Jamaica cause a significant loss of reputation in the US, where the public is more sensitive about certain issues than the public of Jamaica. Such a development alarms the management of the multinational, which interferes in the operations of the subsidiary in Jamaica and alters the subsidiary's actions so that no harm is caused to the firm's reputation in either Jamaica or the US. Because the underlying norms and values of the various national publics differ, the sensitivity of multinationals' attitudes toward social and environmental issues will also differ. Therefore, the multinational will have to operate at the highest level of social and environmental responsibility if it does not want to cause damage to its reputation in any of the countries in which it operates.

Compounding the complexity and importance of CSR for multinationals is the issue of stakeholder salience: who, among the multiple stakeholders, really counts with management (Mitchell, Agle, and Wood, 1997). In other words, which stakeholders from which countries can most strongly influence managerial action? Stakeholder salience depends on the interplay of three potential stakeholder characteristics: power (the probability that one actor within a social relationship would be in a position to carry out his own will despite resistance); legitimacy (a generalized perception or assumption that the actions of an entity are desirable or appropriate within some socially constructed system of norms, values, beliefs, and definitions); and urgency (a situation that is time-sensitive and critical). Obviously, stakeholders possessing all three characteristics (power, legitimacy, and urgency) will have a high level of salience. Stakeholders possessing only two of these characteristics will have moderate levels of salience, while stakeholders with only one of these characteristics will have low levels of salience. In other words, the impact that a particular stakeholder group can have on managerial decisions depends on the amount of power, legitimacy, and urgency that the group possesses. In Shell's case (see the end of this chapter), it was foreign stakeholders, the customers and general public of continental Europe, which, in the end, had the greatest salience in the reversal of the deepwater disposal plan. These stakeholders, having all three characteristics, were able to influence the top management of Shell, and correspondingly the management of Shell UK. So, from the perspective of Shell UK, it was foreign stakeholders with whom Shell UK had to eventually comply. Consequently, the existence of foreign stakeholder salience acts as a mechanism that increases the levels of environmental and social responsibility faced by multinationals.

Indeed there are several factors triggering international convergence of ethical standards and ethical perceptions. A variety of initiatives by MNCs, non-governmental organizations, governments, and international organizations have promoted this tendency. These efforts, along with the critical role of information technology in disseminating news and practices around the world, have elevated the forces working toward universal moral norms. Still, however, the internationalization of business is accompanied by the persistence of national traditions, cultures, and regulatory practices. This applies to CSR, environmental policies, and business ethics as well. International managers must continue to consider divergent societal and governmental pressures in home versus host countries, especially when economic development, political systems, regulatory regime, and social and cultural norms fundamentally differ. The differences in these areas significantly deter the convergence of international ethical standards; and because such differences will not easily disappear, MNCs must continue to be prepared for complying with three sets of social responsibility and ethical requirements: (i) international standards (e.g., International Labor Organization's codes of conduct, social labeling, and other private sector initiatives addressing labor issues; OECD's guideline for MNCs' conduct; the UN's Universal Declaration of Human Rights; the International Chamber of Commerce's business practice mandates); (ii) home country's standards; and (iii) host country's standards. Because a diversified MNC operates in a large number of host countries, it is simply counter-productive to have an organizationally decentralized and yet internally differentiated governing system to monitor an MNC's global CSR. Accordingly, an MNC that is concerned about social responsibility will adopt a universal code composed of the highest standards from among international, home country, or host country standards, regardless of the businesses, countries, locations, and subsidiaries in which they work.

For instance, with respect to foreign employment practices, socially responsible MNCs self-regulate by:

1. providing standards of employment equal to or better than those of comparable employers in the countries in which they operate;
2. maintaining the highest standards of safety and health and providing adequate information about work-related health hazards;
3. giving priority to the employment and promotion of indigenous nationals and contributing to managerial and technical training for local nationals;
4. respecting the right of employees to organize for the purpose of collective bargaining and providing workers' representatives with information necessary to assist in the development of collective agreements;
5. cooperating with governments in providing income protection for workers whose employment is terminated, giving advance notice of plant closures, and mitigating resulting adverse effects;

6. increasing employment opportunities and standards in host countries, providing stable employment for their employees, and cooperating with host governments to create employment opportunities in particular localities; and
7. respecting human rights and fundamental freedoms in host countries and not discriminating on the basis of race, color, sex, religion, language, social, national, ethnic origin, or political opinion.

An MNC's CSR should particularly focus on the relationships with several major stakeholders: (i) host governments (economic and development policies, laws and regulations, political involvement, resisting bribery and corruption, etc.); (ii) the public and environment; (iii) business partners (suppliers, vendors, distributors, joint venture partners); and (iv) consumers and employees (including human rights). Based on several international standards including those mentioned above, Getz (1990) summarized 15 areas of international standards for MNCs dealing with host governments, listed below:

A. Economic and development policies

1. MNCs should consult with government authorities and national employers' and workers' organizations to assure that their investments conform to the economic and social development policies of their host countries.
2. MNCs should not adversely disturb the balance of payments or currency exchange rates of the countries in which they operate. They should try, in consultation with government officials, to resolve exchange rate difficulties when possible.
3. MNCs should cooperate with government policies regarding local equity participation.
4. MNCs should not dominate the capital markets of the countries in which they operate.
5. MNCs should provide necessary information to host government authorities so they can correctly assess taxes due.
6. MNCs should not engage in transfer pricing policies that modify the tax bases on which their entities are assessed.
7. MNCs should reinvest some profits in the countries in which they operate.

B. Laws and regulations

8. MNCs are subject to the laws, regulations, and jurisdications of the countries in which they operate.
9. MNCs should respect the right of every country to exercise control over its natural resources and to regulate the activities of entities operating within its territory.
10. MNCs should use appropriate international dispute-settlement mechanisms, including arbitration, to resolve conflicts with the governments of the countries in which they operate.

11. MNCs should not request the intervention of their home governments in disputes with host governments.
12. MNCs should resolve disputes arising from expropriation by host governments under the domestic laws of the host countries.

C. Political involvement

13. MNCs should refrain from improper or illegal involvement in local political affairs.
14. MNCs should not pay bribes or render improper benefits to any public servant.
15. MNCs should not interfere in intergovernmental relations.

MNCs also need to understand their responsibilities toward the local community and the public's interests. An MNC's strategies and operations should accommodate the need for sustainable development of the local community. In this respect, companies should provide more training and apprenticeship opportunities for people in the community. Technical assistance and investment in the local community's infrastructure, such as in transportation, are examples of MNCs' efforts to participate in social and economic development of the local community. Social accommodation is the extent to which an MNC has been responsive and contributive to the social needs or governmental concerns (e.g., donations to local schools, research, hospital facilities, and sports). Without this accommodation, MNCs are likely to be stereotyped as an "exploiting consortium" by the local community or society. As a result of significant participation by many MNCs in host industries, governments have become increasingly concerned with MNCs' corporate citizenship, pressuring them to be more accommodative to local needs. This implies that MNCs that are more socially responsive to the local community's needs are more likely to maintain productive relationships with local communities, including governmental authorities. The underlying logic is that, in the long run, the bargaining position of firms can be best safeguarded if their business interests accommodate rather than neglect or dominate public interests in host nations. From the host government viewpoint, an MNC's social accommodation shows its commitment to the host society (Luo, 2001).

Environmental protection is an important part of an MNC's CSR. In this respect, MNCs should respect the laws and regulations concerning environmental protection in host countries, cooperate with host governments and with international organizations in the development of national and international environmental protection standards, and supply information to appropriate host governmental authorities concerning the environmental impacts of the projects, products, and processes of their entities. Global pollution, in particular, has been given a great deal of attention in international business. To address this, ISO 14000 (the new European Union pollution guidelines) was established in 1996 to regulate global environment concerns. This standard or certification contains six components, each of which is directly relevant to MNCs:

1. environmental management systems;
2. environmental auditing;

3. performance evaluation;
4. environmental labeling;
5. lifecycle assessment; and
6. environmental assessments of product.

The emergence of this type of international standard means that MNCs need to develop strategies to incorporate concern for the environment into their everyday operations standards. Here are some examples of what is required in a business environment governed by ISO 14000:

- Adopt management strategies that will enable firms to obtain ISO 14000 certification in their industry.
- Reduce pollution and conserve resources as a means of meeting stringent environmental regulations.
- Shift from product changes to behavioral and manufacturing process changes, so as to manufacture products in a more environmentally sound manner.
- Reduce solid waste by incorporating recycling into the manufacturing process.

To respond to these requirements and be socially responsible for global environmental problems, MNCs, in the course of international expansion, investments, and operations, must first comply fully with all host-government environmental and health laws and regulations, and establish workplace health and safety standards that may go well beyond local regulations. Second, they need to make certain that a corporate environmental policy is firmly supported by top executives, widely circulated within the company, and publicized in the host country. Third, MNCs should carry out, and make public, environmental impact assessments for all major investments, including analyses of on-site and off-site environmental effects, technologies for moderating adverse effects, social impacts such as the displacement of local residents and the influx of workers, and ways to manage emergency pollution hazards. Lastly, they should take responsibility for the environmental behavior of joint-venture partners and subcontractors, and should not subcontract hazardous operations to escape direct responsibility for worker and environmental protection.

The simple fact is that MNCs that comply with the highest standards of global environment protection will benefit in the long run. If MNCs spend all their energies complaining about environmental regulations, different standards, increasing costs, and so on, or shifting their capital around the globe in search of yet another pristine unregulated environment, they will miss opportunities to obtain competitive advantages, to build stable relationships in host nations, and to enhance the global quality of life through their own actions. They will also eventually run out of pristine environments to which to move. For individual MNCs, it is difficult to imagine that an MNC could go far if it had a bad record in shirking environmental protection responsibilities or shifting its capital around developing countries searching for unregulated environments.

Consumer protection is another important part of an MNC's CSR in a global setting. To this end, MNCs should respect the consumer protection laws and regulations of host countries and preserve the safety and health of consumers by disclosing appropriate information, proper labeling, and accurate advertising. In addition to the physical attributes of products offered by MNCs, symbolic attributes or interests appear to be gaining importance as international consumers learn to choose products according to an MNC's global performance in CSR. For instance, consumers are increasingly likely to ask how "green" the company is before buying its products. Many symbolic attributes, such as corporate reputation, women and minority employees and directors, company participation in weapons production and nuclear power, product safety, employee safety and health, and environmental protection records, are important dimensions of CSR.

7.3 Corporate Governance and Social Responsibility in International Business

Corporate governance has gained unprecedented prominence in recent years. The failures and successes of modern corporations are equally responsible for this rise in prominence. Modern corporations thus are not simply victims of external conditions that have imposed corporate governance on them, but have also created the very circumstances that made corporate governance imperative. It cannot be denied that spectacular corporate failures and the abuse of managerial power contributed significantly to the rise in prominence of governance. However, neither can it be denied that the phenomenal growth in social power and influence of corporations equally contributed to them taking responsibility for balancing their own interests with those of the societies and the natural environment in which they operate.

CSR is an important part of corporate governance because it helps satisfy the needs of all major stakeholders. MNCs must address social, environmental, and economic demands from stakeholders, as well as financial demands from shareholders. It becomes clear that CSR is a governance issue, which means it belongs squarely on the board's agenda. Directors know that CSR is a corporate governance issue requiring close board overseeing. Both domestic and international companies now face growing pressure to give stakeholders a role in corporate governance, to more transparently disclose social, environmental, and economic policies, to shift many of the previously treated voluntary policies or programs of CSR as mandatory, and to be more responsive to the growing interest by the financial community in the link between shareholder value and non-financial corporate performance. Figure 7.1 schematically shows the corporate governance pyramid addressing the importance of CSR in an MNC's global corporate governance. This pyramid clearly displays the difference between financial corporate governance and responsible corporate governance. The collapse of Enron and WorldCom, among others, reminds us that corporate governance ought to be defined as responsible corporate governance, rather than financial corporate governance. A broader societal role for the firm must be included as the backbone of corporate governance.

Financial corporate governance focuses only on the structures and processes necessary for the pursuit of shareholder value. Important elements in this category are shareholder rights, protection of minority shareholders, and transparency and disclosure issues.

Figure 7.1 Corporate governance pyramid for MNCs

This last issue remains by far the most critical focus of the investment community at home and abroad. Traditionally, attention has been focused on conformance issues in order to attain the goal of good financial corporate governance. Living up to formal standards or benchmarks became the reference point used to judge the quality of corporate governance. Accordingly, companies are disclosing the composition of the board, having the minimum number of independent directors, or establishing special board committees.

This compliance is insufficient to ensure good corporate governance, especially when a firm increasingly engages in complex global businesses. A challenge that is even more important to the quality of governance is to change the fundamentals related to the governance attitudes and behavior of executives and directors. Only then will substance reign over form. We must not forget that corporate governance is not an aim in itself, but a mechanism of structures and processes that allows companies to realize their ambitions and goals and create welfare and economic well-being. The pursuit of shareholder value is hampered if the emphasis on processes and board structures is unequivocally oriented toward control and supervision. Attention must also be given to the complementary issue of performance. Corporate performance in realizing a company's strategic goals and objectives is equally important; without good performance, shareholders and stakeholders, whether customers, governances, suppliers, or community, cannot benefit no matter how complete the company's conformance has been.

The essential difference between financial corporate governance (top of the pyramid) and responsible corporate governance (bottom of the pyramid) lies in the definition of the goal of the firm in general. Financial corporate governance views the firm as the instrument of the shareholders and considers the role of the firm and the duty of its directors to be simply shareholder value maximization. Responsible corporate governance views the firm as a long-term partnership of shareholders and other stakeholders. Therefore, corporate governance should aim at optimizing the long-term return to shareholders while satisfying the legitimate expectations of stakeholders. Understanding the importance of responsible corporate governance now lies at the heart of good corporate governance, and ignoring this broader scope could prove disastrous for corporate branding and financial performance. Responsible corporate governance is also about balancing the legitimate interests of all stakeholders involved, with ethics and sustainable growth being of paramount importance. As I explained in Chapter 1, mechanisms for responsible corporate governance of MNCs are not only market-based, but also culture-based, such as governance culture and corporate integrity, as well as business ethics and other disciplines.

The responsible corporate governance framework necessitates rethinking the principal agent theory in order to include the concept of multiple principals and agents (i.e., stakeholder inclusiveness). In addition, such a broadened role of the firm must lead to a reformulation of the role of the board of directors in general and of the duties of directors and committees more specifically. The challenge for directors will be to help the corporation steer the best possible path among competing claims of shareholders and stakeholders. Boards will have to deepen their appreciation of the relationships – societal as well as financial – that sustain the corporation. They will also have to build their capacity to oversee the corporation's response to intensifying demands for rigor in the management of, and disclosure of information about, social impact. An example to illustrate this is AIG. To bolster its overall corporate governance, AIG, in April 2005, established two new oversight committees to which two outsiders were appointed: (i) Regulatory, Compliance and Legal Committee and (ii) Public Policy and Corporate Social Responsibility Committee.

It should be clear that corporate social responsibility is far more than public relations or reputation management. The societal responsibilities of a firm must be fully integrated into corporate governance and management practice. The view of responsible corporate governance, especially as to the role of the firm in society, should be evident in the firm's products, production process, treatment of stakeholders, system of governance and accountability, and its codes of conduct. It is central to the growth of the firm that CSR not be completely delegated; it must become the final responsibility of senior management and the board of directors.

Because geographically diversified MNCs face a larger number of demanding stakeholders in different countries, corporate social responsibilities are enlarged, requiring more commitment and greater attention from MNCs. Responsible corporate governance requires sharpening CSR not only at the parent level, but at the divisional, regional, and subsidiary levels as well. The second-tier governance explained in early chapters also plays an important role in improving an MNC's worldwide CSR. Because the second-tier board members are more knowledgeable about the societal role of an indigenous business in a host country and are more aware of the needs, concerns, or standards of local employees, suppliers, regulators, and environments, MNC headquarters may delegate some elements of CSR, especially those requiring local adaptations, to subsidiary boards, while emphasizing other elements of CSR that require global harmonizing. Corporate culture and ethical standards, for example, must be globally unified. It is also important to reformulate a new scheme of performance appraisal for frontline executives in different countries. The performance of these country managers should be evaluated not merely by financial corporate governance, namely a bulk of financial indicators, but also by a set of measures that can properly reflect the achievement of corporate social responsibility in the countries they serve.

Many MNCs are making efforts to shift from financial corporate governance to responsible corporate governance. The impact of CSR on the brand image of a corporation is clearly evident in rankings such as those by *Business Week*. Asea Brown Boveri, the Swiss engineering corporation, for instance, is a sponsor of the Global Sustainable Development Facility (GSDF) and an active member of the World Business Council for Sustainable Development (WBCSD). It is a world leader in developing eco-efficient technologies in a wide range of industry areas from electric transmission to transportation and is building a global network to install these technologies in many developing and transition economies. Aracruz Celulose, the world's largest exporter of bleached eucalyptus pulp, is often cited for its efforts to promote sustainable development through tree plantation, harvesting, and pulp production in Brazil. General Motors, the world's largest automobile manufacturer, is involved in various environmental protection initiatives and partnerships. Similarly, Dow Chemical, a US corporation, was selected to participate in the GSDF for, inter alia, abiding by the highest standards of human rights, environment and labor standard norms, as defined by UN agencies. Mitsubishi Group has been actively cultivating an image of environmental responsibility through advertising and specific environmental projects. Novartis, the Swiss life science corporation, is another participant in the GSDF and member of the WBCSD. It is often cited for its efforts in the fields of poverty alleviation and environmental protection. Rio Tinto, a British company, is often cited for its standards of environmental reporting and for promoting continuous social development and sustainable livelihood. CSR provides a number of advantages to business, such as lowering litigation, reduction in taxes, protecting brand image, improving customer satisfaction, reducing absenteeism and employee turnover, and increasing the ability to retain talented employees.

Some MNCs based in emerging economies are also beginning to realize the importance of CSR. For example, Tata Group, India's largest company and founded by Jamsetji Tata, believes in the pioneering concept of trusteeship in management. The profits of many of the companies in the group are channeled back to the people through major philanthropic trusts. During recent years, profits of the company have exhibited a fluctuating trend but their expenditures toward social causes are consistent. Nearly 80 percent of the capital of the holding company, Tata Sons Limited, is held by these trusts. As a result, great national institutions have come into being in the areas of science, medicine, atomic energy, and performing arts.

Failure to pay heed to CSR can dramatically impact a company's reputation and even its value. Multinationals such as Nike, Wal-Mart, Exxon, and Philip Morris have taken hits to their reputations for failing to stay ahead of their stakeholders' expectations. Companies should regard their social responsibilities at least on par with their financial obligations. Too often, financial analysis of companies ignores other risks and resources beyond purely financial matters. A failure to meet environmental, labor market, or even social obligations can have a substantial impact in the longer term.

7.4 Improving Corporate Social Responsibility in International Business

To MNCs actively undertaking and performing geographically diversified businesses in a large array of countries, the required steps or measures to strengthen their global CSR are more sophisticated than those used by domestic businesses, necessitating a significantly greater commitment to designing, implementing, and evaluating their CSR system by all organizational members (directors, executives, country managers, and all employees around the world). In the following paragraphs, I list several areas or measures that MNCs should particularly emphasize in order to improve their global CSR.

1. Following global guidelines and mandates

There are many global guidelines by which MNCs can perform and improve their CSR performance. Most have been issued in the last decade or so by nonprofit international organizations. The more prominent categories of guidelines include the environment, supply chain management, hiring practices, community relations, internal management, information disclosure, and charitable donations. Some of the global benchmarks against which companies' CSR performance is being measured include the United Nations Declaration of Human Rights, the International Labor Organization's labor standards, and several globally recognized voluntary standards, such as the Organization for Economic Cooperation and Development's Guidelines for Multinational Enterprises and the United Nations Global Compact, to name just a few.

Perhaps the most widely accepted reporting guideline, however, is the Global Reporting Initiative (GRI), based in Amsterdam. Launched in 1997 and billed as a common framework for sustainable reporting, the GRI was developed by a group of organizations widely known for responsible business reporting. Among them were representatives of the Association of Chartered Certified Accountants, the United Nations Environment Program, and the World Business Council for Sustainable Development. The GRI took the best practices in the area of human rights, labor relations, environmental management, and sustainable development, and crafted them into guidelines that enable any corporation to produce one comprehensive report. Similar guidelines may have been enacted by home country institutions. For instance, the US Sarbanes–Oxley Act of 2002 has raised the bar for many corporations with mandates that they conduct business with social responsibility in mind. The legislation includes an expectation that companies build effective programs based on adherence to values as opposed to merely laws. Principally through Sarbanes–Oxley Section 302, company executives must now certify that they have effective disclosure controls and procedures in place – and they must continually evaluate them to ensure their ongoing effectiveness.

Many global guidelines, such as the OECD Guidelines for Multinational Enterprises, are voluntary initiatives in nature. These initiatives involve the issuance of codes of corporate conduct setting forth commitments in such areas as labor relations, environmental management, human rights, consumer protection, disclosure, and fighting corruption. These codes are often backed up by management systems that help firms respect their commitments in their day-to-day operations. More recent developments include guidelines on management, reporting and auditing standards, and the emergence of supporting institutions (e.g., professional societies, consulting and auditing services). Note that although the initiatives are often referred to as "voluntary," MNCs are under increasing pressures to adopt them. Such pressures stem from legal and regulatory arrangements, from employees, from the need to protect brand or reputation capital and from civil society.

These global guidelines or voluntary initiatives in corporate responsibility have promoted the accumulation of the management expertise needed to translate legal compliance and ethical norms into the day-to-day operations of companies. The institutional supports for this expertise – management standards, professional societies, specialized consulting and auditing services – help lower the costs of legal and ethical compliance as well as making it more effective. Overall, the benefits for MNCs following these initiatives and guidelines are potentially numerous. They include improved legal compliance, management of litigation risks, brand and reputation enhancement, and smoother relations with shareholders and stakeholders. Finally, MNCs use the initiatives to improve employee morale and to promote a culture of integrity within the firm.

2. Redefining corporate values

Creating a formal CSR program is necessary, but by itself does not guarantee effective ethics management. Recall that Enron had an ethics code, and the board voted to bypass its conflict-of-interest policy. Thus, what matters even more is that everyone, whether directors, executives, managers, or employees, perceive that formal policies go beyond mere window dressing to represent the real ethical culture of the organization. Put simply, for formal systems to influence behavior, they must be part of a larger, coordinated cultural system that supports ethical conduct everyday and everywhere. Ethical culture provides informal systems, along with formal systems, to support ethical conduct.

Corporate social responsibility falls on fertile ground in an MNC that has a tradition of socially responsible activity. An innovative corporate culture that is willing to change also enhances the implementation process. Within such organizations, continuous renewal is encouraged in order to adapt over time to a changing environment. In a forward-looking company, whether CSR initiatives are launched from the top of the organization or grow from the bottom up does not matter very much. What counts is whether both types of process (top-down and bottom-up) can flourish and reinforce each other.

Leaders (directors and executives) at an MNC are responsible for transmitting culture in their organizations, and the ethical dimension of organizational culture is no exception. The powerful mechanisms for embedding and reinforcing culture are: (i) what leaders pay attention to, measure, and control; (ii) leader reactions to critical incidents and organizational crises; (iii) deliberate role modeling, teaching, and coaching by leaders; and (iv) criteria for recruitment, selection, promotion, rewarding, and punishment. Employees in various countries in which an MNC operates need clear and consistent messages that ethics are essential to the business model. Simply telling country managers and foreign employees to do the right thing is not enough. Country managers and foreign employees must be prepared for the types of issues that arise in their particular business, function, and country, and they must know what to do when ethics and the bottom line appear to be in conflict. Executives should tie ethics to the long-term success of each subunit. To underscore the ethical dimension of corporate culture, the reward system is a critical way to deliver a message about what CSR behaviors are expected. Ethical and socially responsible behavior, especially by those country managers or employees in host countries where societal corruption levels are high, can be rewarded by promoting and compensating people who are not only good at what they do, but who have also developed a reputation with customers, unions, suppliers, governments, and the community as being of the highest integrity.

Levi Strauss & Co. illustrates the importance of culture in improving an MNC's global CSR. Levi incorporated its explicitly stated corporate values into its CSR programs and policies. Its corporate values – empathy, originality, integrity, and courage – are the foundation of the company. They underlie how the company competes in the global marketplace and how its executives, directors, and employees behave. These values guide its foundation's giving programs, the support it provides to communities where it has a business presence, and its employee community-involvement programs. In 1991, Levi became the first worldwide company to establish a comprehensive ethical code of conduct for manufacturing and finishing contractors working with the company. Since 2001, the company has been ranked as one of "America's 50 Best Companies for Minorities' by *Fortune Magazine*. Its philanthropy includes a focus on strengthening workers' rights and ultimately improving working and living conditions in communities where third-party contractors make Levi's products. The Levi Strauss Foundation provides innovative "sourcing" grants to local, regional, or global nonprofit organizations to support programs that:

- educate policy makers on the need to include human rights protections in trade agreements;
- increase local monitoring and enforcement of labor and health and safety laws;
- educate workers about their rights and increase their knowledge of financial literacy and health issues; and/or
- create positive partnerships between nonprofit organizations and contractors.

3. Implementing corporate ethics programs

Although MNCs can encourage ethical behavior in informal ways, much effort should still be directed toward implementing formal programs and policies for guiding ethical behavior in these multinationals. As noted earlier, formal ethical programs and informal approaches such as corporate culture are complementary rather than substitutive; they go hand in hand. Common elements of corporate ethics programs include training activities, formalized procedures for auditing and evaluating ethical behavior, disciplinary processes for failures to meet ethical expectations, dedicated ethics telephone lines, formal ethics departments and officers, and cross-functional committees for setting and evaluating ethics policies and procedures. Ethics programs ostensibly bring the behavior of organization members into conformity with a shared ethical standard; they constitute an organizational control system that encourages either shared ethical aspirations or compliance with rules, or both. Ethics programs can enhance company performance, usually by bringing an organization's decisions and actions more into conformity with societal ethical expectations. Ethics programs may help generate legitimacy-enhancing organizational outcomes, a key indicator of corporate social performance and an important contributor to overall organizational success. Ethics programs can also contribute to legitimacy by signaling that the company conforms to societal expectations in its internal organizational processes and structures.

For a globally operated MNC, its most fundamental principles and key components of ethics programs and policies should be universal, requiring the compliance by all employees and subunits regardless of their locations and lines of business. Let us use Levi Strauss again as an example to illustrate this. Levi has approximately 600 sub-contractors in more than 60 countries, but its global sourcing guidelines are universal. These guidelines apply to every subcontractor, no matter of its country of presence. These universal guidelines help Levi to select business partners who follow workplace standards and business practices that are consistent with the company's values. These requirements are applied to every contractor who manufactures or finishes products for Levi Strauss & Co. Trained inspectors closely audit and monitor compliance of these overseas subcontractors. Figure 7.2 lists Levi's Global Sourcing Guidelines.

---

1. Country Assessment Guidelines

The numerous countries where Levi Strauss & Co. has existing or future business interests present a variety of cultural, political, social, and economic circumstances. The Country Assessment Guidelines help us assess any issue that might present concern in light of the ethical principles we have set for ourselves. The Guidelines assist us in making practical and principled business decisions as we balance the potential risks and opportunities associated with conducting business in specific countries. Specifically, we assess whether the:

- **Health and Safety Conditions** would meet the expectations we have for employees and their families or our company representatives;
- **Human Rights Environment** would allow us to conduct business activities in a manner that is consistent with our Global Sourcing and Operating Guidelines and other company policies;
- **Legal System** would provide the necessary support to adequately protect our trade-marks, investments or other commercial interests, or to implement the Global Sourcing and Operating Guidelines and other company policies; and
- **Political, Economic and Social Environment** would protect the company's com-mercial interests and brand/corporate image. We will not conduct business in countries prohibited by US laws.

Figure 7.2 Levi Strauss Global Sourcing Guidelines

II. Terms of Engagement

- **Ethical Standards**

  We will seek to identify and utilize business partners who aspire as individuals and in the conduct of all their businesses to a set of ethical standards not incompatible with our own.

- **Legal Requirements**

  We expect our business partners to be law abiding as individuals and to comply with legal requirements relevant to the conduct of all their businesses.

- **Environmental Requirements**

  We will only do business with partners who share our commitment to the environment and who conduct their business in a way that is consistent with Levi Strauss & Co.'s Environmental Philosophy and Guiding Principles.

- **Community Involvement**

  We will favor business partners who share our commitment to improving community conditions.

- **Employment Standards**

  We will only do business with partners who adhere to the following guidelines:

  Child Labor: Use of child labor is not permissible. Workers can be no less than 15 years of age and not younger than the compulsory age to be in school. We will not utilize partners who use child labor in any of their facilities. We support the development of legitimate workplace apprenticeship programs for the educational benefit of younger people.

  Prison Labor/Forced Labor: We will not utilize prison or forced labor in contracting relationships in the manufacture and finishing of our products. We will not utilize or purchase materials from a business partner utilizing prison or forced labor.

  Disciplinary Practices: We will not utilize business partners who use corporal punishment or other forms of mental or physical coercion.

  Working Hours: While permitting flexibility in scheduling, we will identify local legal limits on work hours and seek business partners who do not exceed them except for appropriately compensated overtime. While we favor partners who utilize less than sixty-hour workweeks, we will not use contractors who, on a regular basis, require in excess of a sixty-hour week. Employees should be allowed at least one day off in seven.

  Wages and Benefits: We will only do business with partners who provide wages and benefits that comply with any applicable law and match the prevailing local manufacturing or finishing industry practices.

  Freedom of Association: We respect workers' rights to form and join organizations of their choice and to bargain collectively. We expect our suppliers to respect the right to free association and the right to organize and bargain collectively without unlawful interference. Business partners should ensure that workers who make such decisions or participate in such organizations are not the object of discrimination or punitive disciplinary actions and that the representatives of such organizations have access to their members under conditions established either by local laws or mutual agreement between the employer and the worker organizations.

  Discrimination: While we recognize and respect cultural differences, we believe that workers should be employed on the basis of their ability to do the job, rather than on the basis of personal characteristics or beliefs. We will favor business partners who share this value.

  Health and Safety: We will only utilize business partners who provide workers with a safe and healthy work environment. Business partners who provide residential facilities for their workers must provide safe and healthy facilities.

Figure 7.2 Continued

4. Understanding the stakeholders' needs

Effective designing of an MNC's global CSR begins with identification of key stakeholders and, more importantly, their respective needs. Because implementing global CSR is not without costs and can be very expensive in some cases, understanding these needs becomes essential. Open and frequent communication with key global stakeholders is key. The *Shell Report*, which is published every year, for instance, is an internal and external communication device to inform its stakeholders on the actions that it has taken to meet its economic, environmental, and social responsibilities. Engagement with the general public also takes place through the "Tell Shell" service. This mechanism is a web-based service that was created to encourage people to have dialogue with the company. In general, companies maximize the benefits of their superior CSR performance when their CSR best matches the stakeholders' needs. Such matches create a mutually beneficial relationship between the company and the stakeholders; the social-purpose initiatives may receive the maximum gains, while the company minimizes costs and diversions. For example, IBM's Reinventing Education initiatives match very well with the needs of their global stakeholders such as foreign governments and local communities. As part of this initiative, IBM contributes financial resources, researchers, educational consultants, and technology at each site, seeking new ways for technology to improve school infrastructure and broad-based systematic change and thereby raise student achievement. In effect, IBM leverages its technological and systems expertise and its experience providing systems solutions to educational clients in order to meet a broader educational challenge.

Thus, contribution complementarity can significantly and cost-effectively enhance an MNC's global CSR. This complementarity concerns the extent to which an MNC's CSR efforts, commitments, or contributions match the stakeholders' desires or needs. For instance, if an MNC transfers technologies or other critical resources to its investment project in a developing country where such technologies and resources are badly needed to advance the local economy, host country governments may be more appreciative of the MNC's business conduct. This complementarity affects the economic incentives of one party as to whether to maintain or increase resources on which the other party depends. Changes of these incentives will alter the economic foundation for developing relationships between MNCs and foreign governments. The interdependence of complementary resources between MNCs and governments glues them together in long-term exchanges. Resource indivisibility between two parties is an important condition for generating synergies from cooperation. When committed resources from each party are complementary, interdependence is enhanced. The dependent party will be expected to be more committed to, and to better cooperate with, the resource provider. Thus, the greater the resource complementarity between two parties, the better inter-party relationships are likely to be. Contributing distinctive resources that are vital to a host economy yet are unavailable or rare locally will be perceived by the governments as a stimulus for the host economy. This, then, increases governmental incentives to maintain good relationships with resource-contributing MNCs. Because resource complementarity is a bilateral alignment, MNCs will also dedicate more to their relationship building with host governments if they have to rely on complementary resources that can only be offered by the host government (e.g., resource acquisition, industry access, preferential treatment, distribution arrangement, and problem solving).

5. Fortifying organizational credibility

Organizational credibility involves the degree of an MNC's organizational trustworthiness or legitimacy as perceived by its global stakeholders. Without this credibility, it will be more difficult for MNCs to build and maintain relations with key stakeholders in a long-term process; both cognitive and relational structures required to understand and evaluate each other will be absent. Improved organizational legitimacy (i.e., increased acceptance by the host country institutional environment) escalates an MNC's local credibility as perceived by political groups, the business community, local employees, and other stakeholders which, in turn, provides a better institutional environment for developing relationships with foreign stakeholders. Sources of credibility include social-responsibility image, adherence to social norms, institutional harmony, corporate reputation, customer loyalty, solidity of relations with the business community (i.e., suppliers, distributors, and competitors), previous trustworthiness, experience in partnering with other local firms, and reciprocal support for network members, among others. For foreign firms in a host country, organizational legitimacy is a key part of their trustworthiness, and this legitimacy increases as social-responsibility image, adherence to social norms, and institutional harmony improve. An MNC's high credibility as perceived by the public or officials in a host country boosts its relationship with authorities and the long-run sustainability of this relationship. This credibility is critical to establishing a desired relationship with a host government because it limits the likelihood of opportunistic behavior in a business environment that lacks developed rules of law or traditionally does not strictly enforce laws. In general, foreign companies are in an inherently disadvantageous position compared to local firms in building organizational credibility. Thus, organizational credibility already accumulated in a host country becomes a strategic asset. An MNC's established credibility will be perceived as its long-term commitment and adaptation to indigenous interests by the society. This not only legitimizes the organization but also stimulates its trust building with authorities.

An illustrative example is Brown & Williamson Tobacco Corp. (now merged with R.J. Reynolds Tobacco Co.). Approximately four years ago, the company began an unprecedented series of dialogues with various stakeholders across the US to improve its image. The question was simple: "What would we need to do to meet your concerns?" The company has held more than 25 dialogues with different constituencies including members of the public, legislators, public health officials, employees, retailers, and wholesalers. Both an external auditor and an internal auditor audited the process. The company's efforts have led to significant change. Brown & Williamson has asked that more of the money that US states receive from tobacco settlement funds be spent by the states on education, prevention, and treatment. It has also requested that the Motion Picture Association of America not feature cigarettes in movies. Moreover, the company will no longer put advertisements on the back of any magazine lest a child see it. Bill White, director of audit for Brown & Williamson, said, "We were impressed by the openness and directness displayed during the dialogue sessions and by the integrity and willingness of management to address the key issues. Our conclusion was that the CSR annual report accurately reflected the issues and management's response to them".

6. Reformulating board roles

Since the board of directors is the first instrument for monitoring the firm, the board should be aware of its enlarged duties relative to CSR. Boards of directors play a leading role in corporate governance and CSR and any significant plans to improve global CSR must be encompassed in their role. The ethical role of directors is critical. Directors have overall responsibility for the ethics and compliance programs of the corporation. The tone directors set by example and action is central to the overall ethical environment of their firms. Their role is reinforced by their legal responsibilities to provide oversight of the financial performance of the firm. Underlying this analysis is the critical assumption that ethical behavior, especially on the part of corporate leaders, leads to the best long-term interests of the corporation. The new board ideal is a multifaceted one that incorporates a broader range of skills, cultures, ages, and industry specializations. But above all, board members must be role models in their core ethical values: honesty; integrity; loyalty; responsibility; fairness; and citizenship.

Institutional shareholders can also become an important driving force for monitoring responsible corporate governance. As trustees of the money of their members (pension funds) or customers (insurance companies and mutual funds), institutional investors have already come under increased scrutiny by the new invisible hand of the media and civil society. Of course, institutional investors are not immune to conflicts of interest and control-bias problems. To remedy these potential problems, corporate governance rules for institutional investors should be developed, or institutional investors will need to monitor their own corporate governance programs. The same holds for the numerous rule-setting bodies and semi-public institutions that perform a supervisory or monitoring function.

7. Formulating a viable sustainability program

MNCs operating in environmentally sensitive industries such as chemical, pharmaceutical, petroleum, mining, and natural resource exploration, to name a few, must establish a viable suitability program as the key element of their global CSR. From these established suitability programs, global stakeholders will be better able to interpret, analyze, and judge these companies' long-term global social responsibility behaviors that can significantly impact the environment and other public interests. Thus, MNCs investing and operating in these industries need to set the right tone and enact a series of sustainability measures that properly balance their short-term financial gains and their long-term social responsibilities. For instance, Baxter International, a manufacturer of pharmaceutical and biomedical products with production facilities in almost

30 countries, has a viable sustainability program in place. The external verification aspect of Baxter's program started in the mid-1990s in response to a stockholder group wanting assurance that environmental data presented to the public was accurate. Initially, Baxter only used its internal personnel at the division and corporate levels to verify environmental data. External auditors were drawn into the verification process as a result of the stockholder group's concerns. Over time, the external report evolved to incorporate the reporting of health and safety data as well as environmental data. Currently, an external consultant, ERM Certification and Verification Services (ERM CVS), and Baxter have an arrangement by which they jointly verify selected data at every facility they audit. ERM CVS maintains overall quality control of the process through recently created verification protocols for use by all their auditors assessing Baxter's facilities.

Another company that is paying more than lip service to sustainable development is French telecommunications giant Alcatel. Having emerged from a major reorganization in 2003, Alcatel, which operates in 130 countries with 60,000 employees, has a comprehensive sustainable development program. Its strategy is based on strict guidelines published in policies and charters, as well as social, environmental, and economic objectives defined by the company's executive management. Alcatel's sites around the world have benefited from an environmental management system, and through its "Digital Bridge" initiative, Alcatel technologies serve development in scores of countries. In 2003, the company joined the UN Global Compact, reinforced its corporate governance practices, updated its "Statement on Business Practices," and elaborated on its Social Charter, which emphasizes Alcatel's commitment to socially responsible practices.

8. Undertaking CSR auditing and assessment

Many MNCs have implemented programs that help them to respond to societal concerns about the economic, social, and environmental impacts of their activities. These help them to manage their compliance with legal or regulatory requirements and their response to "softer" forms of social conduct – in which they commit to norms for appropriate conduct in a variety of areas of business ethics. However, to effectively implement these programs, firms need to have management systems designed to nurture them to respect and honor their commitments. These systems typically employ a range of tools including accounting and record-keeping systems, auditing, and self-assessment. Management control, of course, is a core business function and exists as a separate, well-established discipline within the management field. The extension of this discipline to global CSR and its partial merging with legal risk management has been one of the more important developments in international business of the last two decades.

Chief audit executives need to ensure that CSR is on the board's agenda of corporate governance issues. They should be aware of existing standards and global initiatives as they relate to CSR and use them as yardsticks against which to measure their organization's performance. Additionally, auditors should advise the board on identified best practices and determine whether their organization's core values and code of conduct still reflect the desired position of the enterprise in today's and tomorrow's world. Furthermore, internal auditors should use the international standards and practices designed by independent organizations or competitors as benchmarks against which to measure their organization's CSR performance.

Shell offers a good example on how MNCs take practical steps to conduct social impact assessment (see Figure 7.3). Along with these internal self-assessments of CSR performance, MNCs may also need to invite external organizations that provide external verification services to ensure that their CSR performance complies with the various guidelines and initiatives about which global stakeholders care. Today, there

---

(1) Impact Identification through Integrated Impact Assessments

Experience has shown that the greatest business and societal benefit comes from effective identification and management of operational impacts during planning and design as well as through the operational life. We require that an integrated environmental, social and health impact assessment is carried out prior to any new project or significant modification of an existing one. Conducting environmental, social and health impact assessments provide a structured way of looking ahead at the potential positive and negative impacts that could arise throughout the project's lifecycle. It is a tool to aid design and decision-making.

(2) Stakeholder Engagement Plans

Stakeholder engagement helps us build relationships with communities, governments, NGOs and shareholders. It is also a critical mechanism for problem solving, improving business decisions, and achieving business objectives. Given this importance it is now a requirement for all businesses to establish and implement a Stakeholder Engagement Plan.

(3) Social Performance Plans

Social Performance Plans have now been introduced as a requirement for all of Shell's businesses. Oil Products business has social performance plans in place at the 28 major facilities it operates near communities. Gas & Power will do the same in 2005 at the facilities it operates. The joint ventures where it does not have operational control are encouraged to develop social performance plans. Exploration & Production will put social performance plans in place in 2005 at operations where social impacts could be high. Plans have been in place since 2003 at our nine major Chemicals facilities, four of which surveyed community opinions in 2004 to measure social performance. These social performance plans guide our efforts to engage with stakeholders, reduce disruptive social impacts and generate benefits for the communities where we operate.

(4) Social Performance Reviews

The tools that our businesses use to manage the impact of our operations, include social performance reviews to identify key stakeholders and assess responses to our main social impacts. The first four major social performance reviews have been fundamental in helping the Shell Group develop guidance on how to better and more consistently manage the key social impacts of our operations. The social performance reviews also provide a way to help assure our performance in the social arena and bolster our continuous learning.

Figure 7.3 Social Impact Assessment Steps at Shell

are four categories of organizations that provide external monitoring and verification services:

1. Global accounting firms such as KPMG and PricewaterhouseCoopers.
2. Monitoring firms or NGOs focusing their efforts specifically on inspecting work sites for code of conduct violations.
3. Forensic and investigation firms which typically use a network of professionals to investigate allegations of impropriety or perform due diligence assessments of potential or existing suppliers' ability to comply with codes.
4. Quality assurance or quality registrar or ISO certification firms. Building on the platform established by the International Standards Organization (ISO), an NGO established to promote the development of voluntary standards that govern quality and environmental impact, several quality registrar or quality certification firms have started performing workforce monitoring on codes of conduct and human rights issues.

CASE EXAMPLE 7.1: SHELL'S BRENT SPAR PROJECT

The Royal Dutch/Shell Group – known as Shell – grew out of an alliance between the Royal Dutch Petroleum Company of the Netherlands and the Shell Transport and Trading Company of the UK in 1907. Today, Shell is considered to be one of the largest multinational oil companies, with a significant global presence and five core businesses: Exploration & Production; Oil Products; Chemicals; Gas & Power Generation; and Renewables. In the 1970s, Shell invested heavily in the exploration and subsequent extraction of major oil and gas deposits in the North Sea. It was a profitable investment, since Shell Expro (a 50–50 joint venture between Shell and Esso) discovered a number of rich oil fields, such as the Auk and Brent fields in 1971, the Cormorant and the Dunlin in 1972, the Tern in 1975, and the Eider in 1976.

The Brent Spar, located in the North Sea, was a very large floating oil storage buoy that had been used for storing oil from the Brent "A" platform, and acted as a loading facility for the Brent field. It was first put into operation in December 1976. The unit was owned by Shell Expro, but the management of the Spar was the responsibility of Shell UK. Unlike most other installations in the North Sea, the Brent Spar had most of its bulk (six huge storage tanks) under water. It weighed 14,500 tons, the equivalent of 2000 double-decker buses, and had a displacement of 66,500 tons of water. The Spar had a capacity that could hold the equivalent of four Big Bens. After 15 years of operation, the Spar was decommissioned in 1991, when a review of refurbishment costs showed that further use would not be economical.

After the Spar's decommission, in October 1991, Shell UK started a number of decommissioning studies to find out how to dispose of it. The main problem in the decommissioning of the Brent Spar was its size; it could not be moved around easily, and except for the waters to the North of Orkney, most of the North Sea was not deep enough to accommodate it. In a search for the Best Practicable Environmental Option (BPEO), Shell UK initially considered six options:

1. horizontal dismantling and onshore disposal;
2. vertical dismantling and onshore disposal;
3. infield disposal;
4. deepwater disposal;
5. refurbishment and reuse; and
6. continued maintenance.

From these initial options, after a preliminary study, Shell UK chose to carry out feasibility studies on the options of horizontal onshore dismantling and deepwater disposal. There were a number of technical problems involved in a horizontal onshore dismantling. Calculations on the structural strength of the Spar under various stresses showed that any attempt to rotate it in a horizontal position could pose a significant risk to its structural integrity. The situation was further complicated by the fact that two of the six storage tanks of the Spar had been damaged during operation. In addition, a number of studies conducted by independent engineering firms placed the cost of horizontal dismantling at about $69 million, and the cost of deepwater disposal at about $18 million. Environmentally, an onshore disposal would have been preferable, but the structure was expected to remain intact on the seabed for as many as 4000 years and little leakage and environmental impact was expected from a deepwater disposal. Finally, in February 1994, as a catalyst for subsequent events, an Aberdeen University study endorsed the deepwater disposal.

Based on these studies, Shell UK started formal consultations with local governments, conservation bodies, and fishing interests. In October 1994 a final draft of BPEO and Impact Hypothesis was submitted to the UK government's Department of Trade and Industry (DTI), which is the regulating body for the oil industry in the UK. In February 1995, the UK government announced its intention to approve of the deepwater disposal option and informed, according to international regulations, the OSPAR governments (the Netherlands, Norway, Germany, and Denmark), the other 12 nation states of the EU, and the EU itself. Since no objections were made within the normally allocated time limit, the UK government gave its approval to proceed with its deepwater disposal of the Spar, as the BPEO.

However, Greenpeace opposed this deepwater disposal option. Greenpeace is a global organization, with offices in over 30 countries, campaigning all over the world on environmental issues. Greenpeace was created in 1971 in Vancouver, Canada, when members of the "Don't Make A Wave Committee" renamed their organization to better proclaim their purpose: to create a GREEN and PEACEful world. Greenpeace remains an independent, nonpartisan and nonprofit organization, supported by more than three million members worldwide. It is best known for its nonviolent direct actions, which raise awareness and bring public opinion to bear on decision-makers. Greenpeace had been campaigning against dumping at sea for a long time and saw the deepwater disposal of the Spar as a dangerous precedent and a threat to prior gains such as the international ban on radioactive waste dumping at sea and the prohibition of the dumping of industrial wastes at sea. In September 1994, Greenpeace commissioned a report dealing with the issue of decommissioning and abandonment of offshore oil and gas platforms in general, titled "No Grounds for Dumping," and submitted it to the DTI in December 1994.

Greenpeace opposed deepwater disposal for the following reasons. First, Greenpeace was worried about the precedent the deepwater disposal of Brent Spar would set for the 130 offshore spars existing in the North Sea and coming up for decommissioning in the not so distant future. At this point it should be mentioned that the oil industry and the UK government, despite its public position of assessing the offshore disposal of oil platforms on a case-by-case basis, also saw the Brent Spar case as a test case. This was quite obvious from articles in trade publications of the period and was clearly admitted by DTI minister Tim Eggar in a public briefing issued after 20 June. Second, Greenpeace disputed the environmental assessment of the deepwater disposal option and argued that the damage to the environment would be significantly greater. And third, Greenpeace objected to the deepwater disposal as a matter of principle. As a member of Greenpeace involved in the Spar campaign told the author, "We have been trying for a number of years to teach people not to pollute. Now if one of the largest and richest multinationals in the world can get away with dumping at sea something as big as the Brent Spar, what is the message that it sends to the rest of the world?"

Despite its attempts to get involved, Greenpeace was not included in or invited to the consultations between the DTI and Shell UK that took place in early 1995. So, after the decision for deepwater disposal was reached by Shell UK, the British, Dutch, and German branches of Greenpeace met and the initial occupation of the Spar was decided. In a later meeting, the German division came up with the funds for a prolonged occupation until September, when the weather would make the towing of the Spar to its dumping site impossible. Consequently, on April 30, 1995, around lunchtime, Greenpeace ship *Moby Dick* and an escort of inflatable crafts sped out to the disused Brent field spar loading buoy in the North Sea. Four protesters climbed from their boat onto a steel ladder on the side of the buoy. They climbed part of the way to the top of the buoy on the ladder and the rest of the way using ropes and winches. Five standby vessels were in Brent field at the time but could do little about the invasion.

Despite the occupation, on May 5, 1995, the UK government proceeded and granted the disposal license to Shell UK. However, nobody, not even Greenpeace, was prepared for the publicity that the issue received, especially in Continental

Europe. As a result of this publicity, an increasing number of consumers, politicians, and governments started voicing their opposition to the "dumping of the Spar." For example, on May 9, 1995, the German minister for the environment protested against the deepwater disposal plan. On May 16, 1995, all opposition parties in the UK condemned the dumping of the Spar. And on May 17, 1995, in Belgium, the EU ministers for foreign affairs, the environment and trade, condemned the British government for allowing the dumping of the Spar.

Defending its position, with the support of the British government, Shell UK initiated legal proceedings and the activists occupying the Spar were removed on May 23, 1995. In response, Greenpeace called for a Shell boycott in Continental Europe, and on June 2, 1995, Greenpeace supporters started leafleting gas stations and motorists at over 3000 locations throughout Germany. On June 11, 1995, Shell UK began to tow the Spar to its planned disposal site. In Continental Europe, the opposition to the sinking of the Spar was intensifying. In Germany, some Shell petrol stations reported 50 percent loss in income as protests against dumping the Spar increased. Protesters threatened to damage 200 Shell service stations – 50 were subsequently damaged, two fire-bombed, and one raked with bullets. In addition, on June 15, 1995 Chancellor Kohl protested to the UK prime minister, John Major, at the G7 summit. On June 16, 1995, a second occupation of the Spar began as two Greenpeace activists landed on the Spar by helicopter, and Greenpeace released the results of the samples taken by its members during the first occupation. According to these results, a potential for up to 5000 tons of oil and a significant number of toxic materials were estimated as being on the Spar.

Finally, on June 20, 1995, after a meeting between the top managers of Shell UK, Shell Netherlands, and Shell Germany, Shell UK realized that its position was no longer sustainable, and decided not to sink the Spar. Not all sides involved saw the decision not to proceed with the deepwater disposal of the Spar in the same manner. Greenpeace hailed it as "a victory for everybody, a victory for common sense and a victory for the environment", while Shell described it as a victory of "the heart over the head" and insisted that deepwater disposal was the Best Practicable Environmental Option. In addition, the British government, who alone defended (and one might even say championed) Shell's decision to sink the Spar, felt betrayed and let down. The industry and energy minister said a license to dispose the Spar on shore would not be automatic, and that "Shell would have to convince us that its three years of studies into the Brent Spar disposal were inaccurate". He also added that the British government was considering withdrawing its 50 percent contribution to the disposal costs it was obliged to make under the original license agreement.

Despite the different perspectives with which the reversal decision of Shell was seen, it was the beginning of a new era of compromise and cooperation among a great number of stakeholders in an attempt to find an acceptable solution to the dismantling of the Spar. In brief, the main developments in the aftermath of Shell's decision to reverse the deepwater disposal of the Spar were as follows. On July 7,

1995, the Norwegian government granted Shell permission to moor the Spar in the deep waters of Erfjord in Norway until the new disposal options were considered. On July 12, 1995, Shell UK commissioned the Norwegian certification authority Det Norske Veritas (DNV) to conduct an independent audit of the Spar and verify its contents and recheck Shell UK's previous inventory. On September 5, 1995, Greenpeace apologized to Shell UK for sampling errors and admitted to the inaccuracy of its claims that the Spar contained as much as 5000 tons of oil. In the following two years, a number of Brent Spar Dialogue seminars took place in many European cities, until the Spar was finally decommissioned off the coast of Norway, and the discussion of a possible moratorium on deepwater disposal of offshore installations was initiated in the OSPARCOM meetings.

(Source: Excerpted from Zyglidopoulos, S.C. (2002). The social and environmental responsibilities of multinationals: Evidence from the Brent Spar case. *Journal of Business Ethics*, **36**: 141–52.)

REFERENCES AND FURTHER READING

Ackerman, R.W. (1975). *The Social Challenge to Business*. Cambridge, MA: Harvard University Press.

Aupperle, K., Carroll, A., and Hatfield, J. (1985). An empirical examination of the relationship between corporate social responsibility and profitability. *Academy of Management Journal*, **28**: 446–63.

Barney, J.B. (1991). Firm resources and sustained competitive advantage. *Journal of Management*, **17**: 99–120.

Berman, S.L., Wicks, A.C., Kotha, S., and Jones, T.M. (1999). Does stakeholder orientation matter: The relationship between stakeholder models and firm financial performance. *Academy of Management Journal*, **42**: 488–506.

Carroll, A. (1999). Corporate social responsibility: Evolution of a definitional construct. *Business and Society*, **38**(3): 268–95.

Carroll, A. (2004). Managing ethically with global stakeholders: A present and future challenge. *Academy of Management Executive*, **18**(2): 114–20.

Cochran, P.L. and Wood, R.A. (1984). Corporate social responsibility and financial performance. *Academy of Management Journal*, **27**: 42–57.

Davis, K. (1973). The case for and against business assumption of social responsibilities. *Academy of Management Journal*, **16**: 312–22.

Davis, G.F. and Thompson, T.A. (1994). A social movement perspective on corporate control. *Administrative Science Quarterly*, **29**: 141–73.

Donaldson, T. and Dunfee, W.T. (1999). When ethics travel: The promise and peril of global business ethics. *California Management Review*, **41**(4): 45–63.

Getz, K.A. (1990). International codes of conduct: An analysis of ethical reasoning. *Journal of Business Ethics*, **9**: 567–77.

Graves, S.B. and Waddock, S.A. (1994). Institutional owners and corporate social performance. *Academy of Management Journal*, **37**: 1034–46.

Harrison, J.S. and Freeman, R.E. (1999). Stakeholder, social responsibility and performance: Empirical evidence and theoretical perspectives. *Academy of Management Journal*, **42**: 479–85.

Harrison, J.S. and John, C.H. (1996). Managing and partnering with external stakeholders. *Academy of Management Executive*, **10**(2): 46–60.

Hillman, A.J. and Keim, G.D. (2001). Shareholder, social responsibility and performance: Empirical evidence and theoretical perspectives. *Academy of Management Journal*, **42**: 479–85.

Johnson, R.A. and Greening, D.W. (1999). The effects of corporate governance and institutional ownership types on corporate social performance. *Academy of Management Journal*, **42**: 564–76.

Logan, D., Delwin, R., and Regelbrugge, L. (1997). *Global Corporate Citizenship – Rationale and Strategies*. Washington, DC: The Hitachi Foundation.

Luo, Y. (2001). Toward a cooperative view of MNC–host government relations: Building blocks and performance implications. *Journal of International Business Studies*, **32**(2): 401–20.

Mitchell, R.K., Agle, B.R., and Wood, D.J. (1997). Towards a theory of stakeholder identification and salience: Defining the principle of who and what really counts. *Academy of Management Review*, **72**(4): 853–86.

Pearce, J.A. and Doh, J.P. (2005). The high impact of collaborative social initiatives. *Sloan Management Review*, Spring, 30–9.

Suchman, M.C. (1995). Managing legitimacy: Strategic and institutional approaches. *Academy of Management Review*, **20**(3): 571–610.

Trevino, L.K. and Brown, M.E. (2004). Managing to be ethical: Debunking five business ethics myths. *Academy of Management Executive*, **18**(2): 69–83.

Turban, D.B. and Greening, D.W. (1997). Corporate social performance and organizational attractiveness to prospective employees. *Academy of Management Journal*, **40**: 658–72.

Waddock, S.A. and Graves, S.B. (1997). The corporate social performance-financial performance link. *Strategic Management Journal*, **18**: 303–19.

Welford, R. (2005). Corporate social responsibility in Europe, North America and Asia: 2004 Survey Results. *Journal of Corporate Citizenship*, **17**: 33–54.

Wernerfelt, B. (1984). A resource-based view of the firm. *Strategic Management Journal*, **5**: 171–180.

Wood, D. (1991). Corporate social responsibility revisited. *Academy of Management Review*, **16**: 691–718.

Appendix 1: The Code of Best Practice – The Cadbury Report

(Proposed by the Cadbury Committee of the United Kingdom in December 1992, established by the Financial Reporting Council, London Stock Exchange and the accountancy profession.)

1. Board of directors

1.1. The board should meet regularly, retain full and effective control over the company and monitor the executive management.

1.2. There should be a clearly accepted division of responsibilities at the head of a company, which will ensure a balance of power and authority, such that no one individual has unfettered powers of decision. Where the chairman is also the chief executive, it is essential that there should be a strong independent element on the board, with a recognised senior member.

1.3. The board should include non-executive directors of sufficient calibre and number for their views to carry significant weight in the board's decisions. (note 1)

1.4. The board should have a formal schedule of matters specifically reserved to it for decision to ensure that the direction and control of the company is firmly in its hands. (note 2)

1.5. There should be an agreed procedure for directors in the furtherance of their duties to take independent professional advice if necessary, at the company's expense. (note 3)

1.6. All directors should have access to the advice and services of the company secretary, who is responsible to the board for ensuring that board procedures are followed and that applicable rules and regulations are complied with. Any question of the removal of the company secretary should be a matter for the board as a whole.

2. Non-executive directors

2.1. Non-executive directors should bring an independent judgment to bear on issues of strategy, performance, resources, including key appointments, and standards of conduct.

2.2. The majority should be independent of management and free from any business or other relationship which could materially interfere with the exercise of their independent judgment, apart from their fees and shareholdings. Their fees should reflect the time which they commit to the company. (notes 4 and 5)

2.3. Non-executive directors should be appointed for specified terms and reappointment should not be automatic. (note 6)

2.4. Non-executive directors should be selected through a formal process and their nomination should be a matter for the board as a whole. (note 7)

3. Executive directors

3.1. Directors' service contracts should not exceed three years without shareholders' approval. (note 8)

3.2. There should be full and clear disclosure of directors' total emoluments and those of the chairman and highest paid UK director, including pension contributions and stock options. Separate figures should be given for salary and performance-related elements and the basis on which performance is measured should be explained.

3.3. Executive directors' pay should be subject to the recommendations of a remuneration committee made up wholly or mainly of non-executive directors. (note 9)

4. Reporting and controls

4.1. It is the board's duty to present a balanced and understandable assessment of the company's position.

4.2. The board should ensure that an objective and professional relationship is maintained with the auditors.

4.3. The board should establish an audit committee of at least three non-executive directors with written terms of reference which deal clearly with its authority and duties. (note 10)

4.4. The directors should explain their responsibility for preparing the accounts next to a statement by the auditors about their reporting responsibilities. (note 11)

4.5. The directors must report on the effectiveness of their internal system of financial control. (note 12)

4.6. The directors should report that the business is a going concern, with supporting assumptions or qualifications as necessary. (note 13)

Notes

These notes include further recommendations on good practice. They do not form part of the Code.

1 To meet the Committee's recommendations on the composition of sub-committees of the board, boards will require a minimum of three non-executive directors, one of whom may be the chairman of the company provided he or she is not also its executive head. Additionally, two of the three non-executive directors should be independent in the terms set out in paragraph 2.2 of the Code.

2 A schedule of matters specifically reserved for decision by the full board should be given to the directors on appointment and should be kept up to date. The Committee envisages that the schedule would at least include:

(a) acquisition and disposal of assets of the company or its subsidiaries that are material to the company;

(b) investments, capital projects, authority levels, treasury policies and risk management policies. The board should lay down rules to determine materiality for any transaction, and should establish clearly which transactions require multiple board signatures. The board should also agree the procedures to be followed when, exceptionally, decisions are required between board meetings.

3 The agreed procedure should be laid down formally, for example in a Board Resolution, in the Articles, or in the Letter of Appointment.

4 It is for the board to decide in particular cases whether this definition of independence is met. Information about the relevant interest of directors should be disclosed in the Directors' Report.

5 The Committee regards it as good practice for non-executive directors not to participate in share option schemes and for their service as non-executive directors not to be pensionable by the company, in order to safeguard their independent position.

6 The Letter of Appointment for non-executive directors should set out their duties, term of office, remuneration, and its review.

7 The Committee regards it as good practice for a nomination committee to carry out the selection process and to make proposals to the board. A nomination committee should have a majority of non-executive directors on it and be chaired either by the chairman or a non-executive director.

8 The Committee does not intend that this provision should apply to existing contracts before they become due for renewal.

9 Membership of the remuneration committee should be set out in the Directors' Report and its chairman should be available to answer questions on remuneration principles and practice at the Annual General Meeting.

10 The report and accounts should contain a coherent narrative, supported by the figures, of the company's performance and prospects. Balance requires that setbacks should be dealt with as well as successes. The need for the report to be readily understood emphasizes that words are as important as figures. The Committee's recommendations on audit committees are as follows:

(a) They should be formally constituted as subcommittees of the main board to whom they are answerable and to whom they should report regularly; they should be given written terms of reference which deal adequately with their membership, authority and duties.

(b) There should be a minimum of three members. Membership should be confined to the non-executive directors of the company and a majority of the non-executives serving on the committee should be independent of the company, as defined in paragraph 2.2 of the Code.

(c) The external auditor and, where an internal audit function exists, the head of internal audit should normally attend committee meetings, as should the finance director. Other board members should also have the right to attend.

(d) The audit committee should have a discussion with the auditors at least once a year, without executive board members present, to ensure that there are no unresolved issues of concern.

(e) The audit committee should have explicit authority to investigate any matters within its terms of reference, the resources which it needs to do so, and full access to information. The committee should be able to obtain outside professional advice and if necessary to invite outsiders with relevant experience to attend meetings.

(f) Membership of the committee should be disclosed in the annual report and the chairman of the committee should be available to answer questions about its work at the Annual General Meeting. Specimen terms of reference for an audit committee, including a list of the most commonly performed duties, are set out in the Committee's full report.

11 The statement of directors' responsibilities should cover the following points:

(a) the legal requirement for directors to prepare financial statements for each financial year which give a true and fair view of the state of affairs of the company (or group) as at the end of the financial year and of the profit and loss for that period;

(b) the responsibility of the directors for maintaining adequate accounting records, for safeguarding the assets of the company (or group), and for preventing and detecting fraud and other irregularities;

(c) confirmation that suitable accounting policies, consistently applied and supported by reasonable and prudent judgments and estimates, have been used in the preparation of the financial statements;

(d) confirmation that applicable accounting standards have been followed, subject to any material departures disclosed and explained in the notes to the accounts. (This does not obviate the need for a formal statement in the notes to the accounts disclosing whether the accounts have been prepared in accordance with applicable accounting standards.)

The statement should be placed immediately before the auditors' report which in future will include a separate statement (currently being developed by the Auditing Practices Board) on the responsibility of the auditors for expressing an opinion on the accounts.

12 The Committee notes that companies will not be able to comply with paragraphs 4.5 and 4.6 of the Code until the necessary guidance for companies has been developed as recommended in the Committee's report.

13 The company's statement of compliance should be reviewed by the auditors in so far as it relates to paragraphs 1.4, 1.5, 2.3, 2.4, 3.1 to 3.3, and 4.3 to 4.6 of the Code.

Appendix 2: Summary of Sarbanes-Oxley Act of 2002

Section 3: Commission Rules and Enforcement.

A violation of Rules of the Public Company Accounting Oversight Board ("Board") is treated as a violation of the '34 Act, giving rise to the same penalties that may be imposed for violations of that Act.

Section 101: Establishment; Board Membership.

The Board will have five financially literate members, appointed for five-year terms. Two of the members must be or have been certified public accountants, and the remaining three must not be and cannot have been CPAs. The Chair may be held by one of the CPA members, provided that he or she has not been engaged as a practicing CPA for five years.

The Board's members will serve on a full-time basis.

No member may, concurrent with service on the Board, "share in any of the profits of, or receive payments from, a public accounting firm," other than "fixed continuing payments," such as retirement payments.

Members of the Board are appointed by the Commission, "after consultation with" the Chairman of the Federal Reserve Board and the Secretary of the Treasury.

Members may be removed by the Commission "for good cause."

Section 103: Auditing, Quality Control, And Independence Standards And Rules.

The Board shall:

(1) register public accounting firms;

(2) establish, or adopt, by rule, "auditing, quality control, ethics, independence, and other standards relating to the preparation of audit reports for issuers";

(3) conduct inspections of accounting firms;

(4) conduct investigations and disciplinary proceedings, and impose appropriate sanctions;

(5) perform such other duties or functions as necessary or appropriate;

(6) enforce compliance with the Act, the rules of the Board, professional standards, and the securities laws relating to the preparation and issuance of audit reports and the obligations and liabilities of accountants with respect thereto;

(7) set the budget and manage the operations of the Board and the staff of the Board.

Auditing standards. The Board would be required to "cooperate on an ongoing basis" with designated professional groups of accountants and any advisory groups convened in connection with standard-setting, and although the Board can "to the extent that it determines appropriate" adopt standards proposed by those groups, the Board will have authority to amend, modify, repeal, and reject any standards suggested by the groups. The Board must report on its standard-setting activity to the Commission on an annual basis.

The Board must require registered public accounting firms to "prepare, and maintain for a period of not less than 7 years, audit work papers, and other information related to any audit report, in sufficient detail to support the conclusions reached in such report."

The Board must require a second partner review and approval of audit reports prepared by registered accounting firms.

The Board must adopt an audit standard to implement the internal control review required by section 404(b). This standard must require the auditor to evaluate whether the internal control structure and procedures include records that accurately and fairly reflect the transactions of the issuer, provide reasonable assurance that the transactions are recorded in a manner that will permit the preparation of financial statements in accordance with GAAP, and a description of any material weaknesses in the internal controls.

Section 102(a): Mandatory Registration
Section 102(f): Registration and Annual Fees.
Section 109(d): Funding; Annual Accounting Support Fee for the Board.
In order to audit a public company, a public accounting firm must register with the Board. The Board shall collect "a registration fee" and "an annual fee" from each registered public accounting firm, in amounts that are "sufficient" to recover the costs of processing and reviewing applications and annual reports.

The Board shall also establish by rule a reasonable "annual accounting support fee" as may be necessary or appropriate to maintain the Board. This fee will be assessed on issuers only.

Section 104: Inspections of Registered Public Accounting Firms.
Annual quality reviews (inspections) must be conducted for firms that audit more than 100 issues, all others must be conducted every three years. The SEC and/or the Board may order a special inspection of any firm at any time.

Section 105(b)(5): Investigation and Disciplinary Proceedings; Investigations; Use of Documents.
Section 105(c)(2): Investigations and Disciplinary Proceedings; Disciplinary Procedures; Public Hearings.
Section 105(c)(4): Investigations and Disciplinary Proceedings; Sanctions.
Section 105(d): Investigations and Disciplinary Proceedings; Reporting of Sanctions.
All documents and information prepared or received by the Board shall be "confidential and privileged as an evidentiary matter (and shall not be subject to civil discovery other legal process) in any proceeding in any Federal or State court or administrative agency, . . . unless and until

presented in connection with a public proceeding or [otherwise] released" in connection with a disciplinary action. However, all such documents and information can be made available to the SEC, the US Attorney General, and other federal and appropriate state agencies.

Disciplinary hearings will be closed unless the Board orders that they be public, for good cause, and with the consent of the parties.

Sanctions can be imposed by the Board of a firm if it fails to reasonably supervise any associated person with regard to auditing or quality control standards, or otherwise.
No sanctions report will be made available to the public unless and until stays pending appeal have been lifted.

Section 106: Foreign Public Accounting Firms.
The bill would subject foreign accounting firms who audit a US company to registrations with the Board. This would include foreign firms that perform some audit work, such as in a foreign subsidiary of a US company, that is relied on by the primary auditor.

Section 107(a): Commission Oversight of the Board; General Oversight Responsibility.
Section 107(b): Rules of the Board.
Section 107(d): Censure of the Board and Other Sanctions.
The SEC shall have "oversight and enforcement authority over the Board." The SEC can, by rule or order, give the Board additional responsibilities. The SEC may require the Board to keep certain records, and it has the power to inspect the Board itself, in the same manner as it can with regard to SROs such as the NASD.

The Board, in its rulemaking process, is to be treated "as if the Board were a 'registered securities association' " – that is, a self-regulatory organization. The Board is required to file proposed rules and proposed rule changes with the SEC. The SEC may approve, reject, or amend such rules.

The Board must notify the SEC of pending investigations involving potential violations of the securities laws, and coordinate its investigation with the SEC Division of Enforcement as necessary to protect an ongoing SEC investigation.

The SEC may, by order, "censure or impose limitations upon the activities, functions, and operations of the Board" if it finds that the Board has violated the Act or the securities laws, or if the Board has failed to ensure the compliance of accounting firms with applicable rules without reasonable justification.

Section 107(c): Commission Review of Disciplinary Action Taken by the Board.
The Board must notify the SEC when it imposes "any final sanction" on any accounting firm or associated person. The Board's findings and sanctions are subject to review by the SEC.

The SEC may enhance, modify, cancel, reduce, or require remission of such sanction.

Section 108: Accounting Standards.
The SEC is authorized to "recognize, as 'generally accepted' . . . any accounting principles" that are established by a standard-setting body that meets the bill's criteria, which include requirements that the body:

(1) be a private entity;

(2) be governed by a board of trustees (or equivalent body), the majority of whom are not or have not been associated persons with a public accounting firm for the past two years;

(3) be funded in a manner similar to the Board;

(4) have adopted procedures to ensure prompt consideration of changes to accounting principles by a majority vote;

(5) consider, when adopting standards, the need to keep them current and the extent to which international convergence of standards is necessary or appropriate.

Section 201: Services Outside the Scope of Practice of Auditors; Prohibited Activities.

It shall be "unlawful" for a registered public accounting firm to provide any non-audit service to an issuer contemporaneously with the audit, including: (1) bookkeeping or other services related to the accounting records or financial statements of the audit client; (2) financial information systems design and implementation; (3) appraisal or valuation services, fairness opinions, or contribution-in-kind reports; (4) actuarial services; (5) internal audit outsourcing services; (6) management functions or human resources; (7) broker or dealer, investment adviser, or investment banking services; (8) legal services and expert services unrelated to the audit; (9) any other service that the Board determines, by regulation, is impermissible. The Board may, on a case-by-case basis, exempt from these prohibitions any person, issuer, public accounting firm, or transaction, subject to review by the Commission.

It will not be unlawful to provide other non-audit services if they are pre-approved by the audit committee in the following manner. The bill allows an accounting firm to "engage in any non-audit service, including tax services," that is not listed above, only if the activity is pre-approved by the audit committee of the issuer. The audit committee will disclose to investors in periodic reports its decision to pre-approve non-audit services. Statutory insurance company regulatory audits are treated as an audit service, and thus do not require pre-approval.

The pre-approval requirement is waived with respect to the provision of non-audit services for an issuer if the aggregate amount of all such non-audit services provided to the issuer constitutes less than 5% of the total amount of revenues paid by the issuer to its auditor (calculated on the basis of revenues paid by the issuer during the fiscal year when the non-audit services are performed), such services were not recognized by the issuer at the time of the engagement to be non-audit services; and such services are promptly brought to the attention of the audit committee and approved prior to completion of the audit.

The authority to pre-approve services can be delegated to one or more members of the audit committee, but any decision by the delegate must be presented to the full audit committee.

Section 203: Audit Partner Rotation.

The lead audit or coordinating partner and the reviewing partner must rotate off of the audit every five years.

Section 204: Auditor Reports to Audit Committees.

The accounting firm must report to the audit committee all "critical accounting policies and practices to be used, all alternative treatments of financial information within [GAAP] that have been discussed with management, ramifications of the use of such alternative disclosures and treatments, and the treatment preferred" by the firm.

Section 206: Conflicts of Interest.
The CEO, Controller, CFO, Chief Accounting Officer or person in an equivalent position cannot have been employed by the company's audit firm during the one-year period preceding the audit.

Section 207: Study of Mandatory Rotation of Registered Public Accountants.
The GAO will do a study on the potential effects of requiring the mandatory rotation of audit firms.

Section 209: Consideration by Appropriate State Regulatory Authorities.
State regulators are directed to make an independent determination as to whether the Board standards shall be applied to small and mid-size non-registered accounting firms.

Section 301: Public Company Audit Committees.
Each member of the audit committee shall be a member of the board of directors of the issuer, and shall otherwise be independent.

"Independent" is defined as not receiving, other than for service on the board, any consulting, advisory, or other compensatory fee from the issuer, and as not being an affiliated person of the issuer, or any subsidiary thereof.

The SEC may make exemptions for certain individuals on a case-by-case basis.

The audit committee of an issuer shall be directly responsible for the appointment, compensation, and oversight of the work of any registered public accounting firm employed by that issuer.

The audit committee shall establish procedures for the "receipt, retention, and treatment of complaints" received by the issuer regarding accounting, internal controls, and auditing.

Each audit committee shall have the authority to engage independent counsel or other advisors, as it determines necessary to carry out its duties.

Each issuer shall provide appropriate funding to the audit committee.

Section 302: Corporate Responsibility for Financial Reports.
The CEO and CFO of each issuer shall prepare a statement to accompany the audit report to certify the "appropriateness of the financial statements and disclosures contained in the periodic report, and that those financial statements and disclosures fairly present, in all material respects, the operations and financial condition of the issuer." A violation of this section must be knowing and intentional to give rise to liability.

Section 303: Improper Influence on Conduct of Audits.
It shall be unlawful for any officer or director of an issuer to take any action to fraudulently influence, coerce, manipulate, or mislead any auditor engaged in the performance of an audit for the purpose of rendering the financial statements materially misleading.

Section 304: Forfeiture of Certain Bonuses and Profits.
Section 305: Officer and Director Bars and Penalties; Equitable Relief.
If an issuer is required to prepare a restatement due to "material noncompliance" with financial reporting requirements, the chief executive officer and the chief financial officer shall "reimburse

the issuer for any bonus or other incentive-based or equity-based compensation received" during the twelve months following the issuance or filing of the non-compliant document and "any profits realized from the sale of securities of the issuer" during that period.

In any action brought by the SEC for violation of the securities laws, federal courts are authorized to "grant any equitable relief that may be appropriate or necessary for the benefit of investors."

Section 305: Officer and Director Bars and Penalties.

The SEC may issue an order to prohibit, conditionally or unconditionally, permanently or temporarily, any person who has violated section 10(b) of the 1934 Act from acting as an officer or director of an issuer if the SEC has found that such person's conduct "demonstrates unfitness" to serve as an officer or director of any such issuer.

Section 306: Insider Trades During Pension Fund Black-Out Periods Prohibited.

Prohibits the purchase or sale of stock by officers and directors and other insiders during blackout periods. Any profits resulting from sales in violation of this section "shall inure to and be recoverable by the issuer." If the issuer fails to bring suit or prosecute diligently, a suit to recover such profit may be instituted by "the owner of any security of the issuer."

Section 401(a): Disclosures in Periodic Reports; Disclosures Required.

Each financial report that is required to be prepared in accordance with GAAP shall "reflect all material correcting adjustments . . . that have been identified by a registered accounting firm. . . ."

"Each annual and quarterly financial report . . . shall disclose all material off-balance sheet transactions" and "other relationships" with "unconsolidated entities" that may have a material current or future effect on the financial condition of the issuer.

The SEC shall issue rules providing that pro forma financial information must be presented so as not to "contain an untrue statement" or omit to state a material fact necessary in order to make the pro forma financial information not misleading.

Section 401(c): Study and Report on Special Purpose Entities.

SEC shall study off-balance sheet disclosures to determine (a) extent of off-balance sheet transactions (including assets, liabilities, leases, losses and the use of special purpose entities); and (b) whether generally accepted accounting rules result in financial statements of issuers reflecting the economics of such off-balance sheet transactions to investors in a transparent fashion and make a report containing recommendations to the Congress.

Section 402(a): Prohibition on Personal Loans to Executives.

Generally, it will be unlawful for an issuer to extend credit to any director or executive officer. Consumer credit companies may make home improvement and consumer credit loans and issue credit cards to its directors and executive officers if it is done in the ordinary course of business on the same terms and conditions made to the general public.

Section 403: Disclosures of Transactions Involving Management and Principal Stockholders.

Directors, officers, and 10% owner must report designated transactions by the end of the second business day following the day on which the transaction was executed.

Section 404: Management Assessment of Internal Controls.

Requires each annual report of an issuer to contain an "internal control report", which shall:
(1) state the responsibility of management for establishing and maintaining an adequate internal control structure and procedures for financial reporting; and
(2) contain an assessment, as of the end of the issuer's fiscal year, of the effectiveness of the internal control structure and procedures of the issuer for financial reporting.

Each issuer's auditor shall attest to, and report on, the assessment made by the management of the issuer. An attestation made under this section shall be in accordance with standards for attestation engagements issued or adopted by the Board. An attestation engagement shall not be the subject of a separate engagement.

The language in the report of the Committee which accompanies the bill to explain the legislative intent states, ". . . the Committee does not intend that the auditor's evaluation be the subject of a separate engagement or the basis for increased charges or fees."

Directs the SEC to require each issuer to disclose whether it has adopted a code of ethics for its senior financial officers and the contents of that code.

Directs the SEC to revise its regulations concerning prompt disclosure on Form 8-K to require immediate disclosure "of any change in, or waiver of," an issuer's code of ethics.

Section 407: Disclosure of Audit Committee Financial Expert.

The SEC shall issue rules to require issuers to disclose whether at least one member of its audit committee is a "financial expert."

Section 409: Real Time Disclosure.

Issuers must disclose information on material changes in the financial condition or operations of the issuer on a rapid and current basis.

Section 501: Treatment of Securities Analysts by Registered Securities Associations.

National Securities Exchanges and registered securities associations must adopt conflict of interest rules for research analysts who recommend equities in research reports.

Section 601: SEC Resources and Authority.

SEC appropriations for 2003 are increased to $776,000,000. $98 million of the funds shall be used to hire an additional 200 employees to provide enhanced oversight of auditors and audit services required by the Federal securities laws.

Section 602(a): Appearance and Practice Before the Commission.

The SEC may censure any person, or temporarily bar or deny any person the right to appear or practice before the SEC if the person does not possess the requisite qualifications to represent others, lacks character or integrity, or has willfully violated Federal securities laws.

Section 602(c): Study and Report.

SEC is to conduct a study of "securities professionals" (public accountants, public accounting firms, investment bankers, investment advisors, brokers, dealers, attorneys) who have been found to have aided and abetted a violation of Federal securities laws.

Section 602(d): Rules of Professional Responsibility for Attorneys.

The SEC shall establish rules setting minimum standards for professional conduct for attorneys practicing before it.

Section 701: GAO Study and Report Regarding Consolidation of Public Accounting Firms.

The GAO shall conduct a study regarding the consolidation of public accounting firms since 1989, including the present and future impact of the consolidation, and the solutions to any problems discovered.

Title VIII: Corporate and Criminal Fraud Accountability Act of 2002.

It is a felony to "knowingly" destroy or create documents to "impede, obstruct or influence" any existing or contemplated federal investigation.

Auditors are required to maintain "all audit or review work papers" for five years.

The statute of limitations on securities fraud claims is extended to the earlier of five years from the fraud, or two years after the fraud was discovered, from three years and one year, respectively.

Employees of issuers and accounting firms are extended "whistleblower protection" that would prohibit the employer from taking certain actions against employees who lawfully disclose private employer information to, among others, parties in a judicial proceeding involving a fraud claim. Whistleblowers are also granted a remedy of special damages and attorney's fees.

A new crime for securities fraud that has penalties of fines and up to 10 years imprisonment.

Title IX: White Collar Crime Penalty Enhancements.

Maximum penalty for mail and wire fraud increased from 5 to 10 years.
Creates a crime for tampering with a record or otherwise impeding any official proceeding.

SEC given authority to seek court freeze of extraordinary payments to directors, offices, partners, controlling persons, agents of employees.

US Sentencing Commission to review sentencing guidelines for securities and accounting fraud.

SEC may prohibit anyone convicted of securities fraud from being an officer or director of any publicly traded company.

Financial statements filed with the SEC must be certified by the CEO and CFO. The certification must state that the financial statements and disclosures fully comply with provisions of the Securities Exchange Act and that they fairly present, in all material respects, the operations and financial condition of the issuer. Maximum penalties for willful and knowing violations of this section are a fine of not more than $500,000 and/or imprisonment of up to five years.

Section 1001: Sense of Congress Regarding Corporate Tax Returns.

It is the sense of Congress that the Federal income tax return of a corporation should be signed by the chief executive officer of such corporation.

Section 1102: Tampering With a Record or Otherwise Impeding an Official Proceeding.
Makes it a crime for any person to corruptly alter, destroy, mutilate, or conceal any document with the intent to impair the object's integrity or availability for use in an official proceeding or to otherwise obstruct, influence or impede any official proceeding is liable for up to 20 years in prison and a fine.

Section 1103: Temporary Freeze Authority.
The SEC is authorized to freeze the payment of an extraordinary payment to any director, officer, partner, controlling person, agent, or employee of a company during an investigation of possible violations of securities laws.

Section 1105: SEC Authority to Prohibit Persons from Serving as Officers or Directors.
The SEC may prohibit a person from serving as an officer or director of a public company if the person has committed securities fraud.

Appendix 3: The OECD Guidelines for Multinational Enterprises

Preface

1. The OECD *Guidelines for Multinational Enterprises* (the *Guidelines*) are recommendations addressed by governments to multinational enterprises. They provide voluntary principles and standards for responsible business conduct consistent with applicable laws. The *Guidelines* aim to ensure that the operations of these enterprises are in harmony with government policies, to strengthen the basis of mutual confidence between enterprises and the societies in which they operate, to help improve the foreign investment climate and to enhance the contribution to sustainable development made by multinational enterprises. The *Guidelines* are part of the OECD *Declaration on International Investment and Multinational Enterprises* the other elements of which relate to national treatment, conflicting requirements on enterprises, and international investment incentives and disincentives.

2. International business has experienced far-reaching structural change and the *Guidelines* themselves have evolved to reflect these changes. With the rise of service and knowledge-intensive industries, service and technology enterprises have entered the international marketplace. Large enterprises still account for a major share of international investment, and there is a trend toward large-scale international mergers. At the same time, foreign investment by small- and medium-sized enterprises has also increased and these enterprises now play a significant role on the international scene. Multinational enterprises, like their domestic counterparts, have evolved to encompass a broader range of business arrangements and organizational forms. Strategic alliances and closer relations with suppliers and contractors tend to blur the boundaries of the enterprise.

3. The rapid evolution in the structure of multinational enterprises is also reflected in their operations in the developing world, where foreign direct investment has grown rapidly. In developing countries, multinational enterprises have diversified beyond primary production and extractive industries into manufacturing, assembly, domestic market development and services.

4. The activities of multinational enterprises, through international trade and investment, have strengthened and deepened the ties that join OECD economies to each other and to the rest of the world. These activities bring substantial benefits to home and host countries. These benefits accrue when multinational enterprises supply the products and services that consumers want to buy

at competitive prices and when they provide fair returns to suppliers of capital. Their trade and investment activities contribute to the efficient use of capital, technology and human and natural resources. They facilitate the transfer of technology among the regions of the world and the development of technologies that reflect local conditions. Through both formal training and on-the-job learning enterprises also promote the development of human capital in host countries.

5. The nature, scope and speed of economic changes have presented new strategic challenges for enterprises and their stakeholders. Multinational enterprises have the opportunity to implement best practice policies for sustainable development that seek to ensure coherence between social, economic and environmental objectives. The ability of multinational enterprises to promote sustainable development is greatly enhanced when trade and investment are conducted in a context of open, competitive and appropriately regulated markets.

6. Many multinational enterprises have demonstrated that respect for high standards of business conduct can enhance growth. Today's competitive forces are intense and multinational enterprises face a variety of legal, social and regulatory settings. In this context, some enterprises may be tempted to neglect appropriate standards and principles of conduct in an attempt to gain undue competitive advantage. Such practices by the few may call into question the reputation of the many and may give rise to public concerns.

7. Many enterprises have responded to these public concerns by developing internal programmes, guidance and management systems that underpin their commitment to good corporate citizenship, good practices and good business and employee conduct. Some of them have called upon consulting, auditing and certification services, contributing to the accumulation of expertise in these areas. These efforts have also promoted social dialogue on what constitutes good business conduct. The *Guidelines* clarify the shared expectations for business conduct of the governments adhering to them and provide a point of reference for enterprises. Thus, the *Guidelines* both complement and reinforce private efforts to define and implement responsible business conduct.

8. Governments are cooperating with each other and with other actors to strengthen the international legal and policy framework in which business is conducted. The post-war period has seen the development of this framework, starting with the adoption in 1948 of the Universal Declaration of Human Rights. Recent instruments include the ILO Declaration on Fundamental Principles and Rights at Work, the Rio Declaration on Environment and Development and Agenda 21 and the Copenhagen Declaration for Social Development.

9. The OECD has also been contributing to the international policy framework. Recent developments include the adoption of the Convention on Combating Bribery of Foreign Public Officials in International Business Transactions and of the OECD Principles of Corporate Governance, the OECD Guidelines for Consumer Protection in the Context of Electronic Commerce, and ongoing work on the OECD Guidelines on Transfer Pricing for Multinational Enterprises and Tax Administrations.

10. The common aim of the governments adhering to the *Guidelines* is to encourage the positive contributions that multinational enterprises can make to economic, environmental and social progress and to minimize the difficulties to which their various operations may give rise. In working towards this goal, governments find themselves in partnership with the many businesses, trade unions and other non-governmental organizations that are working in their own ways toward the same end. Governments can help by providing effective domestic policy frameworks that include stable macroeconomic policy, non-discriminatory treatment of firms, appropriate regulation and prudential supervision, an impartial system of courts and law enforcement and efficient and honest public administration. Governments can also help by maintaining and promoting appropriate standards and policies in support of sustainable development and by engaging in ongoing reforms to ensure that public sector activity is efficient

and effective. Governments adhering to the *Guidelines* are committed to continual improvement of both domestic and international policies with a view to improving the welfare and living standards of all people.

I. Concepts and Principles

1. The *Guidelines* are recommendations jointly addressed by governments to multinational enterprises. They provide principles and standards of good practice consistent with applicable laws. Observance of the *Guidelines* by enterprises is voluntary and not legally enforceable.

2. Since the operations of multinational enterprises extend throughout the world, international cooperation in this field should extend to all countries. Governments adhering to the *Guidelines* encourage the enterprises operating on their territories to observe the *Guidelines* wherever they operate, while taking into account the particular circumstances of each host country.

3. A precise definition of multinational enterprises is not required for the purposes of the *Guidelines.* These usually comprise companies or other entities established in more than one country and so linked that they may coordinate their operations in various ways. While one or more of these entities may be able to exercise a significant influence over the activities of others, their degree of autonomy within the enterprise may vary widely from one multinational enterprise to another. Ownership may be private, state or mixed. The *Guidelines* are addressed to all the entities within the multinational enterprise (parent companies and/or local entities). According to the actual distribution of responsibilities among them, the different entities are expected to cooperate and to assist one another to facilitate observance of the *Guidelines.*

4. The *Guidelines* are not aimed at introducing differences of treatment between multinational and domestic enterprises; they reflect good practice for all. Accordingly, multinational and domestic enterprises are subject to the same expectations in respect of their conduct wherever the *Guidelines* are relevant to both.

5. Governments wish to encourage the widest possible observance of the *Guidelines.* While it is acknowledged that small- and medium-sized enterprises may not have the same capacities as larger enterprises, governments adhering to the *Guidelines* nevertheless encourage them to observe the *Guidelines* recommendations to the fullest extent possible.

6. Governments adhering to the *Guidelines* should not use them for protectionist purposes nor use them in a way that calls into question the comparative advantage of any country where multinational enterprises invest.

7. Governments have the right to prescribe the conditions under which multinational enterprises operate within their jurisdictions, subject to international law. The entities of a multinational enterprise located in various countries are subject to the laws applicable in these countries. When multinational enterprises are subject to conflicting requirements by adhering countries, the governments concerned will cooperate in good faith with a view to resolving problems that may arise.

8. Governments adhering to the *Guidelines* set them forth with the understanding that they will fulfil their responsibilities to treat enterprises equitably and in accordance with international law and with their contractual obligations.

9. The use of appropriate international dispute settlement mechanisms. including arbitration, is encouraged as a means of facilitating the resolution of legal problems arising between enterprises and host country governments.

10. Governments adhering to the *Guidelines* will promote them and encourage their use. They will establish National Contact Points that promote the *Guidelines* and act as a forum for

discussion of all matters relating to the *Guidelines.* The adhering Governments will also participate in appropriate review and consultation procedures to address issues concerning interpretation of the *Guidelines* in a changing world.

II. General Policies

Enterprises should take fully into account established policies in the countries in which they operate, and consider the views of other stakeholders. In this regard, enterprises should:

1. Contribute to economic, social and environmental progress with a view to achieving sustainable development.
2. Respect the human rights of those affected by their activities consistent with the host government's international obligations and commitments.
3. Encourage local capacity building through close cooperation with the local community, including business interests, as well as developing the enterprise's activities in domestic and foreign markets, consistent with the need for sound commercial practice.
4. Encourage human capital formation, in particular by creating employment opportunities and facilitating training opportunities for employees.
5. Refrain from seeking or accepting exemptions not contemplated in the statutory or regulatory framework related to environmental, health, safety, labour, taxation, financial incentives, or other issues.
6. Support and uphold good corporate governance principles and develop and apply good corporate governance practices.
7. Develop and apply effective self-regulatory practices and management systems that foster a relationship of confidence and mutual trust between enterprises and the societies in which they operate.
8. Promote employee awareness of, and compliance with, company policies through appropriate dissemination of these policies, including through training programmes.
9. Refrain from discriminatory or disciplinary action against employees who make *bona fide* reports to management or, as appropriate, to the competent public authorities, on practices that contravene the law, the *Guidelines* or the enterprise's policies.
10. Encourage, where practicable, business partners, including suppliers and subcontractors, to apply principles of corporate conduct compatible with the *Guidelines.*
11. Abstain from any improper involvement in local political activities.

III. Disclosure

1. Enterprises should ensure that timely, regular, reliable and relevant information is disclosed regarding their activities, structure, financial situation and performance. This information should be disclosed *for* the enterprise as a whole and, where appropriate, along business lines or geographic areas. Disclosure policies of enterprises should be tailored to the nature, size and location of the enterprise, with due regard taken of costs, business confidentiality and other competitive concerns.
2. Enterprises should apply high quality standards *for* disclosure, accounting and audit. Enterprises are also encouraged to apply high quality standards *for* non-financial information including environmental and social reporting where they exist. The standards or policies under which both financial and non-financial information are compiled and published should be reported.

3. Enterprises should disclose basic information showing their name, location, and structure, the name, address and telephone number of the parent enterprise and its main affiliates, its percentage ownership, direct and indirect in these affiliates, including shareholdings between them.

4. Enterprises should also disclose material information on:

a) The financial and operating results of the company.

b) Company objectives.

c) Major share ownership and voting right.

d) Members of the board and key executives, and their remuneration.

e) Material foreseeable risk factors.

f) Material issues regarding employees and other stakeholders.

g) Governance structures and policies.

5. Enterprises are encouraged to communicate additional information that could include:

a) Value statements or statements of business conduct intended *for* public disclosure including information on the social, ethical and environmental policies of the enterprise and other codes of conduct to which the company subscribes. In addition, the date of adoption, the countries and entities to which such statements apply and its performance in relation to these statements may be communicated.

b) Information on systems *for* managing risks and complying with laws, and on statements or codes of business conduct.

c) Information on relationships with employees and other stakeholders.

IV. Employment and Industrial Relations

Enterprises should, within the framework of applicable law, regulations and prevailing labour relations and employment practices:

1. a) Respect the right of their employees to be represented by trade union and other *bona fide* representatives of employees, and engage in constructive negotiations, either individually or through employers' associations, with such representatives with a view to reaching agreements on employment conditions;

b) Contribute to the effective abolition of child labour.

c) Contribute to the elimination of all forms of forced or compulsory labor.

d) Not discriminate against their employees with respect to employment or occupation on such grounds as race, colour, sex, religion, political opinion, national extraction or social origin, unless selectivity concerning employee characteristics is established by governmental policies, which specifically promote greater equality of employment opportunity or relates to the inherent requirements of a job.

2. a) Provide facilities to employee representatives as may be necessary to assist in the development of effective collective agreements.

b) Provide information to employee representatives which is needed for meaningful negotiations on conditions of employment.

c) Promote consultation and cooperation between employers and employees and their representatives on matters of mutual concern.

3. Provide information to employees and their representatives which enables them to obtain a true and fair view of the performance of the entity or, where appropriate, the enterprise as a whole.

4. a) Observe standards of employment and industrial relations not less favourable than those observed by comparable employers in the/host country.

b) Take adequate steps to ensure occupational health and safety in their operations.

5. In their operations, to the greatest extent practicable, employ local personnel and provide training with a view to improving skill levels, in cooperation with employee representatives and, where appropriate, relevant governmental authorities.

6. In considering changes in their operations which would have major effects upon the livelihood of their employees, in particular in the case of the closure of an entity involving collective lay-offs or dismissals, provide reasonable notice of such changes to representatives of their employees, and, where appropriate, to the relevant governmental authorities, and cooperate with the employee representatives and appropriate governmental authorities so as to mitigate to the maximum extent practicable adverse effects. In light of the specific circumstances of each case, it would be appropriate if management were able to give such notice prior to the final decision being taken. Other means may also be employed to provide meaningful cooperation to mitigate the effects of such decisions.

7. In the context of *bona fide* negotiations with representatives of employees on conditions of employment, or while employees are exercising a right to organise, not threaten to transfer the whole or part of an operating unit from the country concerned nor transfer employees from the enterprises' component entities in other countries in order to influence unfairly those negotiations or to hinder the exercise of a right to organise.

8. Enable authorized representatives of their employees to negotiate in collective bargaining or labour-management relations issues and allow the parties to consult on matters of mutual concern with representatives of management who are authorized to take decisions on these matters.

V. Environment

Enterprises should, within the framework of laws, regulations an administrative practices in the countries in which they operate, and in consideration of relevant international agreements, principles, objectives, and standards, take due account of the need to protect the environment, public health and safety, and generally to conduct their activities in a manner contributing to the wide goal of sustainable development. In particular, enterprises should:

1. Establish and maintain a system of environmental management a the enterprise, including:

a) Collection and evaluation of adequate and timely information regarding the environmental, health, and safety impacts of their activities.

b) Establishment of measurable objectives and, where appropriate, targets for improved environmental performance, including periodically reviewing the continuing relevance of these objectives; and

c) Regular monitoring and verification of progress toward environmental, health, and safety objectives or targets.

2. Taking into account concerns about cost, business confidentiality, and the protection of intellectual property rights:

a) Provide the public and employees with adequate and timely information on the potential environment, health and safety impacts of the activities of the enterprise, which could include reporting on progress in improving environmental performance; and

b) Engage in adequate and timely communication and consultation with the communities directly affected by the environmental, health and safety policies of the enterprise and by their implementation.

3. Assess, and address in decision-making, the foreseeable environmental, health, and safety-related impacts associated with the processes, goods and services of the enterprise over their full life cycle. Where these proposed activities may have significant environmental, health, or safety

impacts, and where they are subject to a decision of a competent authority, prepare an appropriate environmental impact assessment.

4. Consistent with the scientific and technical understanding of the risks, where there are threats of serious damage to the environment, taking also into account human health and safety, not use the lack of full scientific certainty as a reason for postponing cost-effective measures to prevent or minimise such damage.

5. Maintain contingency plans for preventing, mitigating, and controlling serious environmental and health damage from their operations, including accidents and emergencies; and mechanisms for immediate reporting to the competent authorities.

6. Continually seek to improve corporate environmental performance, by encouraging, where appropriate, such activities as:

a) Adoption of technologies and operating procedures in all parts of the enterprise that reflect standards concerning environmental performance in the best performing part of the enterprise.

b) Development and provision of products or services that have no undue environmental impacts; are safe in their intended use; are efficient in their consumption of energy and natural resources; can be reused, recycled, or disposed of safely.

c) Promoting higher levels of awareness among customers of the environmental implications of using the products and services of the enterprise; and performance of the enterprise; and

d) Research on ways of improving the environmental enterprise over the longer term.

7. Provide adequate education and training to employees in environmental health and safety matters, including the handling of hazardous materials and the prevention of environmental accidents, as well as more general environmental management areas, such as environmental impact assessment procedures, public relations, and environmental technologies.

8. Contribute to the development of environmentally meaningful and economically efficient public policy, for example, by means of partnerships or initiatives that will enhance environmental awareness and protection.

VI. Combating Bribery

Enterprises should not, directly or indirectly, offer, promise, give, or demand a bribe or other undue advantage to obtain or retain business or other improper advantage. Nor should enterprises be solicited or expected to render a bribe or other undue advantage. In particular, enterprises should:

1. Not offer, nor give in to demands, to pay public officials or the employees of business partners any portion of a contract payment. They should not use subcontracts, purchase orders or consulting agreements as means of channelling payments to public officials, to employees of business partners or to their relatives or business associates.

2. Ensure that remuneration of agents is appropriate and for legitimate services only. Where relevant, a list of agents employed in connection with transactions with public bodies and state-owned enterprises should be kept and made available to competent authorities.

3. Enhance the transparency of their activities in the fight against bribery and extortion. Measures could include making public commitments against bribery and extortion and disclosing the management systems the company has adopted in order to honour these commitments. The enterprise should also foster openness and dialogue with the public so as to promote its awareness of and cooperation with the fight against bribery and extortion.

4. Promote employee awareness of and compliance with company policies against bribery and extortion through appropriate dissemination of these policies and through training programmes and disciplinary procedures.

5. Adopt management control systems that discourage bribery and corrupt practices, and adopt financial and tax accounting and auditing practices that prevent the establishment of "off the books" or secret accounts or the creation of documents which do not properly and fairly record the transactions to which they relate.

6. Not make illegal contributions to candidates for public office or to political parties or to other political organisations. Contributions should fully comply with public disclosure requirements and should be reported to senior management.

VII. Consumer Interests

When dealing with consumers, enterprises should act in accordance with fair business, marketing and advertising practices and should take all reasonable steps to ensure the safety and quality of the goods or services they provide. In particular, they should:

1. Ensure that the goods or services they provide meet all agreed or legally required standards for consumer health and safety, including health warnings and product safety and information labels.

2. As appropriate to the goods or services, provide accurate and clear information regarding their content, safe use, maintenance, storage, and disposal sufficient to enable consumers to make informed decisions.

3. Provide transparent and effective procedures that address consumer complaints and contribute to fair and timely resolution of consumer disputes without undue cost or burden.

4. Not make representations or omissions, nor engage in any other practices, that are deceptive, misleading, fraudulent, or unfair.

5. Respect consumer privacy and provide protection for personal data.

6. Cooperate fully and in a transparent manner with public authorities in the prevention or removal of serious threats to public health and safety deriving from the consumption or use of their products.

VIII. Science and Technology

Enterprises should:

1. Endeavour to ensure that their activities are compatible with the science and technology (S&T) policies and plans of the countries in which they operate and as appropriate contribute to the development of local and national innovative capacity.

2. Adopt, where practicable in the course of their business activities, practices that permit the transfer and rapid diffusion of technologies and know-how, with due regard to the protection of intellectual property rights.

3. When appropriate, perform science and technology development work in host countries to address local market needs, as well as employ host country personnel in an S&T capacity and encourage their training, taking into account commercial needs.

4. When granting licenses for the use of intellectual property rights or when otherwise transferring technology, do so on reasonable terms and conditions and in a manner that contributes to the long-term development prospects of the host country.

5. Where relevant to commercial objectives, develop ties with local universities, public research institutions, and participate in cooperative research projects with local industry or industry associations.

IX. Competition

Enterprises should, within the framework of applicable laws and regulations, conduct their activities in a competitive manner. In particular, enterprises should:
1. Refrain from entering into or carrying out anti-competitive agreements among competitors:
a) To fix prices.
b) To make rigged bids (collusive tenders).
c) To establish output restrictions or quotas; or
d) To share or divide markets by allocating customers, suppliers, territories or lines of commerce.
2. Conduct all of their activities in a manner consistent with all applicable competition laws, taking into account the applicability of the competition laws of jurisdictions whose economies would be likely to be harmed by anti-competitive activity on their part.
3. Cooperate with the competition authorities of such jurisdictions by, among other things and subject to applicable law and appropriate safeguards, providing as prompt and complete responses as practicable to requests for information.
4. Promote employee awareness of the importance of compliance with all applicable competition laws and policies.

X. Taxation

It is important that enterprises contribute to the public finances of host countries by making timely payment of their tax liabilities. In particular, enterprises should comply with the tax laws and regulations in all countries in which they operate and should exert every effort to act in accordance with both the letter and spirit of those laws and regulations. This would include such measures as providing the relevant authorities the information necessary for the correct determination of taxes to be assessed in connection with their operations and conforming transfer pricing practices to the arm's length principle.

Appendix 4: Sample Company Policies and Procedures Relating to the Foreign Corrupt Practices Act in the United States

[*Author's Note*: These sample policies concerning resisting foreign corrupt practices are provided by the editorial staff of Business Laws, Inc. Business Laws, Inc. is the authority that publishes virtually every aspect of business law needed in international business and domestic transactions. The sample policies in this appendix are excerpted from the "Foreign Corrupt Practices Act" published by Business Laws Inc.]

[*Editor's Original Note*: Most companies with any potential Foreign Corrupt Practices Act (FCPA) exposure have policies requiring compliance with the bribery and/or records sections. Generally, those policies are part of the company policies on legal and ethical conduct, or conflicts of interest. A company's FCPA policy is often treated along with a host of other things, such as honesty in government contracting, insider trading, and antitrust compliance. The following are portions of some of the company policies and procedures which specifically relate to the FCPA.]

1. Improper Influence

No offer of or payment of any gift, loan or gratuity is to be made either directly or indirectly to any business or government entity or any associate of such in exchange for or otherwise in an attempt to procure business for the Company. Gifts and entertainment may be used with representatives of customers or potential customers if they are of limited value, are customary in the situation, are legal, and their public disclosure would not embarrass the Company. Gratuities may be paid to an associate of a government entity to expedite or facilitate the performance of a routine administrative function, where such gratuities are legal, customary, are of limited value and their public disclosure would not embarrass the Company.

2. Business Courtesies Offered to Foreign Government Employees, Officials, and Representatives

The US Foreign Corrupt Practices Act makes it illegal for a US citizen or company to corruptly offer or give directly or indirectly to a foreign government official anything of value in return for that official's action or nonaction resulting in the US citizen's or company's obtaining or retaining business. The fact that a foreign official requested an item of value does not justify such practice under the Act. All employees must strictly adhere to the requirements of the Act. Before offering a business courtesy to a foreign government employee, official, or representative, guidance should be obtained from the appropriate business ethics adviser or the law department.

3. Compliance with Other Laws

Bribery, or the giving of money or anything else of value in an attempt to influence the action of a public official, is unlawful. You are not authorized to pay any bribe or make any other illegal payment on behalf of the Company, no matter how small the amount. This prohibition extends to payments to consultants, agents or other intermediaries when you have reason to believe that some part of the payment or "fee" will be used for a bribe or otherwise to influence government action. It is the policy of the Company to obey both foreign and domestic tax laws and foreign exchange control laws. You are not permitted on behalf of the Company to enter into any transaction which you know or reasonably should know would violate these laws. Neither the Company nor its employees should assist any third party in violating the laws of any country.

4. The Bribery of Government Officials is Forbidden

The Company has had a longstanding policy forbidding bribery of government officials in the conduct of its business in the United States and abroad. The Company also expects its employees to comply with the Foreign Corrupt Practices Act which prohibits the making or offering of any payment to any foreign official to induce that official to affect any governmental act or decision or to assist the Company in obtaining or retaining business. No Company employee anywhere in the world may make a bribe, payment, or gift to any government official whether or not there is an intent to influence. The Company takes this position not only because such bribe, payment, or gift would be in violation of the law, but also because of the Company's commitment to good government and the fair and impartial administration of the law.

5. Payments to Government Employees

No payments of money, gifts, services, entertainment, or anything of value may be offered or made available in any amount, directly or indirectly, to any government official or employee in any country where such payments are illegal or not customary. Such payments are never legal in the United States. Such payments should not be made in other countries, even if legal there, if they are in violation of US laws, regardless of the nationality of the recipient. If in doubt, contact an attorney in the Company legal department. The Foreign Corrupt Practices Act may impose severe penalties for failure to follow the policies stated in this paragraph.

6. Foreign Representatives, Agents, and Consultants

Commission or fee arrangements shall be made only with firms or persons serving as bona fide commercial representatives, agents, or consultants. Such arrangements may not be entered into with any firm in which a government official or associate is known to have an interest unless the arrangement is permitted by applicable law and has been specifically approved by the company's general counsel. All commission and fee arrangements shall be by written contract. Any commission or fee must be reasonable and consistent with normal practice for the industry, the merchandise involved, and the services to be rendered. Payments shall not be made in cash. An associate may not take any action or authorize any action which involves any illegal, unethical, or otherwise improper payment of money or anything else of value.

7. International Business

When conducting business in other countries, laws and local customs and practices will be encountered that differ from those in the United States. The Company's policy is to comply with all laws that apply in the countries where we do business. In countries where common customs and practices might indicate acceptance of standards of conduct different from those to which we aspire, employees should continue to follow the more stringent code of conduct, subject to reasonable business judgment.

The Company's policy prohibits the making of any payment in violation of the US Foreign Corrupt Practices Act. Except as provided in this section, all payments are forbidden to officials or employees of governments or government-owned or related agencies. In some areas of the world, timely action by low-ranking government employees can be obtained only by generally accepted payment of modest gratuities. Payment of modest gratuities to induce a person to do only what he or she is required to do and to which the Company is legally entitled is permissible if it clearly conforms to local custom. However, such payments should not be made as a matter of course; they should be the exception and not the rule, and should be considered only in circumstances where proper alternatives are not meaningfully available. Such payments must be properly recorded on the books of accounts. In no circumstances are any such payments to be made to any official or employee of any governmental entity or government-related entity of any US jurisdiction.

While it is difficult to monetize "modest gratuities," local practice and good judgment should always be applied. In one country, the expediting of customs clearance for a product sample may require payment of a nominal sum, while a commercial shipment of a perishable or urgently needed item might require payment of a greater amount. In any event, should it appear that significant payments are required under conditions that would make failure to deliver extremely expensive, the Chief Financial Officer of the Company should be contacted promptly for resolution. Such disbursements should be recorded as "facilitating payments."

8. Foreign Corrupt Practices Act

The Foreign Corrupt Practices Act prohibits payments, or offers of payments, of anything of value to foreign officials, political parties or candidates for foreign political office in order to obtain, keep, or direct business. Indirect payments of this nature made through an intermediary are also illegal. Company employees and representatives must comply with this Act. This Act also requires that the Company maintain a system of internal accounting controls and keep accurate records of the Company's transactions and assets. The following activities are prohibited: (1) maintaining secret or unrecorded funds or assets; (2) falsifying records; and (3) providing misleading or incomplete financial information to an auditor.

9. US Foreign Corrupt Practices Act

It is the Company's policy to comply with the FCPA in the US and in every jurisdiction in which we operate. The FCPA's basic anti-bribery provision makes it unlawful to pay or offer to pay any money, gift, or item of value to any foreign official for the purpose of influencing any act or decisions made in his or her official capacity. The Act is very broadly construed to cover almost any payment or gift to a foreign official. There is an exception for so-called facilitating payments (payments to obtain such items as licenses, permits, or police protection), but this exception is very narrowly construed and should not be relied upon without consulting with the General Counsel's office. It is the Company's policy to follow both the literal terms of the FCPA and the spirit behind the law; any payment or gift to a foreign official for any reason is a violation of the Business Conduct Policy unless the General Counsel's office has reviewed and approved the gift or payment. The FCPA by its terms is limited to payments to government officials. However, the Company policy goes further and prohibits any similar questionable payment to anyone. Accordingly, no employee of the Company may enter into any agreement or arrangement involving commissions, rebates, bribes, kickbacks or otherwise, when the employee knows or suspects that the probable result is to improperly reward anyone in connection with existing business or prospective business, whether or not the individual is a government official. This policy applies worldwide.

10. Foreign Activities

Business conduct in foreign countries sometimes differs from that in the United States, both in terms of common practice and legality. The simple overriding consideration is that if any unethical or illegal activity is necessary to obtain or retain any business, the Company will not pursue or seek to retain that business. (1) Gifts: No gift intended to corruptly influence any business dealing in which the Company is involved may be given to or received from any foreign national. If an exchange of gifts is both a legal and normal practice, the Company will provide the gift, and any gift received will become Company property; (2) Payments: It is a felony under US laws for the Company, any of its employees, or anyone acting on its behalf, to give, offer, promise, or authorize a payment to a foreign official, foreign political party or official thereof, or any candidate for foreign political office, in connection with obtaining or retaining business for the Company.

US law also makes it a felony to pay money or anything of value to a commission agent, sales representative, or consultant when there is knowledge or firm belief that the payment will be used to corruptly influence a government official in connection with business the Company is attempting to obtain or retain. Political contributions will not be made by or on behalf of the Company in foreign countries. The Company will observe the laws of foreign countries in which it operates concerning payment of agents' fees and commissions, provided these laws are not in conflict with US law. Employees are not to engage in activities designed to circumvent foreign laws concerning retaining or paying sales representatives and consultants.

11. Dealing with Foreign Officials

Do not promise, offer, or make any payments in money, products, or services to any foreign official in exchange for or in order to induce favorable business treatment or to affect any government decision. In some foreign countries, the law may permit minor payments to clerical personnel to expedite performance of their duties. Such minor payments may be made only with the express approval of the country general manager and the Office of the General Counsel, must never exceed a value of $50 (US) per payment and must never be made to gain or retain business.

12. Foreign Corrupt Practices Act

All employees will abide by the provisions of the Foreign Corrupt Practices Act. Business transactions will be governed by Company policies regarding Payments to Foreign Representatives and Foreign Payment Reviews.

13. Facilitating Payments

The Company may on occasion be required to make a minor payment to a foreign government employee whose duties are essentially ministerial or clerical in nature. This minor payment is usually for the purpose of expediting rather than influencing a particular decision. It is made simply to expedite some matter in a more timely or efficient manner. Facilitating payments (sometimes called "grease payments") may not be illegal under the FCPA or foreign government law enforcement policies and customs; however, in certain instances, such payments may be violative of local law enforcement policies or of other Federal statutes, particularly if they involve substantial amounts. If they involve large amounts or if otherwise material, public disclosure under SEC regulations, as noted above, may also be required. Facilitating payments must be strictly controlled and every effort must be made to eliminate or minimize such payments. Facilitating payments, if required, will be made only in accordance with local custom and practice and with applicable Operating Group policy. Recognizing that some confusion may exist as to the propriety of making facilitating payments, such payments should not be made except under the guidance of the Legal Department of the appropriate Operating Group.

14. Improper Payments

As a result of the Foreign Corrupt Practices Act of 1977, any company that has securities registered with, or files a report with the Securities and Exchange Commission, must comply with certain specified accounting control standards. These standards apply to domestic operations as well as foreign and will be enforced by the Securities and Exchange Commission. Basically, these accounting control standards place the burden on a registered company to detect and disclose any improper or illegal use of the Corporation's assets or the misuse of the Corporation's financial accountability system. In compliance with the FCPA guidelines, the Corporation specifically will not tolerate (1) the use of corporate or subsidiary funds or assets for any unlawful or improper purpose; (2) the establishment of any undisclosed or unrecorded funds or assets of the Corporation or any subsidiary; (3) the recording of any false or artificial entries on the books and records of the Corporation or its subsidiaries for any reason, and no employee shall engage in any arrangement that results in any such prohibited act; or (4) a payment on behalf of the Corporation or any of its subsidiaries with the intention or understanding that any part of any such payment is to be used for a purpose other than that described by the documents supporting the payment.

Any employee having information or knowledge of any unrecorded fund or asset or any prohibited act shall promptly report such matters to his Department Head or, where appropriate, to his Division Head, President of the Corporation, or Chairman of the Board. Violators of this policy are subject to appropriate corporate discipline, including dismissal for cause. Employees are reminded that willful violation of this policy may also result in prosecution for violation of the Securities Exchange Act of 1934.

15. Business with Foreign Governments

The Company will comply with the Foreign Corrupt Practices Act which prohibits, for the purpose of obtaining or retaining business, the giving of money or things of value to any foreign official to influence any of his official acts or decisions or to induce him to use his influence to affect any act or decision of his government or one of its agencies. This Act further prohibits giving money or items of value to any person or firm where there is reason to believe that it will be passed on to a government official for this purpose.

16. Illegal or Unethical Payments, Gifts, Bribes, or Gratuities

The Company's policy is to comply strictly with the US Foreign Corrupt Practices Act of 1977. The Act prohibits payments or offers of payments of anything of value to foreign officials, political parties, or candidates for foreign political office in order to secure, retain, or direct business. Payments made indirectly through an intermediary, under circumstances indicating that such payments would be passed along for prohibited purposes, are also illegal. The Act also contains significant internal accounting control and record-keeping requirements that apply to the Company's domestic operations. The Act's intent, in requiring these records, is to ensure that a business enterprise maintains reasonable control over its assets and all transactions involving those assets. All employees are responsible for following Company procedures for carrying out and reporting business transactions.

17. Payments to Foreign Government Officials

The US Foreign Corrupt Practices Act also prohibits Company payments to foreign government officials for the purpose of obtaining favorable government action or keeping government business. Specifically, this law prohibits the Company from directly or indirectly offering, promising to pay, or authorizing the payment of money or anything of value to foreign government officials for the purpose of (1) influencing the acts or decisions of foreign officials; (2) inducing foreign officials to act or fail to act in violation of their lawful duties; or (3) inducing foreign officials to use their influence to assist in obtaining or retaining business for or directing business to any person.

The law also prohibits using intermediaries (for example, foreign affiliates, agents, consultants and distributors) to channel payments to foreign government officials for the same purposes. A minor payment to a foreign government official, made to expedite or secure the performance of routine government action, might not violate US law if the Company can prove that such a payment, often called a "facilitating" payment, is made for the purpose of expediting (rather than influencing) a particular decision that is classified as "routine government action." Because such payments might violate other laws, such as laws outside the United States, or might damage the Company's reputation, consult the Office of General Counselor your subsidiary counsel before making this type of payment. Before making any payment or giving anything of value to a foreign government official or should you have any questions about the proper maintenance of company books and records, consult the Office of General Counselor your subsidiary legal counsel. You can obtain a copy of the Company Foreign Corrupt Practices Act Compliance Manual from the Office of General Counsel.

Appendix 5: OECD Convention on Combating Bribery of Foreign Public Officials in International Business Transactions

Preamble

Considering that bribery is a widespread phenomenon in international business transactions, including trade and investment, which raises serious moral and political concerns, undermines good governance and economic development, and distorts international competitive conditions.

Considering that all countries share a responsibility to combat bribery in international business transactions.

Having regard to the Revised Recommendation on Combating Bribery in International Business Transactions, adopted by the Council of the Organization for Economic Cooperation and Development (OECD) on 23 May 1997, C(97)123/FINAL, which, *inter alia,* called for effective measures to deter, prevent and combat the bribery of foreign put officials in connection with international business transactions, in particular the prompt criminalisation of such bribes in an effective and coordinated manner and in conformity with the agreed common elements set out in that Recommendation and with the jurisdictional and other basic legal principles of each country.

Welcoming other recent developments which further advance international understanding and cooperation in combating bribery of public officials, including actions of the United Nations, the World Bank, the International Monetary Fund, the World Trade Organization, the Organization of American States, the Council of Europe and the European Union.

Welcoming the efforts of companies, business organizations and trade unions as well as other non-governmental organisations to combat bribery.

Recognising the role of governments in the prevention of solicitation of bribes from individuals and enterprises in international business transactions.

Recognising that achieving progress in this field requires not only efforts on a national level but also multilateral cooperation, monitoring and follow-up.

Recognising that achieving equivalence among the measures to be taken by the Parties is an essential object and purpose of the Convention, which requires that the Convention be ratified without derogations affecting this equivalence.

Have agreed as follows:

Article 1: The Offence of Bribery of Foreign Public Officials

1. Each Party shall take such measures as may be necessary to establish that it is a criminal offence under its law for any person intentionally to offer, promise or give any undue pecuniary or other advantage, whether directly or through intermediaries, to a foreign public official, for that official or for a third party, in order that the official act or refrain from acting in relation to the performance of official duties, in order to obtain or retain business or other improper advantage in the conduct of international business.

2. Each Party shall take any measures necessary to establish that complicity in, including incitement, aiding and abetting, or authorization of an act of bribery of a foreign public official shall be a criminal offence. Attempt and conspiracy to bribe a foreign public official shall be criminal offences to the same extent as attempt and conspiracy to bribe a public official of that Party.

3. The offences set out in paragraphs 1 and 2 above are hereinafter referred to as "bribery of a foreign public official."

4. For the purpose of this Convention:

a. "foreign public official" means any person holding a legislative, administrative or judicial office of a foreign country, whether appointed or elected; any person exercising a public function for a foreign country, including for a public agency or public enterprise; and any official or agent of a public international organization;

b. "foreign country" includes all levels and subdivisions of government, from national to local;

c. "act or refrain from acting in relation to the performance of official duties" includes any use of the public official's position, whether or not within the official's authorised competence.

Article 2: Responsibility of Legal Persons

Each Party shall take such measures as may be necessary, in accordance with its legal principles, to establish the liability of legal persons for the bribery of a foreign public official.

Article 3: Sanctions

1. The bribery of a foreign public official shall be punishable by effective, proportionate and dissuasive criminal penalties. The range of penalties shall be comparable to that applicable to the bribery of the Party's own public officials and shall, in the case of natural persons, include deprivation of liberty sufficient to enable effective mutual legal assistance and extradition.

2. In the event that, under the legal system of a Party, criminal responsibility is not applicable to legal persons, that Party shall ensure that legal persons shall be subject to effective, proportionate and dissuasive non-criminal sanctions, including monetary sanctions, for bribery of foreign public officials.

3. Each Party shall take such measures as may be necessary to provide that the bribe and the proceeds of the bribery of a foreign public official, or property the value of which corresponds to that of such proceeds, are subject to seizure and confiscation or that monetary sanctions of comparable effect are applicable.

4. Each Party shall consider the imposition of additional civil or administrative sanctions upon a person subject to sanctions for the bribery of a foreign public official.

Article 4: Jurisdiction

1. Each Party shall take such measures as may be necessary to establish its jurisdiction over the bribery of a foreign public official when the offence is committed in whole or in part in its territory.

2. Each Party which has jurisdiction to prosecute its nationals for offences committed abroad shall take such measures as may be necessary to establish its jurisdiction to do so in respect of the bribery of a foreign public official, according to the same principles.

3. When more than one Party has jurisdiction over an alleged offence described in this Convention, the Parties involved shall, at the request of one of them, consult with a view to determining the most appropriate jurisdiction for prosecution.

4. Each Party shall review whether its current basis for jurisdiction is effective in the fight against the bribery of foreign public officials and, if it is not, shall take remedial steps.

Article 5: Enforcement

Investigation and prosecution of the bribery of a foreign public official shall be subject to the applicable rules and principles of each Party. They shall not be influenced by considerations of national economic interest, the potential effect upon relations with another State or the identity of the natural or legal persons involved.

Article 6: Statute of Limitations

Any statute of limitations applicable to the offence of bribery of a foreign public official shall allow an adequate period of time for the investigation and prosecution of this offence.

Article 7: Money Laundering

Each Party which has made bribery of its own public official a predicate offence for the purpose of the application of its money laundering legislation shall do so on the same terms for the bribery of a foreign public official, without regard to the place where the bribery occurred.

Article 8: Accounting

1. In order to combat bribery of foreign public officials effectively, each Party shall take such measures as may be necessary, within the framework of its laws and regulations regarding the maintenance of books and records, financial statement disclosures, and accounting and auditing standards, to prohibit the establishment of off-the-books accounts, the making of off-the-books or inadequately identified transactions, the recording of nonexistent expenditures, the entry of liabilities with incorrect identification of their object, as well as the use of false documents, by companies subject to those laws and regulations, for the purpose of bribing foreign public officials or of hiding such bribery.
2. Each Party shall provide effective, proportionate and dissuasive civil, administrative or criminal penalties for such omissions and falsifications in respect of the books, records, accounts and financial statements of such companies.

Article 9: Mutual Legal Assistance

1. Each Party shall, to the fullest extent possible under its laws and relevant treaties and arrangements, provide prompt and effective legal assistance to another Party for the purpose of criminal investigations and proceedings brought by a Party concerning offences within the scope of this Convention and for non-criminal proceedings within the scope of this Convention brought by a Party against a legal person. The requested Party shall inform the requesting Party, without delay, of any additional information or documents needed to support the request for assistance and, where requested, of the status and outcome of the request for assistance.
2. Where a Party makes mutual legal assistance conditional upon the existence of dual criminality, dual criminality shall be deemed to exist if the offence for which the assistance is sought is within the scope of this Convention.
3. A Party shall not decline to render mutual legal assistance for criminal matters within the scope of this Convention on the ground of bank secrecy.

Article 10: Extradition

1. Bribery of a foreign public official shall be deemed to be included as an extraditable offence under the laws of the Parties and the extradition treaties between them.
2. If a Party which makes extradition conditional on the existence of an extradition treaty receives a request for extradition from another Party with which it has no extradition treaty, it may consider this Convention to be the legal basis for extradition in respect of the offence of bribery of a foreign public official.
3. Each Party shall take any measures necessary to assure either that it can extradite its nationals or that it can prosecute its nationals for the offence of bribery of a foreign public official. A Party which declines a request to extradite a person for bribery of a foreign public official solely on the ground that the person is its national shall submit the case to its competent authorities for the purpose of prosecution.
4. Extradition for bribery of a foreign public official is subject to the conditions set out in the domestic law and applicable treaties and arrangements of each Party. Where a Party makes extradition conditional upon the existence of dual criminality, that condition shall be deemed to be fulfilled if the offence for which extradition is sought is within the scope of Article 1 of this Convention.

Article 11: Responsible Authorities

For the purposes of Article 4, paragraph 3, on consultation, Article 9, on mutual legal assistance and Article 10, on extradition, each Party shall notify to the Secretary-General of the OECD an authority or authorities responsible for making and receiving requests, which shall serve as channel of communication for these matters for that Party, without prejudice to other arrangements between Parties.

Article 12: Monitoring and Follow-up

The Parties shall cooperate in carrying out a programme of systematic follow-up to monitor and promote the full implementation of this Convention. Unless otherwise decided by consensus of the Parties, this shall be done in the framework of the OECD Working Group on Bribery in International Business Transactions and according to its terms of reference, or within the framework and terms of reference of any successor to its functions, and Parties shall bear the costs of the programme in accordance with the rules applicable to that body.

Article 13: Signature and Accession

1. Until its entry into force, this Convention shall be open for signature by OECD members and by non-members which have been invited to become full participants in its Working Group on Bribery in International Business Transactions.
2. Subsequent to its entry into force, this Convention shall be open to accession by any non-signatory which is a member of the OECD or has become a full participant in the Working Group on Bribery in International Business Transactions or any successor to its functions. For each such non-signatory, the Convention shall enter into force on the sixtieth day following the date of deposit of its instrument of accession.

Article 14: Ratification and Depositary

1. This Convention is subject to acceptance, approval or ratification by the Signatories, in accordance with their respective laws.
2. Instruments of acceptance, approval, ratification or accession shall be deposited with the Secretary-General of the OECD, who shall serve as Depositary of this Convention.

Article 15: Entry into Force

1. This Convention shall enter into force on the sixtieth day following the date upon which five of the ten countries which have the ten largest export shares (see annex), and which represent by themselves at least 60 percent of the combined total exports of those ten countries, have deposited their instruments of acceptance, approval, or ratification. For each signatory depositing its instrument after such entry into force, the Convention shall enter into force on the sixtieth day after deposit of its instrument.

2. If, after 31 December 1998, the Convention has not entered into force under paragraph 1 above, any signatory which has deposited its instrument of acceptance, approval or ratification may declare in writing to the Depositary its readiness to accept entry into force of this Convention under this paragraph 2. The Convention shall enter into force for such a signatory on the sixtieth day following the date upon which such declarations have been deposited by at least two signatories. For each signatory depositing its declaration after such entry into force, the Convention shall enter into force on the sixtieth day following the date of deposit.

Article 16: Amendment

Any Party may propose the amendment of this Convention. A proposed amendment shall be submitted to the Depositary which shall communicate it to the other Parties at least sixty days before convening a meeting of the Parties to consider the proposed amendment. An amendment adopted by consensus of the Parties, or by such other means as the Parties may determine by consensus, shall enter into force sixty days after the deposit of an instrument of ratification, acceptance or approval by all of the Parties, or in such other circumstances as may be specified by the Parties at the time of adoption of the amendment.

Article 17: Withdrawal

A Party may withdraw from this Convention by submitting written notification to the Depositary. Such withdrawal shall be effective one year after the date of the receipt of the notification. After withdrawal, cooperation shall continue between the Parties and the Party which has withdrawn on all requests for assistance or extradition made before the effective date of withdrawal which remain pending.

Index